I0138957

Truman, Congress, and Korea

Truman, Congress, and Korea

The Politics of America's First Undeclared War

LARRY BLOMSTEDT

UNIVERSITY PRESS OF KENTUCKY

Copyright © 2016 by The University Press of Kentucky

Scholarly publisher for the Commonwealth,
serving Bellarmine University, Berea College, Centre College of Kentucky, Eastern
Kentucky University, The Filson Historical Society, Georgetown College,
Kentucky Historical Society, Kentucky State University, Morehead State
University, Murray State University, Northern Kentucky University, Transylvania
University, University of Kentucky, University of Louisville, and Western
Kentucky University.
All rights reserved.

Editorial and Sales Offices: The University Press of Kentucky
663 South Limestone Street, Lexington, Kentucky 40508-4008
www.kentuckypress.com

Cataloging-in-Publication data is available from the Library of Congress.

978-0-8131-6611-7 (hardcover : alk. paper)
978-0-8131-6612-4 (pdf)
978-0-8131-6613-1 (epub)

This book is printed on acid-free paper meeting
the requirements of the American National Standard
for Permanence in Paper for Printed Library Materials.

∞

Manufactured in the United States of America.

Member of the Association of
American University Presses

For Colleen, T.J., Candice, Elizabeth, Alex, and Mom,
and in loving memory of Curtis E. Blomstedt

The United Nations Security Council held a meeting and passed on the situation and asked the members to go to the relief of the Korean Republic. It was unlawfully attacked by a bunch of bandits. . . . And the members of the United Nations are going to the relief of the Korean Republic to suppress a bandit raid on the Republic of Korea.

—President Harry S. Truman,
press conference,
June 29, 1950

Contents

Preface   xi

Introduction: Truman versus Congress   1
1. Into Korea   23
2. The First War, July–October 1950   55
3. The Second War, November 1950–July 1951   93
4. The Forgotten Attempts to End the Forgotten War   135
5. The Third War, July 1951–December 1952   161
6. The Fall of the Trumanites   191
Conclusion   221

Acknowledgments   225
Appendix A: Excerpts from the United Nations Charter   227
Appendix B: United Nations Participation Act of 1945   229
Notes   231
Bibliography   277
Index   295

Photographs follow page 160

Preface

The Korean War stormed onto the world scene on June 24, 1950, when North Korean premier Kim Il Sung launched a massive invasion into South Korea, hoping to unite the peninsula under his leadership. Neither the administration of President Harry S. Truman nor the members of the Eighty-First Congress could have known that their response to this attack would mark a monumental shift in how the U.S. government commits the nation to war. Believing that communist expansion into South Korea threatened American national security, Truman and Congress responded swiftly with military intervention. When China entered the war, however, the U.S. commander in chief and many American legislators became concerned that the regional conflict would escalate into a world war that they were unwilling to wage. As a result, the Korean intervention introduced the American public to the concept of limited war, which contrasted sharply with the Allies' insistence on unconditional surrender of the enemy in World War II. This conflict changed the roles of the president and Congress, as subsequent chief executives dispensed with obtaining congressional declarations of war when it came to major military interventions in Vietnam, the Persian Gulf, Afghanistan, and Iraq.

The war in Korea unfolded quickly. Within three days of receiving news of the attack, Truman dispatched air and naval support to South Korea, inspiring House members to rise and cheer the decision. In addition, he obtained a commitment from the United Nations to give military support to South Korea. On June 28 Congress overwhelmingly approved the president's order to extend the draft for one year and to call up reservists in all branches of the armed services. This bolstered the manpower of the American military, which had dwindled from 12.3 million at the end of World War II to 1.4 million, producing a force of 3.2 million in only fifteen months. After meeting with key members of Congress two days later, Truman issued a statement approving air force missions over North

Korea and noting that "General MacArthur has been authorized to use certain supporting ground units." In just one week, the United States had committed air and ground forces to a significant military intervention overseas. When Secretary of the Army Frank Pace asked the president about obtaining a formal declaration of war from Congress, Truman replied, "Frank, it's not necessary. They are all with me." For the moment, he was right.[1]

Despite the UN's intervention, led by American forces, Kim nearly achieved his goal in the summer of 1950. Dismayed by the speed of the North Korean advance, Lieutenant General Walton Walker, commander of UN ground forces, issued a "stand or die" order on July 29. The UN troops did just that, and by August 15, they and the South Korean forces had secured a small area encircling the southeastern port city of Pusan. There, Walker's forces managed to hold the line until UN commander General Douglas MacArthur launched a daring counterattack at Inchon on September 15, some 150 miles behind enemy lines on the western edge of the peninsula. MacArthur himself underscored the risk of this maneuver, calling it a "five thousand to one shot." The general's gamble paid off, and the Inchon attack swung the momentum to the UN, whose troops quickly took the offensive and reestablished control over South Korea. Admiral William Halsey wired MacArthur: "The Inchon landing is the most masterly and audacious strategic stroke in all history."[2]

Riding the impetus from Inchon on October 7, the UN General Assembly approved a measure allowing the military coalition to take "all appropriate steps . . . to ensure conditions of stability *throughout Korea*," carrying the battle north of the thirty-eighth parallel, the peninsula's original dividing line. The purpose of this change was the "establishment of a unified, independent and democratic Government in the sovereign State of Korea." Although the UN had made reunification of Korea an objective in 1947, this resolution was a significant departure from its initial statement at the war's outset, which had only called on North Korea to withdraw its forces north of the thirty-eighth parallel. Tom Connally (D-TX), chairman of the Senate Foreign Relations Committee, later stated, "I don't recall that any of us reminded the President that his [original] objective had been only to liberate the Republic of South Korea." When UN forces surged into the north, China, perceiving the American advance as a threat to its security, entered the war. By late October, Chinese troops had temporarily halted the UN offensive and then appeared to withdraw from the conflict. A month later, MacArthur initiated another offensive into North Korea, predicting he would have his soldiers home by Christmas. This was not to be. On November 25 some 250,000 Chinese troops overwhelmed MacArthur, forcing a withdrawal that lasted more than two months—the "longest retreat of American military history," according to one historian. In raging winter winds and temperatures that dipped to twenty-five degrees below zero, automatic weapons and vehicle gearboxes froze, forcing the retreating troops to mix kerosene with lubricating oil to keep their equipment functional. Grimly, MacArthur wired Washington: "We face an entirely new war." How to fight this "new" war became the great question.[3]

The result of the Korean War, unlike World War II, was not a clear-cut victory for the United States. Although the UN thwarted Kim Il Sung's bid to bring South Korea under communist rule, the war did not resolve the political strife that had precipitated the conflict, as evidenced by South Korea's refusal to sign the armistice. Testifying to this uneasy peace, nearly 2 million troops currently maintain the 2.5- by 155-mile demilitarized zone between the Koreas. The national boundaries changed only slightly as the negotiators redrew the dividing line between the Koreas close to the prewar boundary of the thirty-eighth parallel. South Korea gained 2,350 square miles of territory, while North Korea gained 850 square miles of land south of the parallel. The United States incurred enormous costs for its part in this intervention: 33,629 dead, 103,284 wounded, and 5,178 missing or captured, as well as $163 billion (in 2013 dollars). For this reason, the Korean conflict is worth remembering and studying in the hope of learning from its mistakes.[4]

Veterans of the Korean War dubbed their conflict the "Forgotten War" because it receded from the public's attention during the prolonged peace negotiations. Yet it is historically crucial. Korea began a trend of American presidents deploying significant numbers of troops overseas without obtaining a declaration of war from Congress. This raises a critical constitutional issue: Should a president have the authority to involve the United States in a major conflict? Did Truman seize this power, or did Congress abdicate it to him? Can Congress help the United States conduct effective international diplomacy, or is this task best left to the executive? The war also played a key role in the 1952 presidential election.

When Truman was considering whether to run for another term, Korea helped slammed the door on the possibility of another campaign for the Missourian. An analysis of his efforts to sell the war is therefore worth another look. Did the president simply do an ineffective job in rallying the nation behind the Korean intervention, or were there other reasons for the decline in his approval rating? How much public support was there for a war in which the unconditional surrender of the enemy was not the objective? Another relevant factor was the role of domestic politics (which is also in the spotlight today in the war on terror). How well did Truman unite Congress behind the Korean cause? Did the Democrats help or hinder those efforts? What role did the opposition Republicans play in the conduct of the fighting? Was Truman committed to a bipartisan approach to foreign policy, and if so, how did he try to woo GOP support?[5]

This study provides new interpretations of events researched by other historians. Concerning the decision to commit troops to Korea, Robert J. Donovan's *Tumultuous Years: The Presidency of Harry Truman, 1949–1953* (1982) blames the president for skirting congressional approval beforehand. James L. Sundquist presents an alternative view in *The Decline and Resurgence of Congress* (1981), faulting Congress for abdicating its responsibility to declare war. I argue that the congressional Democrats are to blame for failing to advise their president to get the legislature's endorsement before committing troops to Korea. Truman's attempt to maintain a bipartisan foreign policy needs to be examined in a new light as well. *The Collapse of the Middle Way: Senate Republicans and the Bipartisan Foreign Policy, 1948–52* (1988) by David R. Kepley is an important study of the Republican side. I expand on Kepley's work by dissecting bipartisanship from the perspective of Truman and his fellow Democrats. Kepley correctly asserts that the president's inclusion of Republicans in the formation of foreign policy left much to be desired, and I explain why.

In addition to these reinterpretations, this book explores fresh topics previously neglected by historians. Ronald J. Caridi's *The Korean War and American Politics: The Republican Party as a Case Study* (1969) describes how GOP factions exploited the war for political gain, crippling Truman's efforts to unite the country. I examine the other side of the coin, analyzing how the Democrats affected wartime unity, as well as how Truman contributed to divisions within his own party. Another overlooked topic is how congressional Democrats influenced the president's path into Korea during that fateful last week of June 1950. Finally, scholars have devoted little attention to Congress's role in getting the belligerents together for peace talks. Although Rosemary Foot touches on this topic briefly in *A Substitute for Victory: The Politics of Peacemaking at the Korean Armistice Talks* (1990), she focuses on the influence of politics once the negotiations began. However, a number of legislators made various peace proposals during the early stages of the war—ranging from the bizarre to the practical. I explain them all.

Finally, this study also addresses other significant historical issues, including Truman's struggle to maintain unity among the Democrats during wartime. Presidents have little chance of success without their party's support, and unpopular presidents can affect their party's strength in Congress. Another important issue is how McCarthyism influenced the Truman administration and Congress. In sum, these topics provide the most detailed political history to date of the Korean War during the Truman administration.

The book is organized chronologically, for the most part, although there is minimal overlap in the analysis of certain topics. The introduction examines the relationship between Truman and Congress following the end of World War II, including the origins of the idea of a bipartisan foreign policy and the strife within the Democratic Party over domestic issues. Chapter 1 covers Truman's decision to commit American military forces to Korea, Congress's role in that decision, and how these events squared with the UN Charter and the UN Participation Act passed by Congress in the 1940s. The next two chapters discuss domestic politics in the context of the war before and after the Chinese intervention in late 1950—treating these periods as two different wars. Chapter 4 traces congressional peace initiatives to end the war, discussing them in the context of McCarthyism. In chapter 5 I explain the political climate as the war stalemated from mid-1951 into 1952. The book concludes with an analysis of the 1952 election, focusing on the Korean War's role in the downfall of the Trumanites.

Americans struggled to define the meaning of the war when it finally ended in 1953. Secretary of State John Foster Dulles declared, "For the first time in history an international organization has stood against an aggressor and has marshaled force to meet force. The aggressor, at first victorious, has been repulsed." Yet a *New York Times* headline read, "Not

Victory, Not Defeat: But Another War, Marked by Shining Deeds as Well as Misery, Passes into History." Harry Truman and Congress had no less of a struggle in conducting the war and deciding when the time was right to begin the process of ending it. The pages that follow tell the story of how they confronted these challenges.[6]

Introduction

Truman versus Congress

President Truman had a couple of things in his favor in the years leading up to the outbreak of hostilities in Korea. The 1948 election returned him to the White House, and it gave control of both houses of Congress to the Democrats, who remained the majority party for the rest of his presidency. It was an era of bipartisanship in foreign policy, as both parties sought to present a unified front to the rest of the world. As the Cold War unfolded, an increasingly hostile Soviet Union, eager to use American political divisions to its advantage, provided a clear incentive for unanimity in international affairs. Nevertheless, Truman had a rancorous relationship with the legislature. The bipartisan approach to international affairs began to unravel in the late 1940s, and Democratic control of Congress did Truman little good as he led the nation into an unexpected and perplexing conflict. Although the Democrats initially united against Republican senator Joseph McCarthy's bombshells alleging a communist infestation in the State Department, their cohesiveness quickly disintegrated. Criticism of Truman from both Republicans and southern Democrats sharpened throughout the remainder of his term, crippling his ability to unite the country behind the war effort.

This introduction examines the causes of the friction between the president and Congress in the late 1940s. Why did the Democrats fail to stick together? Was Truman's leadership to blame? Did Democrats divide over regional agendas, or were other factors involved? What, exactly, was the nature of the bipartisan foreign policy, and why did it begin to falter prior to the war? What was the role of McCarthyism in Democratic Party schisms and foreign policy issues?

Divided Democrats

Civil rights issues contributed heavily to schisms among the Democrats. In 1946 racial violence directed at southern blacks erupted in the form of lynchings and police brutality. To many whites in the region, the Supreme Court's termination of white primaries, surging African American voter registration, and black World War II veterans denouncing discrimination represented threats to the status quo that had to be squashed. Driven by Jim Crow, many black voters left the South and returned to the party of Lincoln, helping to produce a Republican landslide in the 1946 congressional elections. Motivated primarily by revulsion at the racial violence, but also by a realization of the value of the black vote, Truman established the President's Committee on Civil Rights in December. Shortly thereafter the chief executive declared, "We can no longer afford the luxury of a leisurely attack upon prejudice and discrimination." In October 1947 the committee recommended federal legislation to stop lynchings, to prevent various forms of racial discrimination, and to desegregate the armed forces. In February 1948 Truman followed up with an unprecedented speech to Congress dedicated to civil rights in which he strongly endorsed the committee's report and disclosed his intention to integrate the military via presidential fiat. In July the president made good on his promise and issued Executive Order 9981, mandating "equality of treatment and opportunity for all persons in the armed services without regard to race, color, religion, or national origin."[1]

This made Harry Truman public enemy number one in much of the white South. A poll conducted shortly after his February civil rights message indicated a 57 percent disapproval rating in the South, which was typically a Democratic stronghold. A Mississippi woman wrote to the president that surely he would not want his daughter to travel by bus across the country sitting next to a "dirty, evil smelling, loud mouthed negro man." Southerners in the Senate were so outraged that minority leader Alben Barkley (D-KY) would not introduce any of Truman's civil rights initiatives for fear that a filibuster would bottle up other legislation. In the 1948 presidential campaign, southern Democrats vowed to defeat Truman and his pursuit of racial equality. At the Democratic convention, the entire Mississippi delegation and half of Alabama's walked out after passage of a civil rights plank in the party platform, and all the southerners who remained supported Georgia senator Richard Russell rather than Truman as the party's nominee. Soon afterward, disgruntled southerners led by those dissatisfied Democrats formed a third party: the States' Rights Democrats, or the Dixiecrats. The Dixiecrat revolt dealt a second blow to Truman's campaign, which had already been jarred by Henry Wallace's defection to run for president as the Progressive Party's candidate. With the Democrats divided three ways, the Republicans chose a formidable candidate, New York governor Thomas Dewey, their nominee in 1944 and a leader of the GOP internationalists. Even though the Dixiecrats carried four states, Truman overcame the splintering of his party to score the greatest upset in U.S. history. Voicing his understandably hard feelings toward the Democratic defectors a few days after the election, the president told his staff, "I don't want any fringes in the Democratic party, no Wallace-ites or states' righters."[2]

Nevertheless, the victor meted out only a measured punishment to the Dixiecrats. Although Truman purged the Democratic National Committee (DNC) of his southern opponents, he allowed them to retain their positions in the congressional caucuses and as committee chairs. Despite their failure to boot the incumbent from the White House, the Dixiecrats emerged from the 1948 election as determined as ever. Senator Clinton P. Anderson (D-NM), a strong backer of the administration and chairman of the Democratic Campaign Committee, called the southern bloc the "strongest single force in the Senate" from 1949 into the early 1950s. A few southerners, most notably Foreign Relations Committee chairman Tom Connally of Texas, remained staunch Truman allies on international issues in spite of the administration's civil rights policies, but many did not, draining the president's support at the outset of the Korean War. As one historian argued, Truman could have saved himself some grief by having the Dixiecrats removed from their congressional positions of power. Instead of giving in to vindictiveness, the president tried to unite his party and the nation after the election. Truman left the southerners in the saddle—a decision that would both help him and haunt him during the Korean War years.[3]

Truman's determination to build on Franklin D. Roosevelt's New Deal was another bone of contention among southern Democrats. Stymied in his initial attempt to do so immediately after the end of World War II, Truman's upset victory in 1948 motivated him to try again. This time, he gave his initiative a name. In his January 1949 State of the Union address, the president declared that "every segment of our population and every individual has a right to expect from our government a fair deal." The Fair Deal was successful in some respects; it expanded Social Security, raised the minimum wage (from forty to seventy-five cents an hour), and imposed regulations that prevented corporations from buying their competitors' assets. Other measures, such as a national health insurance program and the Brannan Plan, went down to defeat. The Brannan Plan, named after Charles F. Brannan, Truman's secretary of agriculture, was a drastic overhaul of the farm subsidies program that was intended to rectify some of the problems of FDR's Agricultural Adjustment Administration. It would have limited direct income payments to family farmers and imposed ceilings on government payments to any one entity. Most southern Democrats opposed the Brannan initiative because they feared it would damage future cotton and tobacco prices, or they resented it as yet another intrusive federal program. However, no Fair Deal proposal caused more heartache among the Dixiecrats than Truman's attempt to revive the Fair Employment Practices Committee (FEPC), which Roosevelt had established during World War II to eliminate wartime industries' discriminatory pay practices against blacks. When Truman proposed the creation of a permanent FEPC, southern committee chairmen in Congress killed the legislation, as they had done with other Fair Deal programs. Senator James Eastland (D-MS) called the FEPC proposal a ploy to "secure political favor from Red mongrels in the slums of the great cities of the East and Middle West," who aimed to poison the "pure blood of the South."[4]

Truman did not take kindly to the southern recalcitrants. The president, who owed his entry into politics to the Pendergast machine organization in Kansas City, believed in party loyalty as an act of faith. As an aide later noted, Truman believed that one either supported the party or got out of it; he therefore had little patience for Democrats who were not faithful to him as the Democrat occupying the White House. Early in 1950 the chief executive grew increasingly wary of Democratic support for his legislative programs and policies. For the first time during his presidency, White House aides prepared voting record summaries of the Eighty-First Congress to gauge members' support for presidential programs. The State Department got involved as well. Undersecretary of State James E. Webb prepared an analysis detailing which House Democrats supported various versions of a Korean aid bill as it worked its way through Congress. This report, which included a separate tally of southern Democrats' voting patterns, was bluntly titled "Democratic Members Who Voted against H.R. 5330," an indication that the White House was now identifying its enemies within the party.[5]

Rumblings of discontent among the congressional Democrats plagued the president in several ways, beginning with a plan to repeal the House's twenty-one-day rule. Retaliating against the "do-nothing 80th Congress" that Truman had blasted during the 1948 campaign, the president's supporters had passed this protocol in early 1949, empowering committee chairs to bring to a floor vote any bill that the Rules Committee did not act on within three weeks. The aim was to prevent a coalition of Republicans and conservative southern Democrats on the Rules Committee from killing Truman's Fair Deal programs. In January 1950 an aide alerted the president that a move was afoot to repeal the rule, indicating a "serious threat" to his agenda. The Trumanites in the House managed to keep the rule in place throughout 1950, but things would change after that year's congressional elections.[6]

The chief executive had few committee leaders in his corner on Capitol Hill. Writing to a Senate ally in June 1950, Truman admitted, "The main difficulty that I have to contend with is that in both Houses of the Congress there are not over four or five Chairmen of Key Committees who are friendly to the President." He had good reason to be concerned, since Congress had some thirty-four standing committees at the time. Because southerners enjoyed one-party rule in their region, they generally had the most seniority, which translated into control of important committees, particularly in the Senate.[7]

Even the relatively few committee chairmen who were allied with the president struggled with party unity. In May 1950 House Foreign Affairs Committee chairman John Kee (D-WV) was so concerned that fellow Democrats might cause problems on his panel that he requested a meeting with Truman and Secretary of State Dean Acheson to solicit their help. The president took the matter seriously, promising Kee assistance from Speaker Sam Rayburn (D-TX) and majority leader John McCormack (D-MA).[8]

Making matters worse, the White House lacked effective communication with Congress, a problem that continued during the war. Vice President Alben Barkley had little influence in the Senate, even though he was a former majority leader. Moreover, Truman did not dedicate any staffers to congressional relations until his fifth year in office; he preferred to deal with legislative leaders personally and felt that contacting them through his aides was demeaning. Instead, he had the various departments of the executive branch deal with Congress directly. The absence of clear links between the White House and Congress contrasted sharply with the well-defined channels between the administration and the DNC. Even after the president added two Capitol Hill liaisons to the White House staff, his allies in the House and Senate complained about their ineffectiveness. Truman aide Ken Hechler admitted, "Measured by the standards of other administrations, President Truman's machinery for congressional relations left much to be desired."[9]

Members of Congress agreed with Hechler. In a meeting with Secretary of State Acheson, Senator William Benton (D-CT), one of Truman's strongest allies, was "quite critical" of the administration's relations with Congress, complaining that the White House spent too much time "conciliating our opponents and not enough time working with our friends." Acheson concurred. Freshman representative John C. Davies (D-NY) criticized the administration's failure to acclimate a group of enthusiastic Democratic newcomers to the House in 1949, complaining they did not get enough direction or acknowledgment from the White House. As a result, these Democratic rookies started to "look to their home communities and local problems and overlooked Administration legislation."[10]

Why did Truman wait until the fifth year of his presidency to dedicate any staff members to congressional relations, and why didn't he assign stronger assistants to this role? The president's personal philosophy and his past political experiences provide the answers. Truman was comfortable contacting members of Congress personally, and he eschewed a large White House staff. An aide suspected the president remembered his days in the Senate, where he and his colleagues had resented Roosevelt's staffers and their pressure tactics. More important, Truman believed so strongly in party loyalty that he saw no reason to either coddle or twist the arms of his fellow Democrats to maintain their support. If the president had dedicated effective assistants to mentor the large and energetic class of freshman Democrats in 1949, he might have had more congressional allies who were willing to publicly support his policies during the Korean

War. Later, Truman's staff recognized these shortcomings and apparently persuaded their boss to hold weekly meetings with small groups of congressional Democrats. However, things might have turned out better if Truman had initiated such discussions earlier in his presidency.[11]

The president faced open challenges to his leadership of the party as the primaries for the 1950 midterm elections approached. James Byrnes, Truman's former secretary of state, emerged from retirement, publicly attacked the president's Fair Deal agenda, and announced his candidacy in the South Carolina gubernatorial race. This raised concerns in the White House, given the political clout Byrnes wielded throughout the South. When asked about Byrnes's candidacy at a news conference, Truman snapped that Byrnes was a "free agent to do as he damn pleases." This remark provoked Virginia party leaders to boycott the Democratic Party's regional conference in Raleigh, North Carolina. Presidential aide Charles Murphy concluded, "People in control of the party machinery in Virginia are completely out of step with the President." In February Truman went on the offensive and announced plans for a whistle-stop campaign tour. Repeating his successful strategy from the 1948 campaign of stumping from trains, "Give 'em hell Harry" rambled to fifty-seven towns in sixteen states, primarily in the West, covering some 17,000 miles during the first half of May. Built around the theme of "A Report to the People," Truman's campaign circuit was quite successful by all accounts. The president even won grudging praise from GOP operative Victor Johnston, who followed the tour at the behest of the Republican National Committee. After witnessing a turnout of 35,000 people in Ottumwa, Iowa—a crowd equivalent to the town's population—Johnston called Truman's tour a "traveling medicine show" but admitted, "Nobody hates him." Truman even offered Johnston a ride on the train—if he bought a ticket—and told the surprised Republican that he hoped Johnston was as "highly pleased with the reception . . . as I have been." The chief executive was even popular with the livestock on the campaign trail. When a stubborn lamb raised a ruckus as Truman pinned a blue ribbon on it, he called it a "Republican sheep." Immediately, the animal quieted down. The whistle-stop tour went so well that Truman believed he could reverse the trend of the incumbent president's party losing seats in Congress during midterm elections.[12]

Truman's optimism was unfounded. The 1950 primaries brought

bad news when two key incumbent senators who backed the administration's foreign policies went down to defeat. In Florida, fourteen-year veteran Claude Pepper lost to George Smathers in the Democratic primary. Smathers had been a campaign manager for Pepper in the 1930s, and the senator had even procured a U.S. attorney post for Smathers. The challenger equated Pepper's support of Fair Deal programs with a support of socialism and rode a wave of anticommunism to victory. Unscrupulously, Smathers used superimposed photographs and headlines from the communist publication the *Daily Worker* to paint his opponent as an admirer of Joseph Stalin, dubbing the senator "Red Pepper." Although Pepper had voted against the Truman Doctrine appropriation and had clashed with the president on other Cold War issues early on, he was a consistent supporter of the United Nations and had moved closer to Truman's foreign policies of late, voting for the North Atlantic Treaty. Another presidential ally, Senator Frank Graham of North Carolina, lost his primary contest because of a combination of race and red-baiting. Graham's association with organizations such as the American Civil Liberties Union and the Southern Council of Human Welfare made him vulnerable to the latter tactic. Truman told his staff that Graham's defeat was one of the "most serious losses for the administration." In light of the president's struggles with conservative southerners, the political demise of these two liberal Democrats from the region was particularly damaging.[13]

McCarthyite attacks from within the party bludgeoned other pro-Truman Democrats to the brink of defeat in the primaries, which helped the Republicans finish them off in the general election. For example, in the California primary for U.S. senator, Helen Gahagan Douglas's opponent, Manchester Boddy, compared her voting pattern with that of pro-communist representative Vito Marcantonio (D-NY). Boddy accused Douglas of associating with a "subversive clique of red-hots" and called her "the pink lady"—a nickname that her Republican opponent, Richard Nixon, borrowed in the general election. California's Democratic Committee reported that the Republicans got help from "extreme right-wing elements" in the Democratic Party. Something similar happened to Millard Tydings, a steadfastly anticommunist Senate veteran from Maryland who seemed invulnerable to charges of failing to oppose the red menace. Nevertheless, Tydings had to fight off two Democratic challengers in the primary, former congressman John Meyer and Hugh M. Monaghan II.

Tydings had led the committee investigating McCarthy's charges of communist infiltration of the State Department, a probe Meyer criticized as a whitewash. Monaghan latched onto the same theme, calling the committee's dismissal of McCarthy's allegations a "green light to Stalin's agents in this country." Although Tydings breezed to victory against these two Democratic challengers with 66 percent of the vote, Monaghan refused to endorse the incumbent in the general election, thereby contributing to Tydings's upset in the general election.[14]

The Democrats faced another dilemma in Idaho. Incumbent senator Glen H. Taylor, a country-western singer, had bolted the party in 1948 to run for vice president on the Progressive Party ticket headed by Henry Wallace. Taylor now found himself in the uncomfortable position of returning to the fold and trying to win the Democratic primary. Local Democratic leaders were in no mood to back Taylor, complaining that they were being "treated like Dixiecrats" because political favors were going to the ex-Progressive's supporters. This favoritism rankled the Trumanites because the Wallace-Taylor ticket had garnered less than 5,000 of the 200,000 votes cast in Idaho in 1948. The national party chieftains nevertheless stuck with the incumbent Taylor, leading to heartbreak for their candidate and disaster for their party in the general election. Taylor lost in the primary by 948 votes to D. Worth Clark, but he did not go quietly, provoking a probe of the election that yielded some colorful revelations. For instance, there were complaints about a Senate investigator "frequenting Boise clubs often inebriated conducting a propaganda campaign" for the defeated crooner. Although the investigator apparently enjoyed himself, he failed to deliver a win in the primary for Taylor, and Republican Herman Welker thrashed Clark 62 to 38 percent in the general election.[15]

Bipartisanship in Foreign Policy

The idea that Democrats and Republicans should work together to craft foreign policy took shape during World War II. As planners in the Roosevelt administration began to develop an international organization to prevent a third world war, they were determined to avoid repeating Woodrow Wilson's failure to sell the League of Nations to Congress. Wilson's team at Versailles had included himself, three other Democrats, and only one Republican, contributing to disaster when the Senate rejected the treaty. In March 1944 Secretary of State Cordell Hull asked the Senate Foreign Relations committee to form the Committee of Eight to evaluate drafts of what became the UN Charter. Breaking with tradition, committee chairman Tom Connally balanced the subcommittee members evenly by party, rather than giving his Democrats the majority. The Roosevelt administration supplemented the Committee of Eight by including key Republican leaders from both houses in the UN planning process. FDR's team wisely took pains to involve all GOP factions, not just those Republicans who were friendly to the administration. Their strategy paid off handsomely when the Senate approved the UN Charter by a vote of 89–2, marking the official beginning of bipartisan foreign policy.[16]

Truman encouraged bipartisanship when he became president. Following the Truman Doctrine speech of March 1947, the foreign affairs panels in both houses unanimously endorsed aid for Greece and Turkey, as the president had requested (although Republicans were annoyed that he had failed to tell them about the speech beforehand). Truman included prominent Republicans, such as Senator Arthur Vandenberg (MI) and UN representative John Foster Dulles, in early discussions of the Marshall Plan, paving the way for unanimous approval by the Senate Foreign Relations Committee. The committee also backed the North Atlantic Treaty without dissent in 1949, leading the Senate to pass it by an 82–13 landslide. It is noteworthy, however, that these foreign policy successes all dealt with European affairs. After the communist victory in the Chinese civil war, some suggested that the same bipartisanship had been lacking in the formation of Far East policy.[17]

Harry Truman and Dean Acheson defined a nonpartisan foreign policy in different ways. According to Truman, bipartisanship meant "the President can repose confidence in the members of the other party and that in turn the leaders of that party have confidence in the President's conduct of foreign affairs." Truman valued Vandenberg's input on issues; more important, he appreciated that the senator did not attempt to undermine administration policies he disagreed with. To the president, bipartisanship could not work unless there was mutual trust that neither side would use disagreements on foreign policy for political gain. Acheson viewed the idea more cynically, calling it the "holy water sprinkled on a political necessity." The secretary of state believed the president should run foreign policy, and getting the GOP on board would help the administration hurdle the Constitution's checks and balances between the executive and legislative branches. To Acheson, a nonpartisan approach involved proclaiming to Capitol Hill and the public that "politics stops at the seaboard—and anyone who denies that postulate is a son-of-a-bitch and a crook and not a true patriot," and "if people will swallow that, then you're off to the races."[18]

Changes in leadership of the Senate Foreign Relations Committee prior to the Korean War altered the dynamics of the conduct of international affairs. When the Democrats regained control of the Senate following the 1948 elections, Vandenberg relinquished the chairmanship to Connally. The Michigan Republican had been the straw stirring the drink of bipartisanship, and Truman revered him, even though Vandenberg did not always agree with the president and distanced himself from the administration on those occasions. Acheson respected Vandenberg as well, a sentiment that did not extend to Connally. The Texan had an inferiority complex about his Republican counterpart, and this sometimes hampered bipartisan efforts. Connally once tried to have the chief White House usher fired for placing Vandenberg ahead of him in a reception line. Another time, when a reporter asked him about Vandenberg's views during a press conference, Connally railed, "Van, Van; that's all I hear is Van! Who gives a damn what Vandenberg thinks?" Connally was not the student of international issues that Vandenberg was, nor was he as dedicated to the concept of a nonpartisan foreign policy. Moreover, Connally's insistence on being the "first to know" made it difficult for Acheson to have direct dialogues with Republican members of congressional foreign affairs committees.[19]

The power structure in Congress in the late 1940s hindered the task of creating a bipartisan foreign policy. Truman typically relied on an alliance of Democrats and the internationalist wing of the Republican Party led by Vandenberg and Senator William Knowland (CA). An isolationist faction of the GOP led by Robert A. Taft (OH) opposed them. Although Taft was not on the Foreign Relations Committee, he was able to hinder Truman's agenda once Vandenberg fell ill with cancer in the spring of 1950. There were no other GOP heavyweights on the committee, and Vandenberg had been the only Republican the president respected and trusted enough to consult with, thus weakening bipartisanship in foreign policy.[20]

Complicating matters was the fact that some of the GOP internationalists, most notably Senators Knowland, Styles Bridges (NH), and H.
Alexander Smith (NJ), led a loose coalition known as the China Bloc. This
faction vociferously supported the Nationalist regime in China headed by
Jiang Jieshi, who was embroiled in a civil war against the communist forces
of Mao Zedong. The roots of the China Bloc's philosophy can be traced
to the ideas of Senator William Seward (R-NY) in the 1850s and pursuit
of the Open Door policy near the turn of the twentieth century, based on
the belief that the future of American commerce lay in the Far East rather
than Europe. There was a religious component of the China Bloc as well.
Walter Judd (R-MN) had been a Congregationalist medical missionary
in China prior to World War II, and John Vorys (R-OH) was the son of
missionaries. Judd and Vorys, the House leaders of this bloc, saw Jiang not
only as a virulent anticommunist but also as a devout Christian. Although
foes sometimes dubbed the China Bloc the "Asia-firsters," this was a bit of a
misnomer; most members of the coalition simply wanted the United States
to commit an equal amount of resources to stopping communist expansion in Asia as it did to fighting the Cold War in Europe.[21]

The Democrats dampened bipartisanship when they regained control of the Senate following the 1948 elections. The Senate's makeup was
transformed from a 51–45 Republican majority to a 54–42 Democratic
edge, and things changed more than expected. Connally, upon regain-
ing chairmanship of the Foreign Relations Committee in January 1949,
pledged to strengthen bipartisanship, saying, "It is essential that we have
an American foreign policy, rather than a Republican or a Democratic
policy." He reportedly tried to fight off an attempt to increase the Democrats' numerical edge in the committee, but then Vice President Barkley dropped a bombshell: the Democrats would appoint 8–5 majorities
(rather than the usual 7–6) on several key committees, including Foreign
Relations. He justified this move by citing the Democrats' larger majority than that previously held by the GOP. Vandenberg, with his typical
moderation, called the announcement "not particularly impressive in its
bipartisan hospitality." Senator Wayne Morse (R-OR) called it a "shock-
ing repudiation of a bipartisan foreign policy."[22]

Two key events in 1949 brought new challenges to the notion of a
nonpartisan foreign policy. When the Chinese civil war resumed after
World War II, the United States funneled millions of dollars to Jiang

Jieshi's Nationalists. However, popular support in China for Jiang's corrupt regime dropped severely over time, as did military morale. By the spring of 1949, communist victory was imminent, and Secretary Acheson planned to end U.S. aid to the Nationalists due to the futility of their situation. In response to Republican criticism of the administration's handling of China, Acheson generated a 1,054-page white paper on America's China policy in late July 1949. The report asserted that continued assistance to Jiang's regime would be a waste of resources and recommended that the United States concede Formosa, a large island off the coast of mainland China, to the communists. In short, circumstances within China and beyond the control of the United States were ultimately responsible for the communist triumph. The administration found itself on the defensive yet again when it confirmed the first Soviet test of a nuclear weapon in September. Although Acheson and other officials had predicted the Russians would achieve a nuclear capability, they had not expected it to occur until 1950 or 1951. The end of the U.S. monopoly on nuclear weapons would require a complete overhaul of its diplomatic strategies.[23]

Acheson believed it was time to make protecting Europe from communist encroachment a higher priority. By late 1949, the CIA reported that the security of Europe and the Mediterranean was the "most immediate concern of the United States." The State Department's policy planning staff agreed, noting that the "military problem in Europe . . . is at the core of many problems, including not only the arms program but our whole approach to the (Cold) war." As a result, in December 1949 President Truman approved a National Security Council (NSC) recommendation (NSC 48/2) to end U.S. support of the Chinese Nationalists and to assign a higher priority to hindering Soviet expansion in Europe. The following month, Truman asked the NSC to propose a policy response to the USSR's acquisition of nuclear weapons. This document, known as NSC-68, reflected Acheson's belief that the United States needed to contest the Soviet threat around the world—a task that would require a huge increase in defense spending. Specifically, this recommendation called for defense expenditures to expand from $14.3 billion in 1950 to $50 billion by 1955, which meant that the defense budget would grow from 5 percent of gross national product to 20 percent. Acheson's first challenge was to convince the president to support this measure. Truman, however, was far more interested in cutting spending, avoiding tax increases, and preserving his

Fair Deal domestic agenda (for these reasons, Truman ordered that NSC-68 be kept secret). The president was not the only skeptic. The Bureau of the Budget deemed NSC-68's proposed defense increases impossible. Senator Walter George (D-GA), a senior member of the Foreign Relations Committee who was widely respected on both sides of the aisle, was one of the few legislators who got a look at the proposal, but even George, a staunch internationalist, did not buy NSC-68. Neither did President Truman, who promptly ignored its recommendations and proposed a $13.5 billion defense budget for fiscal year 1951, the lowest since World War II. The Senate was in no mood to expand defense spending either, and it reduced Truman's proposal to extend the military draft from three years to two. Thus began Acheson's struggle to change the focus and scope of the American effort to contain communism.[24]

Meanwhile, the Chinese communists had driven Jiang's forces from the mainland to Formosa. Secretary Acheson subsequently became a lightning rod for GOP attacks, a feud that was driven as much by personality conflicts as by policy differences. Acheson regarded the legislative branch as a nuisance due to its penchant for wasting his department's time in endless hearings. Recalling his dealings with Capitol Hill, the secretary of state wrote, "Those who assert that I do not suffer fools gladly . . . do me less than justice for these anguishing hours. Despite current folklore, one could and did learn to suffer." Acheson alienated both Republican and Democratic legislators with his aloofness and, of all things, his preference for British clothing. In their eyes, Acheson did not treat members of Congress with the deference they expected, so he had few Democratic allies when the Republican attacks began. Even though Truman steadfastly backed his beleaguered secretary, many Democrats were more inclined to throw him under the bus.[25]

Although Acheson's July 1949 white paper correctly pointed out that the United States had limited ability to control internal events in China, the Republicans blasted the Truman administration for a defeatist attitude that allowed the communist victory. Senator Styles Bridges led the initial attacks, claiming that the State Department had plunged to a "new low in governmental integrity and rectitude of high principles." Bridges argued that the United States' commitments to prevent the spread of communism were inconsistent in different parts of the globe, asking, "Have we manhood in Europe and none anywhere else in the world? Are we men in Europe and mice in Asia?"[26]

The geopolitical complexities of the Cold War worked against the administration and in favor of black-and-white perceptions such as those articulated by Bridges and his allies. Recalling the American victories over the twin evils of the Japanese and Adolf Hitler, the right wing of the Republican Party viewed communism as equally evil and therefore advocated forceful opposition to it, at all costs, anywhere in the world.

Acheson disagreed. In a January 12, 1950, address to the National Press Club, he pointed out that prioritizing opposition to communism was "putting the cart before the horse." Although the secretary's statement was valid, it seemed to contradict the 1947 Truman Doctrine, which proclaimed that it was U.S. policy to "support free peoples who are resisting attempted subjugation by armed minorities or by outside pressure." Did the Chinese Nationalists merit American support, regardless of the ineptness of their leadership? Acheson implied that in some situations, opposition to communism was in the nation's interest; in other cases, such as Formosa, it was not necessarily vital to prevent a communist takeover. The secretary went on to define the nation's Pacific "defense perimeter" along a line running from the Ryukyu Islands and the Aleutian Islands off the coast of Alaska, south to the Philippines. (This line of defense did not include the Korean peninsula, a point the Republicans would later pounce on when the war broke out.) Acheson flatly asserted that U.S. aid for the Nationalists was not justified because Jiang's support in China had "melted away." Even though it was unfathomable to Bridges and company that the Nationalists had lost due to poor leadership rather than inadequate American assistance, the secretary portrayed the situation accurately. Initially, Senate Democrats agreed. In a rare show of unity, they responded to Bridges by unanimously endorsing the administration's decision, arguing that continued aid to the Chinese Nationalists could draw the United States into a war.[27]

House Democrats then threw the administration a curveball. Despite a sizable 263–171 Democratic majority, on January 20 the House rejected Truman's proposed $11 million aid package for Korea by one vote, the first major foreign policy bill rejected by Capitol Hill in four years. Although Congress passed the Korean aid bill the following month, it came with a price: the administration had to postpone cutting off funds to the Chinese Nationalists until June.[28]

Secretary Acheson then generated another controversy. On January

21, after a sensational trial, former State Department official Alger Hiss was convicted of lying under oath about his connections to the Communist Party. At a press conference four days later, Acheson declared that despite the guilty verdict, he would not turn his back on Hiss. Even though the secretary was expressing his personal loyalty to Hiss rather than governmental policy, his statement produced a firestorm of criticism. In the House, Richard Nixon (R-CA) and minority whip Les Arends (R-IL) described Acheson's response, respectively, as "disgusting" and an "affront to the nation." Democrats chimed in as well. Representative James C. Davis (GA) asked, "How long can Americans be expected to show respect for Acheson when he hugs to his bosom those who have betrayed their country?" Senator James Eastland (D-MS) presented a resolution from his state's legislature that described Acheson's backing of Hiss as a "dangerous precedent to the security of the nation." No Democrats defended the secretary, including President Truman.[29]

Then came another bombshell for the administration. On February 3 Klaus Fuchs, a German refugee who had worked as a physicist on the Manhattan Project, confessed that he had been a spy for the Soviet Union. Fuchs's information probably helped speed the Soviets' acquisition of a nuclear capability and led to the conviction and execution of Julius and Ethel Rosenberg for espionage. Politically, Fuchs's confession, coming so soon after the Hiss conviction, rendered the Truman administration increasingly vulnerable to charges of being soft on communism.[30]

In this environment, the administration tried to explain to the American people why the United States had been powerful enough to stop the Nazis and the Japanese in World War II but not the communist Chinese in 1949. Moreover, Truman struggled to explain the speed with which the Soviets had ended the U.S. monopoly on the atomic bomb. The answers proposed by a little-known Republican senator from Wisconsin, Joseph McCarthy, were as follows: the United States had "lost" China because communists like Alger Hiss were running the State Department, and the Russians had the A-bomb because of lax security against spies like Fuchs. McCarthy launched himself from obscurity into prominence on February 9, 1950, less than a week after Fuchs's confession, with a speech to a Republican women's group in Wheeling, West Virginia. In it, he made the startling claim that he had a list of 205 communist infiltrators working in the State Department. The next day in Salt Lake City, he said he had 57 names. During a six-hour speech on the floor of the Senate on February 20, McCarthy changed his story again, declaring that he knew of 81 communists in the State Department. This speech quickly created a rumpus as a trio of Democratic senators tried repeatedly, but unsuccessfully, to pin McCarthy down. Majority leader Scott Lucas (IL), Brien McMahon (CT), and Herbert Lehman (NY) interrupted McCarthy's speech sixty-one, thirty-four, and thirteen times, respectively, to no avail. Despite his elusiveness, the Wisconsin senator had struck a nerve.[31]

The Senate convened a special committee chaired by Millard Tydings (D-MD) to investigate the charges. Twelve weeks of hearings began on March 8. Committee members included Democrats Tydings, McMahon, and Theodore Green (RI), along with Republicans Henry Cabot Lodge Jr. (MA) and Bourke Hickenlooper (IA). McCarthy deemed it a good committee. From the Democrats' perspective, Tydings seemed to be the perfect choice to lead the investigation. His reputation as both an able senator and an ardent anticommunist would insulate him from any charges of being "soft on communism." Hickenlooper was the only McCarthy adherent on the panel, and Lodge, the other Republican, had a solid history of supporting Truman's foreign policy. Tydings thus hoped to get some Republican help as he attempted to rein in the Wisconsin senator's wild charges. But Tydings also had, in one historian's words, a "political killer instinct." He detested McCarthy and intended to plow him under. The chairman's eagerness to do so would eventually backfire.[32]

Tydings made no attempt to conduct impartial hearings. Minutes after the proceedings began, they degenerated into a partisan donnybrook. The chairman immediately attacked McCarthy, refusing to let him finish his opening statement. As the chairman, Tydings should have postured himself as the mediator of the hearings rather than the chief protagonist, regardless of McCarthy's infuriating evasiveness in spelling out the specific charges. Tydings worked closely with the State Department behind the scenes, determining which issues to emphasize and which witnesses to call, giving credence to McCarthy's claim that the Democrats were conducting a whitewash.[33]

Early in the hearings, Senator Bridges added to McCarthy's charges, declaring that the Soviet government had planted a "master spy" who was "using our State Department as he wills." Bridges promised that a group of fellow Republican senators would be demanding Acheson's head

in the weeks ahead. Democrats replied to these charges with a deafen-
ing silence for two and a half weeks. Finally, freshman senator William
Benton (D-CT), a former State Department official, stepped forward to
defend the secretary, saying of the alleged problems in the department,
"You certainly do not cure a man's headache by cutting off his head." Representative Stephen M. Young (D-OH) called McCarthy a "rabble rouser"
and insisted that the State Department employed no subversives. Senator Warren Magnuson (D-WA) noted that McCarthy's charges "probably
caused great joy in Russia." The problem with these courageous rejoinders
was that they came from congressional lightweights. The only influential
Democrat who consistently and publicly backed the Truman administration during the Tydings hearings was Senator Connally, chair of the
Foreign Relations Committee. However, even Connally did not defend
Acheson on the Senate floor until six weeks into the hearings.[34]

The White House and party liberals grew concerned about the congressional Democrats' abandonment of Acheson during the initial weeks
of the Tydings hearings. Charles Murphy, preparing the president for a
routine meeting with the "Big 4" congressional leaders (Vice President
Barkley, House Speaker Rayburn, and the majority leaders of the Senate and House), suggested that Truman ask them "if anyone will defend
Acheson in the Senate." At its national convention just a few days later,
the Americans for Democratic Action (ADA), a liberal lobbyist group,
expressed outrage at "the reluctance of many Democratic Senators and
Congressmen to reply to these attacks with the truth which is common
knowledge to every one of them and which, had it been spoken, would
long since have disposed of the whole contemptible campaign."[35]

The administration, however, fought back in a couple of ways. The
State Department created a special group, consisting of people both
inside and outside the government, to investigate and rebut McCarthy's
charges. Truman counterattacked the GOP vigorously. In a press conference the president said he was "fed up" with the criticism, declaring that
this attempt to "torpedo" his nonpartisan policy was "just as bad . . . as it
would be to shoot our soldiers in the back." After praising key Republicans such as Senators Vandenberg and Leverett Saltonstall (MA) for their
support, the president singled out minority leader Kenneth Wherry (NE)
and Bridges as McCarthy's chief cohorts in undermining the administration's foreign policy. In the middle of the press conference Truman

paused to rephrase his assessment for the record: "The greatest asset that the Kremlin has is the partisan attempt in the Senate to sabotage the bipartisan foreign policy of the United States."[36]

Soon, however, the president tried to shore up his relationship with the influential Bridges. The Tydings committee proceedings, which began to sour for the Democrats in April, and Vandenberg's illness probably nudged Truman in that direction. Bridges's position as the ranking minority member of the Armed Services Committee and his subsequent ascendance to GOP floor leader indicated his clout. Truman met with the senator and the secretary of state on April 18, and they had a fruitful conversation on a range of international issues. All agreed that such discussions needed to continue in order to maintain a bipartisan foreign policy. The president publicized his "very satisfactory talk" with Bridges in a press release, pledging not only to keep the Republicans informed but also to "solicit their views and take them into serious account in both the formulation and implementation of our foreign policy." He then instructed Acheson to set up meetings with senior Senate Republicans to discuss an upcoming foreign affairs summit. Connally, who reportedly "snorted like a Texas longhorn" and called the president's olive branch a "blunder" and an "affront," stepped in and limited the secretary's meetings to Republicans on the Foreign Relations Committee. Truman's efforts paid off in the short term, as Bridges stifled his attacks on Acheson for a year.[37]

Connally's reaction complicated Truman's efforts to enhance nonpartisanship in foreign affairs. Although "Texas Tom" had good relationships with Republicans Alexander Wiley (WI) and Lodge on his committee, his animosity toward Bridges proved counterproductive. If a president as partisan as Truman could extend the olive branch to Bridges in spite of the latter's attacks on Acheson, Connally should have done the same. Disputes over turf drove the Texan's refusal to invite Republican leaders to confer with the secretary of state, and he insisted that only the Foreign Relations Committee could have a say in diplomatic issues.[38]

The Democrats worked in other ways to foster harmony with the Republicans during the Tydings hearings. Representative Brooks Hays (D-AR) visited Acheson and asked him to rekindle bipartisanship, suggesting that GOP congressmen such as Walter Judd actually "held a kinder feeling" toward Acheson than some of their public comments indicated. The secretary responded positively, but he had to be skeptical:

Judd, a leader of the China Bloc, had been screaming for his resignation. Acheson was remarkably conciliatory when Thomas Dewey, the Republican governor of New York, phoned to clear an upcoming speech with him. Dewey's draft noted in "strong terms" that the Democrats had given China away at Yalta, and it blamed the communist victory on the administration's policy reversals regarding support for the Nationalists. Secretary Acheson accepted these criticisms without complaint. He did, however, ask Dewey to amend a passage characterizing Formosa as the only hope of the Far East, which the governor agreed to do. Moreover, at Acheson's suggestion, Dewey agreed to reword a couple of sections that seemed to condone McCarthyism. For his part, Truman took pains to congratulate former president and GOP stalwart Herbert Hoover for his speech exhorting unity of moral purpose in the struggle against communism. Notably, Truman refused to criticize Hoover's call to oust all communist nations from the UN, a position the administration opposed.[39]

The president added two Republicans to the State Department in an effort to bolster bipartisanship. In March the administration named John Sherman Cooper, a Kentucky Republican, as a consultant to the secretary of state. Unfortunately, Cooper turned out to be a lackluster choice due to his lack of foreign policy experience. Truman did better when he appointed John Foster Dulles to a similar position on April 6. Just two weeks earlier the president had said he would never appoint a "stuffed shirt" like Dulles, despite the Republican's extensive experience in foreign affairs. But fallout over the Tydings hearings and pressure from the ailing Vandenberg probably persuaded Truman to change his mind. Political expediency entered into the equation as well. Acheson confided to Senator Herbert Lehman (D-NY), who had recently ousted Dulles from his Senate seat, that this move would prevent Dulles from running for the Senate in 1950. On the day the White House announced his appointment, Dulles was still haggling with Acheson about his new job title. Rebuffed after bucking for the title of ambassador at large, Dulles claimed he "personally was not concerned about rank," but his actions said otherwise. Wanting to make sure he outranked Cooper, he asked that the word "top" be added to his job title of consultant to the secretary. Truman refused to placate Dulles on the wording, but the appointment accomplished its purpose, and the administration made sure the press understood its importance. A *New York Times* headline proclaimed, "Dulles Named U.S. Adviser to Renew Bipartisan Policy."[40]

As the Tydings hearings raged on, the administration announced a reorganization of the Foreign Relations Committee designed to enhance congressional input into policy formation. The new system created eight bipartisan subcommittees corresponding to principal areas of the State Department, such as European affairs, UN affairs, and Far Eastern affairs. Area leaders in the State Department would meet with these subcommittees monthly to consult about regional issues. Although Connally took credit for the reorganization, he merely blessed the final product. Jack McFall, assistant secretary of state in charge of congressional relations, recalled that he initiated the plan and convinced the chairman to go through with it by allowing him to call it the "Connally Plan." Francis Wilcox, chief of staff for the Foreign Relations Committee, claimed *he* was the one who proposed it to Connally. McFall most likely hatched the scheme as a way to quell Republican attacks during the Tydings hearings. He probably pitched it to Wilcox, who had Connally's ear and convinced the senator to restructure the committee.[41]

The reorganization of the Foreign Relations Committee ultimately became a missed opportunity to enhance bipartisan support for Truman's policies. It seemed that the new system could not help but improve communication between the State Department and the Senate, and it was an effective symbolic gesture. Committee member H. Alexander Smith promptly telegrammed his congratulations to Connally when he found out about the reorganization. Yet the devil was in the details, and some subcommittees were more bipartisan than others. Four senators (two Democrats and two Republicans) made up the UN Affairs and European Affairs Subcommittees, the foreign policy areas with the strongest tradition of cooperation between the parties. The remaining subcommittees, most notably Far Eastern Affairs, contained two Democrats and one Republican. Since the communist triumph in China in 1949, Republicans, including Vandenberg, had complained that the Democrats were not soliciting their input on Asian issues. The imbalanced representation on the Far East subcommittee lent credence to GOP complaints.[42]

Meanwhile, the Tydings hearings took an interesting turn. Early on, the press had supported Tydings in spite of his aggressive tactics, and McCarthy seemed headed for irrelevance. However, things changed when the chairman's zeal to bury his Wisconsin adversary led observers to believe that he was not delving into the charges as deeply as he should. Events came to a head over the investigation of Owen Lattimore, a professor accused of having communist ties. Tydings pronounced Lattimore innocent, but Lodge disagreed and asked for more testimony. Newspaper stories now blamed Tydings as much as McCarthy for the partisan and sometimes chaotic hearings. The public took notice; a poll released in May 1950 revealed that only 14 percent of Americans were unaware of McCarthy's charges against the State Department. Behind the scenes, Tydings continued his quest, reportedly telling Truman that he intended to "finish the discrediting of McCarthy." But the negative press was taking its toll. After receiving a call from the senator, Truman quipped that Tydings was the "most nervous individual" he had ever seen. By June, the embattled chairman was in a panic, besieging the White House with daily phone calls and even asking the president to set a deadline for completion of the hearings. Wisely, Truman refused to interfere; he believed Tydings had totally botched the hearings and now wanted the president to save him. As the hearings wound down, the chairman continued to openly refute McCarthy's charges, while the other Democrats on the committee either sat in silence or skipped sessions altogether. One journalist called the probe "an inquiry which in its bitterness and partisanship was unique in the annals of Congress."[43]

Conversely, Dean Acheson's fortunes were changing for the better as the hearings wound down. By May 1950, he could see the light at the end of the tunnel, despite the relentless Republican attacks. More Democrats came to his defense, highlighted by a performance on the Senate floor "unparalleled in recent years." In a well-orchestrated attack, the likes of which veteran Capitol Hill aides had never seen, the Democrats, led by majority leader Scott Lucas (IL) and majority whip Francis Myers (PA), pointed out the inconsistencies in McCarthy's accusations and the lack of evidence presented. At one point, Vice President Barkley ordered Lucas to sit down when he called McCarthy a liar. Another senator roared that if McCarthy's charges turned out to be unfounded, the Wisconsin senator should be "scourged by public opinion from the society of decent men and women." Acheson subsequently wrote to an acquaintance that it seemed "this storm is about over." It would not be his last.[44]

1

Into Korea

Harry Truman's presidency was distinctive: he was the only American president to serve as commander in chief during two major wars, and the first of these significantly affected the way he approached the second. When World War II ended with the use of nuclear weapons, the United States was the only nation that possessed them. By the time of the Korean conflict, things had changed dramatically; the Soviet Union was now an open adversary with its own nuclear capability. Much as he wanted to stop the expansion of Soviet communism in the Far East, Truman was equally determined to avoid a third world war. Nor had the president forgotten that the 1938 Munich Conference had given part of Czechoslovakia to the Nazi regime to quench Hitler's thirst for lebensraum. In 1950 Truman believed that Stalin, like Hitler, craved world domination. The commander in chief thus interpreted the North Korean invasion as nothing less than a land grab orchestrated by the Soviet Union in its quest to conquer the globe.

This chapter examines the decision to intervene in Korea. Why did the president go to war in the first place? How did he determine there was no need for congressional approval? Did Truman bully Congress out of its authority to declare war, or did the legislators abdicate their constitutional responsibility? How did the U.S. role in the United Nations play into the dynamics of the situation? Could the commander in chief have mitigated the political thrashing he suffered at the hands of his Republican adversaries after China's entry into the war? Ultimately, the Eighty-First Congress, controlled by the president's party, never exercised its war-making power in a conflict that produced more than 130,000 American casualties. The Korean decision had enormous historical implications, as subsequent presidents followed Truman's lead, sending American forces into major confrontations without a declaration of war from Congress.

The Decision to Intervene

Trouble in Korea hit the Truman administration like a thunderbolt. At 3:00 p.m. on Saturday, June 24, the president was flying from Washington to his home in Independence, Missouri, for what he thought would be a relaxing weekend. Little did he know that before he landed, Kim Il Sung's forces would thunder across the thirty-eighth parallel with almost 110,000 soldiers, more than 1,400 artillery pieces, and 126 tanks. Word reached Washington that evening, and at 11:20 p.m., Secretary Acheson phoned his boss: "Mr. President, I have very serious news. The North Koreans have invaded South Korea." That night, State Department officials began to work on a request for an emergency meeting of the UN Security Council. Ambassador at Large Philip Jessup recalled that the attitude was, "We've got to do something, and whatever we do, we've got to do it through the United Nations."[1]

The attack made only a ripple when it was first reported in the American press. Events in Korea were relegated to page 20 of the Sunday edition of the *New York Times,* which reported there was "no indication that the United States intends to take direct military action." The *Washington Post* placed the story in a section near the back, noting that North Korea had formally declared war on Saturday at 9:00 p.m. eastern daylight time.[2]

Meanwhile, Sunday began very early for American diplomats. Ernest A. Gross, acting U.S. ambassador to the United Nations, telephoned UN secretary-general Trygve Lie at 3:00 a.m. to request a Security Council meeting as news of the invasion spread to governments around the globe. If the Soviets ended their boycott of the Security Council to veto any actions against North Korea, the United States planned to call for an emergency gathering of the General Assembly. At 8:00 a.m. Washington got word that a North Korean regiment had occupied Kaesong, only forty miles northwest of the South Korean capital of Seoul (see figure 1). Acheson rushed back to the State Department from his Maryland home at around 11:00 a.m., giving reporters a whiff of the crisis in the air when he arrived coatless and disheveled. Minutes later, after getting reports that the communists were strafing nearby installations, John J. Muccio, U.S.

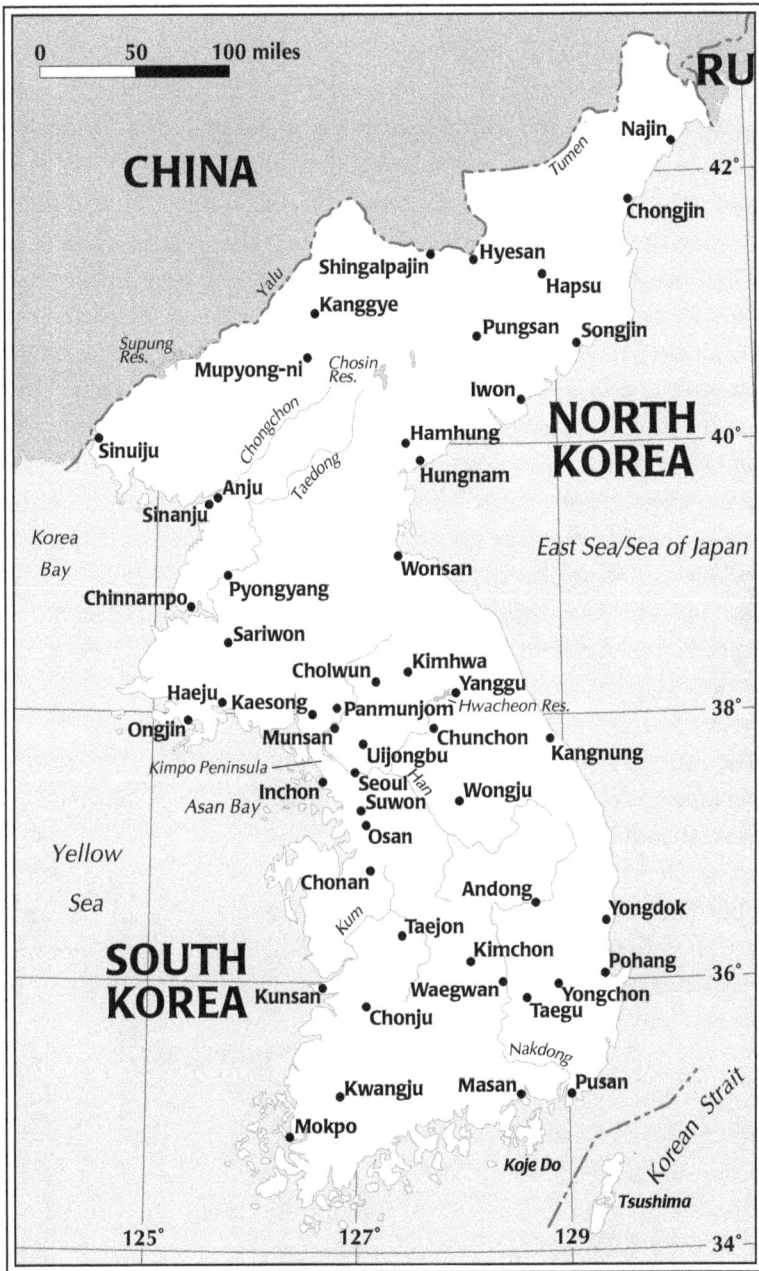

Figure 1. The Korean peninsula, June 1950. (Map by Dick Gilbreath, University of Kentucky cartography lab. Source: www.paulnoll.com. Used by permission.)

ambassador to South Korea, ordered the evacuation of the families of embassy staff members from Seoul.[3]

After receiving a call from Acheson at 2:45 p.m., describing the deteriorating situation for the South Korean forces, Truman decided to return to Washington. The president believed that North Korea would ignore the expected Security Council resolution calling for a cease-fire and withdrawal due to the "complete disregard" of the UN displayed by Kim Il Sung and his "big allies" (the Soviets) in the past (the Soviets had refused to allow North Korea to participate in UN-supervised elections in the peninsula in 1948). If that happened, Truman felt the United States would have to do something, and he wanted to get back to Blair House (where he was living temporarily while the White House was being renovated) as quickly as possible. Leaving some of his staffers behind, the president rushed to the airport, boarded his plane, and impatiently asked a Secret Service agent why they were not taking off. When the agent reported that the pilot was waiting for his navigator, Truman insisted that they take off without him. Obediently, the pilot removed the boarding ramp and closed the door. As the pilot prepared to taxi to the runway, the navigator's car sped up to the plane, and he climbed a rope ladder to board the aircraft.[4]

The president had military intervention in mind from the start. As he prepared to leave for Washington, he told reporters, "Don't make it alarmist. It could be a dangerous situation, but I hope it isn't." However, Brigadier General Wallace H. Graham, Truman's personal physician, told journalists, "The boss is going to hit those fellows hard." Margaret Truman had spent that weekend with her father and wrote in her diary, "Northern or Communist Korea is marching in on Southern Korea and we are going to fight."[5]

As Truman traveled back to Washington, the UN Security Council met, and Congress weighed in on the situation. Curiously, the Soviets continued their boycott of the Security Council rather than vetoing the resolution calling for North Korea to withdraw. In the Soviet Union's absence, the Security Council voted 9–0 for the resolution, with Yugoslavia abstaining. John Kee (D-WV), chairman of the House Foreign Affairs Committee, told reporters that, based on what he knew at the time, South Korea was in a "fairly good position to take care of itself." (Kee's comment reflected the thoughts of the executive branch, which had removed all

American combat troops from Korea in mid-1949, leaving behind only a military advisory group.) Senator H. Alexander Smith claimed the United States had a moral imperative to look after the "infant Korean Republic." Other Republicans assailed the White House. Representative Paul W. Shafer (R-MI) said Korea had been "flung into the Soviet orbit" by the State Department. Senate minority leader Kenneth Wherry (R-NE) attributed the crisis to China policy, trumpeting, "The Administration should stand up and do something and then we'll stop those Commies."[6]

The president convened the first meeting on the Korean crisis with his National Security Council on Sunday evening. Attendees included the Joint Chiefs of Staff (JCS) and officials from the State and Defense Departments. As they waited for dinner to be served, two of them recalled that Truman was seated near a window repeating softly to himself, "We can't let the U.N. down!" After discussing the situation, the commander in chief directed the Seventh Fleet to head toward Formosa and await further instructions, and he ordered American air and naval support to secure Seoul during the evacuation of American citizens. They did not discuss obtaining congressional approval, and the president stressed, "We are working entirely for the United Nations."[7]

Congress got more involved on Monday, June 26. In the first Senate session after the invasion began, five Republicans and one Democrat mentioned Korea in the floor debate. Only two House members, both Republicans, did the same. Most of the GOP legislators blasted the administration for permitting these events to occur, and Senator William Knowland asked whether the United States would "sit back and twiddle our thumbs and do nothing" if the USSR blocked UN action. Senator Tom Connally shook his finger at the critics and questioned their "splendid attitude of doubt," asserting, "the President . . . is not going to tremble like a psychopath before Russian power." Despite the partisan sparring, when Republicans emerged from a GOP Policy Committee meeting, Senator Eugene D. Millikin (CO) reported that his colleagues seemed "unanimous that the incident should not be used as a provocation for war."[8]

News from Korea worsened as the day went on. During a morning conversation with Congressman Kee, Acheson said South Korea was in "pretty good shape." However, by 2:00 p.m., the White House learned that the government of the Republic of Korea (ROK) had fled Seoul. The president got varying advice from congressional Democrats. Representa-

tive Franklin D. Roosevelt Jr. (NY) suggested a joint ultimatum delivered by the United States and the USSR demanding a cease-fire and that
the North and South Koreans return to their original positions. Roosevelt
believed that if the Soviets declined, they would be exposed as a "party
of interest in the present invasion . . . disrupting the peace of the world."
Significantly, Truman asked Senator Connally whether he needed to ask
Congress for a declaration of war before sending American forces to Korea.
Although the Texan later regretted it, he answered, "If a burglar breaks into
your house you can shoot him without going down to the police station
and getting permission." Fearing a "long debate in Congress which would
tie your (Truman's) hands completely," Connally asserted, "You have the
right to do it as Commander-in-Chief and under the U.N. Charter."[9]

Truman reconvened the NSC that evening. General Omar Bradley,
chairman of the JCS, shared General Douglas MacArthur's assessment
that a "complete collapse [of the ROK] is imminent." When one of his
generals reported that the United States had shot down its first North
Korean plane (built by the Soviets), the commander in chief remarked,
"I hope it's not the last." After hearing out his advisers, Truman decided
to have American naval and air forces assist the South Koreans as needed
below the thirty-eighth parallel, removing the previous restrictions that
limited U.S. military activities to assisting with the evacuation of Americans. Notably, when one of the generals asked for permission to conduct operations in the north, the president replied, "Not yet." He also
ordered the Seventh Fleet to prevent any skirmishing between the Chinese Nationalists on Taiwan and the communists on mainland China.
The NSC did not discuss asking Congress for a declaration of war, and
John Hickerson, assistant secretary of state for UN affairs, later asserted
that such a request would have been premature. Truman nevertheless felt
it necessary to have a dialogue with the legislators and scheduled a briefing
with congressional leaders for the following morning. A statement summarizing his decisions was prepared for release to the press the next day.
Implementation, however, began immediately.[10]

Hickerson, one of the last to leave the meeting, later shared some poi-
gnant comments made by Truman that Monday night. Relaxing with a
drink after a taxing day, the president confided, "I have hoped and prayed
that I would never have to make a decision like the one I have just made
today." The president expressed disappointment that the lack of American

support had probably contributed to the failure of the League of Nations, underscoring his determination that the UN succeed in its first crucial test. Revealing his belief that the Soviets had ordered the North Korean invasion, the chief executive declared, "Now is the time to call their bluff," asserting, "in the final analysis, I *did this* for the United Nations."[11]

The president reiterated this conviction when he met with lawmakers on the morning of Tuesday, June 27. At this gathering of fourteen congressional leaders (nine Democrats and five Republicans), Truman had NSC and military officials update them on the situation. He then read the statement prepared the night before, telling the group he would release it to the press at the conclusion of the meeting. During the ensuing discussion, the president affirmed the U.S. commitment to defending South Korea. Republicans stressed the importance of adhering to UN orders, and Senator Connally assured the group that the United States would not intervene alone. The JCS clarified that Truman's orders did not commit U.S. ground troops. Connally recalled that no one dissented, and Acheson attributed the consensus to the fact that the United States had responded with force. The commander in chief informed, but did not consult, the legislators.[12]

Truman's initial public statements reflected how quickly the situation had escalated. Radio and television stations began interrupting broadcasts on the afternoon of Sunday, June 25, with updates on the situation, and Korea was front-page news in major newspapers the following morning, yet the White House did not issue a statement until almost noon on Monday. The announcement commended the UN Security Council for its swift passage of a U.S.-sponsored resolution calling for the withdrawal of North Korean troops and assistance from UN members to support this directive. Tuesday, after the meeting with congressional leaders, Truman issued his second press release, asserting that the June 25 Security Council resolution justified deploying U.S. air and naval forces to "give Korean Government troops cover and support." He also announced the dispatch of the Seventh Fleet to the Straits of Formosa to keep the peace between the Chinese communists on the mainland and the Nationalists. The June 27 statement was significant for several reasons. The previous day, the culprit had been identified as the "forces of North Korea," but now the offender was "communism," an intentionally ambiguous term that could mean North Korea, China, or the USSR. The statement discussed the motivation for the North Korean attack, calling it a clear indication that "communism has passed beyond the use of subversion to conquer independent nations and will now use armed invasion and war." It also represented a policy reversal regarding Formosa. Due to the North Korean invasion, a communist occupation of the island was now deemed a "direct threat to the security of the Pacific area and to the United States forces" in the region. Formosa had become a vital American interest. This policy change delighted the China Bloc Republicans in Congress, who had criticized Truman and Acheson for enabling the communist victory in China in 1949. There is no doubt that the move to protect Formosa helped Truman solicit broad support for the Korean intervention. House members lauded Truman's statement with a standing ovation. One voice, however, dissented. New York congressman Vito Marcantonio of the American Labor Party said the president had undermined Congress's constitutional authority to declare war. "For all purposes," Marcantonio stated, "we are at war." He called the president's move a calamitous decision that could bring "disastrous consequences on the people of the United States unless checked by the people themselves."[13]

Tuesday, June 27, concluded with two momentous events. Just before midnight, the UN Security Council adopted a resolution that member nations "furnish such assistance to the Republic of Korea as may be necessary to repel the armed attack and to restore international peace and security in the area." This wording was more aggressive than that of the earlier resolution, which had called on members to "render every assistance to the United Nations" in persuading North Korea to withdraw north of the thirty-eighth parallel. The Security Council approved the resolution 7–1, with Yugoslavia opposed, Egypt and India abstaining, and the USSR absent. Meanwhile, North Korean troops had overrun Seoul, prompting a triumphant Kim Il Sung to cable his troops, "Hail the united Korean people!"[14]

Nevertheless, the president hardly mentioned Korea during his previously scheduled addresses on June 27 and 28. Expecting Truman to discuss the Korean situation in person for the first time in his June 28 speech to the American Newspaper Guild, the major networks arranged to broadcast his message to the nation. But the commander in chief disappointed them, saying only that the United States must "do everything we can to prevent such aggression."[15]

Congress united behind the president. Senator Henry Cabot Lodge Jr. (R-MA) backed Truman's dispatch of air and naval support and hoped the commander in chief would "not shrink from using the Army," if necessary. A Senate-House conference committee assembled a bill in less than an hour, extending the selective service for a year and giving Truman broad powers of implementation. The House passed the bill 315–4 and forwarded it to the Senate, which passed it 76–0 on Wednesday, June 28, after "not a word of debate." Only two days earlier, both houses had seemed to be in a "hopeless deadlock," haggling over restrictions on the president's use of the draft in peacetime. The outbreak of hostilities in Korea changed all that, and editorials lauded Congress's response. Interestingly, the press overlooked the fact that 120 House members and 20 senators did not bother to show up to vote (although 12 of the absentee senators sent verbal word to colleagues that they supported the bill). The most likely explanation for the poor turnout was the overwhelming approval of military support to Korea. Members knew their individual votes would not affect the bill's passage.[16]

Senator Robert A. Taft (R-OH) was an important exception to the rally around the president. The GOP's lead isolationist delivered a major speech that, like Marcantonio's, accused the president of exceeding his constitutional authority by committing American air and naval forces to Korea. "We are now actually engaged in a de facto war," Taft declared, arguing that if this intervention went unchallenged, the president could "go to war in Malaya, or Indonesia, or Iran, or South America without congressional consent." Claiming that Truman had "no legal authority" for his action, the Ohioan warned his colleagues that if they did not respond, they would be terminating "for all time the right of Congress to declare war as provided by the Constitution." Taft also brought up the UN Participation Act of 1945 (UNPA), which required the president to get congressional approval before committing American armed forces to UN missions. The law authorized the commander in chief to negotiate special agreements with the Security Council "providing for the numbers and types" of U.S. armed forces, along with "their degree of readiness and general location," to support UN military actions. Although the UNPA required congressional approval of such an agreement, none was in place in June 1950. Taft believed that intervention in Korea was the right thing to do, but there was a constitutional principle at stake. He would endorse Truman's action if the president requested Congress's approval.[17]

Taft's speech drew immediate criticism. As soon as the Ohio senator sat down, majority leader Scott Lucas (D-IL) rose to the administration's defense, asserting that the UN Charter gave Truman the authority
he needed. Lucas reminded his colleagues of the "traditions and precedents established more than 100 times" by previous presidents, including
Thomas Jefferson's dispatch of the navy to combat the Barbary pirates and
the use of American forces to quell the Boxer Rebellion in China. Senator Connally later read into the record a portion of the June 27 Security
Council resolution calling on UN members to assist the South Koreans.
Senator Ralph Flanders (R-VT) said Truman's action was legal as long as
military activity remained south of the thirty-eighth parallel. The *Washington Post*, conceding Congress's right to declare war, argued, "Police
action to halt aggression is not war, as American history testifies." Secretary Acheson later dismissed Taft's opposition as "typical senatorial legal-
istic ground for differing with the President."[18]

The administration continued to inch deeper into the Korean affair.
On the morning of Thursday, June 29, the Pentagon began to receive
reports that the ROK army was in a continuous retreat and suffering 50
percent casualties. Truman convened another NSC meeting at 5:00 p.m.,
where the JCS recommended the introduction of American ground forces.
General Bradley emphasized that the troops would only secure the port
of Pusan for the protection of American evacuees; no troops would go to
the invasion front. The generals, however, wanted permission to bomb
targets in North Korea. The president urged restraint, saying he did not
want the United States to become "over-committed to a whole lot of other
things that could mean war." He authorized attacks only on ammunition
dumps, air bases, and supply storage facilities in the north, claiming he
"only wanted to restore order to the 38th Parallel." Apparently, none of
the attendees knew that General MacArthur had already ordered the air
force to make strategic strikes into North Korea.[19]

The president finally elaborated on the Korean situation at a routine
press conference on Thursday, June 29. More than half the reporters' questions dealt with the conflict. They were hungry for information:

QUESTION: Mr. President, everybody is asking in this country, are
we or are we not at war?
THE PRESIDENT: We are not at war.

Truman described the North Korean attack as a "bandit raid" and agreed with a reporter's characterization of the UN response as a "police action." In both cases, the journalists confirmed these descriptors with the president before going to press, and both terms would come back to haunt him. Bandit raids do not conjure up images of tanks, airplanes, and infantry. Critics would later pound the president's description of the conflict as a "police action" as American casualties mounted. One rhetorician explained: "'Bandits' are usually 'suppressed' through capture and incarceration by the 'police.' But Truman mixed the metaphor: The Security Council's resolution called only for the 'police' to ensure that the 'bandits' withdraw to their hideout in North Korea." The bandits were looking more formidable by the hour.[20]

The decision to intervene in Korea culminated the next day, Friday, June 30. General MacArthur, who had conducted a personal inspection of the front, cabled Washington in the middle of the night and warned, "The only assurance of holding the present line, and the ability to regain later lost ground, is through the introduction of U.S. ground combat forces into the Korean battle area." He asked for a combat regiment immediately, followed by two divisions for a counteroffensive. When this request reached the president at 5:00 a.m., Truman was already awake and getting dressed for his morning walk. He approved the regiment but held off on the two divisions until he had a chance to meet with his military advisers. At 8:30 a.m. the president and the NSC discussed Jiang Jieshi's offer of 30,000 Chinese Nationalist troops to help fight the North Koreans. Truman liked the idea because it got other UN members involved and avoided the involvement of American ground forces. Acheson felt otherwise, fearing that use of the Nationalist troops would invite communist China to join the fight. The JCS backed the secretary, citing logistical and tactical problems with the deployment of Jiang's forces. Truman, bowing to their judgment, declined the offer. The commander in chief then made a momentous decision: MacArthur could have his two divisions of American troops.[21]

Truman briefed sixteen congressional leaders later on the morning of June 30. He read aloud a summary of his decisions, which he released to the press while the meeting was in progress. "In keeping with the United Nations Security Council's request," the president had authorized the hitting of targets in North Korea and the use of "certain supporting ground units." A long silence ensued before the legislators began asking questions. Most dealt with contributions by other UN members, and several senators urged the use of token combat forces from other nations to emphasize that this was a UN action rather than an American response. At one point, Truman claimed the United States had sent no troops into "actual combat" yet; the plan was simply to secure communication and supply lines at Pusan. This was a stretch of the truth, given the president's approval of two divisions for a counteroffensive just hours earlier.[22]

Only one of the sixteen, Senator Wherry, challenged the president. Rising as though he were speaking on the Senate floor, the minority leader asked Truman if he intended to advise Congress before dispatching ground forces to Korea. Truman responded that he had already ordered the troops into Korea but would advise Congress in the event of a "real emergency." When Wherry argued that Congress should be consulted *before* the president made such moves, Truman gave a confusing response. Apparently referring to the events of June 25, the president claimed he could not confer with Congress because it had been a weekend emergency, asserting, "I just had to act as Commander-in-Chief, and I did." Thus, Truman promised he would advise Congress in the event of a major crisis, yet in the next breath indicated he did not have time to consult the legislature during emergencies. The president assured the congressmen that if any major actions occurred in the future, he would *tell* them. Wherry did not go quietly, rising again and repeating his demand. Truman again tried to placate the senator, replying, "If there is any necessity for Congressional action, I will come to you. But I hope we can get those bandits in Korea suppressed without that." Later in the meeting, Wherry raised the issue a third time, correctly surmising the significance of the final sentence in the president's press release authorizing the use of American ground troops. This time, a House colleague, Dewey Short (R-MO), sawed Wherry off at the knees, extolling Truman's leadership and stating that nearly everyone in Congress shared his sentiments.[23]

Yet Wherry's objections apparently pricked the conscience of another key GOP senator in attendance. Although he called Truman's response an "answer to prayer" in his diary, H. Alexander Smith had been wrestling with the issue since Senator Taft had raised it earlier in the week. Smith agreed with Taft's assertion that the UNPA did not authorize the president's action because there had been no previous congressional approval of American military support of a UN mandate. However, he also reasoned that the statute did not bar the president from using military force, and he bought into Truman's argument that the president's constitutional powers as commander in chief allowed him to deploy military force. Like the administration, Smith believed the precedents cited by the State Department gave Truman plenty of justification for bypassing Congress. Nevertheless, as a compromise (and perhaps to throw a political bone to the powerful Taft), Smith proposed a joint resolution approving the president's action. Truman agreed to look into the idea and asked Acheson to make a recommendation.[24]

Despite the president's talk of suppressing bandits, the congressional leaders clearly understood the weight of his decisions. Acheson noted in his memoirs, "We were then fully committed in Korea." Senator Connally recalled that as he and the other congressmen filed out, "All of us were shocked by the realization that only five years after World War II, American youth were once more involved in military combat."[25]

Congressional Approval Considered

Truman revisited the question of obtaining a congressional endorsement of the intervention on Monday, July 3. As Congress recessed for the Independence Day holiday, the president called a meeting (at Acheson's request) of the cabinet, the service secretaries, and the "Big 4" representatives of the Democratic leadership on Capitol Hill. Of the Big 4, only Senator Lucas bothered to attend. Acheson pointed out that several legislators were quite nervous about what they perceived as "excessive Presidential independence." The attendees therefore discussed whether Truman should address Congress on the Korean crisis and whether he should seek a joint resolution supporting the war effort, as Senator Smith had suggested during the June 30 briefing. Acheson distributed a proposed resolution that he had reworded; rather than endorsing American intervention to maintain peace in the "Pacific area," the revised resolution discussed the need to ensure security in the "Korean situation," a change designed to avoid reopening the debate over China policy.[26]

Lucas was indecisive during the meeting, which was particularly problematic because he was the lone voice from Capitol Hill. When Truman asked for his opinion on the proposed resolution, the senator was reluctant to respond without talking it over with his colleagues. After more prodding, Lucas admitted the president "had very properly done what he had to without consulting the Congress." The majority leader therefore opposed the resolution, even though he deemed it "satisfactory" and believed it could pass. Yet Lucas reported that many colleagues had expressed the opinion that Truman should "keep away from Congress and avoid debate," and he worried that a discussion of the resolution would last at least a week. The senator appeared to be sensitive to Republican criticism. When Lucas noted that most legislators were "sick of the attitude" demonstrated by Taft and Wherry, the president correctly surmised that the latter had lightened up a bit following the June 30 briefing (Lucas disagreed). Still, the majority leader's position was baffling. If most members of Congress were sick of Taft and Wherry, why did he fear a floor debate? Confounding his recommendation further, Lucas said that if Truman reconvened the congressional leaders from the Friday briefing, they would probably unanimously endorse the resolution, ensuring its passage. The senator also worried that a presidential speech to Congress on Korea would be "practically asking for a declaration of war."[27]

The cabinet members and service secretaries in attendance did not serve the president well, either. Few offered their views on a congressional sanction. General Bradley was an exception, opposing the resolution in order to avoid a lengthy debate in Congress on "matters which now seemed to be taken for granted." The rest made neutral comments. Even Acheson, after opening the meeting and sharing his drafts of the revised resolution and a proposed address to Congress, said little else.[28]

Truman himself raised the issue of the constitutionality of his actions. However, when Lucas pointed out that a presidential speech to Congress could be perceived as asking for a declaration of war (and therefore should be avoided), Truman agreed, clarifying that he "had not been acting as President, but as Commander-in-Chief of our forces in the Far East." Later, he noted he had to be "very careful" to avoid the appearance of "trying to get around Congress and use extra-Constitutional powers." The president spoke of the challenges involved in keeping the legislators informed, but he showed no inclination to seek their advice or approval. Truman refused to introduce the resolution, maintaining that it was up to Congress to do so. The discussion ended with a decision to take no action until after the legislators returned from their recess. By the time the legislature reconvened, Acheson recalled, "We were pretty well won over to Senator Lucas' view."[29]

The July 3 meeting was the last meaningful discussion about obtaining congressional approval to send American forces into Korea. After meeting with the Big 4 a week later, Truman told Acheson they had advised him not to address Congress, making no mention of any discussion about a joint resolution. However, Senator Alexander Wiley (R-WI) passionately pleaded with the White House to submit a resolution for a congressional endorsement. Wiley contended that a resolution would safeguard Congress's "integrity," even if it occurred after the fact. He declared, "No single military action taken by the executive branch . . . has had as many widespread implications as this one," reflecting concerns that Korea was only the first Soviet foray and that others would follow elsewhere. Complaining that Congress had been yielding "more and more of its authority . . . to the executive branch," Wiley asked whether he and his colleagues should "sit by silently while the President takes actions which might lead us into a third world war." Wiley's pleas fell on deaf ears, including his GOP colleagues on the Foreign Relations Committee. White House aide George Elsey noted that a congressional resolution was "discussed half-heartedly from time to time, but the issue was never clearly thrashed out." When Elsey told Truman in mid-July that drafts of such a declaration had been floating around the White House, the president said he had never heard of them and expressed scorn for the idea. Elsey later concluded that his boss had been "dreadfully wrong." Speaking of the president, Elsey lamented, "We of the staff had served him poorly by not . . . seeking congressional involvement in the opening days of the conflict. It was soon too late. We had 'Truman's War' to deal with."[30]

Response to Intervention

The president was slow to deliver a war message to the public. Acheson pushed Truman hard during the July 3 meeting, urging him to address the nation about Korea within a couple of days, but to no avail. At a press conference three days later, the president refused to comment on the status of the conflict, even though the first contingent of 500 American troops had been on the ground for more than a day, enduring withering attacks. When a reporter asked Truman on July 13 whether he intended to speak to Congress and the public about the conflict, he replied that he was thinking about it. The president thought about it for another week before his first major speech about the Korean situation.[31]

Nevertheless, the president's decision to intervene against North Korea was wildly popular, and *Newsweek* reported that the nation was "revived by Harry S. Truman's immediate counterpunch." *New York Times* reporters in all parts of the country printed descriptions such as "real unanimity," "99-to-1 in favor," "virtually unanimous approval," and "no dissenting voices" to characterize public opinion. The *Roanoke World-News* said the president "spoke for every true American," adding, "we should be glad this showdown has come." Joseph C. Harsch of the *Christian Science Monitor*, who had lived in the capital for twenty years, declared he had never "felt such a sense of relief and unity pass through the city." Telegrams and letters deluged the White House, running ten to one in favor of intervention. Support for the war came from some astonishing places. Socialist Party leader Norman Thomas and former Progressive Party presidential candidate Henry Wallace bucked their parties to support the intervention because it was a UN action. Even the Carnegie Foundation for International Peace jumped on the bandwagon. As historian Eric Goldman wrote, "For one moment, suspended weirdly in the bitter debates of the postwar . . . the bold response of Harry Truman had united America . . . as it had not been since that distant confetti evening of V-J."[32]

Most members of Congress initially supported the war. Responding to mail from constituents, Senator Theodore F. Green (D-RI) echoed the president's belief that the Soviets were "testing the limit to which our appeasement . . . might go." Green also cited the League of Nations' failure to respond to Italy's attack on Ethiopia in 1936 to justify the UN action in Korea. Preaching the doctrine of Truman, Green wrote, "We are interested in a street fight where there is shooting, even if we are not shot at ourselves." A member of the Foreign Relations Committee, Green nevertheless held that "the President, and not the Congress, has the conduct of our foreign affairs." The Rhode Islander made a distinction that most Americans probably did not notice, writing, "We did not go into Korea to fight communism" but to "help the United Nations fight aggression."[33]

Senator Paul H. Douglas (D-IL) presented a scholarly defense of the administration. Sparked by Taft's questioning of the president's authority to lead America to war, Douglas reviewed James Madison's notes from the 1787 Constitutional Convention to justify Truman's approach. The Illinois senator said the founding fathers had substituted the word "declare" for the word "make" in the clause giving Congress the authority "to declare war," thus allowing the commander in chief to "repel sudden attacks" without obtaining congressional approval. Douglas cited Lincoln's call for volunteers following the attack on Fort Sumter as one of many precedents. Since time was of the essence in responding to the Korean emergency, Truman, like Lincoln, could deploy troops without a formal declaration of war. Douglas conceded that previous presidents had dispatched the military to defend against *direct* threats to American lives and territory. However, because there was no doubt that the communists would attack elsewhere if they were not stopped in Korea, America's "ultimate security" was at stake, justifying Truman's action. Douglas implied that presidents could wage limited war but not world war, observing that it "would be below the dignity of the United States to declare war on a pigmy state."[34]

Douglas's assertion of the president's authority to respond to a crisis militarily echoed sentiments expressed by Senator Edwin C. Johnson (D-CO) five years earlier. Johnson, who typically opposed Truman, had admitted that the use of atomic weapons to end World War II had reversed his views on congressional declarations of war and convinced him not to tie the commander in chief's hands. In the midst of debate on the UNPA, Johnson had decried efforts to set limits on the number of troops the president could deploy without congressional consent. Believing there would be no time for consultations in the nuclear age, Johnson had warned, "Nations not set to get under way trigger-quick will be whipped before they start."[35]

Senator Douglas acknowledged that there were "grave dangers" in giving the chief executive the power to use military force. But he believed that a president's personal sense of responsibility to the institution of the presidency and Congress's power to impeach would act as restraints. Both arguments were weak. Presidents are generally forceful people who lead the country as they see fit, and the power of the office does not necessarily make executives more cautious about using it. Impeachment is too cumbersome and is unlikely to be used at the outset of a war. Even after months of protests over the Vietnam War, Congress never seriously con-

sidered impeaching Lyndon Johnson or Richard Nixon as a means of getting the United States out of that conflict.[36]

Other Democrats supported Truman's decision for different reasons.
According to Senate Armed Services Committee chairman Richard Russell (GA), Congress could not declare war on North Korea because the
United States had never recognized its existence as a sovereign state. Senator Guy Gillette (IA) held that articles 39 through 42 of the UN Charter, which describe directives by the Security Council to remedy breaches
of the peace, gave Truman the right to go to Korea. Curiously, Gillette
(and nearly everyone else, except for Senator Taft) ignored section 6 of
the UNPA, which required the president to get congressional approval
before sending American armed forces to respond to a Security Council
request.[37]

Sometimes, the zeal of the president's Democratic allies went into
overdrive. Representative John Walsh (IN) issued a statement declaring that "an irate America" would soon "deluge Russia itself with atom
bombs." Skeptical that the USSR had a nuclear capability, he continued, "It won't be just a one-bomb attack either. . . . We have at least 250
bombs." According to Walsh, "The only way to destroy an octopus is to
strike at its heart," and he warned, ominously, that the United States was
"not going to continue fighting secondary nations." A White House aide
described the senator's comments as "rather bad" but worried that if anyone said anything to the independent Walsh, it would "probably excite
him to the point that he would make a statement far worse."[38]

At the time, the GOP overwhelmingly endorsed the commitment of
American forces to Korea as a legitimate action by the commander in
chief. Three of the five Republican members of the Senate Foreign Relations Committee backed the president and expressed no concerns about
the lack of congressional approval. Senator Vandenberg, writing to Truman from his sick bed, applauded the decision and said he only wished
the United States had pushed for UN action sooner. Recalling Hitler's
aggression prior to World War II, Senator Flanders said, "We have the
invasion of the totalitarian power [in Korea] according to the old pattern,"
and he was pleased that the UN was not following the "pusillanimous
policy of the League of Nations." Flanders declared, "All the world knows
that it is Russia which is on the move and not North Korea." He wove
a creative rationalization for the legality of the president's police action,

reasoning that since the United States had accepted the Japanese surrender in southern Korea and had overseen free elections forming its government in 1948, America had "certain responsibilities of military protection against military invasion" of South Korea. Flanders pointed out that the ROK needed U.S. protection because the UN had not formed its own police force. According to Flanders, the United States did not need a declaration of war because it was simply carrying out an "existing obligation," provided it did not send forces north of the thirty-eighth parallel. Advancing into North Korea would "constitute action of a very different sort," requiring a congressional declaration of war. Even Senator Knowland, who normally opposed Truman's Far East policies, voiced support. Echoing the president's characterization of Korea as a "police action," Knowland acknowledged that Truman had the right to commit troops as commander in chief. The urgency of the situation made the use of such power acceptable. All these arguments translated into staunch, albeit brief, support for the president from the opposition party. H. Alexander Smith noted that the GOP was "elated," while Senator Styles Bridges announced, "I approve completely what has been done." Representative Charles Eaton (R-NJ), an ordained Baptist minister, proclaimed, "We've got a rattlesnake by the tail and the sooner we pound its damn head in, the better." Even Senator Taft, Truman's most persistent nemesis, admitted that he supported the "general policies" laid out by the commander in chief, causing White House press secretary Charlie Ross to exclaim, "By God! Bob Taft has joined the U.N. and the U.S." Despite its limited nature, Taft's response "caused great joy at the White House."[39]

The administration did what it could to maintain this unity. Acheson contacted Senator Wiley, the second-ranking Republican on the Foreign Relations Committee, early during the first week of the crisis to apprise him of the situation. Significantly, the secretary turned down a request from Senator Elbert Thomas (D-UT), a staunch administration ally, to speak at a state Democratic gathering in late July. Acheson demurred, with Truman's blessing, and noted there was a "great deal of business to get through on a unified basis" in the upcoming months. This showed a deliberate avoidance of political partisanship, despite the looming midterm elections. The president took the time, in the midst of the crisis, to pen a heartfelt letter to Vandenberg, who was recovering from surgery. Although part of Truman's response was a refutation of the senator's criticisms of Far East policy prior to the war, he also made it clear that he respected the ailing Republican's views. The president forthrightly justified his policies and noted that he believed Vandenberg had "decidedly wrong information and wrong impressions" about the causes of the Korean crisis. Despite their differences, Truman concluded his letter wistfully, reminding the senator, "We have never needed you so badly."[40]

One group of Republicans intended to maintain bipartisan support of the administration's Far East policy through the upcoming midterm elections. A progressive GOP bloc from the public and private sectors calling itself the Republican Advance emerged from a secret gathering with a thirteen-page Declaration of Republican Principles. This faction aimed to separate itself from Taft's attack-dog tactics against Truman's foreign policy. The Republican Advance called for the party to stop its "purely negative opposition" to administration objectives, ranging from domestic issues to Far East policy, and to create progressive party initiatives. Although this group opposed some aspects of Truman's Asian policies, it formally endorsed the Korean intervention. The declaration of principles attracted the support of only twenty-one GOP congressmen and four senators, but several publicly backed the proposal.[41]

The administration did nothing to enlist the Republican Advance in its quest for a bipartisan foreign policy. This was a mistake. Unlike the Taft wing of the GOP, this group seemed willing to put aside opposition for the sake of opposition. The progressive Republicans, despite their lack of numbers in Congress, counted some powerful members among their ranks, including Representative Walter Judd, who enjoyed significant influence in Far East policy, and Senator Smith of the Foreign Relations Committee. While it would not have guaranteed broad Republican support for a nonpartisan foreign policy, a Democratic overture toward this faction could have been helpful.

Analysis

Some historians have endorsed, in varying degrees, Truman's decision to intervene militarily in Korea. David Rees sees the Korean crisis as a sign of Soviet aggression; he believes that U.S. intervention prevented World War III and strengthened the Western alliance. Biographer Alonzo Hamby emphasizes the expectations of America's Cold War allies, arguing that the nature of the North Korean attack magnified its geopolitical importance. With the eyes of the world on America, Truman had to act or risk losing current or potential allies against the Soviets. Arthur Schlesinger Jr. agrees that the president had to go to war, but he hedges his endorsement. Although Truman was wrong to assume that the Soviets were the sole instigators of the attack (we now know that Kim Il Sung begged Stalin for the green light), he still did the right thing. Schlesinger posits that if the president had not intervened, Stalin might have been tempted to encourage local communist offensives elsewhere.[42]

Revisionist historians have been less sympathetic to Truman's approach. Joyce Kolko and Gabriel Kolko suggest that the American determination to create a sphere of capitalist countries to trade with U.S. businesses following World War II drove the president to intervene. Bruce Cumings describes the conflict as the United States injecting itself into a Korean civil war. This intervention inflicted nothing less than genocide on the Korean people, yet it halted American expansionism in Asia. Stephen Pelz argues that Truman painted himself into a corner due to his inept policies and leadership. The president committed to supporting a trusteeship of South Korea; then he backed away by pulling American forces out of the country as he sought to shrink the military budget. Pelz argues that this invited the North Korean attack. Because Truman's rhetoric had promised support for the South Koreans, he had no choice but to respond militarily.[43]

Of the naysayers, only Barton J. Bernstein has discussed Truman's political alternatives, bluntly positing that the president could have avoided war "without producing a backlash at home or disrupting the alliance system." Bernstein suggests that Truman could have blamed the Republicans for resisting aid to Korea earlier in 1950; the GOP therefore invited the invasion by rendering South Korea powerless to stop it. Since John Foster Dulles, a GOP adviser in the State Department, was worried that military intervention could produce a quagmire akin to Dunkirk in World War I, Bernstein believes that Truman could have convinced other Republicans to support a decision to stay out of Korea. Bernstein does not discuss the potential damage to U.S. credibility with its allies had it walked away from Korea. However, it is difficult to imagine a significant change in the quality of the nation's alliances. The Americans had a firm military presence in Japan, and European allies such as Britain and

France were not going to jump into the arms of the Soviets just because the Americans distanced themselves from Korea.[44]

Truman went to war in Korea for multiple reasons. Although he often spoke passionately about the need to preserve the UN's credibility, the president also noted that had the Soviets attended the Security Council meetings and vetoed UN action in Korea, he would have intervened unilaterally. During the first week of the war, the commander in chief told a group of legislators, "If we let Korea down, the Soviets will keep right on going and swallow up one piece of Asia after another," and possibly the Middle East and Europe as well. Since the president would have gone to war with or without the UN's sanction, his *primary* reason for sending American troops to Korea could not have been to ensure UN credibility. Nevertheless, Truman felt it was vital to keep the UN from collapsing like the League of Nations had. Another motive for the administration was to uphold American prestige in the international community. In his memoirs, Truman observes that a failure to act would have negatively affected the "confidence of peoples in countries adjacent to the Soviet Union," particularly if the United States did not protect a nation "established under our auspices." Acheson agreed, calling American prestige the "shadow cast by power" and noting that it had "great deterrent importance."[45]

Did McCarthyism lead the president into a war that he otherwise would have avoided? The communists' victory in China's civil war in 1949 and Senator McCarthy's antics in 1950 certainly pressured Truman to respond forcefully to the Korean crisis. Moreover, the president quickly changed his policy toward Formosa once the situation in Korea ignited. Whereas he had been prepared to concede Taiwan to the communists before the war, Truman swiftly dispatched naval forces to protect the Kuomintang from the communists on the mainland (and vice versa) following the North Korean attack, gladdening the hearts of his GOP foes. Nevertheless, McCarthyism was a negligible factor in Truman's decision to respond militarily. He had resisted political pressure and stayed out of the Chinese civil war, and he would do so later when he recalled MacArthur. The president possessed enough antipathy of his own toward communism; he did not need additional encouragement from McCarthy and company. The nature of the North Korean attack motivated Truman more than any fear of the McCarthyites. When North Korea launched a large-scale armed invasion (with equipment supplied by the Soviets), the president interpreted it as a replay of the 1930s. Thus, the main reason Truman committed the United States to war was to stop what he perceived as Soviet expansionism. In Truman's eyes, Stalin had replaced Hitler and Mussolini.

The president had ample reason to be wary of the Soviet leader. Even though we now know that Kim Il Sung initiated the invasion, Stalin could have prevented it. He chose not to. (In contrast, although Syngman Rhee would have gladly attacked North Korea, the United States did not allow him to do so.) Stalin's willingness to unleash Kim came as no surprise, given the former's behavior during the previous decade. The USSR had taken control of the Baltic states and parts of Finland in 1939, followed by Bulgaria and Romania five years later. In 1945 the Red Army occupied Poland, and Stalin demanded (unsuccessfully) that Turkey give him access to the Dardanelles, linking the Black Sea to the Mediterranean. When the Soviet leader made his famous 1946 speech declaring that world war was inevitable as long as capitalism existed, it had a profound effect on Americans, Truman included. These circumstances understandably led the president to jump to the erroneous conclusion that Stalin had ordered the attack on South Korea.[46]

Another relevant question is whether it was legal for Truman to commit American forces to Korea without congressional approval. Since the United States went to war under the auspices of the United Nations, some background on the implementation of the UN Charter is in order. Articles 39 through 43 of the charter deal with breaches of the peace (see appendix A). They define the steps the Security Council can take to restore international order, leading up to the use of force. Article 39 identifies the act of aggression and makes recommendations on how to respond, while article 40 empowers the Security Council to call for "provisional measures," such as cease-fires. Article 41 covers economic and political sanctions, and if the actions allowed under article 41 are ineffective, article 42 empowers the Security Council to "take such action by air, sea, or land forces . . . to maintain or restore international peace and security," using forces of member nations. Article 43 delineates how to implement article 42. To provide military resources for the UN, the Security Council and member nations negotiate a "special agreement or agreements" to provide "armed forces, assistance and facilities, including rights of passage," for the council's use. These special agreements define the "numbers and types of forces, their degree of readiness and general location." Such agreements are "subject to ratification by the signatory states in accordance with their respective constitutional processes." In 1945 Truman had taken pains to assure Congress that he did not intend to circumvent the legislative branch through these special agreements to commit American forces. As the Senate debated ratification of the charter, Truman sent a message from the Potsdam Conference to Senate president pro tempore Kenneth McKellar (D-TN), stating that he would "ask the Congress by appropriate legislation to approve" such special agreements.[47]

After approving the charter in July 1945, legislators wrestled with implementing it. A key issue was how to reconcile Congress's constitutional authority to declare war with these special agreements to provide U.S. military forces to the UN. Senator Connally introduced the UNPA bill to integrate the UN Charter with American law. After a week of debate on the Senate floor, both houses approved the bill and sent it to Truman, who signed it in December 1945. Based on the debates, it is clear that Congress intended to approve any commitment of American forces to the UN. Section 6 of the statute (see appendix B) authorized the president to negotiate special agreements with the Security Council per article 43. Congress then had to approve these special agreements before the UN could use American military resources. However, once Congress endorsed a special agreement, the president did *not* have to get its approval to dispatch forces for an article 42 situation, so long as the scope of the deployment did not exceed the conditions set out in the special agreement.[48]

The intent of article 43 was to provide, in advance, a contingent of forces from member nations that could be used if the Security Council needed them. In February 1946 the Security Council directed the UN Military Staff Committee to make recommendations for the special agreements, and the General Assembly subsequently asked the Security Council to "accelerate as much as possible the placing at its disposal of the armed forces mentioned in Article 43 of the Charter." The committee produced its report in late June 1947, but the five permanent Security Council members never reached a consensus on special agreements. Discussions continued for another year, but they were fruitless because the Soviets were usually at odds with the others. Thus, when the Korean crisis occurred, no special agreement per article 43 of the UN Charter (or congressional approval to use American forces per section 6 of the

UNPA) was in place to provide American troops for an article 42 military intervention.[49]

The UN intervened in Korea based on an article 39 Security Council *recommendation* rather than an outright UN military action declared under article 42. Truman did not publicize this distinction, but it was problematic because the UNPA did not mention congressional approval of resolutions under article 39. The president therefore decided there was no need to involve Congress, claiming that the Security Council recommendation to assist the South Koreans and his constitutional powers as commander in chief justified his actions.[50]

A couple of analysts have affirmed the chief executive's right to forgo congressional approval, for disparate reasons. Historian Ronald Caridi claimed the UNPA permitted Truman to skirt Congress, citing the following portion of section 6:

> The President shall not be deemed to require the authorization of the Congress to make available to the Security Council on its call in order to take action under article 42 of said Charter and pursuant to such special agreement or agreements the armed forces, facilities, or assistance provided for therein: Provided, That nothing herein contained shall be construed as an authorization to the President by the Congress to make available to the Security Council for such purpose armed forces, facilities, or assistance *in addition to the forces, facilities, and assistance provided for in such special agreement* or agreements.

Caridi misread the legalities in two ways. He mistakenly treated the Security Council's June 27, 1950, resolution recommending assistance to South Korea as a special agreement. In addition, Caridi interpreted the above-quoted portion of the UNPA as allowing the president to bypass Congress when supporting an article 42 military action. This passage actually means that the president does not repeatedly have to get congressional approval to dispatch military forces to the UN, so long as the deployment does not exceed the scope of the original special agreement approved by Congress.[51]

According to political scientist Edward Keynes, Truman had sound legal footing to circumvent Congress. Keynes argued that the president did not need to declare war because World War II was not yet officially over (the Japanese peace treaty was not signed until April 1952). Therefore, statutes legalizing American involvement in World War II still applied when the Korean fighting erupted. From a practical standpoint, this reasoning is difficult to swallow, since few believed that World War II was still under way in 1950. Furthermore, Keynes claimed that since Truman intervened in support of a UN resolution, and since the UN Charter was a binding treaty, he had no need to get a declaration of war from Congress.[52]

More often, analysts have taken the position that the president violated the Constitution or the UNPA in the Korean intervention. Political scientist Louis Fisher harked back to the debates over the charter. To help get it passed, Dean Acheson (undersecretary of state at the time) assured a House panel, "It is entirely within the wisdom of Congress to approve or disapprove whatever special agreement the President negotiates" with the Security Council. Fisher argued that Truman clearly violated the substance of the UNPA and ignored its history. Arthur Schlesinger Jr. was also critical of Truman's method, if not the decision to intervene. Schlesinger correctly pointed out that the State Department's report describing eighty-five instances of chief executives using force without congressional approval was suspect, in that none of these examples involved a military action against another nation. (Though not officially recognized by the UN, North Korea was a sovereign state for all practical purposes.) Moreover, all the incidents listed in the report involved military actions of a considerably smaller scope than the Korean crisis. Historian Arnold Offner conceded that during the first days of the crisis, Truman did not know how large the American military commitment would be; therefore, he could be excused for bypassing Congress in the initial commitment of air and naval support. However, when the president received MacArthur's request for two divisions, Offner correctly argued that Truman knew he was making a major commitment to Korea and should have sought congressional approval immediately.[53]

Why did the administration eschew a congressional endorsement of the war effort? Paradoxically, Truman and Acheson justified their action by citing both support and opposition in Congress. When Secretary of the Army Frank Pace asked Truman about getting congressional approval, the president replied, "Frank, it's not necessary. They are all with me." Acheson later affirmed, "We had complete acceptance of the President's policy by everybody on both sides of both houses of Congress." They were right. The president's archenemies, Taft and Wherry, guaranteed that Congress would pass a resolution endorsing the military action. Yet the administration shied away from a resolution, fearing the political lumps they would take during the floor debate. The secretary later said he did not want to answer "ponderous questions" that could have "muddled up" Truman's policy.[54]

The administration had plausible reasons for not requesting a formal declaration of war early on. There was a possibility the North Koreans would back down upon an initial show of American force, and a congressional declaration might have rendered such a tactic useless. A more important reason is that Truman did not want to inflame the situation, fearing that a declaration of war would draw the Soviets or the Chinese into the fray. Another justification was that American forces were acting under UN authority. Even though American military preparations began before the Security Council passed its resolutions authorizing intervention in Korea, U.S. forces ultimately acted on behalf of the UN. A congressional declaration of war would have been inappropriate for what was technically an international peacekeeping operation.[55]

Nevertheless, Truman briefly considered seeking Congress's blessing. Early in the first week of the crisis, the president asked Connally for his opinion regarding congressional input. A few days later, Truman directed Acheson to research the history of presidential use of military force without Congress's approval. Acheson's list of eighty-five precedents did not build a convincing case. For example, the most recent use of force cited in the State Department report was the dispatch of about 2,800 troops to China in 1932 to protect Americans at the international settlement in Shanghai. Such incidents bore little resemblance to the Korean situation.[56]

The State Department's report, however, reinforced Truman's belief that he did not need congressional approval of any kind. His comment at the July 3 meeting, explaining that he "had not been acting as President, but as Commander-in-Chief of our forces in the Far East," provided hints of his reasoning. The Korean crisis was not a war; it was a police action enforcing a UN directive. Therefore, a declaration of war was not necessary. Because the United States was acting at the behest of the UN, Truman believed he had the constitutional right as commander in chief to deploy American forces as he wished. The president desperately wanted the United Nations to become an effective peacekeeping entity. More-over, he was not about to weaken the office of the presidency. As an aide wrote to a Republican senator concerning congressional endorsement of the intervention, "It is quite certain that the President would never have asked for a resolution."[57]

Truman should have sought some form of congressional approval (other than a declaration of war) to commit American forces to Korea. The president and the secretary of state knew from their experiences guid-ing the UN Charter and the UNPA through Congress that the legisla-ture believed it had the power to approve the use of American troops on behalf of the UN. Technically, one could argue that the president acted legally because the Security Council did not implement article 42 in the Korean crisis. (The UNPA required Congress's approval to send American troops to support an article 42 intervention, but it was silent on article 39 interventions.) The administration had tried and failed for two years to hammer out an article 43 special agreement with the Security Council. Truman's intense desire for an effective UN response led him to take some short cuts. Still, it was unnecessary to circumvent Congress. If the admin-istration did not violate the letter of the law, it clearly ignored the intent.

Congress, however, contributed significantly to Truman's abuse of presidential power, a topic that historians have not yet fully investigated. The legislative branch performed weakly in various ways, one of which was failing to show up for work. The tumultuous first week of the conflict ended on Friday, June 30, with the commander in chief's announcement that he was committing ground troops to Korea. This was an opportune time for members of Congress to push the administration to seek legis-lative endorsement. Instead, they took a weeklong Fourth of July recess, giving the president another reason not to consult them. During the July 3 meeting, Truman indicated that he preferred not to call Congress back to Washington to discuss Korea. Presidential counsel Charles Murphy later recalled legislators' antipathy toward special sessions, which may explain the president's reluctance to call one. Congress's lack of attention to the UNPA was a more important factor. Two-thirds of the senators and 256 of the 435 House members were holdovers from the Congress that had debated congressional approval of U.S. military commitments to the UN in 1945. Most had been in office when amendments to the UNPA were approved in 1949. Yet only Taft seemed to remember the provisions of this law. Neither the urgency of the Korean crisis nor the lack of precedent for a UN military intervention excused Congress's lack of attention to the UNPA.[58]

The Republicans could have done more to encourage Truman to seek Congress's approval. After Truman's June 27 statement about sending air and naval support to Korea, Senator Arthur V. Watkins (R-UT) immediately questioned the legality of this decision. However, he reluctantly accepted Senator Lucas's defense that the Security Council resolution made the president's action legitimate. After the war turned sour, Watkins published a cogent article explaining the importance of the UNPA, but he could have pushed back harder in 1950. In the aftermath of the firing of General MacArthur, Senator Karl E. Mundt (R-SD) pointed out that the United States had not adhered to the UNPA or article 43 at the outset of the war. Mundt therefore argued that the United States had the right to push for total victory in Korea, regardless of the UN's desires. Although Taft and Wherry, leaders of the Senate Republicans, publicly asked the president to get the consent of Congress, most of their colleagues sat on their hands. Had the Republicans rallied to their leaders' cause while professing their support for intervention in Korea, Truman may have reconsidered his decision.[59]

McCarthyism was an even larger factor. Although anticommunist fanatics did not drive Truman to intervene in Korea, they had a lot to do with his reluctance to seek Congress's approval. This is the only explanation for why the administration and the Democratic leadership paradoxically feared congressional debate on intervention, despite overwhelming approval on Capitol Hill for involvement in Korea. If Congress debated a war resolution, Acheson predicted the McCarthyites would subject recent Far East policy to a chorus of "endless criticism."[60]

The Democrats—the president's fellow party members—were even more culpable than the Republicans. Senator Connally made a mistake on June 26 when he advised Truman that congressional approval was unnecessary. As chairman of the Foreign Relations Committee, Connally was in the right place at the right time. Had he advised the president to ask for Congress's blessing, the Democratic leadership could have started the process of obtaining congressional consent to commit troops by the end of the week. In his memoirs, the Texan admitted the error as a "matter of political strategy" and recalled that the GOP used the decision against Truman in 1951. Strangely, Connally said nothing about the UNPA, which he had introduced in 1945, even though the law's clear intent was to ensure congressional approval before committing American forces to UN action. Majority leader Lucas's indecisiveness during the July 3 meeting could not have given the president much confidence in the Democratic leadership's ability to obtain congressional endorsement. Had the Democratic leaders told Truman he needed Congress's approval, he would have had no choice but to comply. The president deserves the most blame for skirting constitutional checks and balances, but the Democratic leadership should have steered him toward a wiser path. Consequently, a White House aide wrote that there was "no serious discussion" of a resolution from Congress, and "there was no strong Congressional leadership to push one through."[61]

A final question is whether congressional sanction of the war at the outset would have helped the president politically. Hamby claims the political value of congressional endorsement has been overblown. He argues that the GOP was so keen to usurp Democratic control that it would have criticized Truman's foreign policy harshly during the 1952 election season even if Congress had approved a declaration of war. Hamby is right. The Republicans may have tempered their attacks on "Truman's War" had they endorsed it, but a congressional war resolution would not have saved the president much political grief in 1951–1952. Nor would a declaration of war have helped Truman's mobilization program. Congress readily gave the president the power to implement wage and price controls in September 1950, only three months into the war, even though it had not officially sanctioned sending troops to Korea. When Truman struggled to extend his mobilization program in mid-1951, a congressional declaration of war would not have helped his cause. The limited scope of the war, the lack of rationing of consumer products, and the start of armistice talks in July 1951 caused lawmakers to lose enthusiasm for economic controls. Moreover, although Truman largely lost the battle to extend economic controls (see chapter 5), he was wildly successful in obtaining massive increases in defense spending to fight the Cold War in places other than Korea. Offner contends that authorization from Congress up front might have allowed the legislators to prevent the UN from going north of the thirty-eighth parallel, or at least forced a debate on it. This seems unlikely. The UN's military momentum had most Americans in a state of euphoria, including members of Congress. The legislative branch was as eager to seize an opportunity to roll back communist expansion as the executive branch was. Congressional approval at the outset would have made no difference in subsequent war policy.[62]

On June 30, 1950, just moments after the White House announced the commitment of American troops to Korea, Senator John Stennis (D-MS) prophesied, "I believe we are creating precedents which will constitute new rules of international law." He was half right. The Eighty-First Congress was helping to create new rules of domestic (not international) law, allowing presidents to send Americans to war without congressional consent. Congress was perfectly content to let Truman take the heat for the Korean War. A couple of weeks later, a political scientist wrote in the *New York Times,* "We seem to have come to the point where Americans are willing to accept the President as sole and undisputed master of our actions abroad in time of international crisis. Somehow we have moved a long way from the conceptions of 'checks and balances' that set some limit to the Chief Executive's role in making war and peace." Several members of the administration, along with Senator Connally, later regretted their failure to work harder to persuade the president to obtain Congress's blessing before going to war. Disconcertingly, they all focused on the political ramifications of Truman's actions. None of them worried about the violation of the spirit of American governance.[63]

Ironically, the president made several comments during the first weeks of the war that revealed how dangerous Congress's passivity could be. When an aide asked about a congressional resolution approving the Korean intervention, the commander in chief snapped, "It was none of Congress's business. . . . I just did what was in my power." Yet he told another staffer, "I sit and shiver . . . at the thought of what could happen with some demagogue in this office I hold."[64]

2

The First War,
July–October 1950

The Korean War was actually three wars. From July to October 1950, North Korea was pitted against UN forces led by the United States. Communist China's entry into the fray, coinciding with midterm congressional elections in the United States, constituted a "new" war that raged from November 1950 until the beginning of the armistice talks in July 1951. The final two years of the conflict constituted the third war, a bloody stalemate in which the two sides simply tried to inflict maximum casualties to obtain a negotiating edge at the peace talks.

This chapter delves into how Congress and the Truman administration managed the first war, the effect of partisan politics on war policy, and the war's influence on American politics through the 1950 elections. One theme is President Truman's struggle to maintain a bipartisan foreign policy in spite of the efforts of the Taft wing of the Republican Party, which tried to use the conflict to its political advantage. Another theme is how the president's own party contributed to his headaches as much as the opposition GOP did. Nevertheless, the sharply partisan Senate vote on the Tydings committee report, initial military setbacks for UN forces, the political ambitions of Senators Taft and McCarthy, and Truman's shortcomings as a seller of the war did surprisingly little damage to public support for the Korean intervention. In addition, I examine the administration's fateful decision to change the scope of the war by authorizing UN forces to advance north of the thirty-eighth parallel. McCarthyism had motivated Truman to bypass a congressional declaration of war at the outset. Did it similarly prod him to try to reunify the peninsula by force?

Did the momentum of General MacArthur's smashing success at Inchon give the commander in chief little choice but to proceed northward? In the end, war policy and the upcoming midterm congressional elections were inextricably linked.

Truman Addresses the Nation

Nearly three weeks passed between the commitment of American forces to Korea and President Truman's first public speech on the crisis to an increasingly impatient nation. As UN forces suffered early setbacks, journalists called the administration "secretive" and a "beehive of indecision." Senator Margaret Chase Smith (R-ME) complained, "The gruesome reality of a shooting war should be brought home to the American people instead of being glossed over by the Truman administration." Nervousness edged toward panic. Senator Owen Brewster (R-ME) suggested allowing General MacArthur to use the atomic bomb as he saw fit, and Senator Lyndon Johnson (D-TX), a Truman ally, worried that Korea could become a "slaughterhouse for democracy." The Reverend Billy Graham phoned the president, warning him that the public was in the grips of a "fear you could almost call hysteria."[1]

Despite the negativity on the home front, Truman was already thinking ahead to a potential unification of the Korean peninsula. During his July 13 news conference, the president refused to rule out carrying the fighting into North Korea. Four days later, Truman asked his National Security Council to propose a policy that could be implemented once UN forces had fought their way to the thirty-eighth parallel. Throughout July, the State Department internally debated the pros and cons of carrying the fighting into the north. Hawks such as John M. Allison, director of Northeast Asian Affairs, asserted that it was time to "be bold and willing to take even more risks than we have already." Eventually, the president would agree.[2]

Meanwhile, Truman prepared to speak to the nation on the Korean situation. He was not a spell-binding orator. With the exception of campaign stump speeches, Truman typically spoke from a prepared text. Clark Clifford, the president's head speechwriter in the early part of his administration, remembered that his former boss "read poorly from written texts, his head down, words coming forth in what the press liked to call a 'drone.'" Clifford lamented the contrast between Truman and the "brilliant and compelling style of his predecessor," which "made the problem all the more serious." *Time* described one key speech on the war as "painfully deliberate" at times, noting that Truman moved "occasionally with a breakaway rush to the end of a jumbled phrase." Probably recognizing his limitations, the president treated speech making as an unsavory chore to get through as soon as possible, which contributed to his ineffective delivery. Whereas a skilled orator like Franklin Roosevelt spoke at 95 to 120 words per minute, Truman zoomed through his speeches at 150 words per minute.[3]

Yet there was a more important reason for the president to delay his first major speech on Korea. Kim Il Sung's invasion had taken him (and the rest of the nation) by surprise, and he needed some time to decide how to respond. Truman determined early on that the UN had to restore the integrity of the ROK if the international body was to have any credibility in the future. The primary goal of the intervention was to avoid a repeat of 1930s appeasement; however, the commander in chief was equally determined not to start another world war. Truman therefore downplayed the crisis in his public statements and took his time before addressing the nation.

Finally, on July 19, Truman spoke about Korea to an estimated 130 million Americans via a radio address. He listed his reasons for intervening but was short on specifics regarding how a communist takeover of South Korea endangered America's national interests in the short term. He portrayed the North Korean invasion as a replay of Munich, saying, "Appeasement leads only to further aggression and ultimately to war." The Soviets, through Kim Il Sung, were continuing their quest for world dominance, and the United States had to stop them. The president injected a moral component, a consistent theme of his war rhetoric. He said that America was "united in detesting Communist slavery. . . . We believe that freedom and peace are essential if men are to live as our Creator intended us to live. It is this faith that has guided us in the past, and it is this faith that will fortify us in the stern days ahead."[4]

The speech attempted to rally the public—judiciously. Truman did not call for victory. Instead, he urged the nation to meet the challenge "squarely" to "drive the Communists back," and he characterized the intervention as an effort "to help the Koreans preserve their independence." The president, reflecting his decision to embrace the tenets of NSC-68, prepared the public for a military buildup "over and above what is needed in Korea." Truman asserted that Korea was likely the first of many communist attacks to come. Declaring that improved defense would "require considerable adjustment" to the economy, Truman stated his determination to keep inflation under control by limiting credit purchases of agricultural commodities and housing, for starters. He warned the public to expect "substantial increases" in taxes—necessary contributions to national defense that all Americans "should stand ready to make."[5]

Initial response to the address was mostly positive. To some, Truman's speech lacked the "inspiration that the occasion called for"; it had no "ringing phrases of a Churchillian or Rooseveltian performance" or a "compelling call to arms." Columnist Drew Pearson wrote that compared with Roosevelt's "master at the helm" image during World War II, Truman came across as a "sincere, somewhat inadequate little guy who was trying to do his best." Some thought the public was ahead of the president on Korea. *Time* characterized the public's attitude as "a willingness to do whatever had to be done, but an irritated sensation of not being told what to do. A suspicion that the Administration doesn't quite trust the country, hesitates to give it bad news or require hard sacrifices." Nevertheless, the White House received five times more supportive letters than critical ones. One journalist commended the president for waiting several weeks to give a "calm yet forceful statement." Another called the address a "bold answer to communism's drawn sword."[6]

The timing of Truman's first major public speech about Korea could have been better. Secretary of State Acheson had suggested that the president take his case directly to the American people during the first week of July, rather than waiting two more weeks. A speech by the president could have calmed the nation down as the initial negative reports from the war front rolled in. Truman should have made a preliminary speech in early July, explaining why the United States was intervening and what American national interests were at stake. He could have followed up with the details about what the war would mean for Americans at home.

The president approached mobilization cautiously at the war's outset. Despite his belief that the North Korean attack represented a serious threat of communist expansion, the commander in chief was determined to maintain a balance between domestic spending (for his Fair Deal programs) and national defense without creating permanent budget deficits. In the short term, the president feared the inflationary pressures inherent in deficit spending; he also believed the public would not accept the sharp tax increases required by his pay-as-you-go philosophy, particularly as the nation was enjoying relief from the high taxes necessitated by World War II. Truman had suffered through the politically bruising process of demobilizing after the war and probably had little desire to reenter the inferno of wage and price controls. Moreover, the president did not want the populace or the international community to equate Korea with World War II. Nevertheless, at a July 8 cabinet meeting, the president briefly considered a government takeover of the Rock Island Railroad because labor strikes were holding up manganese and copper shipments needed for the war effort. The railroad issue aside, Truman worried that immediate, comprehensive mobilization would hamper production for domestic purposes, to the detriment of the overall economy. The president also recognized that any proposals to fund mobilization through tax increases or deficit spending would rile conservative Republicans in Congress, who were even more hawkish on taxes and deficits than Truman was. A provoked GOP could hinder the president's chances of passing *any* budget increase for the military and its efforts in Korea.[7]

Truman's July 19 speech therefore took a limited approach to mobilization. Although the president asked for the authority to control production and the allocation of raw materials, he stopped short of asking for the power to set prices. Political expediency contributed to his conservative approach. House Speaker Sam Rayburn had advised Truman that congressional approval would be easier to obtain if the president's request for mobilization powers did not include wage and price controls, which had been unpopular during World War II. Some have argued that Rayburn's advice did not serve his president well; Truman should have demanded and imposed price controls immediately to curb inflation, which would become problematic later in the war. Although this argument has some validity, it is based on information that Truman did not have at the time. We now know that inflation tracked with anticipated escalations in the war; such expectations led to increased demand for wartime commodities, driving prices up. For example, inflation rose from 2.1 to 3.8 percent after the September 1950 Inchon landing and escalated to over 9 percent following China's entry into the war. However, in July 1950 the president could not have known the degree of mobilization needed to prosecute the war, which was only a few weeks old. Thus, Truman might have been able to mitigate some of the subsequent inflation had he imposed wage and price controls from the outset, but at this early stage of the war, there was no way he could have known the extent of the economic controls that would be necessary.[8]

The president attempted to calm consumer fears. As he explained to the nation in his July 19 speech, "If I had thought that we were actually threatened by shortages of essential consumer goods, I should have recommended that price control and rationing be immediately instituted. But there is no such threat. We have to fear only those shortages which we ourselves artificially create." Nevertheless, Americans promptly created such scarcities. By late July, lawmakers were already getting complaints from their constituents about the hoarding of goods and profiteering. Remembering the dearth of consumer items during World War II, people started "hoarding everything from automobile tires to metal hair curlers," buying 100-pound bags of sugar and coffee by the case. Panic buying through the end of 1950 drove the price of rubber from $0.34 to $0.86 per pound and tin from $0.76 to $1.84 per pound, causing needless shortages and sharp inflation. Some companies responded creatively to food shortages. New Jersey Bell Telephone added pot roast of whale to the menu in its employee cafeteria. A Toledo, Ohio, car wash added a frozen meat section for its customers' convenience, charging them $1.75 per pound for filet mignon, compared with $1.50 for a car wash. Runs on consumer goods flowed with the military fortunes in Korea, spiking initially, subsiding after the UN success at Inchon, and then running rampant again when China intervened.[9]

Despite his fiscal conservatism, in early July 1950 Truman recognized the realities of the war and canceled the $13.5 billion defense budget ceiling for fiscal year 1951, asking the Department of Defense (DOD) to draft a new spending measure not just for Korea but "to increase our common defense, with other free nations, against further aggression." At the same time, the commander in chief instructed his new budget director to scrutinize the Pentagon's proposed budget increases, "with the idea of not putting any more money than necessary at the time in the hands of the Military." The army asked that the revised budget include three more divisions of troops to replace units sent to Korea, the navy wanted to reactivate four aircraft carriers that had been mothballed after World

War II, and the air force requested funding to bring combat planes out of retirement. Truman responded by asking for a defense budget increase of $10 billion beyond the original $13.5 billion, which passed Congress easily. The president took this opportunity to increase the draft-eligible pool to 2 million men and called up an additional 25,000 volunteer reservists. Before July was over, the DOD requested and received an additional $1.2 billion that was tacked onto the $13.5 billion supplemental appropriation. The demands for resources kept coming. On January 2, 1951, its last day in session, the Eighty-First Congress blessed another defense request of $16.8 billion, which included $9.2 billion for the army, $3.0 billion for the navy, and $4.6 billion for the air force. Interestingly, Congress added a supplemental appropriation of $365 million for the DOD that included no money for the military; these funds were designated for broad Cold War programs such as civil defense and the Voice of America radio broadcasts into communist countries. Finally, lawmakers added another $6.6 billion to the budget, most of which went to the DOD. Thus, by the end of fiscal year 1951, some $48 billion had been appropriated for the military—about the same amount as the budgets of 1947–1950 combined. The postwar contraction of the nation's defense budget disappeared with the onset of the Korean crisis.[10]

McCarthyism and the First War

Political unanimity for the decision to go to war faded quickly. As UN troops retreated to Pusan and headlines screamed "G.I.'s Curse Lack of Tanks, Planes," legislators returned to their partisan ways. Senator Bourke Hickenlooper (R-IA) demanded an accounting of all defense spending since 1947, lamenting in a "choking voice" that the United States seemed incapable of stopping the "alleged bandit raid." When majority leader Lucas replied that he would speak when Hickenlooper stopped choking, the Republican shot back that the war was "enough to make a great many of the American people choke." Senators Homer Capehart (R-IN) and Tom Connally had a sharp exchange over the number of troops that European allies had sent to Korea. When Connally asked Capehart if America should surrender because it was fighting alone at the moment, the Indiana Republican called him a "clown" and accused him of putting on a "vaudeville act."[11]

Thus, the Republican "rally 'round the flag" at the outset of the war did not last long. Nor did it include a vote of confidence for Secretary of State Acheson. During the first week of the war, and even before the commitment of American troops, Senator Taft led a Republican chorus demanding the secretary's resignation. Senator McCarthy chimed in, blaming war casualties on a "group of untouchables" in the State Department that had gutted Korean aid prior to the war. Shortly thereafter, conservative Republicans seized on Acheson's January 12, 1950, speech that had excluded Korea from America's "defense perimeter" against communist expansion in the Pacific. This exclusion, the GOP argued, was nothing less than a tacit message that the United States would not defend South Korea from an invasion. Republicans claimed the secretary of state had "electrified all Asia because Korea and Formosa . . . were designated as abandoned by America."[12]

Ironically, Acheson had obtained his definition of the U.S. defense perimeter from General MacArthur, whom many Republicans regarded as the foremost American authority on Far East policy. In a March 1949 interview with a British journalist, the general had explained his idea of the American line of defense in the Pacific, matching the one Acheson articulated in January 1950. The secretary later regretted his reference to MacArthur's strategy, calling it an example of the danger of using military positions to explain the nuances of foreign policy. Acheson's speech was ambiguous at best. After excluding Korea from the geographic line of defense, he emphasized that if an attack occurred in a region outside the defense perimeter, other countries (in addition to the United States) should repel the aggressor by virtue of their commitments to the United Nations. The secretary also implied that Korea and Japan could expect American assistance in the event of an attack. Interestingly, Acheson's remarks produced antagonistic statements from the North Koreans, who blasted him for *subjugating South Korea into the American orbit.* However, documents released after the end of the Cold War provide circumstantial evidence that Kim Il Sung and Stalin took Acheson's remarks as a signal that the United States would not intervene in a Korean civil war. Less than a week after Acheson's January 12 speech, Kim renewed his pleas to Stalin for permission to invade the ROK. By the end of the month, Stalin had relented and was making plans to provide Soviet assistance to the North Koreans. An internal Soviet report on Stalin-Kim meetings in Moscow between March 30 and April 25, 1950, provides insight into the Soviet leader's thinking. Stalin was encouraged by the fact that the United States had "left China," and he believed the recent (February 1950) Sino-Soviet pact would discourage American meddling. Moreover, the Soviet premier believed that "according to information coming from the United States . . . the prevailing mood is not to interfere" with communist activities in Asia. Some historians argue that Acheson's speech was a key source of this "information"; others argue that his speech clearly did not represent an American abandonment of Korea. Although the Stalin-Kim meeting notes make no *explicit* mention of Acheson's January 12 remarks, his GOP critics were probably justified in blaming the secretary's speech, given the timing of Stalin's green light to Kim.[13]

Nevertheless, Democrats dutifully defended the secretary of state in the initial weeks of the conflict. Senator Millard Tydings (whose committee was finishing its report on McCarthy's allegations against the State Department) led the charge. Tydings defended the administration's foreign policy, pointing out that Korea was likely only one of many places where the Soviets planned to test their ability to expand. Curiously, the Democrats never pointed out that MacArthur had originally articulated the Pacific defense perimeter cited in Acheson's controversial speech. With better communication between the secretary and congressional Democrats, the latter could have used this as ammunition against Republican attacks.[14]

The GOP also tried to use Truman's bipartisan foreign policy rhetoric against him. Senator William Knowland, king of the "Asia-firsters" on Capitol Hill, suggested that the president give the opposition more say in foreign policy matters by replacing some of the Democrats in his cabinet with Republicans. FDR had created a bipartisan cabinet in 1940 by nominating Republicans Frank Knox and Henry Stimson to the posts of secretary of the navy and secretary of war, respectively. While Roosevelt clearly did this to gain Republican support for his foreign policies, he had additional motives. Roosevelt was preparing for a third run for the White House and wanted to remove international affairs as a campaign issue. The end of his second term was the logical time to make changes to his inner circle. Moreover, Knox's and Stimson's predecessors had become difficult to work with, and Roosevelt was more than willing to replace them. Things were different in 1950. Truman had just appointed two

Republicans to high-ranking positions in the State Department, and there were no cabinet members he wanted to get rid of at the moment. Defense secretary Louis Johnson's open warfare with Acheson led the president to replace him several months later, presenting the best opportunity to add a Republican to the cabinet. This exception aside, Truman was in the middle of his term, and arbitrarily asking cabinet members to step down because they were Democrats was unthinkable for the president, who was loyal to a fault. In addition, such changes would have heightened the sense of crisis surrounding Korea, which the administration was trying to downplay at this early stage of the war.[15]

Knowland followed up with an even worse idea, suggesting that Truman should not stump for Democrats in the 1950 congressional elections. Asking a sitting president, the leader of his party, to remain on the sidelines veered from the purpose of a nonpartisan foreign policy. Republicans rightfully asked Democrats to consult them on international issues as a way to seek a national consensus, but Knowland's suggestion was an attempt to manipulate the bipartisan foreign policy issue for political gain. Nevertheless, his wish largely came true. Truman campaigned little in 1950, but not because he was trying to placate the Republicans; he was simply too busy with the war to hit the campaign trail.[16]

The day after Knowland's demand for more GOP input into the conduct of the war, John Foster Dulles met with Republican senators to get their views. Dulles, a prominent Republican adviser to Acheson, handled the situation deftly. Knowland and company's main demand was that the administration push other UN members to send soldiers to bolster the ground troops in Korea. Dulles heard them out and then assured them that the administration could achieve such ends by "working quietly." After the meeting, Senator H. Alexander Smith said that although there had been no bipartisanship in Far East policy up to that point, he felt the administration was moving in that direction. Smith was right. Senator Taft felt otherwise, saying, "I haven't seen any evidence that the Administration wants any [Republican input]." This was an unfair criticism, given Truman's recent appointment of two Republicans, Dulles and John S. Cooper, to State Department posts. It was true that the president often used the mantra of bipartisanship as a club to bludgeon his GOP opponents, but the Dulles and Cooper appointments had been practical ways to obtain Republican input into policymaking. Neither these appointments nor Truman's rapport with Senator Vandenberg swayed Taft. Although he knew little about foreign affairs, Taft was the de facto Republican leader in the Senate, putting him in a good position to oppose the administration. By mid-July 1950, Taft and other Republicans were already plotting to use "Mr. Truman's War" as a campaign issue in the midterm elections. Writing to a friend, Taft stated, "The only way we can beat the Democrats is to go after their mistakes. . . . There is no alternative except to support the war, but certainly we can point out that it has resulted from a bungling of the Democratic administration."[17]

Meanwhile, the Tydings committee wrestled with partisan acrimony as it drafted its final report on Senator McCarthy's allegations of communist infiltration of the State Department. The three Democrats on the committee tried in vain to get the endorsement of at least one of the two Republicans, with Senator Henry Cabot Lodge Jr. the obvious choice. Even though Tydings tried to entice him with a trip to Europe to "investigate" State Department security from abroad, Lodge refused to sign the report. The Massachusetts Republican correctly believed that the Democrats were more interested in attacking McCarthy than investigating the State Department. With no hope of getting Lodge's support, the Democrats rammed through their findings, submitting their report to the full Senate for debate. The majority statement, which called the charges a "fraud and a hoax," concluded that no one accused by the Wisconsin senator had committed any wrongdoing. Moreover, it called McCarthy's accusations "perhaps the most nefarious campaign of half-truths and untruths in the history of the republic," and it ripped the Republicans on the committee for their poor attendance and lack of zeal.[18]

Tempers boiled over when the full Senate began to debate the report on July 20, the day after Truman's speech to the nation. As the session began, minority leader Kenneth Wherry asked that Edward Morgan, counsel for the committee Democrats, be removed from the Senate floor. When this effort failed, Wherry cornered the lawyer near the back door and called him a "dirty son of a bitch" for writing the report. The GOP leader (and former undertaker) then threw a wild punch at the athletic Morgan, grazing his shoulder. Others quickly stepped in and separated them, and the lawyer later quipped, "I could have punched his lights out." William E. Jenner (R-IN) lambasted Tydings for overseeing the "most scandalous and brazen whitewash of treasonable conspiracy in our history," provoking the chairman to charge across the room, shaking his fist at Jenner. Ultimately, the Senate voted three times on the report, and each time *all* 96 senators voted with their party members on the committee, thereby accepting the majority report. On a positive note for President Truman, these votes marked the peak of Democratic Party solidarity during the Korean War.[19]

Bad news from Korea rocked the nation throughout the summer of 1950. UN forces continued to retreat until early August, when they finally stalled the North Korean advance near Pusan on the southeast coast of the peninsula. Even then, American troops could do no more than hold their position until late September. Reports of retreat contrasted sharply with Americans' memories of World War II victories, and they responded erratically. Panic purchasing of consumer goods continued, creating needless shortages. Yet the American people stayed solidly behind the war effort during the "first war." A Gallup poll indicated that only 20 percent thought involvement in Korea was a mistake, while 65 percent believed it was not a mistake. Truman's approval rating stood at 43 percent in late August, up from 37 percent in June. Nonetheless, correspondents around the country reported that many Americans were chafing at the prospect of fighting "small brush fires" against the Soviets around the globe, sparking calls for a preemptive nuclear attack on the Russians. *Time* reporters often heard phrases such as "Let's end it before it starts."[20]

At least two congressmen had other ideas about how to end the fighting. In August 1950 Representative Charles E. Bennett (D-FL) recommended that Truman ask the Russians to accept a cease-fire and to allow the UN to station police forces throughout the Korean peninsula to oversee free elections. Bennett, a freshman congressman, admitted the proposal was a long shot, but he was naïve to even suggest it, given that the Soviets' refusal to accept such elections had hardened the division of Korea in the first place. Later that month, H. Alexander Smith met with Truman foreign policy adviser Averell Harriman and suggested that the United States propose peace terms. Harriman rejected the idea, countering that the United States should pressure other UN members to propose such initiatives. Although Smith was a veteran of the Foreign Affairs Committee, his idea was nearly as bad as Bennett's. With UN troops struggling to hold on to a small piece of South Korea, Kim Il Sung would not have agreed to a cease-fire unless it were accompanied by his enemy's surrender.[21]

The Republican assault on Acheson continued throughout the summer of 1950, straining Democratic unity. Senator Wherry launched a vicious attack on the secretary, declaring, "The blood of our boys in Korea is on his shoulders, and no one else." The minority leader argued that since the American intervention amounted to a repudiation of Acheson's prewar Korea policy, Truman should replace him. The commander in chief took off the gloves, calling Wherry's comment a "contemptible statement and beneath comment." The Nebraskan retorted, "The President's failure to remove Acheson, after repudiation of his stupid foreign policies, is contemptible." Representative Robert Sikes (D-FL) countered that what the United States needed was a change in military leadership in the field. Without mentioning MacArthur by name, Sikes pointed out that the UN forces were taking a "terrific licking" and suggested that they needed someone in Korea "who can and will get on with the job." Sikes attracted little support from his Democratic colleagues, and no one publicly seconded his proposal. Nevertheless, his counterattack questioning the effectiveness of MacArthur, the darling of conservative Republicans, was a bold move. Then, just two weeks after the Tydings report, a journalist shocked Truman by informing him that House Democratic whip J. Percy Priest (TN), a consistent backer of his programs, believed that both Acheson and Secretary of Defense Louis Johnson should resign to help unify the country. The president, incredulous that a party leader had made such a statement, told the reporter to inform Priest that Acheson and Johnson would stay on. (Ultimately, Truman retained Acheson but fired Johnson, replacing him with George Marshall.) The president showed increasing sensitivity to this issue in his correspondence with Bennett. The Florida Democrat noted that replacing Acheson was a topic "pressed with great vigor by quite a number of my constituents," and he recommended that the secretary step down. Truman fired back that Democrats "should not be accepting lies and propaganda put out by people like McCarthy." Nonsoutherners also began to grow concerned about the secretary of state, and Senator Paul Douglas (D-IL), a staunch Fair Dealer, confided to a colleague that Acheson had become a "political liability."[22]

Ultimately, concerns about possible communist subversion in the government drove the largest wedge between Truman and his Democratic comrades during the first phase of the Korean War. Senate Judiciary Committee chairman Pat McCarran (D-NV), like McCarthy, had made anticommunism his signature issue, and McCarran was the primary cause of this intraparty friction. His quest to fight communism at home as well as in Korea came to fruition with the Internal Security Act of 1950, better known as the McCarran Act. A strident Truman nemesis, McCarran patterned the bill after a similar one sponsored by House *Republicans*. The McCarran Act required all members of the Communist Party to register with the Justice Department, and it directed the department to compile membership and financial information about all communist-related organizations. It banned the federal government and defense contractors from employing communists, and it blocked aliens who advocated totalitarianism from entering the country. Indicative of the power of McCarthyism during an election year, only seven of fifty-four Democrats voted against the McCarran Act, despite its restrictions on civil liberties.[23]

With such overwhelming Democratic approval, and amidst daily Republican attacks on his secretary of state for being soft on communism, it seemed the president had no choice but to sign the bill. But he did not. Truman courageously vetoed it, motivated in part by his longtime personal dislike of McCarran, whom he once described as having a "record for obstruction and bad legislation . . . matched by that of only a few reactionaries." Another more worthy reason was the president's belief that the bill was a tyrannical infringement on the First Amendment right of free speech. The president saw the McCarran Act as another sedition bill. In his veto message of September 22, Truman declared, "In a free country, we punish men for the crimes they commit, but never for the opinions they have," and he argued that the bill would put the government into the "thought control business."[24]

Truman was no match for the McCarthyesque atmosphere of the day, and Congress overwhelmingly overrode his veto. House members who were infuriated by the veto chanted, "Vote! Vote!" forcing Speaker Rayburn to plead with them simply to allow Truman's veto message to be read on the floor. Emotions ran high. Republican maverick William "Wild Bill" Langer (ND) collapsed on the Senate floor while filibustering against the bill, prompting emergency personnel to cart him off on a stretcher. After all this excitement, the House voted 286–48 (161–45 among the Democrats) to override—just one hour after the president's veto. The next day, the Senate voted 57–10 to do the same, with twenty-six Democrats voting to override and an additional ten agreeing in principle, although they were conveniently absent. The ten Democrats voting to sustain the veto took care to issue a press release distinguishing themselves from the "dastardly group" of communists opposing the bill, and they urged the public to work for its repeal through anticommunist organizations. Only three Democrats running for a Senate seat in 1950 voted against the measure, and two of them lost.[25]

Despite its bluster, the McCarran Act had little lasting effect. The courts ruled several portions of the law unconstitutional, and the parts that survived touched few individuals. No "communist" organizations ever bothered to register with the Justice Department. In the short term, however, Congress's vote reflected the public's communist phobia, and the nation seemed willing to sacrifice civil liberties to battle communism at home while its soldiers fought the "reds" in Korea. Truman's inability to scrounge up the handful of Senate votes needed to sustain his veto emphasized the divisions in his party forged by McCarthyism.[26]

Top officials in Truman's government did not help matters when they sent confusing signals to the public about his war policies. General MacArthur released a message for the Veterans of Foreign Wars extolling the value of Formosa for American military purposes and asserting that it was wrong to assume that an American defense of Formosa would antagonize communist China. MacArthur's statement contradicted the president's policy of neutrality regarding Formosa, a tactic designed to avoid arousing Mao's regime. To the administration's alarm, Secretary of the Navy Francis P. Matthews advocated a preventive war with the Soviets, declaring, "To have peace we should be willing to pay . . . any price—even the price of instituting a war to compel cooperation for peace."[27]

A Change of Direction

The president responded in a speech to the nation on September 1. Emphasizing his determination to keep the conflict in Korea from expanding into a general war, Truman stated that the United States had no interest in taking over Formosa. He rejected the idea of preventive war, calling it the "weapon of dictators, not of free democratic countries like the United States." Yet the address also laid the groundwork for a change in the scope of the intervention: "We believe the Koreans have a right to be free, independent and *united*—as they want to be." Though consistent with the

UN's post–World War II intention to eventually reunify the peninsula, this line in the speech revealed that the administration was seriously considering carrying the fight north of the thirty-eighth parallel. Such discussions within the State Department had begun as early as July. On August 17 the American ambassador to the UN, Warren Austin, told the General Assembly in a televised address that it should expand the mission to prevent a future invasion by North Korea, asking, "Shall only a part of the country be assured this freedom? I think not." Truman's remarks, coming on the heels of Austin's speech, clearly signaled an interest in changing the aim of the war from that set out in the initial UN resolution, which had been to restore the integrity of South Korea. If the United States wanted to keep other countries from getting involved in the war, why did its objective become more aggressive? *Time* was one of the few publications to criticize the speech, stating, "By every kind of wigwag and smoke signal . . . the Administration seemed to be trying . . . to tell the Chinese Communist Boss Mao Zedong that he had nothing to worry about the U.S." However, most of the major media paid little mind to the apparent change of direction by the administration.[28]

The American people continued to support the war and then some, crying out for more government action at home. One poll indicated that 70 percent of Americans favored higher taxes to increase the size of the military, and they backed universal military training by a margin of four to one. Pollster George Gallup wrote, "Rarely has the [Gallup] Institute in its fifteen years of measuring public opinion found such heavy majorities expressing a willingness to pay more taxes for any public purpose." In the early months of the war, Americans clamored for total wage and price controls. High employment rates throughout the nation likely contributed to this fearlessness regarding economic controls. In August 1950 New York State had so few unemployment claims that it fired 500 state employees from its compensation division. By September 1950, overall employment in the nation exceeded 62 million people, an increase of 2 million over the number employed on V-J Day. More important, the populace expected Washington to mobilize for victory as it had during World War II, and constituents bombarded their representatives on Capitol Hill in a sign of "profound public reaction." One journalist wrote, "One could almost hear Congress saying to the citizen in the White House: 'Say, you—don't you know there's a war on?'"[29]

Heeding the public outcry for mobilization, Congress passed the Defense Production Act (DPA) of 1950. The final bill reflected a compromise between President Truman and congressional Republicans. Initially, the GOP pushed for the total mobilization demanded by the public, including price ceilings across the board. The White House's economic team was concerned about potential challenges in administering full-scale controls and feared that this approach would hamper the long-term defense escalation advocated in NSC-68, the State Department's proposal to counteract the perceived Soviet threat. In the end, the bill rejected mandatory universal price caps and gave Truman the flexibility to impose controls on wages, prices, and rents when and where he saw fit. However, the DPA did require the president to impose wage controls when commodity price constraints had been implemented. In addition, the law gave the federal government the power to expand defense production plants, restrict credit, allocate commodities to prevent shortages, and settle labor disputes related to economic controls.[30]

Truman announced the passage of the DPA in a forceful speech to the nation on September 9. To help keep inflation in check while increasing defense spending, the president demanded a "pay-as-you-go" policy. Declaring that the nation had borrowed too much during World War II, he warned that Korea would mean "heavier taxes for everybody." Truman told consumers to "buy only what you really need and cannot do without," and he asked workers not to ask for raises beyond what was required to keep pace with cost-of-living increases. Unfortunately, the president did not exercise his power to cap prices or wages for several months, but his address bluntly exhorted Americans to sacrifice for the war effort. Truman also announced that he would ask for funding to add 3 million military personnel, a move greeted warmly by the public.[31]

The Truman administration took a couple of proactive measures to ensure continued public support of the DPA. Mindful that small businesses had been largely ignored during World War II mobilization, Secretary of Defense George Marshall and the Munitions Board took steps to include them. The board even encouraged small firms to band together as quasi-cartels to help them land war contracts. To prevent the appearance of a garrison state during initial mobilization, the Office of Price Stabilization intentionally took a decentralized approach when implementing and enforcing price caps on commodities.[32]

Passage of the DPA precipitated some interesting dynamics within labor unions, as well as in the relationship between the federal government and labor. Despite enjoying strong support from American communists in the 1930s, union leaders took a hard anticommunist stance during the Korean War. In United Automobile Workers (UAW) plants, right-wing gangs physically attacked antiwar workers in "run-outs" on the shop floor. A Milwaukee UAW employee suffered a broken back at the hands of his union brethren simply because he had signed a peace petition. At Ford Motor Company's Linden, New Jersey, factory, liberal workers made the mistake of trying to distribute "Hands-Off Korea" pamphlets. Conservative workers, vowing to "make every gate in the Linden plant a 38th parallel," beat up the radicals and kicked them out of the plant. National UAW leaders responded with a statement condemning the attacks but otherwise took no action. However, the unions' gung-ho attitude about fighting communism had its limits. Right off the bat, labor unions refused to pledge to avoid strikes, as they had done during World War II. UAW education director Victor Reuther declared, "While we are prepared to accept the added responsibility which national economic mobilization may place on the U.S., we are determined to surrender no rights in the process." Reuther was probably trying to protect some of the recent fruits of collective bargaining. In May 1950 General Motors workers had approved a five-year contract that included annual cost-of-living raises, boosted by an additional "annual improvement factor" based on the company's anticipated profitability. Interestingly, Ford and Chrysler had agreed to similar contracts with the UAW just a few weeks before passage of the DPA, possibly in an attempt to avoid wage controls. The Truman administration ultimately took a middle position between business and labor in implementing the DPA. Although unions had little meaningful input regarding manpower management and other policymaking decisions, they did have influence in issues directly affecting workers, such as wages, hours, benefits, and working conditions.[33]

The limited mobilization that began in the fall of 1950 produced one huge aftershock. Three weeks after Truman signed the DPA, he officially approved NSC-68. Although the American people were unaware of the document's existence (it was not declassified until 1975), they would soon feel its effects in the form of tax increases, credit restrictions, and, eventually, creation of the Cold War industrial-military complex. By the time

Truman left office, defense spending had increased from 5 percent of gross domestic product in 1950 to 14.2 percent.[34]

Election Politics—1950

As the nation mobilized for war, Democrats and Republicans mobilized for the 1950 midterm elections. Roused by the acrimonious vote on the Tydings committee report, Republicans who had previously been friendly to the administration's foreign policy were planning to attack the Democrats' Korean strategy. Senator H. Alexander Smith decided to push for a GOP statement on Far East policy "so that the Democrats will not claim that they saw the issues" correctly. On August 13 Smith and the other minority members of the Senate Foreign Relations Committee released a manifesto covering Cold War policies since 1945. Three of the four authors—Smith, Henry Cabot Lodge Jr., and Alexander Wiley—were members of the party's Vandenberg faction. They believed their statement reflected the spirit of a nonpartisan foreign policy, taking a compromise position between the Taft-Wherry wing, which was demanding Acheson's resignation, and Truman's approach. The statement declared, "The major tragedy of our time was the failure and refusal of American leadership in 1945 to recognize the true aims and methods" of the Soviets. The Democrats had tried to convince the Republicans that Chinese communism was "only a great agrarian reform movement." The Republican internationalists blamed the opposition party for Korea's division at the thirty-eighth parallel in the first place, due to agreements at Yalta. Far East policy had given the Kremlin a "green light to grab whatever it could in China, Korea, and Formosa." In Asia, the Republicans claimed, "This was never a bipartisan policy. It was solely an Administration policy." The GOP senators warned, "The American people will not now excuse those responsible for these blunders."[35]

One historian has characterized the Republican statement as "temperate." This is a bit generous. Taft endorsed the manifesto, which he never would have done unless he believed it would help his party hammer the Democrats. The fact that Smith came up with the idea for the statement with an eye toward the election was apparent in its threat that the public would hold the "blunderers" accountable for their foreign policy gaffes. In a *New York Times* story (headlined "Truman Is Blamed") about the statement, Republicans nonetheless insisted, "In this crisis there can be no 'politics as usual.'" Such double-talk foreshadowed the GOP strategy of supporting the war effort while criticizing the policies leading up to it. As one Republican senator quipped, "We'll man the pumps and unroll the hose, but damned if we'll sing, 'Hail to the Fire Chief.'"[36]

The Democrats justifiably perceived the GOP statement as an attack and responded in kind. Tom Connally called it a purely political statement and suggested that if the Republicans really wanted international peace, they should pursue "unity at home instead of quarrelsome and pettifogging attacks on the Administration." He pointed out that John Foster Dulles had been in Korea only days before the war erupted and had reported no imminent danger. Senator Brien McMahon (D-CT) chimed in, "These masters of hindsight seek to cut themselves in on the victories of our foreign policy and to divorce themselves from our defeats." Although the president's advisers discouraged him from reacting in any way that might be perceived as harmful to the bipartisan foreign policy, Truman confided his belief that Republicans such as Taft, Wherry, and McCarthy had invited the North Korean invasion through their criticism of the administration, presenting a picture of a divided America to the communists. Privately, the president accused Dulles of instigating the GOP manifesto, calling it "demagogic."[37]

The nature and source of the GOP's August statement made it nearly impossible for the president and his party to pursue any semblance of a bipartisan foreign policy until after the 1950 elections. The Republicans on the Foreign Relations Committee laid the blame for Korea on the Democrats and made it a campaign issue. They believed that Truman had cut them out of Far East policymaking from the beginning, that Acheson had made a mess of it, and that the Democrats needed to pay. As journalist William S. White wrote, the Republicans were "genuinely and profoundly bitter about the Far East, where, they think, some sort of Socialist virus within the Administration has worked a great, historic wrong." Since 1945 the Foreign Relations Committee, under Vandenberg's influence, had been the one governmental entity in which party affiliations had been put aside. But given the strident criticism now coming from people like Smith, Wiley, and Lodge, Truman's minions had no choice but to hit back.[38]

Nevertheless, the president backed up his bipartisan foreign policy rhetoric with several Republican appointments in the midst of the campaign mudslinging. Pundits praised Truman for selecting people based on competency rather than as payback for political favors. Most notably, the president named Robert A. Lovett and Walter S. Gifford to the posts of deputy secretary of defense and ambassador to Great Britain, respectively. Gifford's was a noteworthy appointment, in that Truman had promised the job to one of his chief fund-raisers but then reneged and gave the position to the GOP businessman. Lovett, an experienced bureaucrat, added another Republican to the top echelons of the State Department, supplementing Dulles and Cooper. Yet the GOP cared little about these gestures. Their chief interest lay in improving their numbers in Congress.[39]

The Republicans followed up with a white paper on Far East policy, *Background to Korea*. The nearly sixty-page pamphlet, designed for GOP candidates and the public, traced American policy in China and Korea from the late 1940s forward. It opened with a blunt statement: "The area of bipartisan foreign policy is clearly defined. Asia, including China and Korea, has been excluded." Moreover, it declared that a "spirit of consultation" was "totally lacking." This was a valid criticism, up to a point. As the Korean crisis unfolded, Truman met with bipartisan groups of Congress, but strictly to inform them of his decisions rather than to solicit their input. Reaching back to George Marshall's 1948 testimony that defending Korea was infeasible, the pamphlet was an "I told you so" document. It included a chronology of events and was sprinkled with quotes criticizing Democratic policies, such as the one from Senator Homer Ferguson (R-MI). Ferguson, reacting to the administration's January 1950 decision not to send American troops to Formosa to bolster the Jiang regime, sputtered that the bipartisan foreign policy had been "kicked out the window" by Truman and Acheson. The white paper also reproduced portions of a July 1950 speech made on the House floor by Walter Judd (R-MN), who complained, "In Europe we insisted that . . . the governments must keep the Communists out, but in China we insisted that . . . the government must take Communists in." Judd's comment overlooked the fact that postwar Europe's communist presence was smaller than China's. More important, Allied troops occupied much of western Europe following World War II; this was not the case in China. The United States was therefore in a much better position to ward off communist influence in Europe than in China. This reality, however, did not prevent the Republicans from attacking the administration as the 1950 election season began.[40]

A solitary Republican voice spoke out against using foreign policy missteps as campaign fodder. In September, Senator Lodge wrote an article for the *New York Times* analyzing the response to the GOP's August statement (which he had helped write) and describing his definition of bipartisanship. In Lodge's view, the statement's primary value was its recommendations for future policy directions, rather than its critique of the past. He was dismayed that the statement had been "cheered by many Republicans as a blow for party victory in November" and "denounced by many Democrats as an ending of the bipartisan foreign policy." Rebuking the Taft faction, the Massachusetts senator wrote, "The opposition should not follow the desires of some Republicans who say that we . . . should always oppose the Democrats no matter what they do," lest they be accused of "me-tooism." He also criticized Democrats who defined bipartisanship as the GOP going along with the administration, no matter what. Lodge argued that Republicans should steer Truman toward the best possible policy. Unfortunately, the heat of campaign rhetoric obliterated his wise counsel. Even internationalist Republicans continued to attack the administration, while the Trumanites branded their opponents as isolationists. By ignoring Lodge, the Democrats missed a chance to foster the idea of a bipartisan foreign policy.[41]

Instead, the Democrats made GOP opposition to a bipartisan foreign policy a campaign issue. Averell Harriman, the president's foreign policy guru who rarely engaged in political mudslinging, attracted attention across the nation with a speech he made at an organized labor convention. Ripping Taft's "constant guerilla warfare" against administration foreign policy, Harriman declared that, after examining the senator's record, "You cannot escape the conclusion that if the Congress had adopted his positions, Communist objectives would thereby have been furthered." When asked at a press conference whether he agreed with Harriman's harsh assessment, Truman said he did; Taft's record spoke for itself. Not to be outdone, the senator replied that until recently, Harriman and the president had believed "Joe Stalin was 'Good old Joe.'"[42]

Democrats used foreign policy issues in other clever ways, such as their Senate Campaign Committee's defense of William Benton (CT), who was accused of being a communist because he frequently voted with

Claude Pepper (D-FL) and Glenn Taylor (D-ID). (Thanks to red-baiting tactics, Pepper and Taylor both lost their primaries.) Examining thirty key votes on foreign policy issues, the committee reported that Pepper had voted "against the Communists," and therefore in favor of the bipartisan foreign policy, twenty-seven times, for a "batting average" of .900. Taylor, the erstwhile Progressive, had a much less spectacular average of .344. Both Pepper and Taylor, however, came in with higher anticommunist batting averages than thirty-two Republican senators, most notably, minority leader Kenneth Wherry at .233. The committee's point was that Benton's voting with Pepper and Taylor was not such a bad thing.[43]

Truman pounded on the bipartisanship issue in his only speech of the campaign, broadcast nationally just days before the election. Repeatedly taking care to note that *some* Republicans *were* working with Democrats on international affairs, the president labeled opponents of his foreign policy as isolationists. Truman railed that the isolationists had "dragged foreign policy into politics" and wanted the United States to "shut ourselves off from the rest of the world and abandon our friends and allies." This prompted cries from the crowd of "Give 'em hell, Harry." He proceeded to do just that, chastising certain Republicans for besmearing bipartisanship in foreign policy and for losing "all proportion, all sense of restraint, all sense of patriotic decency."[44]

Truman's attack on Republican isolationism was a questionable tactic. The GOP's main beefs had been inadequate support of the Chinese Nationalist regime; Acheson's defense perimeter speech, which had invited the North Korean attack; and steady complaints about the White House's failure to consult Republicans. The president would have been better off pointing out the decision-making roles of Republicans Dulles and Cooper, along with the recent appointment of Lovett, emphasizing his selection of them in a spirit of bipartisan cooperation. With such a tactic, Truman could have argued that it was impossible to satisfy the GOP no matter what he did.

Some Democrats found ways to defend themselves from Republican attacks on "Truman's War." In the face of GOP criticism in his state, Senator Warren G. Magnuson (D-WA) simply stood firm, believing his constituents would rally behind the president in wartime rather than second-guessing the policies leading up to the war. Although the national press did not publicize their views, a few Democrats reacted to Republican condemnation a bit more creatively. Representative Emmanuel Celler (D-NY) argued that all Americans shared blame for the North Koreans' attack due to the demobilization mentality following World War II. Senator Tydings and Representative Robert Sikes (D-FL) presciently noted that the American military needed a new paradigm because its existing planning was based on fighting a major power rather than a regional war. Recalling the context of Acheson's defense perimeter speech, Representative Mike Mansfield (D-MT) reminded his colleagues that the plan had always been for the United Nations, not solely the United States, to protect Korea.[45]

Democrats tried to turn the war from a political liability into an asset, despite the bad news from the battlefront. The Democratic National Committee (DNC) decided to highlight the defeat of a $150 million Korean aid bill in the House in January 1950. Senate majority whip Francis J. Myers (D-PA) planned to emphasize that some politicians who had previously demanded military cutbacks "are the loudest now in criticism of the lack of preparedness." However, this strategy presented challenges to party unity. Responding to Republican attacks on Acheson following the vote on the Tydings committee report, Michael J. Kirwan (OH), chairman of the House Democratic Campaign Committee, issued a nineteen-page summary of legislators' voting records against Korean aid packages in 1949 and early 1950, proclaiming, "The isolationist bloc of the House must shoulder the responsibility for the Communist attack on South Korea." The rub for the Democrats was that forty-two of their own members, primarily southerners, had voted against all aid packages for Korea and therefore fell into the "isolationist" category. Interestingly, in preparing this statement, the DNC took pains not to blame the Republican Party by name, targeting the isolationists in both parties. Kirwan's report underscored the political dilemma for the Trumanites: to defend Secretary Acheson, they had to attack the voting records of many in their own party.[46]

An anecdote from Texas illustrates the problems the unpopular secretary of state created for his party. Jack Carter, a member of the State Democratic Executive Committee, wrote to Sam Rayburn expressing serious concerns about an anti-Truman faction of delegates challenging the pro-administration slate officially adopted at the Tarrant County convention. The group had attacked the president harshly, passing a resolution blaming the State Department for creating the "darkest hour and the most crucial period that ever existed in the state of Texas," including the initial division of Korea, which had caused the war in the first place. To remedy this sorry state of affairs, the delegates demanded that "Congress should take a common everyday weeding hoe and chop down every Pansy that exists in the State and other Departments of the United States Government." Carter noted that this resolution "could have been written by Senator McCarthy himself."[47]

By the autumn of 1950, few Democrats publicly supported Acheson. Only twelve out of forty-nine Democratic senators spoke out in his favor during the election campaign. Of this dozen, seven had joined the Senate since 1948, meaning that their statements carried little political clout. The party was thus at an impasse regarding foreign policy. Truman adamantly stood up for Acheson, while most Capitol Hill Democrats ran from the beleaguered secretary of state.[48]

Domestic issues also contributed to divisions within the Democratic Party during the 1950 election season. Fair Deal initiatives such as national health insurance and civil rights drew the ire of southern Democrats, prompting concerns about support for the administration in key states such as Texas. Truman crony Henri Warren worried that antiadministration delegations from the large metropolitan areas of Houston, Dallas, and Fort Worth could control the upcoming state Democratic convention. He predicted that "delegates will be brought in from East Texas who definitely know that President Truman and Roosevelt want their daughters to marry negroes" and who believe that a "federal police force will require that negroes be employed in the shops and factories and on the farms." Warren complained that Truman's congressional allies rarely appeared at such state gatherings, and he urged the president to pressure them to attend and thus blunt attacks on the administration.[49]

As the 1950 campaign continued, the Democrats did a number of things to counter criticisms of Truman's Far East policy. In response to candidates who were clamoring for fact sheets justifying the war, the Democrats' Senate Campaign Committee prepared "The Truth about Korea." Of the sixteen pages in the document, less than three were devoted to explaining why the administration had intervened; the remainder were dedicated to refuting Republican criticisms of Korean policy before the war. Arguing that Kim Il Sung's strike was the first time the "international Communist movement" had used overt military force, the Democrats declared that inaction would have encouraged additional attacks elsewhere. Interestingly, the tract did not mention reunification of the peninsula, asserting that the UN had acted simply to "check and throw back the aggression."[50]

The State Department was heavily involved in the campaign, collaborating with the White House to provide ammunition for Democrats running for office. One pamphlet effectively defended Acheson's heavily criticized January 1950 speech in which the secretary had declared, "*Initial* reliance must be on the people attacked to resist it and *then* upon the commitments of the entire civilized world under the Charter of the United Nations." This was exactly how the Korean intervention had transpired. Recalling the evils of appeasement, one tract noted, "We have learned by hard experience in the 1930s that when we allow aggression to succeed anywhere in the world we invite aggression everywhere in the world." Another publication stressed that the communists had changed tactics in Korea. Rather than relying on subversion, the "international communist movement, for the first time, adopted open warfare to achieve its purposes." The State Department distributed "Information Objectives for the Rest of 1950" to guide its personnel in making public statements. These guidelines stressed past successes of the containment policy in Europe and Turkey and reminders that similar efforts would need to continue for an "indefinite period." The department also published a Korean War "fact sheet" for Democrats on the campaign trail to help them answer questions about Far East policy. In August Acheson met with a group of Democratic lawmakers who were concerned about increasing public support for a preventive war with the Soviet Union. Acheson came down firmly against the idea of a preemptive attack. In a response as relevant today as it was in 1950, the secretary told them, "Any nation embarking upon a preventive war would . . . find itself immediately without any Allies and would ultimately find itself in the unenviable position of having the world against it."[51]

The administration also took its case directly to the American people by publishing a booklet entitled *Our Foreign Policy.* White House aide George Elsey had come up with the idea to explain the administration's objectives in Korea in lay terms. Truman suggested only a few editorial changes, but they were telling. For instance, the president disliked this passage: "Three times in recent years we have been forced to sacrifice peace

. . . to preserve the independence and freedom that we value even more highly." "We haven't 'sacrificed peace,'" Truman told Elsey. "We got into Korea to *preserve* peace." Capitalization of "Communist" and "Communism" also irritated the president, who demanded that these words appear in lowercase. To make the document more compelling, Elsey circulated drafts to scholars such as Arthur Schlesinger Jr., asking for their input.[52]

Our Foreign Policy explained why the United States went to war in Korea, but it obfuscated the goals of the mission. Noting that the Soviet Union had gained control of 7.5 million square miles of territory and 500 million people since 1945, it declared there were "no more side lines for a nation to sit on." The fact that a totalitarian nation was "seeking to extend its power and to impose its system of communism over others" justified the intervention in Korea. Moreover, the Soviet Union had reneged on its "solemn pledge" to work with the United States, Britain, and China to restore Korean independence, and it had "sealed off the northern area of Korea from all outside contact," a reference to proposed reunification elections under UN supervision. However, the document contradicted the UN's stated objective at the time—restoration of the ROK—stating that America's purpose was "helping the Koreans to become a united and independent people." Did this mean South Koreans, or all Koreans?[53]

The initial printing of 50,000 copies of *Our Foreign Policy* was quickly exhausted, and the State Department eventually printed more than 400,000 booklets. The administration sent thousands of them to industrial leaders to educate them on defense preparations, to public and university libraries, and to principals of all secondary schools. Another 20,000 copies were sent to civics teachers, and 2,500 went to college professors teaching courses in international relations; organizations representing women, labor, religion, and business also received the booklet. The *Washington Post* used it as a source in a series of question-and-answer articles about foreign affairs. Although critics dismissed the publication as a hasty and erroneous rebuttal to the Republicans' *Background to Korea,* most of the press responded favorably. Edward R. Murrow of CBS endorsed it, and Earl Godwin of NBC called it a "very timely bit of reading matter" that was "as easy to read as a mystery tale."[54]

The Korean crisis severely curtailed Truman's ability to stump for Democrats. He made a whistle-stop tour in the spring but had to cancel a second one planned for the fall. Truman involved himself in only two

Senate races. In his home state of Missouri, the president wanted to oust incumbent Republican Forrest C. Donnell, a harsh critic of the administration. Although Truman boosted the candidacy of state senator Emery W. Allison, former congressman Thomas C. Hennings Jr. prevailed in the primary, much to the president's irritation. Ironically, this helped Truman in the long run. Hennings triumphed in the general election, making him the only Democrat to unseat a GOP incumbent. Moreover, Missouri's new senator became a dogged opponent of Joseph McCarthy. The president also lent some support to the campaign of Representative Helen Gahagan Douglas for an open Senate seat in California, even though he had once referred to her as "one of the worst nuisances." Again, the chief executive's backing was to no avail, as Republican Richard Nixon trounced Douglas in the general election. Except for his one speech on the eve of the election, this was the extent of Truman's involvement in the 1950 races. As Ken Hechler wrote of the president, "He put on his commander in chief's hat and his political hat gathered dust."[55]

The Republicans intended to "keep the Communist pot boiling" during the campaign, with the junior senator from Wisconsin as the head chef. The GOP saw Joseph McCarthy as its "new political alchemist" in 1950, a man who could "turn fear and mistrust into votes." Although he campaigned in fifteen states, "Tailgunner Joe," as he liked to call himself, had a direct influence in only one race—the one between incumbent Democrat Millard Tydings and Republican John Marshall Butler, a political newcomer. In July McCarthy took over Butler's campaign and overhauled its organization from top to bottom. He brought in a Chicago public relations man to organize the day-to-day details and used his personal contacts to raise money for Butler, enabling the challenger to outspend Tydings three to one. The coup de grace that discredited the incumbent's long record of steadfast opposition to communism was a widely publicized photograph that showed Tydings apparently sitting and listening thoughtfully to Earl Browder, chairman of the Communist Party USA. The picture was a fake, produced by merging two separate photos; the two men had never met until Browder testified before the Tydings committee. Maryland's veteran senator, behaving with the confidence of an incumbent running for a fifth term, did not respond directly to the smear campaign until October. By then, it was too late to stop the momentum of McCarthy's onslaught.[56]

The Democrats reacted to McCarthy in curious ways during the campaign. For example, the DNC distributed a booklet titled *Scare Words,* a collection of Republican quotes and predictions that had failed to materialize. Despite McCarthy's notoriety, it barely mentioned his red scare. The Democratic Senate Campaign Committee circulated a flyer lambasting the Wisconsin senator for publicly defending German SS troopers accused of killing American prisoners of war in the Malmedy murders case, suggesting that he would similarly "leap to the defense of the North Korean war criminals." The harshness of this attack prompted one committee member to criticize it as being so badly written that it would damage the panel's credibility, calling the charges against McCarthy "preposterous" and "gutter politics against a gutter snipe." Unsurprisingly, Tydings and Senator Brien McMahon, another McCarthy target, had crafted the document. After being on the receiving end of the Wisconsin Republican's salvos, they were ready to plunge into the muck and slug it out.[57]

General MacArthur's daring and successful counterattack at Inchon in mid-September changed the UN's military fortunes and seemed poised to affect the elections. Cautious optimism turned to euphoria in the Democratic camp. McMahon proclaimed, "The lessons of this victory will be carefully studied both in Moscow and in the capitals of the free world," and he wrote in a published letter to the State Department that Korea had "exploded the legend of the Red invincibility." Connecticut's other incumbent senator running for reelection, William Benton, thought Korea would help the Democrats get out the vote. Apparently, the Republicans agreed; they sent cynical letters to their opponents' campaign headquarters, accusing them of timing the victory in Korea to coincide with the elections. The Democratic elation, however, would be brief.[58]

A Fateful Decision

The Inchon landing was one of several factors contributing to President Truman's momentous decision to authorize UN forces to carry the fighting north of the thirty-eighth parallel. With the victory at Inchon, unification of the Koreas—a stated goal of the UN since 1947—appeared to be within reach. MacArthur wanted the freedom to forge northward to finish off his adversary. The Joint Chiefs of Staff believed that proceeding north would enable UN forces to maneuver into more defensible positions. Moreover, having expressed doubt that MacArthur's risky Inchon plan would work, the Joint Chiefs were in no position to oppose him now. Truman also had powerful political incentives to reunify the peninsula. After suffering relentless disparagement from the Republicans since 1949 for losing China to Mao Zedong, Truman's failure to proceed north of the thirty-eighth parallel could have branded him an appeaser of communism. Britain provided key assistance to Truman's decision to change the scope of the war. Hoping to realize the UN's objective in Korea and, more importantly, to ensure U.S. troop commitments to NATO (see chapter 3), the British initiated a resolution supporting Ambassador Austin's August proposal to carry the battle northward. Following some revisions suggested by the Americans, the UN General Assembly passed it overwhelmingly on October 7, changing the aim of the war. Two days later, the U.S. Eighth Army crossed into North Korea. No longer content with repelling the communist invaders from the north, the UN's objective became enforcing "conditions of stability throughout Korea" and establishing a "united, independent and democratic government in the sovereign state of Korea."[59]

The Truman administration encountered few problems in persuading the UN to change the official objective of the war. The composition of the 500,000 international military forces in Korea at the time was a roughly fifty-fifty split of American and ROK troops. By war's end, fifteen additional UN members had contributed an additional 44,000 personnel, the bulk of them from the British Commonwealth. Thus, only the United States and the ROK had large military contingents in the conflict. Although the Soviet Union had ended its boycott of the UN Security Council by this time, the administration avoided a potential Soviet veto by pushing the resolution through the General Assembly, where the United States enjoyed broad political support.[60]

President Truman did little to sell the American public on the need to broaden the scope of the war. It was hardly necessary. One poll indicated that nearly three-quarters of Americans supported the decision to advance into North Korea. Most major newspapers endorsed the change in policy. *Life* rejected the notion of stopping at the thirty-eighth parallel, deeming such "timidity . . . quite worthless." The possibility of Chinese intervention caused no concern to *Life*'s editors, who believed that Mao Zedong was awestruck by American air and sea power and must be "quaking in his boots." Both political parties backed the northern advance. Senator Joseph O'Mahoney (D-WY) wrote to Truman that the United States, which had "given so much of its blood and manhood" in Korea, should not allow the communists to reestablish the "iron curtain" from which to launch future attacks. Representative Hugh D. Scott Jr. (R-PA), a former GOP National Committee chairman, accused the State Department of planning to "cringe behind" the thirty-eighth parallel. In his September and October press conferences, the president scarcely mentioned the subject, other than to dodge questions about whether he had authorized MacArthur to go north. Truman's October 17 address to the nation from San Francisco was his only major speech during this critical phase of the war, and he touched on the policy change only briefly. Noting that his discussions with MacArthur at Wake Island a few days earlier included plans to ensure a "unified, independent and democratic" government in Korea (the purported Allied intent after World War II), the chief executive warned that the "evil spirit of aggression" still presented a "clear and present danger." Nevertheless, Truman assured the public that the UN would shortly "restore peace to the whole of Korea."[61]

Could the president have persuaded the American people that UN forces should stop at the thirty-eighth parallel? Historian Alonzo Hamby points out that Truman had to consider that halting at the boundary would have left open the possibility of a future North Korean attack. In light of current international friction with North Korea, this argument seems even stronger. Scholars Halford R. Ryan and Melvyn Leffler, however, suggest that Truman could have stopped at the thirty-eighth parallel and proclaimed victory. Leffler notes that despite the popularity of taking the battle into the north, many Americans were ready for a negotiated settlement to end the war in the fall of 1950. Moreover, Truman had withstood criticism before, and he would soon weather one of the worst political storms in American history when he fired MacArthur (see chapter 3). However, the temptation to grab a rousing victory against the tide of Soviet communist expansion ultimately motivated the president's decision. Such a victory would also throw a badly needed counterpunch against the McCarthyites, who had been tormenting Truman since Mao's 1949 victory in China.[62]

Three days after MacArthur assured the president at the Wake Island meeting that China would not enter the conflict, Chinese troops crossed the Yalu River into North Korea, engaging South Korean troops for the first time on October 25. The new war ushered in a new campaign for the Democrats. During the week leading up to Election Day, newspaper headlines screamed "U.S. Units Retreat 50 Miles in Korea," "Another Acheson Betrayal," and "Red Counterblows Again Throw Allies Back in Furious No. Korea Clashes." On election eve, the magnitude of the Chinese intervention became obvious to the nation, and the Republican National Committee immediately responded with a press release. It declared that the crisis highlighted "the ineffectiveness of our United States foreign policy where it has not been a united policy," contrasting it with bipartisan measures such as the Marshall Plan. Criticizing a State Department that was "intent on appeasing the Chinese Communist Revolution," the Republicans charged that the administration had "inexcusably turned its back on those patriotic Chinese groups," referring to the Nationalists. The GOP asserted that this was the "issue on which the American people are called upon to express themselves as they go to the polls on Election Day." On November 7, in the midst of nothing but bad news from Korea, Americans went to the polls to elect their legislators. Reminiscing about that day two decades later, Representative Richard Bolling (D-MO) said, "We could feel the ground slipping out from under us."[63]

Election Results

Surprisingly, the 1950 contests left the Democrats in control of Congress. However, the elections robbed Truman of key congressional allies and shrank his party's numerical margins over the Republicans in both houses. Overall, as in the 1946 elections, nonsouthern liberals were the most common casualties, particularly in the House. In the Senate the top two Democrats, majority leader Lucas and majority whip Myers, went down in defeat. So did Tydings, along with three-term senator Elbert Thomas (D-UT), another staunch Truman backer. The elections repudiated the Democratic power structure in the Senate, as six of the thirteen members of the party's steering committee lost in either the primaries or the general election, decimating those leaders who were strong supporters of the president. With the defeat of so many Truman allies in the Senate, the election was more of a setback for him than for his party. Truman recognized this as he watched the results roll in. Although the president frequently enjoyed his bourbon over a poker game with friends, an aide recalled that election night in 1950 was the only time he saw the chief executive using liquor to drown his sorrows.[64]

Several factors led to the Democrats' losses in 1950. Truman staffers and some members of Congress blamed the DNC leadership of William Boyle, even though the party outperformed the Republicans in fund-raising from 1949 through 1951. One congressman groused, "The only time the Democratic National Committee shows any signs of life is at the cocktail hour." More specifically, some Democrats complained about the DNC's failure to staff a permanent research division, which had been so effective in 1948 in gathering facts to spotlight Republican inconsistencies and Democratic successes. Another weakness was the selection of a rookie senator, Clinton Anderson, to chair the Senate Campaign Committee. Anderson had been a three-term member of the House and Truman's secretary of agriculture before his election to the Senate in 1948. However, because he was from a small state (New Mexico) and had only one Senate campaign under his belt, putting Anderson in charge of all Senate races across the nation did not make sense.[65]

At the time, most Republicans and Democrats agreed with Arthur Schlesinger Jr.'s assessment of the 1950 election as a "triumph for McCarthyism." This, however, was an overstatement, as demonstrated by the fate of House Democrats who had voted against the McCarran Act. Supporting that bill did not provide political sanctuary, as twenty-three of the twenty-eight Democrats who had backed the McCarran Act lost in November. Conversely, only five of the twenty-one House Democrats who had opposed the bill suffered defeat, and three of those five lost in quests for Senate seats. Voting to override Truman's veto of the McCarran Act failed to carry most of these Democrats to victory in 1950. Democrats bucking the McCarthyite push for this largely symbolic statute to squash internal communism did just fine in the elections.[66]

A closer examination of McCarthy's effect on specific races yields some interesting discoveries. Although McCarthy liked to take credit for Lucas's defeat in Illinois, other factors affected the results. Senator Anderson and at least one historian blamed the majority leader's defeat on a highly publicized probe into organized crime led by Senator Estes Kefauver (D-TN); this investigation uncovered corruption in the Chicago police department, and Lucas was deemed guilty by association. Curiously, Lucas's campaign focused on farm issues, attempting either to cut into opponent Everett Dirksen's strength in rural areas or to deflect attention from the Kefauver investigation. Anderson and Truman had different takes on how support of the president contributed to Lucas's defeat. The president claimed the majority leader lost because he was too wishy-washy, while Anderson suggested that Lucas's unwavering support of the White House was to blame. In light of electoral trends elsewhere, Anderson's explanation is closer to reality. Democrats known for backing Truman exhibited significant vulnerability in the election.[67]

No one, however, could deny McCarthy's role in Tydings's defeat in Maryland. Senate Democrats followed up with an inquiry into the unscrupulous methods used to engineer Butler's surprise victory. As Anderson pointed out in a letter to the *St. Louis Post-Dispatch,* the Democrats pushed for and obtained this probe as a matter of principle. Tydings was not asking for a new election, and the Democrats had no hope of obtaining any immediate political gain from the investigation; instead, they hoped to teach McCarthy and those who employed his tactics a lesson for future campaigns. Imploring his colleagues to pursue the matter, McMahon produced a copy of *Common Sense,* a fascist publication used against him in his contest, bearing the headline, "McMahon—Communist Dupe." The Connecticut senator warned his colleagues, "I beat it, boys, but maybe you can't in 1952." After investigating allegations of unlawful fund-raising practices, the use of fraudulent campaign literature, and improper involvement by groups outside the state of Maryland in Butler's organization, a Senate rules subcommittee agreed that Tydings had a legitimate complaint. Although the subcommittee called Butler's campaign tactics "despicable" and declared that McCarthy had played a "leading and potent" role, the Senate stopped short of denying the victor his seat or formally censuring either Butler or McCarthy. An outraged Senator Benton reacted to the report by delivering the "most outspoken attack on McCarthy that had ever been heard in Congress" and submitting a resolution demanding the Wisconsin senator's resignation. Benton's outburst sparked a chorus of "amens" from a trio of Democratic colleagues and a commendation from columnist Drew Pearson for accurately documenting McCarthy's falsehoods. However, most of Benton's fellow Democrats did not immediately leap to his defense, and one of them half-jokingly remarked that the Benton-McCarthy feud could produce the "ideal double murder."[68]

Thus, McCarthy's direct effect on the 1950 elections was spotty. This, however, was not the public perception. By 1951, Americans were buying anticommunist comic books and enjoying movies such as *I Was a Communist for the FBI*. Congress feared McCarthy, too. Even though an investigative subcommittee *unanimously* agreed that the Wisconsin senator had acted unethically and unlawfully in the Maryland campaign, the Senate, with its Democratic majority, let him off with a slap on the wrist. *Newsweek* aptly declared, "Democrats Fume at McCarthy, But He Has Them Terrorized."[69]

Korea loomed larger than Joseph McCarthy in the 1950 campaign. A survey of lead editorials in more than sixty small-town newspapers by a Democratic Party staffer underscored the war's importance. Although the author of this analysis had intended to highlight tax policy as a campaign issue, it actually showed that the war was a more prominent concern in small-town America. Despite the considerable efforts of the Truman administration, Democratic incumbent senators running for reelection struggled to respond to common questions raised by the GOP on the campaign trail, such as, "Why did we stop the communists in Europe [via the Marshall Plan], but left Asia [China and Korea] 'wide open'?"[70]

Key Truman supporters recognized shortcomings in their party's promotion of the administration's Korean policy during the 1950 campaign. Bolling believed that when candidates adequately explained the "facts" of foreign policy, they did well. He conceded, however, "It is an unfortunate fact that a great many politicians do not know those facts and do not understand our foreign policy. Obviously they cannot make it understandable to their constituents." Presidential aide Ken Hechler agreed, saying that in spite of its efforts, "the administration has not succeeded as well as it should in convincing the people, in simple terms, of the rightness of the course we are pursuing." The problem was that foreign policy was more complicated than it had been during World War II. As Hechler observed, there was "no great, unified, patriotic" feeling about Korea, lamenting, "the people do not fully understand how much better off they are than if this should develop into an all-out war."[71]

The 1950 election results stiffened the resolve of Truman's congressional enemies, adding to the challenges of keeping his party together during wartime. The president accurately described Congress as nominally controlled by the Democrats but conceded, "The majority is made up of

Republicans and recalcitrant Southern 'Democrats'—who are not Democrats." In his diary, Truman wrote, "My 'friend,' Harry Byrd [D-VA] says he has the professional southerners lined up against Yugoslav Aid. Wonder if he'd like being branded Stalin's No. 2 helper in the Senate." Although individuals such as Representative Hale Boggs (D-LA) informally organized small groups of legislators to support the president, Truman faced an even steeper uphill battle as the Eighty-Second Congress went to work.[72]

Nonetheless, some in the administration believed that the 1950 elections had not necessarily ruined the president's ability to carry out his foreign policies. A White House analysis began with a summary of how frequently senators had supported the administration on thirty key foreign policy votes between 1947 and the outbreak of the war (see table 1). Nine of the thirty-two "100 percenters" had lost their seats in the 1950 elections. Opponents of Truman's foreign policy replaced four of these nine, and the remaining five were supplanted by either Democrats or Republicans who were expected to back the administration. In Missouri, a Democrat expected to staunchly back Truman had unseated a Republican, resulting in a net reduction in the 100 percent category from thirty-two to twenty-nine. The elections produced no net change in the 90–99 percent category, leaving the White House with forty-four senators expected to support foreign policy issues 90 percent of the time or better. Since the administration would need forty-nine votes to win, the remaining five votes would have to come from the eleven senators in the 80–89 percent bracket. Because this group included four Republicans perceived as "internationalists," along with four Democrats, the White House believed it could scrounge up the five votes needed from this group on nearly all foreign policy initiatives.[73]

Regardless, the elections clearly affected the dynamics of lawmaking on Capitol Hill. In the House, the Democrats' numerical edge slipped from ninety-two to thirty-six, and Truman's opponents took this as a cue to flex their political muscles. On Congress's first day in session in 1951, Edward E. Cox (D-GA) proposed a vote to end the twenty-one-day rule, which would restore the Rules Committee's power to bottle up legislation indefinitely. Majority leader John McCormack (D-MA) and Adolf J. Sabath (D-IL), the dean of the House, spearheaded the effort to protect the rule. As chairman of the Rules Committee, Sabath's support for the

Table 1. Senators' Support for Truman on Key Foreign Policy Issues, 1947–June 1950

Number of Senators	Frequency of Support for Truman (%)
32	100
15	90–99
11	80–89
10	70–79
4	60–69
7	50–59
17	0–49

rule seems surprising, since its repeal would have restored enormous power to his panel. However, with the Rules Committee's five southern Democrats (of eight Democrats in total) joining forces with the four Republican members, the chairman could not ensure that Truman's legislation would reach the House floor for a vote. Sabath therefore decided that the best way to support the president was to back the twenty-one-day rule, allowing committee chairs to force floor votes on bills not acted on by the Rules Committee within three weeks. When Truman's congressional allies tried to persuade their colleagues to keep the rule, his opponents countered that Fair Deal initiatives such as national health insurance and the Brannan Plan for agricultural assistance were the real reasons behind the dispute. At the mention of these programs, the entire floor demanded a vote to end the rule. The administration lost decisively, 244–179, with 92 (of 235) Democrats joining 152 Republicans in voting to restore power to the Rules Committee, despite the fact that House Speaker Rayburn and McCormack were strong administration allies. An examination of the southern states having only Democrats in their congressional delegations indicates the antipathy toward Truman. Only 19 of 99 Dixie Democrats voted to back the president and retain the rule. McCormack observed that the Republicans appeared content to ride along on the "tail of the Dixiecrat kites." This combination of GOP opposition and southern dissidents would create even more challenges as Truman grappled with a far more dangerous war, featuring China as the new adversary.[74]

3

The Second War,
November 1950–July 1951

Communist China proved to be an unpredictable foe as the next phase of the fighting in Korea began. After their jolting entry into the war in late October, Mao's forces abruptly broke off the fighting shortly after the November 7 elections and withdrew for nearly three weeks. This lull in the conflict gave the United States time to reassess its attempt to reunify the peninsula. General MacArthur prevailed on the Truman administration to allow him to continue his quest to destroy the enemy army, launching a UN offensive on November 24 and promising to have the troops home for Christmas. Eighth Army, under the command of Lieutenant General Walton H. Walker, formed a broad front across the western and central portions of the peninsula and pushed northward. Major General Edward M. Almond led X Corps, composed chiefly of the First Marine Division and the army's Seventh Infantry Division. Following an amphibious landing at Wosan on the northeast coast, X Corps moved northwest to disrupt enemy supply lines. A formidable mountain range separated these two armies, which operated virtually independently of each other. On November 25 communist Chinese forces launched massive counterattacks, with disastrous results for both UN contingents. Walker ordered the longest retreat in American military history, some 275 miles, culminating south of the thirty-eighth parallel by mid-December. Meanwhile, six Chinese divisions trapped the First Marine Division at the Chosin Reservoir, precipitating the most famous and miraculous breakout of the war. By the time the escaping marines were evacuated by sea from Hungnam on the east coast of North Korea, they had killed an estimated 40,000

Chinese troops while suffering losses of 743 Americans dead or missing, 2,894 wounded, and 3,600 nonbattle injuries (mostly from frostbite). The second war—very different from the first—was under way.[1]

China's intervention in Korea alarmed both Congress and the American public. Some lawmakers wanted to attack China and drive for total victory; others advocated a complete pullout of American troops, while a third faction supported Truman's ultimate course of salvaging whatever was possible without expanding the war's scope. A November 1950 poll, taken before the public knew the extent of Chinese involvement, indicated that only 39 percent of Americans favored carrying the battle into China if that country entered the conflict. According to a January 1951 Gallup poll, 49 percent of Americans now regarded the war as a mistake, versus 20 percent four months earlier. In a poll taken shortly after Chinese troops crossed the Yalu River into North Korea, more than half the respondents said they believed World War III had begun.[2]

The second phase of the Korean War thus created a severe test of President Truman's ability to maintain national unity. Preserving Democratic Party harmony proved equally challenging. A combination of sharp GOP criticism, rebellion within his own party, and the possibility of losing the war forced the chief executive to actually practice the gospel of bipartisan foreign policymaking that he so often preached. As he prepared to declare a national emergency in response to the Chinese involvement, Truman reached out to congressional Republicans like never before. The bipartisan mood, however, soon vanished, demonstrating the impracticalities of a foreign policy jointly implemented by the president and Congress.

Democrats in Disarray

Truman and the congressional Democrats failed each other in important ways at the outset of the China crisis. For his part, the president was slow to rally the American people to respond to the Chinese invasion. He did not mention it publicly until his November 16 press conference, which he opened with a statement that condemned China's involvement but reassured the Chinese that the UN had no designs on their territory. However, the president refused to answer questions about the issue. At his next news conference two weeks later, he fielded questions on China's intervention, which was the predominant topic, and dropped a figurative bombshell when he repeatedly asserted that the use of atomic weapons was an option in Korea, at General MacArthur's discretion. Although the president's staff swiftly clarified his remarks to reassure allies that he had *not* given his field commander the authority to use the bomb, these comments fueled the public's growing fear that another world war was at hand. Truman waited another two weeks to address the American people directly about the new situation they faced. By that time, American forces had been fighting Chinese communists for more than a month.[3]

Why did the president wait so long to discuss the Chinese intervention with the public? A number of factors contributed to this delay. As noted in the previous chapter, Truman was not much of a speech maker; clearly, he was more comfortable with press conferences than with prepared speeches. Although he normally enjoyed the friendly banter with journalists, the president could become defensive, cutting reporters off in midsentence and answering their questions before they finished asking them. Although most of the White House press corps liked Truman personally, even when they disagreed with him, press conferences were no more effective than formal speeches in getting the president's message across to the public. Moreover, breaking with a tradition begun by Woodrow Wilson, Truman held only one press conference per week, rather than two. The administration tried to compensate by issuing more press releases than the Roosevelt team had, but these statements were not nearly as useful to reporters as question-and-answer sessions. In retrospect, Truman's slow start in his personal promotion of the war effort was not surprising. Salesmanship was not his thing, unless he was on the campaign trail.[4]

More important, political and personal shocks contributed to Truman's delayed response. In a matter of days, the commander in chief went from expecting the war to end within a few weeks to facing an enemy with several hundred thousand troops and the possibility of a world war. However, he could not have been totally surprised. China had issued warnings in October, through Indian diplomats, that it would get into the war if UN forces crossed the thirty-eighth parallel, and some in the State Department had taken them seriously. The sudden death on December 5 of press secretary Charlie Ross, a close friend of Truman's, did not help the president's morale or the effectiveness of White House communications. As had been the case at the outset of the war, the commander in chief waited an unacceptably long time before making a speech to the nation about this new international crisis, even as the public and his party grew increasingly anxious.[5]

Undersecretary of State James E. Webb tried to help the president improve his relationship with southern senators in the midst of the China crisis. A North Carolinian with experience in regional politics, Webb explained to Truman that southerners felt they were spending a lot of energy defending themselves against the president's civil rights initiatives. He also pointed out that southerners had generally supported the administration's foreign policy; for example, Senator Richard Russell (D-GA) had shared the president's belief in the futility of continued funding of Jiang Jieshi in 1949. Suggesting that the administration could find common ground with southerners in areas other than racial issues, the undersecretary floated a "what if" scenario in which Truman and Russell agreed to warn each other privately of impending disagreements over policy before going public with them. The president, who had once disparaged Russell as the "great Georgian Senator, representative of the National Chamber of Congress, the Coca-Cola Company, etc.," expressed appreciation for Webb's suggestions, but little else. Although there is no evidence of a rapprochement along these lines, Russell later helped the administration immensely during the Senate inquiry into the firing of General MacArthur. However, the residual enmity between the president and the South over civil rights was probably too much for either Russell or Truman to overcome.[6]

This hostility manifested itself as Democrats and Republicans formed coalitions to thwart Truman's policies. Early in 1951 Clarence Cannon (D-MO), the powerful chairman of the House Appropriations Committee, faced open revolt as a bipartisan group voted to remove his power to name members of subcommittees. Fortunately for the chairman, the mutiny lasted only a few days, probably due to his long tenure in the House. Southerners organized the "Committee of 78," an unofficial group whose purpose was to oppose pro-Truman leaders in both houses. In addition, House Democrats from the eleven former Confederate states and Kentucky built a Dixiecrat-Republican alliance in early 1951, headed by William G. Colmer (MS), that became an imposing political force. Originally formed to oppose civil rights legislation, the group's scope grew to include controlling the fate of all appropriations bills. Each state had a designated member of this secret committee, and most named an alternate as well. A subset of these Democrats formed a "liaison committee" with key Republicans, who supplied a GOP staffer to scrutinize appropriations bills and plan amendments as needed.[7]

The Dixiecrat-GOP alliance grew powerful enough to challenge House Speaker Sam Rayburn. After taking the floor to promote a project for his own district, Rayburn watched in dismay as his colleagues scuttled it. He reportedly cornered Eugene Cox (D-GA) and asked, "Gene, you knew that item was my pet baby. Why did you oppose it?" Cox replied, "Sam, you should have informed our group that you were interested in this item." An incredulous Rayburn asked, "What group?" Cox retorted, "Our special group to consider what items should be defeated." According to an observer, the Speaker was "infuriated to the point that he had to restrain himself to keep from taking a swing at Cox." All the House Democrats knew how important the project was to Rayburn, and the purpose of killing it was to "chastise" him. This defeat of the Texan's bill, along with his ignorance of the coalition's existence, illustrated how far Truman's congressional allies had fallen in political influence.[8]

Dean Acheson resumed his role of political lightning rod at the outset of the Chinese intervention, straining Democratic Party unity—again. Before the Christmas 1950 recess, both the Senate and the House Republican conferences submitted resolutions to Truman demanding that he fire Acheson, claiming the secretary had lost the support of Congress and the public. Undersecretary Webb conceded that legislators were being bombarded by letters from the public demanding Acheson's resignation. As columnist James Reston noted, Acheson's problem was not with Republicans but with *Democrats* who, based on election results, believed he had become a drag on the party and needed to step down. Of the six Democratic senators up for reelection in 1950 who had strongly backed Acheson, only three won: Herbert Lehman of New York, and William Benton and Brien McMahon of Connecticut. Some Republican operatives even suggested easing off the attacks on Acheson and letting the president's party do the job. Webb wisely recommended enlisting moderate Democrats, such as Carl Hayden (AZ), Lister Hill (AL), and Harley Kilgore (WV), to defend Acheson, rather than staunch Trumanites; however, there is no evidence that they stepped forward or that Truman asked them to do so. A handful of House Democrats endorsed Secretary Acheson, with one declaring, "He and his accomplishments will live in history long after the names of his detractors are forgotten." In the Senate, however, "not one Democrat rose . . . to defend Acheson."[9]

Representative Richard Bolling (D-MO) blamed public animosity toward the State Department on a combination of things. In analyzing the Democrats' losses in the recent congressional elections, Bolling claimed that Republicans had intentionally employed the "McCarthy technique of big lies, little lies, [and] half-truths" to confuse the public about the administration's foreign policy aims. Since he believed that voters who understood Truman's policies would support the president, Bolling saw the "get Acheson" movement as an education problem. Moreover, he attributed voter confusion to Democratic legislators, admitting in a letter to the president that it was "an unfortunate fact that a great many politicians do not . . . understand our foreign policy."[10]

This problem festered for the Democrats as the Korean conflict continued. Limited war was a new concept to the American public and to its political leaders. On the heels of the unconditional surrender of America's foes in World War II, how could the administration convince the electorate that total war against North Korea and China was not wise, particularly when the top military commander in the field advocated just that? As a result, most Democrats stood aside and allowed Truman to take the heat as he firmly supported his secretary of state. In his diary the president fumed, "There are liars, trimmers and pussyfooters on both sides of the aisle in the Senate and the House."[11]

Bipartisanship in War Policy

China's entry into the Korean fray redefined the nature of Truman's battle to maintain a bipartisan foreign policy. From this point on, most of the commander in chief's Republican adversaries were not isolationists trying to prevent American entanglement in other nations' business. Rather, much of the opposition disagreed with the president on the locale and degree of U.S. involvement in international situations. Specifically, Truman had to convince them how far the United States should go to contain communism in Asia.

The president believed that a nonpartisan foreign policy was in the national interest. At a staff meeting in November 1950, he called attention to an article in *Pravda* reporting how divided the American peo-

Table 2. White House Appointments with Republican Congressmen and Other Leading Republicans

Year	Number of Meetings
1948	25
1949	28
1950	38

ple were over the Korean War. According to the president, this article indicated that foreign policy opponents were at least partially responsible for China's entry into the war. Yet Truman had inconsistently nurtured bipartisanship earlier in his presidency. A White House report (see table 2) provided a rough but indicative measure.

The second session of the Eightieth Congress in 1948 was one of the most contentious in history. In the 1948 elections the Democrats had regained control of Congress as Truman pulled off his upset victory. They were in no mood for bipartisanship in 1949, and the Democrats loaded up key committees with inordinate majorities. The number of presidential consultations with Republicans increased by only three from 1948 to 1949, indicating that there was no special effort to reach out to them. In 1950 Truman dramatically increased his meetings with Republicans, driven by McCarthyism and Korea, particularly after China entered the conflict.[12]

Changes in GOP leadership and behavior contributed heavily to the inconsistency of bipartisanship through 1950. Taft began to voice his views in foreign affairs as he contemplated a run for the White House in 1952, seeking to fill the Republican void created by Vandenberg's illness and subsequent passing. Unlike his Michigan colleague, Taft believed that pointing out the parties' differences on international issues would help the Republicans politically. The 1950 elections seemed to prove him right, encouraging the conservative senator to aggressively critique administration policy.

A combination of Democratic losses in the 1950 elections and the specter of another world war resulting from the Chinese invasion led Truman to push anew for bipartisan support. The Republican leadership did not make it easy for him. In late November Senators Taft and Wherry called for the president to reexamine his policies in response to the election results. Acheson responded by likening the "re-examinists" to a farmer who pulls up his crops every morning to see how they did overnight. Senator Eugene D. Millikin (R-CO) called the secretary's policies "Achesonian Jackassery." As *Time* bluntly observed, "There was no harmony of suggestions." At a press conference, Senator Connally announced Acheson's forthcoming meetings with congressional foreign affairs committees to discuss the world situation. Initially, Connally responded calmly and positively when reporters asked him about Republican demands for input, saying that the administration was "always prepared to reexamine anything we don't think is right." But when the journalists continued to harp on the subject, the Texan "pounded the table and let fly," barking, "that's all they have been doing—reexamining, complaining and growling." Asserting that the Democrats had consulted the Republicans all along, Connally asked of the GOP, "Do they want to undo all of these things? I don't think they do," even if "some of their big-mouthed advocates do." Weary of the ongoing questions, Connally's final commentary on the idea of bipartisanship was, "To hell with all that."[13]

Nevertheless, Acheson and Truman kept trying to include Republicans in the process. The secretary reported that his meetings with the House Foreign Affairs Committee and Senate Foreign Relations Committee had gone well, and he thought both groups had come away "sobered by the events in Korea" and more fully cognizant of what the nation faced. On December 1 the president had the Joint Chiefs of Staff brief thirty top congressional leaders from both parties. The Republicans asked questions about troop commitments by American allies and poor intelligence regarding Chinese troop strength, but they emerged from the meeting in a spirit of cooperation. Noting that Truman had asked for increased military appropriations, Wherry said, "He's going to get it." Within two hours, lawmakers began drafting the legislation. A couple of days later, the State Department hastily summoned floor leaders from both parties, along with the ranking members of the foreign relations committees from both chambers, to solicit their input on the worsening situation in Korea. Undersecretary Webb bluntly asked the attendees what they thought the administration should do. Representative John Vorys (R-OH) exemplified the lawmakers' mood as they exited the meeting, saying, "I think I had better keep my trap shut." Soon afterward, a group of eight legislators, four from each party, sent Truman a letter commending his decision not to abandon Korea in the face of the Chinese intervention. For now, the idea of a bipartisan foreign policy still showed signs of life.[14]

Interestingly, China's initial rout of UN forces drew peace proposals from both sides of the aisle in the House. Frank W. Boykin (D-AL), a staunch ally of the president, advocated a U.S. withdrawal from Korea to enable an improved defense of its "outer ramparts" of Japan, Formosa, and the Philippines. Boykin reasoned that retreat and retrenchment would be less humiliating than caving in to demands for UN recognition of the communist Chinese regime in exchange for UN control of South Korea. Francis Case (R-SD) submitted a more involved proposal that included abolishing the UN Security Council and setting up an annual system for reviewing the admittance of new member nations. The aim of both measures was to facilitate seating communist China in the UN. Case also wanted to withdraw the American fleet from the Formosa Strait by October 1951, which addressed China's insistence that Korean armistice talks include other regional issues in the Far East. Truman responded politely to both suggestions, then ignored them. In retrospect, a more opportune time to propose an armistice would have been during the lull between China's first two offensives in November 1950. Apparently, no lawmakers made any such suggestions during this interval.[15]

Just as the parties began to inch closer on Korean policy, a careless remark by Truman started a chain of events that threatened to unravel Democrat-GOP cooperation. Responding to reporters' questions during a November 30 press conference about MacArthur's options for dealing with the Chinese intervention, the president said he was considering the use of atomic weapons. When astonished journalists repeated the question, probably to allow the president to qualify his response, he not only confirmed his answer but also made it sound as if MacArthur could use nuclear weapons at will.[16]

The president's loose talk about nuclear weapons created quite a stir among America's key allies. Historian William Stueck notes that "alarm in western Europe and elsewhere reached a new peak" with regard to the Korean situation. Within a few hours of Truman's press conference, French prime minister Rene Pleven and foreign minister Robert Schuman flew to London to discuss restraining the United States. The Dutch government swiftly voiced its concerns to the British. India, a significant international player as leader of the Arab-Asia contingent in the UN, told the British that the immediate need was to prevent expansion of the war in Korea. The Indians also proposed a meeting of the major powers to link resolution of the Korean War with that of the China-Taiwan situation, an idea strongly opposed by the United States. Even Australia, a staunch American ally, asserted that nuclear weapons should be used in Korea "only after fullest consultation." British prime minister Clement Attlee therefore hurried to Washington for a five-day unscheduled meeting with Truman. He wanted assurances that the Americans were not about to start another world war.[17]

Attlee's summit with Truman made many Republicans uneasy. They justifiably feared that the Brit would try to convince Truman to withdraw from Korea and endorse the seating of China in the UN. The day the talks began, Senator Knowland challenged Britain's reliability as an ally. Hinting that future American support for Europe could be at stake, Knowland said the United States hoped to meet future threats with staunch allies "in the common cause of freedom, not just regional freedom, Mr. Prime Minister." Democrats, including Connally, chose not to respond to Knowland, possibly to avoid drawing attention to him. GOP criticism intensified the next day when Taft demanded that the president give the nation "more complete information" about the Korean crisis. The Ohioan complained that the administration was informing congressional Republicans about decisions after the fact, rather than consulting with them beforehand—conveniently ignoring Webb's recent session with legislators. He also proposed that the president make a public report on his talks with Attlee. Senator George Malone (R-NV) was harsher: "I prophesy that we will do exactly what England and France tell us to do, for we still have officials without the backbone to stand up to Europe leaders."[18]

Republican paranoia peaked on the third day of the Attlee-Truman talks. Twenty-four GOP senators submitted a resolution requiring the president to obtain Senate approval before making any "understandings or agreements" with the prime minister. The Republicans intended to stretch the Senate's constitutional power to approve international treaties as far as possible, fearing that the president might agree to withdraw from Korea or restrict American use of nuclear weapons in the conflict. Lame-duck majority leader Lucas and Connally swiftly blocked the resolution from coming to a floor vote, but the Democrats generally continued their "passive spirit" with regard to these opposition outbursts, which included—

again—a demand for Acheson's ouster. Since three of the six Democrats on the Foreign Relations Committee had just been defeated in the 1950 elections, it must have been particularly difficult for them not to lash out at the GOP. Nevertheless, the State Department "appealed in the strongest terms" for Democrats not to counter with attacks on General MacArthur, the darling of the Old Guard Republicans, for his failure to anticipate the Chinese intervention. Acheson showed notable restraint, since the GOP was trying to have him fired. Senator Paul Douglas (IL) demonstrated the Democrats' stance, quipping, "It's about time we stopped fighting one another and started fighting the Chinese Communists."[19]

The Republican uproar forced the administration to take notice. Truman recalled that during dinner with Attlee one evening, he had discussed his problems with opponents in the Senate, "who seemed to be violently determined to disrupt the nation's foreign policy." Acheson displayed his sensitivity to GOP concerns during "one of those close calls that lurk in summit meetings." On the last day of the talks, the president and the prime minister emerged from a private meeting, happily announcing that they had agreed that neither the United States nor the United Kingdom would use nuclear weapons without consulting the other first. A perplexed Acheson reminded Truman that he had repeatedly insisted that no other country or entity could limit his use of atomic weaponry if it were necessary for defense of the United States. Moreover, the resolution of the twenty-four Republican senators had given "fair warning of the temper of Congress," which would never stand for such an agreement. The secretary argued that going public with the proposed measure would provoke a "most vicious offensive" against both Truman and Britain by the Republican opposition. Acheson was persuasive, and the two heads of state agreed to less specific language: Truman said he hoped never to have to use atomic weapons and that he planned to "keep the Prime Minister at all times informed of developments which might bring about a change in the situation."[20]

Acheson's reaction highlighted how sensitive the administration had become to Republican criticism in the wake of China's entry into the war. Most of the twenty-four Republicans who had signed the resolution were anticommunist hawks like Wherry and McCarthy. Curiously, Taft, the Republican most feared by the Truman team, did not sign the resolution. Neither did any of the GOP senators from the Foreign Relations Committee, who were perceived as being the easiest to work with. Thus, even though only the hard-core Republican opposition endorsed the resolution, the administration greatly feared their wrath in the event of a misstep during the Attlee meetings. The Truman administration knew that its gamble to reunify the Korean peninsula had backfired, making it vulnerable to Republican criticism.

The White House therefore responded to GOP cries for inclusion. Several congressional Republicans were invited to a luncheon aboard the presidential yacht during the Attlee-Truman summit, producing a victory of sorts for bipartisanship. The icy atmosphere melted when Senator Wiley of Wisconsin, the ranking Republican on the Foreign Relations Committee, spotted dessert. Wiley, grinning broadly, announced, "Mr. Prime Minister, you are privileged to eat America's choice dessert"—Wisconsin blue cheese. Once the meals and meetings had concluded, the president followed Taft's suggestion and issued a press release summarizing what the two heads of state had discussed. Reaction from the Republican Right was mixed. Wherry complained about the lack of additional allied troop commitments to battle the Chinese. Senator Owen Brewster (ME) stayed on the fence, saying that the agreements "are very good, as far as they go," but cautioning, "the proof of the pudding is in the eating." Acheson followed up the next day by providing a synopsis of the world situation and the Attlee talks to the Senate Foreign Relations Committee. Connally and Wiley issued a joint statement acknowledging the meeting with the secretary and noting that Acheson had "made [it] clear that the United States is definitely and firmly opposed to any appeasement in the Far East."[21]

The same day, White House aide Charles Murphy proposed that Truman begin a series of monthly meetings with legislators from both parties to discuss international issues. Murphy suggested that the floor leaders from both chambers, the chairs and ranking minority members of the committees dealing with defense and foreign affairs, the Speaker of the House, and the vice president be invited to attend. Interestingly, even though Taft was not on any of these committees, Murphy asked the president to give "serious consideration" to including the Ohio senator, who was "seriously concerned about the present situation and would honestly like to try to help." This, combined with Taft's influence in the Senate, convinced Murphy that the Ohioan should sit in on the meetings. It probably took a bit of courage for Murphy to make this suggestion, given the president's weariness of Taft's naysaying.[22]

Truman did not follow up on Murphy's suggestion, but he did resume impromptu sessions with Republicans following the Attlee summit (these meetings had been suspended during the 1950 campaign season). Although the White House did not keep notes on the topics of these meetings, it is reasonable to assume that the chief executive was more likely to consult with Republicans on foreign affairs than on domestic issues. Whatever the topics, Truman was keeping the lines of communication open.[23]

A National Emergency

One of the most crucial issues of the war—and one that demanded bipartisanship—was the president's decision to declare a national emergency. China was not the only threat. The war continued to pressure Americans at home, with the consumer price index rising by 8 percent from June 1950 to March 1951. Liberals began to call for price controls to curb inflation and wartime profiteering. Up until this point, Truman had resisted ordering a full mobilization, for a couple of reasons. Mobilization would require more sacrifice, and Americans would be far less inclined to accept higher taxes and consumer rationing for a limited and unpopular war in Korea than had been the case during World War II. More important, Truman did not want Americans or the international community to believe that a third world war was under way. Nevertheless, by December 1950, the commander in chief decided that mobilization was necessary not only for Korea but also for the Cold War taking place elsewhere around the globe. As historian Paul Pierpaoli notes, the Truman administration hoped the nation would accept rearmament and more stringent government controls in exchange for a healthy economy. The president's immediate challenge was to get Congress on board. On December 11, three days after the end of the Attlee talks, Truman announced that he was convening a meeting of key congressional leaders from both parties to solicit their input on foreign policy. This gathering was not merely a response to Taft's December 5 demand for Republican input; Jack McFall of the State Department had been pushing for such a meeting since late November.[24]

This bipartisan conference marked some notable changes in the president's dealings with the GOP. For the first time in more than three years, Truman included Senator Taft in a consultative meeting at the White House. This was a significant gesture; although Taft was not a member of either the Armed Services or the Foreign Relations Committee, he held the powerful post of chairman of the Republican Policy Committee. Moreover, the president was asking for Republican input *before* making a final policy decision, unlike at the war's outset, when he had simply called congressional leaders to inform them that he had decided to commit armed forces to Korea. This change in approach attracted attention from the national media.[25]

Eighteen congressional leaders, eight of them Republicans, arrived at the White House at 10:00 a.m. on December 13 to share their thoughts on foreign policy. As they filed in, Senator Wherry greeted Acheson by saying, "You are looking square at your opposition." When the secretary reddened and Wherry's GOP colleagues squirmed in their chairs, the Nebraskan quickly added, "I mean your constructive opposition."[26]

Truman began by reading a summary of a CIA report titled "Probable Soviet Moves to Exploit the Present Situation." He then recommended that the legislators read the top-secret report in its entirety and showed surprising deference when he merely said he hoped they would not leak the information it contained, rather than ordering them to keep their mouths shut. The president appeared particularly interested in soliciting Taft's support, which was a tall order. When Truman discussed the possibility of declaring a national emergency, Taft tried, unsuccessfully, to pin him down on the degree of mobilization he envisioned. Their dialogue exemplified a typical struggle between the executive and legislative branches during wartime. The commander in chief requested the power to make the necessary preparations in case the country had to mobilize fully, without actually committing the nation to full mobilization. He wanted flexibility. Taft argued that Truman should explain exactly what he believed the country needed in terms of defense appropriations and tax increases and then periodically come to Congress to get its approval as needed. The president opposed the senator's approach as being too time-consuming.[27]

The meeting, which lasted twice as long as its scheduled duration of one hour, proceeded with Truman going around the table and asking each congressman his views on declaring a national emergency. House minority leader Joe Martin (MA), the first Republican called on, said he was unsure what a declaration of a national emergency involved. Truman responded by handing Martin a list of powers automatically afforded the president during a national emergency. Martin ultimately said he was not against declaring an emergency. Taft was the next Republican to give his views. He began tentatively, saying he spoke only for himself and "with some hesitation." The Ohioan questioned the psychological value of declaring a national emergency, which Truman had touted, and he said he believed the "exact size of the military program ought to be decided." In the end, he was "generally inclined against" declaring a national emergency without knowing the specifics of the military buildup. Senator Wherry spoke next, and like Taft, he preferred that Truman come to Congress with specifics on the resources and authority needed. Again, the president rejected this approach, declaring, "Time is of the essence." Wherry then suggested that Truman should ask for all powers short of declaring a national emergency (whatever that meant). After agreeing with Taft, Senator Millikin said the United States needed to strengthen itself immediately, "pounding the table with his fists" in excitement as several of his colleagues responded, "Aye, aye." Three Republicans, Representative Charles Eaton (NJ), Senator Wiley, and House veteran Dewey Short (MO), endorsed the national emergency declaration outright.[28]

The Democrats lined up behind the commander in chief with varying levels of courage. Vice President Barkley was the first Democrat called on to express his views, and he gave a persuasive explanation of why he had abandoned his initial skepticism. House Speaker Rayburn showed little leadership, declining to comment because he wanted to hear from the committee chairmen first. Senator Tydings, smarting from his recent electoral defeat, said he was speaking only because Truman had asked him to, noting, "I've had my horse shot out from under me." Nevertheless, Tydings gave Truman a ringing endorsement, as did several other Democrats. Connally responded in a surprisingly diplomatic fashion, supporting the declaration of an emergency while agreeing with the Republicans that the public needed to be given details about what such a declaration would mean for the nation. Walter George (GA), completing his thirtieth year in the Senate, emphasized the importance of bipartisan backing and endorsed Taft's call for details on how mobilization would affect taxes.

Lucas made a more pointed appeal for bipartisanship, imploring Taft, Wherry, and Martin not to tell the press they opposed Truman on the issue of declaring a national emergency.[29]

Taft and company heeded Lucas's plea. Before leaving the White House, the Ohio senator drafted a statement for the press and cleared it with Truman before releasing it. It noted Taft's agreement with the administration that a "dangerous emergency" existed, and his endorsement of a rapid military escalation. However, because the Republicans had not been "sufficiently advised as to the legal effect" of a declaration of a national emergency, they could not take a "final position on that question." The president's press release about the meeting accurately reflected the concerns of Taft and his GOP comrades.[30]

Truman's gathering with congressional leaders marked the peak of bipartisan cooperation during the war. The administration's gesture might have seemed like a charade because of widespread reports that the president was planning to declare a national emergency before he met with the congressmen. However, the meeting was valuable because of how Truman conducted it. Instead of simply giving the legislators a sneak preview of an impending press release on war policy, the president took the time to hear the opposition's views and respond to their concerns. He also made a special effort to reach out to Taft—a distasteful chore, since the Ohio senator had been largely responsible for making foreign policy a political issue in the 1950 elections. Truman also deserves credit for his respectful treatment of the GOP legislators even though many of them were trying to force Acheson out. Each side portrayed the meeting in a positive light to the press, emphasizing common ground and qualifying their differences. This was good for the country in a time of crisis.[31]

The commander in chief then went before the American people to declare the Korean situation a national emergency and to explain what he planned to do about it. Truman emphasized that there would be no appeasement of the communists, harking back to the fateful Munich agreement of 1938. Therefore, the nation would implement an accelerated mobilization by adding 1 million people to active military duty and calling up two National Guard divisions. To keep inflation under control, selected wage and price controls would be necessary. The president also discussed tax increases to fund the war effort. To coordinate domestic support for the war, Truman announced the creation of a new agency, the Office of Defense Mobilization. Although he did not say so in his speech, this agency would have more power than its World War I counterpart, the War Industries Board.[32]

Truman's address on the national emergency went over well, with a few exceptions. *Time* criticized the delivery of the speech, saying it had a "thin, overworked and flat quality" and noting that it "had gone through ten draftings and . . . showed it." More commonly, the president earned high marks. Reports from *New York Times* regional correspondents across the country indicated that people accepted the sacrifices Truman had outlined, and some were ready to go even further. A California man wrote, "My partner and I expect to lose our small business as a result of the defense effort. . . . That is not important. Our only concern is the safety of our country, and of free people everywhere."[33]

Critics have pointed out several flaws in Truman's declaration of a national emergency, with varying degrees of accuracy. A valid complaint is that the president again stopped short of full mobilization, electing to implement only selected wage and price controls. If the nation was facing a true emergency, why not impose price controls across the board, which would have put the consuming public at ease? Less convincing is criticism of Truman for making only four nationally broadcast speeches between the start of the war and the announcement of a national emergency. The fact is, when presidents address the nation too often, the speeches lose their dramatic effect. Another dubious critique is that the declaration of a national emergency was merely a psychological ploy to rally the public behind the commander in chief. He had a valid reason for making this speech: the public needed to be reassured that the government was responding decisively to the new war. Because Truman was planning to draft more Americans into the military and demanding more economic sacrifice from the rest, he had to impart a sense of urgency.[34]

The president's address told the nation what lay ahead, using both familiar themes and new ones. As in previous speeches, Truman reminded the nation about the dangers of appeasement and his determination to finance the war on a pay-as-you-go basis. In the most inspiring line of the speech, the president recalled the theme of personal sacrifice: "Each of us should measure his own efforts, his own sacrifices, by the standard of our heroic men in Korea." To underscore the fact that a national emergency existed, Truman emphasized the threat to Americans at home, repeating a dozen times that the United States was in danger. As indicated by the immediate public reaction to the speech, Americans were ready to deal with the Chinese intervention, and they believed that communist expansionism was a real threat.[35]

Bad news from Korea continued. On December 23 General Walker was killed in a jeep accident, prompting MacArthur to replace him with Matthew Ridgway. The new leader of Eighth Army found morale and discipline in a deplorable condition. Ridgway's woes continued when the Chinese launched a major offensive on New Year's Eve, hoping to conquer the entire peninsula. Seoul fell to the communists—again—on January 4, 1951, creating a horrific scene as UN soldiers rebuffed civilian refugees at bayonet point while abandoning the ROK capital. Yet thanks to Ridgway's superb leadership, a couple of weeks later his forces established a stable front across the peninsula near Wonju, about seventy miles south of the thirty-eighth parallel. Meanwhile, the Joint Chiefs of Staff rejected MacArthur's requests for reinforcements. His new objective was simply to hold Korea, if possible, and to inflict as many casualties on the enemy as he could.[36]

Meanwhile, as Mao's forces prepared to cross the thirty-eighth parallel into South Korea, the Truman administration began to push for a UN resolution condemning the Chinese "aggressors." However, the United States' UN allies were less pliable than during the initial decision to intervene in Korea and the subsequent resolution to carry the war into the north. Immediately, the Arab-Asia contingent, Canada, and the United Kingdom stated they would not support the measure until the UN presented a cease-fire proposal to the Chinese (a proposal Mao's regime ultimately refused to entertain). Due to Arab-Asian influence, the British and Canadians then revised the resolution to require the approval of the General Assembly for any additional measures (i.e., sanctions) against China. As a Canadian diplomat warned, "If the West is not careful, China, instead of being regarded as a menace, will be looked on as a rallying point for an independent East." The United States agreed to the changes, and the General Assembly subsequently passed the first resolution in UN history condemning a nation as an aggressor. Although the resolution passed easily, America's allies had successfully delayed and then amended the resolution. However, the challenges posed by multilateralism in the

UN paled in comparison to the trials of maintaining a bipartisan foreign policy at home.[37]

The Great Debate

The bipartisan cooperation exhibited at Truman's December 13 meeting with congressional leaders vanished quickly. Two days later, Republicans in both houses renewed their demands for Acheson's resignation by large majorities. Even GOP senators who normally cooperated with the administration joined in the call for a "thorough housecleaning of the State Department." Congressional Democrats were mute, with the exception of Senator Lucas, who denounced the resolution as an "invitation for Stalin to strike" in the midst of American disunity. The president, as usual, defended Acheson vigorously, opening his December 19 press conference with a statement of support for the secretary. Equating the assault on Acheson with demands for President Lincoln to fire William Seward, Truman asserted that "communism—not our own country—would be served" by sacking the secretary of state. Leaks from executive sessions of the Foreign Relations Committee added fuel to the fire. In one instance, General Omar Bradley testified that the UN should probably abandon Korea; his words appeared in newspapers three hours later. Such breaches created a dilemma for the administration. If the leaks continued, the executive branch would be reluctant to share confidential material or frank assessments with the committee. If Truman's team withheld information, the Republicans would blast the Democrats for failing to consult them.[38]

Meanwhile, Acheson traveled to a meeting of the North Atlantic Treaty Organization (NATO) in Brussels on December 17, setting the stage for even more partisan rancor. At the outset of the Korean War, Truman and other Western leaders believed the Soviet Union had ordered the North Korean attack and feared it might be a prelude to communist aggression elsewhere. Europe looked vulnerable, with only twelve poorly equipped NATO divisions (two of them American) in West Germany to defend against twenty-seven Russian divisions and 60,000 military police in East Germany. When the president announced his plans to dispatch four additional divisions to Europe on September 9, 1950, his political opponents said nothing. However, Acheson's trip to Brussels three months later, the appointment of Dwight Eisenhower as supreme

NATO commander the same week, and Truman's announcement that he planned to deploy American troops to Europe as soon as possible drew renewed attention from the president's political foes. A Republican ex-president proved to be the surprising spark that ignited a new debate over Truman's conduct of foreign policy.[39]

Herbert Hoover's December 20, 1950, speech kicked off the so-called Great Debate over Truman's desire to send troops to Europe. Hoover's address, delivered in New York City and broadcast on national radio, cas-tigated the current administration's foreign policy. The former president argued that deploying U.S. ground troops in both Europe and Asia was expensive and would play to the communists' strength, which in his view was a ground war. The UN's "defeat" in Korea, he contended, illustrated the futility of relying on combat troops to fight wars on communist turf. Hoover argued that Truman's policies would create an unsustainable tax burden on Americans and federal budget deficits leading to "economic disaster." The former president also pointed to the United States' dispro-portionate burden in Korea compared with other UN members. Western Europe, claimed Hoover, should bear the main responsibility for defend-ing itself. The former president recommended a policy in which the United States would control the Atlantic and Pacific via the navy and air force, establishing a "Western Hemisphere Gibraltar of Western Civilization."[40]

Congressional conservatives responded swiftly to Hoover's exhorta-tions. On the day the Eighty-Second Congress convened for the first time, Representative Frederic Coudert (R-NY) bluntly challenged Truman's authority to deploy troops abroad and introduced a joint resolution speci-fying that "no additional forces be sent or maintained outside the United States . . . *without the prior approval of Congress in each instance.*" Five days later, minority leader Wherry introduced a weaker version in the upper house that would prohibit the deployment of ground forces for NATO, "pending the formulation of a policy with respect thereto by the Con-gress." Senator Taft delivered a 10,000-word speech the same week, his longest on foreign policy. Taft echoed some of Hoover's themes, includ-ing the primacy of air and naval forces over ground forces and the need to limit American commitments elsewhere in the world. The GOP leader saw Truman's foreign policy as fostering either constant war or prepara-tion for battle, both of which would lead to "dictatorship and totalitarian government." Taft viewed the increases in military spending as threats to the nation's economic security and the "American values" of a balanced federal budget and a stable dollar. Philosophically, Taft contrasted his conservative approach, designed to "maintain the liberty of our people," with Truman's policy, which meant to "spread sweetness and light and economic prosperity to people who have lived and worked out their own salvation for centuries."[41]

Once the gauntlet had been thrown down by the conservative wing of the Republican Party, the Great Debate on the Wherry resolution began. Arguments continued for some three months in what one historian called the first showdown between the executive and legislative branches over the power to commit American troops abroad. A few prominent Democrat senators, most notably Harry Byrd (VA) and Walter George, expressed some interest in joining the efforts led by Taft and Wherry. Moreover, key internationalist Republicans such as Senators Vandenberg, Lodge, and H. Alexander Smith actually supported Truman's troop deployments to NATO, if not his disinterest in seeking congressional approval. Nevertheless, the Great Debate was largely partisan. Much of the discourse veered back to Far East policy, based on the premise that since Truman had botched Korea, Congress needed to take control of foreign affairs. Lodge called the office of the Senate Foreign Relations Committee to complain that he could not get an answer to a question that "everybody in the country" was asking: "Why do we stay in Korea?" Francis Wilcox, the committee's chief of staff, admitted privately that it was "entirely possible that no policy has yet been worked out." Smith complained that the administration's relationship with Republicans amounted to "complete non-cooperation" on Far East issues. Senator Margaret Chase Smith (R-ME) foolishly insisted that Truman's foreign policy would not be legitimate unless he consulted Republicans such as Joseph McCarthy, even though she had publicly castigated McCarthy's methods only months before. Republican senator William Jenner (IN), who had previously voiced no concern about the lack of a formal declaration of war, suddenly stated that if Congress had a "shred of courage and patriotism left" it should "lay down an ultimatum to the President demanding either a declaration of war or the bringing back of American G.I.s to home shores." When Taft argued that the Soviets would not necessarily attack Europe if the United States did not station forces there, Connally replied that Soviet puppets were presently killing Americans in Korea. "In Texas," he snorted, "we are strongly of the opinion that when a person shoots at you, he is being unfriendly."[42]

Four issues provided the tinder for the Great Debate ignited by Hoover's December 20 speech. One was the current status of the fighting in Korea. With the nation's hopes of having the troops home for Christmas dashed by the Chinese entry into the war, Hoover's address occurred during the depths of American military misery. On the verge of victory only a few weeks before, UN troops had been driven nearly 300 miles south of the thirty-eighth parallel, the nadir of the longest retreat in American military history. Chinese forces had regained control of Seoul. Lawmakers therefore struggled to answer questions from their constituents, such as "Why does my son have to stay in Korea?" And they wondered how sending American military forces into Europe could be justified, given the struggles in Korea. Truman ally Senator Brien McMahon argued that the Korean intervention was "equally applicable in connection with the right of the President to send troops to Europe," and he asked his colleagues, would it be "better to wait until invaders land on Cape Cod before we start defending the United States?" Conversely, Senator Taft argued, "We could not have a better lesson than has been taught us in Korea" to *not* send additional troops to Europe.[43]

Budgetary concerns over Truman's mobilization plans provided a second motivation for the Great Debate. The opening of the debate coincided with initial discussions of the fiscal year 1952 budget. Truman caused considerable ire among conservative Republicans when he asked for a $72 billion budget, despite projected revenue of only $55 billion. Truman declared that the deficit would have to be covered by a tax increase. Moreover, the budget request arrived on the heels of the December 1950 declaration of a national emergency, which included a general mobilization of the economy not only to support the Korean conflict but also to buttress the Cold War in general. Conservative Republicans who had criticized Truman for allowing China to fall to communism now saw no end in sight to Cold War defense spending. Senator John Bricker (R-OH) declared that the "Acheson containment plan involves policing the 20,000 mile Soviet perimeter," which would "bleed us white both physically and financially." Many in the GOP associated the combination of the national emergency mobilization and the proposed deployment of troops to NATO as a threat to a balanced budget, economic prosperity, and civilian control over the military. As Bricker proclaimed, "We can wipe out all traces of communism in the world, but if we lose the Constitution we are doomed to slavery."[44]

Conversely, Truman and his supporters saw mobilization and higher defense spending as vital moves to *ensure* American freedom. Democratic legislators reasoned that the lesson to be learned from Korea was the importance of ground troops, arguing that this proved the fallacy of Hoover's reliance on air and naval forces. The Trumanites were convinced that America's economic future was inextricably tied to that of western Europe. Acheson posited what would happen if western Europe's wealth of technical knowledge and natural resources fell under the control of the Soviet Union. Defending the Europeans via NATO would add "more than 200,000,000 free people" to the fight against communist aggression in the Cold War. Democrats therefore felt there was no choice but to defend Europe. As Senator Hubert H. Humphrey (D-MN) declared, while Congress argued about the legalities of the president sending troops to Europe, Stalin could inflict a "deathblow."[45]

A third issue fueling the Great Debate was the perception that the Europeans were not pulling their weight in the struggle against communist expansion. Truman's opponents wondered why the United States should send troops to support NATO when the Europeans were contributing little to the Korean War. The numbers did not lie: as of January 1953, the United States had 350,000 troops assigned to the UN Command, versus only 44,000 from allies other than South Korea. The Truman administration felt that western Europe was simply not strong enough to defend itself against an openly expansionist Soviet Union; after all, Stalin had just initiated the Korean War (or so they thought). Two key Republicans who were supportive of Truman in the Great Debate, William Knowland and Henry Cabot Lodge Jr., flatly stated that Taft had failed to grasp the reality of European weakness. In the midst of the debate, Acheson testified to Congress that a reluctance to fortify NATO with troops would be a poor signal to send to the communist world. Conservatives saw the situation quite differently. Referring to the recent Chinese intervention in Korea, the *Chicago Tribune* fumed, "At the very moment when the Red onslaught has developed its surprise fury, Britain and France, the slacker empires, prove their utter undependability as allies." Even the State Department privately expressed concerns that "as yet none of our NATO allies is acting with the same sense of urgency as we are in speeding defense programs," opining that the British "could well support a substantially larger defense outlay without danger."[46]

Nevertheless, the biggest factor driving the Great Debate was the power struggle between Congress and the president over the authority to commit American troops overseas. During his first press conference following the introduction of the Wherry resolution, Truman bluntly asserted that "under the President's constitutional powers as Commander in Chief of the Armed Forces, he has the authority to send troops anywhere in the world." When reporters questioned Truman about the nature of his consultations with Congress on overseas troop deployments, he clarified, "I don't ask their permission, I just consult them." An enraged Taft retorted that Congress needed to "reassert its constitutional right to pass upon fundamental principles of foreign policy" in response to this "constitutional crisis."[47]

One historian described the Great Debate as a "dispute over policy masquerading as constitutional conflict." In addition to the fiscal policy dispute described earlier, Truman's opponents saw his plans to deploy American troops to Europe as a deviation from the original intent of the NATO Treaty. In one exchange, Senator Bourke Hickenlooper (R-IA) reminded Acheson of the latter's assurance to Congress in 1949 that the NATO Treaty would *not* entail the deployment of American troops to Europe beyond those already stationed there. The secretary responded that conditions in the world had changed. In fact, the administration had sold the NATO Treaty to the Senate based on the premise of providing arms, not troops, to Europe. This clear change in policy, along with Truman's lack of political finesse, escalated the rancor of this debate.[48]

The Great Debate finally ended in early April 1951. A rally by UN forces in Korea, highlighted by the reoccupation of Seoul in mid-March, helped ease the political tension in Congress. A compromise crafted by Truman's congressional allies and proposed by Senator John McClellan (D-AR) amended the Wherry resolution, approving the four divisions for Europe initially sought by the president but banning the dispatch of additional troops without Senate approval. Over Truman's strenuous objection, the Senate passed this nonbinding resolution by a vote of 69–31. Both parties claimed victory. Despite his irritation at having to share control of military deployments with Congress, Truman got the troops he wanted for Europe. Conservatives convinced themselves that they had reined in Truman's conduct of the Cold War. However, the Great Debate damaged the mutual respect exhibited by the legislative and executive branches for their separate responsibilities for national defense.[49]

The administration nevertheless continued to promote bipartisanship as best it could. The president vigorously rejected GOP calls for Acheson's resignation, calling them "old, in the sense that they are the same false charges." Yet Truman carefully acknowledged that there were "some Republicans who recognize the facts and the true reasons for these attacks on Secretary Acheson, and who do not agree with their colleagues." Dean Rusk, assistant secretary of state for Far Eastern affairs, met with H. Alexander Smith in an unsuccessful attempt to alleviate the moderate Republican's concerns about Far East policy. The White House and the State Department took the time to thank some Republicans simply for commending the president's State of the Union address. In February 1951 Truman asked his staff to prepare a report showing the "extent of bipartisan cooperation and congressional cooperation in foreign policy" for Vice President Barkley to use in an upcoming speech. The president suggested the inclusion of Republican appointments in the State Department and UN delegations, bipartisan agreement regarding the Marshall Plan, and GOP support of the Defense Production Act. Unfortunately, Barkley's speech attracted scant coverage in the national media, and there was no mention of bipartisanship. Aide Ken Hechler ultimately compiled a list of all meetings between the president and Republicans, even though he had little proof of their content. And when a Democratic senator suggested, "Let's have our foreign policy, let them have theirs and may the best man win," Hechler argued that bipartisan foreign policy was "too much of a sacred cow to trample underfoot."[50]

Firing MacArthur

President Truman's dismissal of General Douglas MacArthur just a week after the close of the Great Debate was the most dramatic confrontation between a president and a military commander in the nation's history. This event marked a turning point in the battle over the future viability of a bipartisan foreign policy. Senator Taft had been trying to declare the death of nonpartisanship in foreign affairs for years. In 1948 he proclaimed that Truman's election marked the end of bipartisanship; he asserted again that bipartisanship was dead when Dean Acheson became secretary of state in 1949; then, after the Korean War erupted in 1950, he decreed that a bipartisan foreign policy had been dead for months. Although Taft's pessimistic assessment arguably represented an extremist viewpoint at the time, it became the national consensus by the summer of 1951. The commander in chief's decision to fire a revered military hero, who also happened to be a Republican, delivered the final blow to interparty cooperation in foreign affairs. Responding to the GOP explosion that followed, the administration lashed out at its enemies while trying unsuccessfully to save the Holy Grail of bipartisanship. Yet, although Truman's dismissal of an American icon initially looked like a golden opportunity for the president's McCarthyite tormentors, it ultimately proved to be a relatively brief crisis.[51]

Ironically, Truman had rejected a key *Republican's* advice to remove MacArthur from command at the outset of the war. As it happened, State Department adviser John Foster Dulles had been in the Far East for consultations with the general when the North Koreans invaded the south. Dulles's report to the president painted an unflattering portrait of MacArthur's performance. When news of the attack initially reached the general in Tokyo, he downplayed it, saying the South Koreans could handle it alone. Later that evening, MacArthur's staff refused to wake him to tell him that ROK forces were in full retreat, fearful of disobeying his "strict orders" not to disturb him after office hours. Dulles himself had to wake the general and give him the bad news. The next day, a despondent commander told the diplomat and the rest of the delegation, "All Korea is lost." When Dulles returned to Washington, he recommended that Truman recall MacArthur immediately. But given MacArthur's status in the Republican Party, the president knew that such a move would provoke a massive reaction. Ultimately, Truman could have saved himself some grief by removing MacArthur in July 1950. It would have precipitated a political firestorm (and possibly sacrificed the success at Inchon), but the president could have used Dulles's influence to mitigate the GOP uproar. By 1951, the political climate had worsened, and Dulles could not help the president justify the general's removal, even if he had wanted to do so.[52]

MacArthur's path to dismissal started with his public disagreement with the administration over the role of Formosa in the war. Jiang Jieshi's Nationalist Chinese government occupied the island and had offered more than 30,000 troops to assist UN forces at the outset of the Korean conflict. Truman had given the offer serious consideration but eventually opted against it. Instead, the administration had dispatched the Seventh Fleet to the Formosa Strait to deter clashes between the Nationalists on the island and the communists on mainland China, which he feared would expand the war. A neutral policy regarding Formosa also aimed to counter Soviet charges that the United States was using the Korean crisis to grab nearby territory and intended to occupy the island. General MacArthur disagreed with this policy in a public speech, saying that the administration "do[es] not understand the Orient."[53]

The general ensured his demise in March 1951, even as he took the offensive against Chinese forces. By the middle of the month, UN forces had retaken Seoul and controlled most of South Korea. To take advantage of this military momentum, the United States and its allies planned a diplomatic initiative: they would propose armistice talks before sending the UN army north of the thirty-eighth parallel for a second time. The statement, drafted by the Truman administration, proposed a cease-fire and indicated a willingness to discuss other Far East issues with the combatants once the Korean situation was settled. The Joint Chiefs of Staff provided input and then passed the statement along to General MacArthur. But before the UN could offer this olive branch, the general torched it by issuing his own "proposal" for ending the war. Calling the power of the communist Chinese army "exaggerated," the UN commander threatened to invade mainland China unless the enemy surrendered immediately. A journalist noted that one could "almost hear the swish of the MacArthur sword as it cut through the air."[54]

MacArthur's announcement forced the UN to shelve its peace overture, and according to Truman's memoirs, it was what convinced the president to fire him. The final straw was the general's letter to House minority leader Joe Martin (R-MA), endorsing the use of Nationalist Chinese forces against communist China and criticizing the administration's determination to deploy American military resources for the defense of Europe. The letter, which Martin read aloud on the House floor, stated, "It seems strangely difficult for some to realize that here in Asia is where the Communist conspirators have elected to make their play for global conquest." MacArthur added that it was in Korea that "we fight Europe's war with arms." To Truman, this portion of the letter was the "real clincher," since it undermined his firm commitment to linking the mobilization effort for Korea to the Cold War at large. The president could not have his military commander actively trying to unravel administration policy. At 1:00 a.m. on April 11, at a hastily arranged press conference, Truman recalled the "Caesar of the Pacific."[55]

The commander in chief followed this up with a radio address to the nation at 10:30 p.m. The most important aspect of the speech was that, for the first time since China's intervention, Truman publicly stated his intention to limit the war's scope. Although he had mentioned preventing another world war in his national emergency speech the previous December, he had never explained precisely what he meant. Now, however, the president declared that contrary to MacArthur's desires, the UN forces would not expand the war into China, observing, "It is easier to put out a fire in the beginning when it is small than after it has become a roaring blaze." Concluding his comments, Truman clarified his disagreement with MacArthur, saying the question was "whether the Communist plan of conquest can be stopped without a general war." This speech came at a pivotal moment in the president's quest to sell the war—with its revised objective—to the nation. However, it represented a missed opportunity. Preoccupied with the removal of MacArthur, Truman inadequately prepared the public for his revised war objective. The new policy of limited war, as opposed to driving communist rule from the peninsula, would challenge the nation's enthusiasm for both the war and Truman's mobilization program.[56]

The firing of MacArthur, whom many considered a living legend, produced an unprecedented eruption. "President Truman must be impeached and convicted," proclaimed the front page of the *Chicago Tribune,* which went on to call the president "unfit, morally and mentally, for this high office." Thousands of letters and telegrams swamped the White House, initially running two to one against the president. Joseph McCarthy and his Republican allies vented their outrage. McCarthy called the firing a "Communist victory won with the aid of bourbon and Benedictine," adding that if the Democrats did not remove Truman, they risked labeling themselves the "party of betrayal." The president remained unflappable, writing in his diary, "Quite an explosion. Was expected but I had to act. Telegrams and letters of abuse by the dozen."[57]

The GOP wasted no time putting their deposed general to political use. On the day of the firing, a cadre of key Republicans, including John Foster Dulles of the State Department, held a number of meetings to plan a congressional inquiry into Far East policy. Since MacArthur had "unsurpassed knowledge of the political and military conditions" in the region, they decided to invite him to address a joint session of Congress. Democrats, fearing public backlash if they balked, agreed to both the speech and the hearings. Senator McMahon defended the administration as effectively as anyone. Speaking at a fund-raiser, McMahon called MacArthur a fine soldier but emphasized the ideal of civilian authority over the military. The senator, "disturbed" by the Republicans' reaction, nevertheless welcomed their demands for an investigation into Far East policy, commenting, "Let's find out why the isolationists on the European front want an all-out war in the Far East."[58]

MacArthur's stirring address to Congress made April 19, 1951, a day to remember. Asserting that China's entry into the war required changes in diplomatic policy to enable changes in military strategy, the general lamented, "Such decisions have not been forthcoming." Continuing his lambasting of the Truman administration, he declared, "War's very object is victory, not prolonged indecision," and he railed against those who "would appease Red China." After thirty-seven minutes, during which the audience interrupted to applaud thirty times, the American icon ended with this famous line: "Why, my soldiers asked of me, surrender military advantages to an enemy in the field? I could not answer." Representative Dewey Short (R-MO) declared, "We heard God speak here today, God in the flesh, the voice of God." President Truman was less impressed, privately calling the hoopla "nothing but a damn bunch of bullshit."[59]

In the aftermath of the general's recall, Republicans took their attacks to a new level, not only renewing their calls for Acheson's scalp but also going after Truman like never before. This time, Acheson's crime was creating policies that General MacArthur did not like. McCarthy proclaimed the secretary should resign and go to the Soviet Union, "for which you have been struggling and fighting so long." Some demanded impeachments. Others, such as Representative Frederick R. Coudert Jr. (NY) and Senator Robert C. Hendrickson (NJ), who recognized that Truman had not committed an impeachable offense, proposed constitutional amendments to enable the recall of the president. A radio debate over Acheson's policies between Senator Homer Capehart (R-IN) and

Democrats Hubert Humphrey (MN) and Herbert Lehman (NY) escalated into a "little brawl" at the station. When Democrats called the GOP the "war party" for backing MacArthur's desire to invade China, Republicans came up with a new epithet of their own when Senator Wherry proclaimed, "This is Truman's war."[60]

Not all Republicans subscribed to these assaults. Senator James H. Duff (PA) was one of the few GOP senators calling for national unity in the aftermath of MacArthur's firing, and the Massachusetts duo of Senators Lodge and Saltonstall publicly backed Truman's decision. H. Alexander Smith privately hoped he could get some Democrats to support a centrist policy. Determined to hit Truman's "fear-ridden appeasement mentality hard," Smith wanted to enlist Jiang's help while avoiding a wholesale invasion of China. Smith believed that supporting the Nationalists might encourage the collapse of the communist regime. Interestingly, he mused that, in this scenario, Jiang's forces could "precipitate themselves into a wider sphere of action," requiring the United States to "go ahead and back them up," which sounded a lot like an American invasion of mainland China. Smith exemplified the quandary of the eastern internationalist wing of the GOP, which rejected the general's strategy for winning the war before and after his firing. Thinking ahead to the 1952 presidential race, these moderates feared that if the party backed MacArthur's aggressive strategy, they would push Dwight Eisenhower into the Democratic camp. The partisan atmosphere around MacArthur's firing, however, led them to express such concerns quietly.[61]

To President Truman's dismay, many Democrats jumped on the conservative GOP bandwagon to oust the secretary of state. Representative Omar Burleson (D-TX), correctly believing he had no chance of convincing Truman to fire Acheson, sent a private letter to the secretary asking him to resign, citing a loss of confidence in his leadership. Later, he released the letter to the press. Senator Paul Douglas, a Fair Deal ally of the president, agreed that Acheson should leave, declaring, "In a war you recognize your casualty, take him out of the field and put him in a field hospital." Douglas claimed he had even asked the Republicans to ease up on their sniping to allow the secretary to resign honorably. As Acheson prepared to testify at the "MacArthur hearings," a probe organized to criticize administration policy, a cohort of influential congressional Democrats reportedly visited Truman and asked for the secretary's resignation, including new Senate majority leader Ernest McFarland, Senator Connally, Senate Democratic whip Lyndon Johnson, Senate Campaign Committee chairman Clinton Anderson, House majority leader John McCormack, and Speaker Rayburn. A knowledgeable Senate staffer who observed Acheson's testimony at the hearings noted that several committee members were clearly out to get the secretary, who increasingly looked like an albatross for the Democrats.[62]

A surprise policy reversal by Acheson's own department added to the Democrats' problems. In a May 1951 speech, Dean Rusk, the assistant secretary for Far Eastern affairs, affirmed American support for the Chinese Nationalists, saying the United States would not "acquiesce in the degradation that is being forced upon them" and adding that the Nationalists would "continue to receive important aid and assistance from the United States." Rusk's remarks attracted significant attention—and rightfully so, since Acheson's 1949 white paper on China had concluded that such aid no longer made sense. The State Department swiftly issued a statement insisting that Rusk's remarks did not mean a policy change, further muddying the waters. One Democrat telegrammed Truman that Rusk's speech "seems worse than MacArthur's program" and observed that in the upcoming elections, the State Department's constant "apologizing and backing water" would "get a lot of Democrats beat unnecessarily."[63]

The DNC did not help much, either, to the displeasure of the Truman administration. The day after MacArthur's firing, senators were already asking the White House staff for information they could use to answer questions from constituents and defend Truman against the GOP. Ken Hechler expressed his frustration with Charlie Van Devander, DNC public relations director; the two men had three conversations in one day, encompassing "the exploratory, the explanatory, and the hortatory." Hechler wanted the DNC to help provide ammunition for the Democrats. Van Devander, however, thought the controversy was a "national issue, and should not be made a partisan football"; he believed it would be "dangerous to have the news circulate that the Democratic National Committee is spreading propaganda." The DNC told another Truman aide that it wanted to stay "non-partisan" regarding MacArthur—an amazing statement from a partisan organization. Hechler thought it was amazing, too, telling Van Devander that the Republican National Committee was "shooting information up to the Hill in an endless belt," and he did not think the Democrats should "sit around with our hands tied." Eventually, the DNC relented. Yet, when asked to put together some speeches, Van Devander claimed he was "not too clear" about what they should contain.[64]

The attacks on Acheson took their toll on Truman's allies. In a letter to Truman, Senator William Benton reported that Eleanor Roosevelt was pleading with him to participate in a debate on her television program because "the Republicans are eager to talk and I [Roosevelt] can't find Democratic senators to talk against them." Sam Rayburn, normally a beacon of optimism, lamented to former vice president John Nance Garner, an old friend, that the Democrats were "as low as the bottom of the ocean now and do make many mistakes." John A. Carroll, a former congressman who joined the White House staff in 1951, wrote that the "liberal Democratic forces seem to have lost their fighting spirit."[65]

Meanwhile, the American public continued to struggle with the concept of fighting for something less than the enemy's unconditional surrender. A congressman told a White House aide that China's involvement in Korea was "very hazy in the public mind." People he talked to did not realize that the Chinese soldiers were not volunteers but were fighting on the authority of their government. The presence of such misconceptions as late as July 1951 underscored the administration's challenges when it came to selling the war. Newspapers reported that UN forces were taking nameless hills and then losing them a few days later. Soldiers in Korea wrote home that the "idea of this war as an endless one is almost universally accepted here." Truman's political allies warned him, "The public may not understand the dangers of MacArthur's proposals for an expanded war in China, but . . . they do understand the impact of veal cutlets at $1.50 and 'low cost' house dresses at $11.95." With Americans hearing mostly military news, they were "beginning to confuse military policy with foreign policy." Such confusion was understandable, since the decision to give up on reunifying the peninsula by force divorced the UN's military objective from its political goal of uniting the Koreas.[66]

Republicans planned to make the hearings on Far East issues the sequel to MacArthur's address to Congress in their quest to discredit Truman's policies. The Senate decided on joint hearings of the Armed Services and Foreign Relations Committees, featuring MacArthur as the headliner for a parade of witnesses to include cabinet members and the Joint Chiefs of Staff. The probe, which began in early May and ran through mid-June 1951, produced some surprising political effects.

H. Alexander Smith's correspondence as he prepared for the hearings reveals the GOP's partisanship. In his diary, Smith mused not only about getting MacArthur's views but also about how to "best protect him" and get his colleagues' agreement to do so. Despite his seemingly cordial relationship with Acheson, Smith dedicated most of his preparatory work to drafting questions for the secretary of state. Although the New Jersey Republican held no personal animosity toward Acheson, he clearly hoped to force the secretary from office. Moreover, the senator thought MacArthur's recall had helped persuade GOP isolationists to go along with Smith on U.S. involvement in Europe and the Far East, and he hoped he could make them feel included in foreign affairs. Nevertheless, Smith had some concerns as the hearings began, writing to a friend, "I am trying to find the hemlock to drink before my political demise."[67]

Senator Richard Russell (D-GA), chairman of the Armed Services Committee, successfully jockeyed for leadership of the joint MacArthur hearings. He hoped to get through the proceedings with minimal political damage to his party. In addition, Russell probably saw this as an opportunity to bolster his presidential candidacy in 1952. Democrats and Republicans on the panel immediately clashed over whether to conduct the hearings in closed session. Several GOP members preferred open hearings to maximize the media attention to their attempts to crucify Truman and Acheson. Russell and his Democratic colleagues wanted closed hearings due to concerns over publicizing military secrets and the possibility of creating a media circus. Ultimately, the chairman forged a compromise: the committee barred cameras and reporters from the proceedings, but it released edited transcripts of the testimony to the press on an hourly basis. Despite the portentous connotation of "edited" transcripts, the system worked well. As a typist transcribed each page of testimony, two officials, one from the Defense Department and one from the State Department, looked it over, removed any sensitive material, and then released it to the press "practically automatically." Years later, Senate historian Donald Ritchie reviewed the unedited transcripts and reported that the editors held back only a "very small percentage" of the testimony. This underscores why Russell won so much praise from Republicans and even MacArthur for his conduct of the hearings, in striking contrast to Tydings's performance a year earlier.[68]

The hearings began with the testimony of the GOP's star witness, Douglas MacArthur. Senator McMahon exposed the general's weak spots. For instance, when MacArthur assured the senator that the Soviets would not intervene if the war extended into mainland China, the following dialogue ensued:

> McMAHON: Suppose, General, you are wrong about that? You could be wrong, couldn't you?
> MacARTHUR: Most assuredly.
> McMAHON: You did not believe at one time that the communists of China would come into the conflict in Korea?
> MacARTHUR: I doubted it.
> McMAHON: They did.

After some additional give-and-take, McMahon concluded, "And now, of course, we can all agree that there's a possibility that the Soviets will come in if we adopt the recommendations that you propose to carry out." When the senator pressed MacArthur about how to defend the United States in an all-out war with the Soviet Union, he responded, "That doesn't happen to be my responsibility, Senator. My responsibilities were in the Pacific." That prompted McMahon to whisper to a staffer, "Now I've got him. I've really got him. He is a theatre commander; he doesn't know anything really about what's happening in the rest of the world. The Joint Chiefs of Staff are the only ones who have a knowledge of the whole military responsibility of this government."[69]

Next, the panel quizzed Secretary of Defense George Marshall and members of the Joint Chiefs of Staff, who backed Truman at MacArthur's expense. Marshall contended that MacArthur should have resigned due to his strident differences of opinion with the president. Although the Joint Chiefs backed MacArthur's recommendation of increased aid to Formosa, they disagreed with his ideas to blockade China and bomb Manchuria. General Omar Bradley, chairman of the Joint Chiefs, noted that MacArthur's policies would "increase the risk of global war and that such a risk should not be taken unnecessarily." He continued, "The Joint Chiefs of Staff . . . are in a better position than is any single theatre commander to assess the risk of general war." Most famously, Bradley opined that MacArthur's proposals for dealing with China would involve America "in the wrong war, in the wrong place, at the wrong time, with the wrong enemy."[70]

By the conclusion of Bradley's testimony, Democrats and some Republicans had found common ground on several issues. Truman had the right to remove MacArthur and had twice ordered the general to keep his policy views to himself. They also established that MacArthur had disagreed with the military restrictions imposed on him and had lobbied publicly and privately for months to change the policy. A number of GOP senators now believed that MacArthur had been out of line. Nevertheless, after the hearings, the president largely abandoned the rhetoric of bipartisanship in foreign policy.[71]

Senator Russell, reasoning that the public had already heard the various viewpoints on MacArthur's removal and Far East policy, persuaded an 18–5 majority of the committee not to issue a final report. The chairman believed that such a commentary would be divisive and might negatively affect the peace negotiations that had just gotten under way in Kaesong. Nevertheless, eight Republican committee members decided to issue their own statement after failing to persuade any of the Democrats to join them. The Republican report called Truman's Far East policy a "catastrophic failure," rejected any suggestion that it had been "achieved under bipartisan sponsorship," and denied that "all must share the responsibility for the failure." The Truman-bashing aside, it is noteworthy that these eight Republicans were expected to support Taft as the GOP's 1952 presidential nominee, whereas the other four Republicans on the committee were thought to favor the more moderate Eisenhower.[72]

The MacArthur hearings thus produced a fractured GOP, in contrast to the united Democrats. When Republicans attempted to remove Acheson by cutting off his salary as part of an appropriations bill, the Democrats dug in their heels. John J. Rooney (D-NY) led the charge on the House floor, shouting that the people of his district did not like "slippery, snide, and sharp practices" and accusing the Republicans of using "lynching" tactics against the secretary. The House defeated the measure 171–81, with only two Democrats voting for it—a remarkable turnabout in the party's support for Acheson. The Far East inquiry thus solved a major public relations problem for the administration surprisingly quickly, blunting the assaults on the secretary of state.[73]

Senator Russell, an erstwhile foe of Truman on civil rights issues, boosted the president's credibility with regard to MacArthur's removal. He ran the hearings with a minimum of controversy and banned reporters, microphones, and cameras from the proceedings. By avoiding live television broadcasts that could have been viewed by some 30 million Americans, Russell defused emotions and focused the public on the content of the daily transcripts. Under his leadership, the inquiry eventually exposed MacArthur's insubordination and ignorance of international issues outside the Far East, dousing the political firestorm over the general's removal. The leader of the southern Democrats became, in one historian's words, the "hidden rock against which MacArthur was shattered."[74]

MacArthur, who had considered running for president in 1948 and doubtless had similar ambitions for 1952, saw his political fortunes sink in the aftermath of the hearings. Anticipating the politics of the Far East policy probe, Bill Max, director of circulation for the *Chicago Sun-Times* and a friend of Truman's, wrote of MacArthur, "The stupid G.O.P. is using him as a political football, and it will kick him in the teeth. They will be looking for a way to dump him." Max's prediction came true. By the fall of 1951, the ruckus over the firing of MacArthur, along with his chances to be the GOP's 1952 presidential nominee, had faded away like an "old soldier."[75]

Challenges of Mobilization

In the midst of the twin dramas of the Great Debate and the termination of General MacArthur, the nation geared up for the national emergency declared in December 1950. This mobilization was designed to meet the Truman administration's dual goals of neutralizing China in Korea and preparing for a broader Cold War. However, this military escalation differed from preparations for World War II in several respects. There were no severe labor shortages in the defense industries, as there had been in the early 1940s. Shortfalls of key materials never directly affected the Korean War, nor did American consumers experience the rationing of household goods that became the norm during World War II. Because the administration patterned its mobilization bureaucracy after that used for the world war, it prepared for conditions that, to a large extent, did not occur. In other words, Truman's team geared up to fight a much larger war—"just in case." Although such preparations were prudent, they also generated fear that a combination of economic controls and Cold War defense spending was creating an American garrison state. To combat such concerns, the administration took pains to decentralize decision making within the mobilization agencies, particularly in the implementation of wage and price controls. Truman's team also recruited corporate executives to run the Controlled Materials Plan rather than relying solely on government bureaucrats, as they did in the Office of Defense Mobilization and the Defense Production Administration. In this manner, the administration took a "sometimes perilous middle course between the extremes of totalitarian Communism and dictatorial Fascism."[76]

Overall, the administration was successful in managing the key task of equipping the military. However, a couple of disputes arose during the initial year of the program. NATO commander Dwight Eisenhower pushed hard for more military equipment in Europe in early 1951 and called for an even higher level of war materials production, reflecting the wrangling over manpower issues during the Great Debate. Some have questioned why President Truman did not use Eisenhower, a World War II hero, to promote the mobilization effort. One theory is that Truman did not want to shift the focus from Korea to Europe. However, it is more likely that the president preferred to fight his own battles. Truman's personality would not allow him to admit that he needed one of his generals to promote military escalation. The unwillingness of civilian producers to convert the manufacturing of machine tools to the war effort created problems in the latter half of 1951, and as a result, the nation failed to meet its military production targets. Fortunately, this did not affect the Korean War, but it did slow defense buildups elsewhere. Nevertheless, mobilization transformed military spending in ways that would have been unbelievable only six months before the war started. U.S. military resources grew dramatically between the beginning of 1950 and the conclusion of Truman's presidency in January 1953. Military production of hard goods increased sevenfold, and the size of the armed forces doubled. From June 1950 to January 1953, the size of the army increased from 10 full divisions to 21; the navy increased from 7 carrier groups to 16 and ballooned to a fleet of 400 warships, doubling in size; and the number of wings in the air force mushroomed from 48 to 100. By fiscal year 1953, Truman had increased military spending by a factor of four since 1949. NSC-68 had become a reality.[77]

Mobilization put a significant strain on the relationship between the Truman administration and organized labor, a key stakeholder in the Democratic Party. The trouble began when the president created the Office of Defense Mobilization, an umbrella agency to coordinate economic control activities during the national emergency declared in December 1950. Truman named Charles E. Wilson, the president of General Electric (GE), to run the new agency—a job Wilson accepted only when he was given broad authority to implement full mobilization. From the administration's perspective, Wilson was a good choice, given his corporate background and his experience as the number-two man on the War Production Board during World War II. Politically, the GE mogul happened to be a moderate Republican, making him an asset in Truman's continual quest for bipartisan support. However, Wilson, a "big, bull-necked Irishman from New York's Hell's Kitchen," hated unions. As Truman made other appointments to the new mobilization organizations, the unions perceived that business representatives would dominate the bureaucracy. In response, the AFL, CIO, railroad unions, and machinists' unions swiftly created the United Labor Policy Committee (ULPC) to get the president's attention. The battle lines had been drawn.[78]

Rumblings of labor discontent quickly developed over the credit policies implemented during the national emergency. Reasoning that consumer access to credit needed to be tightened to get inflation under control, the Federal Reserve raised the down payments required for the purchase of homes, automobiles, and appliances, and it shortened the duration of loans for such items. This policy, of course, limited the ability of the working class to purchase these items. When UAW head Walter Reuther asked Federal Reserve chairman William Martin why the Fed had not imposed similar credit restrictions on banks, a "shocked and amused" Martin replied that "bankers simply would not tolerate such control."[79]

A bigger controversy erupted after the Economic Stabilization Agency announced a freeze on all wages and prices (except farm commodities) on January 25, 1951. This hastily arranged policy was designed to be a temporary one, until a more detailed wage and price control scheme could be devised. The Wage Stabilization Board (WSB), composed of three representatives each from government, business, and labor, immediately began working on a formula that would allow wages to increase somewhat, giving workers a cushion against inflation. By a vote of 6–3, the WSB approved a measure in mid-February that would allow unions to negotiate wage increases up to 10 percent above freeze levels. Union representatives on the WSB walked out after voting against the measure, having argued unsuccessfully for raises up to 12 percent, exclusive of fringe benefits and inflation allowances in long-term contracts. In support of the WSB's union members, the ULPC ordered labor representatives in *all* mobilization agencies to walk off their jobs at the end of February. President Truman now had a political problem with organized labor. More important, there was a real possibility that labor strikes would be the next step, crippling the mobilization effort.[80]

Public opinion was divided over the labor dispute. Surprisingly, *Business Week* sympathized with the unions, calling the mobilization program an "uneven stabilization." Predictably, the president of the National Association of Manufacturers called the walkout an "inexcusable filibuster against the national welfare." The White House was divided as well, with its more liberal staffers siding with the unions. Truman was unhappy with both sides and told his cabinet that the situation was a "conspiracy between labor and management to gouge the country without regard to the public interest." Nevertheless, the administration adroitly brought labor back into the fold by mid-April 1951. Despite his disdain for unions, Wilson adopted a more conciliatory approach (for the time being), and the WSB agreed to add cost-of-living increases to the 10 percent wage boost it had approved in February. The administration created a National Advisory Board for Mobilization Policy composed of representatives from business, agriculture, and labor to give unions a voice in policymaking. Finally, the WSB was given the authority to resolve certain types of labor disputes associated with mobilization. Although none of these measures gave unions significantly more power, they were enough to convince labor to participate once again in the defense buildup.[81]

Workers experienced other positive effects early in the mobilization effort. In anticipation of the declaration of a national emergency, several companies resolved strikes with terms favorable to unions. The UAW and John Deere resolved a 107-day strike, and coal mine operators and miners signed their first agreement without confrontation in a number of years. In addition, a major railroad workers' dispute was rectified (albeit temporarily). The government exempted UAW–Big 3 automaker contracts (which had been signed just prior to the declaration of the national emergency) from wage freezes as part of the resolution of the WSB controversy. Despite these material gains for union members, labor never acquired a major political voice in broader issues such as the allocation of resources and manpower.[82]

Mobilization affected the nation's economy in multiple ways. As expected, the economy expanded at an astonishing pace, with an 18 percent growth in gross domestic product for 1950 alone. With this rapid growth came the challenge of inflation, which was a major reason for the implementation of wage and price controls. The president had not forgotten his economic battles in 1946–1948, when inflation had risen to nearly 20 percent. As the nation mobilized following China's entry into the war, inflation rose most steeply between December 1950 and May 1951, hovering around 9 percent in the early months of 1951 before tapering off to about 2 percent by early 1952. Inflation trends proved frustrating to Americans who were subject to wage freezes. Ironically, one analysis indicates that military spending was not the main cause of inflation; instead, the stockpiling of goods by businesses and consumers was the primary culprit. In other words, Americans were creating artificial shortages by needless hoarding.[83]

Despite localized unemployment issues, joblessness did not present a major problem, with unemployment hovering between 3 and 4 percent following the decision to mobilize. Although members of Congress frequently complained that small businesses suffered during the war, they actually enjoyed good profitability, possibly due to the efforts of the Munitions Board and Secretary Marshall (see chapter 2). Income distribution improved, particularly for farmers, who were exempt from the initial price freezes. Historian Eric F. Goldman shares a relevant anecdote about a conversation that took place at a county fair on Long Island during the war. A stockbroker observed, "The people who used to have it [money] don't. The workingman does. . . . One of my best customers is a potato farmer in Hicksville [believe it or not, an actual community on Long Island]; I've sold him $19,000 worth of mutual funds."[84]

Consumers did suffer a few inconveniences due to the mobilization effort. Tungsten was in short supply by the spring of 1951, owing to its use in high-velocity ammunition; nickel, used to manufacture tanks and airplanes, also became scarce. Sales of durable goods began to suffer in

May 1951 as a result of excessive inventories and the credit restrictions imposed by the government. These inventories had been expanded intentionally, anticipating defense orders for household appliances and automotive goods that never materialized. In a trend that started with the mobilization for World War II and continued during the Korean War, industrial jobs declined in the Northeast and Midwest, as manufacturing associated with the defense buildup expanded in the South and West. By the summer of 1951, the military situation in Korea had stabilized, and defense spending became more focused on the Cold War, prompting the Truman administration to slow the mobilization effort accordingly. Based on one measure, the defense expansion program was already successful: the "year of maximum danger from the Soviets," projected to be 1954 in NSC-68, had now been delayed by two to three years.[85]

The nation did not hear much from President Truman during early 1951; therefore, the public saw little leadership of the war effort. In the four months following the declaration of a national emergency, Truman addressed the nation only once. White House staffer George Elsey recalled that his boss "hunkered down and worked harder than ever at his desk." Recognizing that Truman needed a higher profile, Elsey proposed a series of informal visits to military and defense industry establishments. However, the chief executive took only one brief trip, dismissing the tour as "gimmickry." Trying another approach, Elsey suggested that they have a friendly senator publicly ask Truman why the nation was still involved in Korea, allowing him to respond for the benefit of the nation. The president flatly rejected this idea as a publicity stunt.[86]

The gung-ho spirit that greeted the declaration of a national emergency withered by the spring of 1951. A California congressman said a Ford dealer in his district had sold sixty-seven cars per month prior to price controls; now he was selling only two per month. Another legislator blamed beef shortages on price controls. Television manufacturers complained about weak sales. The arrest of a Cadillac dealer for overcharging a customer made national headlines because it was the first time a citizen had been jailed for violating price controls. Preparing for a nuclear holocaust, Californians shopped for bomb shelters outfitted with Geiger counters. Children were not exempt from the national fear of communism. In 1951 communists began to appear as villains in comic books. Bowman Gum Company, which produced baseball cards, published a new series of cards, titled the "Children's Crusade against Communism," depicting various communist leaders as demons. By early March, resistance against the administration's overall defense buildup was beginning to take shape.[87]

To improve the American people's understanding of the purposes of the mobilization program, the Truman administration formed the National Consumer Advisory Committee (NCAC) in the summer of 1951. With representatives from some twenty-six national organizations, such as Parent-Teacher Associations, the YWCA, and labor unions, the NCAC established local committees of volunteers ("the housewives," as the administration referred to them) in ten cities to publicize and educate consumers about price controls. These local committees also had some input into price limits. Despite this effort, Truman never won the public over. Although some people were nervous about the potential for a nuclear showdown, most Americans did not perceive an imminent threat once the Chinese invasion into Korea had been neutralized. A regional war of containment did not inspire the spirit of sacrifice that had dominated America during the early 1940s. As Truman lamented to a friend, each segment of the economy was "interested only in its own selfish interests and is making an effort to grab all the traffic will bear."[88]

Public support for "Truman's War" eroded alongside the discontent over the mobilization program, despite the improved battlefield situation for UN forces. One congressman wrote to the president that his district overwhelmingly wanted out of Korea and out of Europe as well. Polling data throughout the spring of 1951 indicated that Americans were losing their enthusiasm for reuniting the Koreas. One survey indicated that 46 percent of the public was willing to end the war with a division of Korea at the thirty-eighth parallel, versus 36 percent against. Another survey reported that more than half of Americans were unwilling to sacrifice their lives or those of loved ones to prevent a communist takeover of Asia. Surprisingly, 57 percent said they would accept the seating of the communist Chinese government in the UN in exchange for peace in Korea. Peace, it seems, was on the minds of several members of Congress as well.[89]

4

The Forgotten Attempts
to End the Forgotten War

"Korea has become a meat grinder of American manhood," declared a congressman in the spring of 1951. As the war headed into its second year, several legislators began to openly express interest in ending the conflict, which was starting to look like a stalemate. From Congress's perspective, two political issues came into play as some members tried to stop the shooting in Korea. One was power. Due to the constitutional constraints on the legislative branch, a lawmaker had a reasonable chance of affecting foreign policy only by being a political heavyweight on Capitol Hill or by wielding influence on a pertinent committee. The other issue was the red scare. The Korean conflict occurred just as Joseph McCarthy's anti-communism crusade gathered momentum, giving his quest a significant shot in the arm. Political dissent, particularly on the issue of communism, was widely perceived as a dangerous thing. Many viewed President Harry Truman's decision to intervene in Korea as a long-overdue response to the spread of communism. No one in Congress would dare to suggest a peaceful resolution of the war short of unconditional surrender of the enemy, making them vulnerable to the dreaded charge of being soft on communism. Or would they?[1]

This chapter examines how lawmakers tried to end the war during the last two years of the Truman presidency. How did members of Congress respond to peace overtures by the enemy prior to the Kaesong talks? What was the nature of congressional efforts to stop the fighting? Did legislators' proposals influence the administration? Of particular interest is how these lawmakers could openly recommend anything short of total victory during the height of McCarthyism. Several historians argue that the anticommunist vitriol of the day squelched most criticism of the war, yet legislators from both parties felt secure enough to try to push the nation toward peace. The answers reveal proposals ranging from the bizarre to the pragmatic to the idealistic as Capitol Hill, like the White House, struggled to end the war and claim victory without the unconditional surrender of the communists.[2]

Peace Proposals before the Armistice Talks

Although Truman had to shelve the peace initiative torpedoed by MacArthur in March 1951, several members of Congress continued to push for an end to the war. One idea was particularly unusual. In a letter to Truman, Representative Albert Gore Sr. (D-TN) proposed planting radioactive waste between the Koreas, producing an "atomic death belt." After notifying all the belligerents, the United States would deliberately lace a strip of land across the peninsula with nuclear waste; American troops would then recontaminate it periodically until the UN and the communists hammered out an official agreement to end the war. Radio broadcasts would warn intruders that entering the zone "would mean certain death or slow deformity to all foot soldiers." As a member of the Appropriations Committee, which allotted funds to the Atomic Energy Commission, Gore probably had access to research projects on the theoretical uses of nuclear material. His idea was similar to MacArthur's unpublicized plan to cut off the communist Chinese forces from their supply lines by planting radioactive waste along the border between Manchuria and Korea. To supplement his "dehumanized belt," the Tennessee congressman proposed protecting Japan from invasion or submarine attack by making available "such variety of atomic bombs and other weapons as might be necessary."[3]

Gore's plan got some attention when he publicized his letter to the president. The *Los Angeles Times* made the proposal a headline story, while the *New York Times* and *Washington Post* covered it for several days. Brien McMahon, chairman of the Joint Congressional Committee on Atomic Energy and a proponent of nuclear weaponry, downplayed the feasibility of Gore's idea. However, the army was not as pessimistic. One report suggested dispersing one pound of nuclear material per square mile and pointed out that, fortunately, such waste was already available. Acknowledging that no type of warfare was good, the army observed that such a tactic had "humane possibilities greater than those of most other weapons of modern war." Telling the president that Korea called for "something cataclysmic," Gore later asserted that although some called his idea lunacy, "other people think it is crazy to keep swapping American lives for Chinese lives."[4]

The administration disregarded Gore's idea, but soon thereafter it considered reviving a more conventional method for achieving a cease-fire. At an April 24, 1951, meeting, Truman's team agreed to revise the planned armistice initiative scuttled by MacArthur because, as an aide noted, "The old draft is like damp cotton, you can't see through it and you can't make anything of it." Figuring out when to use it was the problem, as the Chinese forces had launched an offensive two days earlier, producing the largest single battle of the war. Making a peace offer in the midst of this attack would be perceived as a sign of weakness. Moreover, sources that became available after the end of the Cold War indicate that the Chinese and North Koreans had previously committed to an offensive that they believed would bring victory. Hopes by American allies that MacArthur's removal would make China more amenable to an armistice turned out to be futile. Throughout late April the Chinese claimed the general's firing meant nothing because U.S. policy in Korea had not changed. Even though the communist offensive subsided at the end of the month, the administration did not issue the revised proposal.[5]

The Senate majority leader initiated a push for peace through an atypical avenue. In mid-May Ernest McFarland talked with Secretary Acheson about a potential feature in *Cosmopolitan* on Cold War tensions. The magazine wanted to publish an article on how to ensure a peaceful world and had asked several senators for their views. McFarland outlined his own six-point plan for the secretary, who had concerns about two of them: "End the arms race by establishing a truce in the rearmament process of the Soviet Union," and leave Germany and Japan permanently disarmed. Acheson grew agitated when McFarland turned down his offer to send someone from the State Department to "assist" the senator with his comments for the article. The secretary worried that such a quote from McFarland could be "quite serious." Acheson therefore had a State Department staffer make up an excuse to visit the senator on other business, who then used the opportunity to water down the statement.[6]

Senator McFarland toed the administration line, but other senators who provided comments for the article did not. Instead of calling for an end to the arms race, the majority leader now suggested an *"armament program . . .* for police purposes only." Rather than disarming Japan and Germany, McFarland proposed peace treaties to "insure the establishments of free governments." Paul Douglas, however, called on UN forces to "complete the liberation of Korea," an idea the administration had abandoned. In an obvious slap at the Soviet Union, Henry Cabot Lodge Jr. suggested changing the UN Charter to enable it to "expel members who want to destroy the organization." Estes Kefauver (D-TN) declared, "To get peace, we shall have to surrender a part of our sovereignty." Criticizing the administration for considering his measure "too drastic a step," Kefauver quipped, "They overlook the fact that war is a drastic problem demanding a drastic solution."[7]

Meanwhile, another peace blueprint surfaced from a most unlikely source. On May 17 Senator Edwin C. Johnson (D-CO) submitted a resolution outlining his plan for an armistice in Korea. Calling the war a "hopeless conflict of attrition and indecisiveness and a breeder of bitter racial hatreds," he proposed a cease-fire effective June 25, the first anniversary of the fighting. UN troops were to relocate south of the thirty-eighth parallel, and the communists would move north of the parallel. Johnson called for all non-Koreans to leave the peninsula and for an exchange of all prisoners by the end of the year. The Coloradan justified his suggestion by arguing that there was "no way to keep the limited war with China from developing into a full-scale war."[8]

Johnson's resolution was a reversal of his views on the conflict. A month earlier he had called MacArthur's firing a "tragic development," presumably because he agreed with the general's desire to expand the war. Four months after submitting his peace proposal, the senator reversed field again. Asking why the United States did not use "these fantastically ferocious lethal weapons," Johnson dismissed the dangers of nuclear war, claiming that the possibility of Soviet retaliation was "too absurd to consider."[9]

Coincidentally, on the same day Johnson presented his proposal, Truman's National Security Council (NSC) issued an internal report recommending a way to move forward in the war. Like Senator Johnson, the NSC suggested a military armistice guaranteeing the autonomy of the South

Korean government to the thirty-eighth parallel. However, the NSC did not provide a year-end deadline for troop withdrawals and asserted that following an armistice, the United States would pursue a "united, independent and democratic Korea" by "political, as distinguished from military means." As is typically the case, the executive branch took a longer view than legislators, who tend to focus on the here and now.[10]

Initially, Senator Johnson's peace initiative made few headlines. The Senate did not debate it at all; it was referred to the Foreign Relations Committee, which tabled it. The major U.S. newspapers barely mentioned the proposal. Most of the political world probably dismissed the resolution as pie-in-the-sky posturing by an isolationist. The editor of the *Denver Post* did not doubt the senator's sincerity but called his idea a "proposal of despair" from "Colorado's senior ostrich."[11]

However, the proposal leaped into prominence two days later. Soviet radio covered the resolution extensively, and *Pravda,* the Soviet Communist Party newspaper, printed it in its entirety, suggesting that some American leaders were "beginning to realize that Wall Street's gamble in Korea is hopeless." The *New York Times* noted this was the first U.S. peace initiative published by the Soviet press in quite a while. Two communist newspapers in Vienna also printed the resolution, one running a headline that proclaimed: "Cease-Fire in Korea, June 25." Marxist dailies in the West, such as the *New York Daily Worker,* also took notice, running the story on the front page for almost a week.[12]

The communist press coverage of the Johnson resolution attracted the attention of the noncommunist world. A news story from London speculated that the senator's proposal had apparently sparked a sudden concession by Andrei Gromyko, the Soviet representative at a meeting of deputy foreign ministers. Despite the State Department's concern that the plan did not provide for supervision of the cease-fire or troop withdrawals, Secretary Acheson mentioned the proposal in a report to the American contingent in the UN. Although the State Department noted no new peace gestures from the communists, it resurrected the possibility of submitting a revised version of Truman's March 1951 peace initiative to the United Nations once the new Chinese offensive ended. Acheson also indicated a willingness to discuss seating communist China in the UN, provided it was not linked with a Korean settlement. Western diplomats in Moscow speculated that Soviet interest in Johnson's resolution could be "significant." Moreover, the proposal reportedly "stirred interest" at the UN. According to India's representative, Sir Benegal N. Rau, the plan motivated him to remind the General Assembly of General Matthew Ridgway's earlier comment that it would be a "tremendous victory" if UN forces controlled the ROK to the thirty-eighth parallel. Warren Austin, U.S. ambassador to the United Nations, prepared an alternative proposal to Johnson's that called for UN troops to stop pursuing the communists upon reaching the thirty-eighth parallel. He reasoned that if the Chinese and North Koreans wanted peace, they would stop shooting as well. Unlike Johnson, Austin suggested that the United States remain in the south long enough to train and arm ROK troops and that it continue air reconnaissance of the north. Journalist Stewart Alsop speculated that once the UN weathered the May 17–22 offensive, the communist reaction to the senator's plan could be a step toward a cease-fire.[13]

Senator Ralph Flanders (R-VT) also aired his views on Johnson's resolution, worrying that the communists might prevail in reunification elections held shortly after the withdrawal of foreign troops. Instead, he said the UN should rebuild North and South Korea before holding elections to improve the odds of keeping Korea in the "anti-communist camp." Others who took notice of the Johnson initiative included activists from the Denver Peace Council. They slipped into the audience at an international affairs forum sponsored by the Democratic Party and asked Averell Harriman about the proposal. Harriman responded that there was "no indication" the communists desired a cease-fire. When the meeting broke up, members of the Peace Council passed out leaflets urging the Democratic National Committee to endorse Johnson's resolution. A few days later, the leadership of the Mine, Mill, and Smelter Workers Union sent a telegram to Senate Foreign Relations Committee chairman Tom Connally, asking for quick action and calling Johnson's plan an "honorable method whereby war in Korea can be halted."[14]

Surprisingly, given the McCarthyesque atmosphere, Senator Johnson refused to shy away from the communist press's embrace of his resolution. Brushing aside criticisms of his proposal as appeasement, he called Russian media coverage a "great opportunity" because it was a sign of Soviet interest. He was one of the few politicians who publicly questioned the wisdom of demanding the absolute capitulation of an enemy that had not been totally routed. The senator blamed slogans such as "unconditional surrender" and "no separate peace" for dividing the Allies after World War II, and he believed the United States should not repeat that error in Korea. In a nationwide broadcast on NBC, Johnson said that no interest group had driven the initiative; he had come up with the idea himself. He contrasted the communist press coverage with that of most U.S. newspapers, accusing the latter of treating his resolution like a "hot potato." Perhaps some of them shared the sentiments of a South Korean diplomat who called Johnson "absurd beyond imagination—like a daydreamer."[15]

Johnson's plan elicited no known response from Senator McCarthy. The MacArthur hearings were under way at the time, prompting the Wisconsin senator to focus his attacks on the secretary of state. "We must impeach Acheson, the heart of the octopus," declared McCarthy, predicting that the secretary would be ousted shortly. Interestingly, he floated his own suggestion for getting the United States out of Korea, proposing that Nationalist Chinese troops be substituted for American forces to "let our Chinese friends fight our Chinese enemies."[16]

Despite the international attention generated by Johnson's resolution, there is no concrete evidence that it helped induce the communists to take up armistice negotiations. Historians who have scoured recently opened Chinese and Russian archives make no mention of the proposal, nor do accounts by major diplomatic players of the time. Although the senator's resolution encouraged India to push for peace in the General Assembly, this was nothing new, for the Indians had actively pursued peace from the outset. Johnson, who publicly thrashed about on the Korean issue, bouncing from one position to another, succeeded mainly in creating media speculation and a headache for the Truman administration, forcing it to clarify U.S. policy for the international community.[17]

The late spring of 1951 also marked the beginning of a game of cat and mouse between American and Soviet diplomats. It all began with a simple gesture of politeness. Soviet UN representative Jacob Malik and his alternate offered their U.S. counterparts a ride into Manhattan after a meeting and engaged them in a freewheeling discourse. According to the Americans, the Russians were "enjoying a frank exchange of views with two antagonists." Significantly, the Soviets suggested that the Korean War could and should be settled via discussions between the United States and the USSR (rather than China). Malik challenged the Americans' insistence that the United States wanted peace, noting "speeches of Senators which advocate dropping atomic bombs on Moscow." Even though the discussion revealed the deep mistrust between the superpowers, the State Department interpreted Malik's openness as an opportunity for further communication and sent Soviet expert George Kennan to talk with the ambassador. Kennan's work would come to fruition several weeks later.[18]

Speculation in the press about a cease-fire quickened in late May and early June. Thomas J. Hamilton of the *New York Times* reported on a Soviet offer to negotiate with the United States based on the prewar division of the Korean peninsula. Hamilton noted that this gesture was consistent with recent communist rhetoric about the Johnson resolution. Although a spokesman for Malik denied the offer, other diplomats confirmed its legitimacy and speculated that Soviet officials had backed away due to China's irritation at the peace feeler. In a radio address sponsored by the UN, Canadian foreign minister Lester Pearson declared that the scope of the war was limited to restoring South Korea and did not require the complete destruction of the enemy. Similarly, UN secretary-general Trygve Lie said a cease-fire based on a boundary near the thirty-eighth parallel would satisfy the resolutions of the summer of 1950, ignoring the October 1950 resolution authorizing UN forces to advance into North Korea to reunify the peninsula. Responding to these and other rumors, the State Department, in Acheson's words, "cast about like a pack of hounds searching for a scent." The hounds, however, had to search quietly. As another State Department official recalled, "McCarthyism was then active and the MacArthur uproar was at the forefront of attention."[19]

Kennan met informally with Malik on May 31 and June 5. Although Kennan was not officially attached to the U.S. government at the time, his status as a Soviet expert coaxed the Russian to open up a bit on the Korean issue. Malik said that although his government wanted peace in Korea "at the earliest possible moment," the USSR should not be directly involved in armistice talks because it was not involved in the fighting. He recommended that the United States approach the North Koreans and the Chinese communists. In his reports to the State Department, Kennan worried that although the USSR did not want war, it had a "mortal apprehension" about the specter of American troops in Manchuria or on the Korea-Soviet border. The Soviet guru warned, "The hour of Soviet action, in the absence of a cessation of hostilities in Korea, may be much closer than we think."[20]

Privately, the administration did not share Kennan's belief that Malik wanted peace. Shortly thereafter, Truman met with Acheson and Secretary of Defense George Marshall on "a *most* important matter." Based on that meeting, the president surmised that the Soviets' weariness of the Korean situation had made them "want to quit." Yet his reaction was, "Well, we'll see." A day after the Kennan-Malik meetings concluded, the State Department vented its frustrations internally in a mock letter to the Russian:

Rumors of Peace in Korea

Somebody has started these peace rumors . . . but who? This time they can't accuse the Western powers of starting them. For—on this issue, peace—we have never dealt in rumors. Our cards are on the table. We have put it on the line every time. We want peace, and, what's more, we're not ashamed of wanting it.

But there are, perhaps, other people who are a little bit ashamed of it.

Ahhh Mr. Malik, dear Mr. Malik, no one could ever accuse you of starting such rumors. You would not be ashamed of it, would you? You'd never beat around the bush, would you? You'd never deal under the table, would you? Of course not. . . .

Then why don't you say it? Straight out! The one word the whole world is waiting for. Speak up like a man. Gain yourself honor. Cover your nation with glory. Speak, Mr. Malik. Speak! . . .

We know who can stop the war. Stalin! . . .

So I'm writing him a letter. . . . My message is simple: . . . Stop the killing![21]

Finally, Malik spoke, making a key diplomatic move that helped trigger the armistice talks. In a radio address broadcast throughout the United States on June 23, the Russian called for a cease-fire and for peace based on the withdrawal of forces from the thirty-eighth parallel. The significance of Malik's remarks, however, lay in what he did not say. He dropped previous demands that all foreign troops leave Korea, that the UN seat communist China, and that Formosa be transferred to Mao. The speech attracted significant media and diplomatic attention in the United States.[22]

The congressional response to Malik's address varied. Senator William Jenner (R-IN) criticized the initiative as reminiscent of the Yalta agreement and Secretary Marshall's failed attempt to reconcile the Chinese civil war a few years earlier. Jenner called the Russian's "mock-peace terms" repulsive because they played on humanity's natural desire to stop the bloodletting. From the other side of the aisle, Senator Walter George (D-GA) complained that the proposal would not reunify the peninsula. Senator Harry P. Cain (R-WA) declared that the UN should reject appeasement and attack the enemy "with everything we've got" until the two sides reached a peace that was satisfactory to the United States. Eugene Millikin, chair of the Senate Republican Conference, said Malik's initiative sounded "completely false to me."[23]

A more prevalent reaction in Congress was guarded optimism, sometimes from surprising sources. GOP senators James Kem (MO) and Bourke Hickenlooper (IA), usually harsh critics of the administration, were willing to give the Soviet peace feeler a chance. Though cautioning against appeasement, Kem said the United States should "examine carefully any approach that has the possibility of leading to an honorable peace." Speculating on whether withdrawal meant "only that they [the Chinese] back away 10 feet from the thirty-eighth parallel," Hickenlooper added that if China did withdraw, "I don't think we should hesitate" to reciprocate. House minority leader Joseph Martin Jr. (MA) said he wanted to hear more about the Soviets' intentions.[24]

Other legislators from both parties responded to Malik's speech cautiously. Representative Mike Mansfield (D-MT) recommended following up on the proposal and stressed the need to ensure South Korea's security and (unrealistically) the withdrawal of communist troops from *all* of Korea. Senator Zales M. Ecton (R-MT), anticipating that Malik would probably not be providing additional details, nevertheless urged the administration to follow up on the Soviet gesture. Chet Holifield (D-CA), a member of the House Foreign Affairs Committee, offered the most prescient advice, suggesting that the United States explore Malik's offer but proceed with caution because the offer did not come from China. Senator Lyndon Johnson (D-TX) expressed the wariness of many of his colleagues, saying his initial reaction was to "beware of any wolves parading in the clothing of peace."[25]

Some of Truman's strongest allies on Capitol Hill were more bullish on Malik's address. Brien McMahon expressed his concern about previous dealings with Malik but added, "This country will never slam the door on any efforts to negotiate an honorable peace." Senator Theodore Green (D-RI) publicly echoed McMahon's cautious optimism, saying that Malik's offer merited "careful consideration" from the UN, despite suspicions that it was "only a political move." Green declared that although the United States should avoid demonstrating "any apparent unwillingness" to end the war, the country should accept "peace based on the removal of the causes which brought about the war." Privately, some of the president's supporters were less inhibited about endorsing the Malik initiative. Tom Connally told Acheson that the United States should carefully scrutinize the proposal and "not turn it down cold." Representative John A. Blatnik (D-MN) urged Truman to accept a cease-fire at the thirty-eighth parallel because there was no hope for an absolute victory. Blatnik feared the conflict could expand into another world war and advised the president not to worry about the "political shysters and demagogues" who were calling him an appeaser. The congressman, a former World War II combat soldier, declared, "War is a form of insanity."[26]

Senator McCarthy thereupon exhibited some political insanity. In mid-June, as rumors of peace talks continued, he launched an attack on George Marshall with a 60,000-word speech calling the former secretary of state's Far East policy a "carefully planned retreat from victory." Marshall, a revered World War II commander and one of the most respected men in Washington, was a questionable target, leading key Republicans to distance themselves from McCarthy. As one historian noted, this was likely an attempt by the senator to recapture the spotlight. Although McCarthy made no immediate public comment on the Malik speech, a few days later he referred to the peace rumors as the "planned betrayal of 1951" and accused the State Department of signing the "death warrant of every American boy who has died in Korea."[27]

The Truman administration responded to Malik's speech guardedly. A State Department press release expressed a willingness to talk peace but also noted, "The tenor of Mr. Malik's speech again raises the question as to whether this is more than propaganda." Admiral Alan G. Kirk, the U.S. ambassador to the Soviet Union, was more optimistic. In a message to Acheson, Kirk called the address a "significant new turn" in the Russians' approach to Korea and recommended following up on "any element

of sincerity" in Malik's communication. Truman apparently delayed
the release of advance press copies of his June 25 speech in Tullahoma,
Tennessee, due to the Soviet offer (presumably, to revise his remarks).
The president's address conveyed wariness, noting that the United States
should "always keep the door open" to peace but insisting that a cease-
fire had to be a "real settlement." A few days later, Truman told an aide
he was "not too optimistic," quipping that Malik's sudden unavailability
to the press might mean that the Soviet was "in the doghouse with the
Kremlin."[28]

The president took action six days after Malik's speech. Secretary
Acheson notified leaders of the congressional foreign affairs committees
that the administration had authorized UN commander General Matthew Ridgway to discuss armistice terms with his communist counterpart. The proposal included a cease-fire around the thirty-eighth parallel
and the establishment of a demilitarized zone. Acheson attempted to
quell concerns, such as those expressed by Representative Charles Eaton
(R-PA), who was convinced that Malik's speech was a trick. The White
House press corps noted that some on Capitol Hill were already grum-
bling that peace under such terms would constitute appeasement.[29]

Senator Flanders seemed to approve of the administration's response,
yet he used the occasion to deliver a strong dose of criticism. A tireless
proponent of peace, Flanders acknowledged Truman's "cautious acceptance" of Malik's proposal. Nevertheless, with the MacArthur hearings
winding down, the senator could not resist pointing out the administration's decision to have military commanders in the field (rather than
representatives of government) negotiate an armistice. Flanders argued
that MacArthur had advocated the same approach and Truman had fired
him; however, the senator failed to acknowledge that the general's statement had been unauthorized and had threatened China with annihila-
tion. Moreover, Flanders took Acheson to task for not admitting sooner
that he had changed his mind about trying to reunify Korea through military conquest. Recalling his unsuccessful attempts to pin Acheson down
on the issue during the MacArthur hearings, the senator likened Acheson
to God's description in the book of Job of people who "darkeneth counsel
by words without knowledge." Despite his vengeful ramblings, Flanders
made a valid point: Malik had seized the initiative in the quest for peace.
The senator noted that had the UN made the first move (perhaps includ-

ing his idea to rebuild the peninsula), it could have "put the Communists on the spot." As recently as two weeks earlier, the administration had been revising drafts of its aborted March peace initiative. The Soviets, however, beat the Americans to the punch.[30]

The communist Chinese responded curiously to Malik's speech. Although they knew about the Soviet peace feelers of the past several weeks, they had no advance notice of Malik's address. Thus, China did not broadcast Malik's offer locally until June 29, the same day Ridgway broadcast the UN's armistice proposal. Interestingly, when the Chinese publicized Malik's initiative, they also included details of Senator Johnson's May 17 resolution. The Johnson proposal differed from the UN's in that he called for the withdrawal of all foreign troops from Korea and a full exchange of prisoners, regardless of whether the POWs wanted to go home. These points of the Johnson resolution foreshadowed China's negotiating position once the talks began.[31]

On July 1 the Chinese agreed to begin armistice negotiations within a couple of weeks, and a few congressional figures expressed hopefulness. Senator Connally said he was happy about the possibility of peace. Senate minority leader Wherry echoed Connally's pleasure, provided the terms included "positively no appeasement." However, most members of Congress who were interviewed on the subject gave either noncommittal or negative comments. House Speaker Rayburn preferred to wait before expressing his views. Taft was suspicious that the communists did not want to begin the cease-fire immediately and complained, "Rather than punishment, it looks like a reward for aggression." Pat McCarran (D-NV) declared he had "no confidence in that Communist group," insisting (erroneously) that the UN would be negotiating with the Soviets rather than the Chinese, making the process more difficult. Senator Karl Mundt (R-SD) hoped the talks would be a "prelude to peace" but prefaced his remarks by warning the public of "possible Trojan horse tactics by the Russian bear."[32]

The start of the peace talks at Kaesong on July 10 figured little in the administration's promotion of the Korean cause. When asked about the negotiations at his press conference, the president declined comment. Truman could have used the occasion to express his hope for a quick and just armistice and to remind the negotiators of the high stakes involved, but he probably anticipated the long road and tough talks ahead and did not want to get the nation's hopes up for a speedy settlement. We now know, thanks to correspondence revealed after the end of the Cold War, that the hard-liners in Congress and the administration were appropriately skeptical about the communists' motives in agreeing to armistice talks in July 1951. Encouraged by Stalin, the Chinese agreed to open negotiations primarily to buy time for their military forces to regroup and dig in on the battlefield. Although some correspondence indicates that China *might* have concluded an armistice had the terms been to its liking, the Chinese agreed to the talks mainly for strategic military reasons. Mao's negotiators embarked on a strategy of prolonging the war until American resources were exhausted. Public statements by the Truman administration and budget debates in Congress influenced Chinese thinking. Peng Dehuai, China's military commander in Korea, took notice when UN ambassador Warren Austin remarked that the United States could not send more troops to Korea due to its commitments in western Europe. However, Peng misinterpreted defense expenditure debates, believing that U.S. military spending had already reached $75 billion to $80 billion per year. (In reality, the Department of Defense had *requested* $60 billion for its fiscal year 1952 budget, *on top of* Korean War costs. Actual total defense outlays were $29 billion in fiscal year 1951 and $52 billion in fiscal year 1952.) Noting Senator Taft's estimate that America's limit was $70 billion to $72 billion per year, Peng concluded that the United States was "on the verge of an economic crisis." For these reasons, Peng telegrammed Mao that dragging out the war would "compel the enemy to yield to peace."[33]

Peace Proposals during the Armistice Talks

Coincidentally, shortly after the armistice talks got under way, a congressional peace initiative months in the making finally came to fruition. It originated from another unlikely source: Senator Brien McMahon. Cochair of the Joint Committee on Atomic Energy, McMahon had previously promoted himself as "Mr. Atom" and had once called Hiroshima "the greatest event in world history since the birth of Jesus Christ." At times, he seemed to believe there was no way to avoid eventual war with the Soviets and expressed no qualms about the prospect of nuclear conflict. Nevertheless, in early 1951 McMahon began crafting a "friendship resolution" directed at the Russian people, seeing it as part of a "great moral crusade for peace akin . . . to the Fourteen Points and the Four Freedoms."[34]

The Connecticut senator's resolution sought to counter a communist "peace offensive" begun before the Korean War broke out. In March 1950 a series of international conferences promoting world peace and a ban on the use of atomic weapons culminated in Stockholm, Sweden. Communists from around the world dominated these meetings, with French communist Frederic Joliot-Curie chairing the permanent committee of the World Peace Congress. In Sweden, Joliot-Curie's group began to circulate a petition demanding a ban on nuclear weapons. By August 1950, more than 273 million people around the globe had signed the petition, some one-eighth of the world's population. Eighty-six percent of the signatures came from the Soviet bloc and China. However, 1.4 million people in the United States also signed the petition, or one out of every 111 Americans—a total much larger than the estimated number of communists in the nation. As one journalist noted, the timing of the American intervention in Korea "caught the United States in about as tight a propaganda trap as any it has fallen into in the post-war years." McMahon crafted his own call for peace to neutralize the "spurious but unprecedentedly successful Stockholm Petition."[35]

The friendship resolution took more than six months to come to fruition. McMahon did his homework, lobbying the Foreign Relations Committee and involving the White House in the preparation. On February 8, 1951, the senator submitted the first version of the resolution from the Senate, endorsed by twenty-two of his colleagues. Among the cosponsors were nine Republicans, including Foreign Relations Committee members Alexander Wiley and H. Alexander Smith, giving the resolution bipartisan clout. The lengthily titled "A Declaration of Friendship from the American People to All the Peoples of the World, Including the Peoples of the Soviet Union" sought to assure the world that the United States was not a warmongering nation. It expressed regret over the "artificial barriers" separating the American people from their Russian counterparts and ended by challenging the Soviet government to share the resolution with its citizens. Commending the bill to the Senate, McMahon noted that the USSR was calling Americans "atomic barbarians" and said it was a "great tragedy that the Communists have stolen the word peace from the free nations of the world."[36]

Representative Abraham Ribicoff—like McMahon, a Connecticut Democrat—sponsored the House version of the bill on the same day. A bipartisan group of eight representatives cosponsored the measure with Ribicoff, and the friendship resolution enjoyed favorable press coverage across the nation. Like McMahon, Ribicoff took the moral high ground, noting, "Spiritual power and not material power—is the key to the world's ills."[37]

The State Department strongly supported the friendship resolution. Responding to a request from the Senate Foreign Relations Committee for an analysis of the bill, Secretary Acheson expressed a "most sympathetic interest" in the proposal. Acheson's department even helped reconcile the House and Senate versions of the bill, consulting with McMahon and Ribicoff for their input. The legislators suggested that the overall critiques of the Soviet government be toned down and recommended the addition of details about past instances when the State Department had kept its people in the dark about UN activities. Acheson agreed to the changes and generated a four-page evaluation of the McMahon-Ribicoff bill for Foreign Relations Committee chairman Tom Connally, which the *New York Times* printed in its entirety. The secretary expressed his pleasure that the resolution clarified that Americans would "not sell [their] souls" to end the war, insisting on a peace based on "moral principles."[38]

Progress on combining the McMahon and Ribicoff resolutions into a joint bill slowed considerably following Acheson's March 20 assessment. The full Senate did not approve its version of the bill until May 4. Things went worse in the lower chamber. The full House did not vote on Ribicoff's resolution until a month later, and only 43 representatives showed up for the vote, passing it 36–7. Many thought it was a mistake not to make a quorum call to get more members on the floor for the vote. Although there was widespread support for the bill in the House, the low turnout sent a negative message to the world, which was detrimental for a measure designed to combat Soviet propaganda. One Democrat attributed the poor turnout to everyone's belief that the resolution would pass easily. Nevertheless, referring to American radio broadcasts beyond the Iron Curtain, he conceded that the vote was "hard to explain on the Voice of America."[39]

The House incorporated a couple of substantial changes into the final joint resolution that Truman signed into law. These amendments tough-ened the bill. One asserted Congress's policy to "exert maximum efforts to obtain agreements to provide the United Nations with armed forces." Another, referring to the "artificial barriers" between the American and Soviet peoples, suggested, "The Soviet government could advance the cause of peace immeasurably by removing those artificial barriers, . . . permitting the free exchange of information." Finally, on July 6, President Truman invited McMahon and Ribicoff to the White House for a signing ceremony to celebrate the peace initiative. Malik was so impressed that he sailed out of New York harbor to begin a two-month vacation.[40]

It is not clear from the historical record why it took Congress and the president more than five months to pass the friendship resolution. One possibility is that they considered it a low priority. Although the bill began its trek from Capitol Hill to the White House in the midst of the Great Debate over U.S. troop deployments to Europe, Congress and the State Department acted promptly on the bill during February and March. A more likely explanation for the delay is MacArthur's torpedoing of the administration's peace efforts in late March. Once the White House shelved its plans to offer armistice talks to the communists, it is likely that Truman's team quietly put the brakes on the McMahon-Ribicoff resolution for a couple of months. As the momentum toward armistice talks reappeared in May, lawmakers and the president were probably encouraged to revive the friendship message to the Soviet people.

The administration swiftly executed the official transmittal of the McMahon-Ribicoff resolution to the USSR government. Truman, however, did not approach this communication haphazardly. Noting speculation in the press that the Democrats might propose an official congressional endorsement of the impending armistice talks for political reasons, the president was not enthusiastic about McMahon's plans to make a speech extolling the administration's peace efforts on the day of the bill signing. "This is a very delicate matter," Truman told his staff, "and if those fellows up on the Hill start making speeches they'll blow the whole thing out of the water." The senator did not deliver his address, probably due to White House concerns. An aide noted, "The President does not feel that this is a time for Congressional action, or a time for Congressional consultation." With the legislators under control, the White House dispatched the McMahon-Ribicoff resolution to the Soviet Union two hours after Truman signed it.[41]

The administration sent the declaration to Soviet president Nikolay Shvernik under a cover letter from President Truman. In the spirit of McMahon's hope that this would be an "extremely effective weapon in the battle for the minds of men," the first and last paragraphs of Truman's letter urged Shvernik to release the resolution to the Soviet public. He pointed out, "We shall never be able to remove suspicion and fear as potential causes of war until communication is permitted to flow, free and open, across international boundaries." However, the president's message did not include something else that McMahon and Ribicoff had suggested: an invitation for Stalin to come to the United States and confer with Truman. The Voice of America broadcast the text of the letter and the accompanying resolution twice an hour for three days. Truman waited to see how the USSR would respond to his dare to communicate a message of peace from the United States to the Soviet people.[42]

The McMahon-Ribicoff resolution attracted significant attention in the United States. After Assistant Secretary of State Dean Rusk's May 1951 speech on China policy, in which he voiced surprisingly staunch support for the Nationalists, he asserted that he was simply expressing American support for the Chinese people as the friendship resolution had for the Russian populace. The *New York Times* endorsed the resolution, and Senator McFarland publicized it as a significant accomplishment of the Eighty-Second Congress. More than anyone else, McMahon worked to keep the initiative in the public eye. In a speech to the International Federation of War Veterans Organizations eleven days after the transmittal of the peace message, he blasted the USSR for failing to release it to the Soviet people. The senator also suggested exchange visits between Russian and American veterans as a pathway to peace. A couple of weeks later, in a speech on the Senate floor, he chastised the USSR's inaction. Mocking President Shvernik's lack of response and figurehead status, McMahon posed a series of sarcastic questions: "Where is the man hiding? . . . Has Mr. Shvernik been liquidated? . . . Has he won . . . a one-way ticket to the salt mines of Siberia?" The senator then added a new challenge, offering to send a congressional delegation to the Soviet Union to deliver its message of goodwill personally. McMahon declared, "The Kremlin crowd has been caught without an answer."[43]

Shvernik broke his silence on August 6, when he released a personal response to Truman's challenge, accompanied by a resolution from the

USSR's Presidium of the Supreme Soviet. Using language similar to that in the McMahon-Ribicoff resolution, Shvernik declared that the Soviet people had "no basis for doubting that the American people also do not want war." He blamed tensions on forces in the United States that were "striving to unleash a new world war" for "their own enrichment." The Presidium's lengthy message was primarily a litany of American diplomatic offenses against the Russians. Nevertheless, it noted, "It goes without saying that one can only welcome the approach of the Congress . . . for the strengthening of friendly relations between the U.S. and the Soviet Union." The substantive response of the letter included a reiteration of Soviet demands for a five-power peace pact to reduce the arms race, a position the United States had consistently opposed because it considered the UN the proper forum for such issues. Shvernik released his response, the McMahon-Ribicoff resolution, and Truman's cover letter to the Soviet press simultaneously. For the first time since World War II, the people of the USSR heard a message from an American president.[44]

Shvernik's response to the friendship resolution did not impress the Truman administration. Although the State Department called the Kremlin's answer a "step forward" and expressed pleasure that the Russians had "finally seen fit" to communicate American goodwill to the Soviet public, Secretary Acheson publicly and bluntly declared his doubt that it signified a change in Soviet policy. Again rejecting the call for a five-power agreement, the State Department called the counterproposal a "propaganda trap." When an aide brought the president a copy of Shvernik's letter, he quickly scanned it and then tossed it back to his underling, snorting, "Bunkum."[45]

Some shared the administration's skepticism. Ribicoff said the Russian response fell "far short" of answering his friendship resolution, while Senator Wherry said it "should not be taken at its face value." His adversary across the aisle agreed, and majority leader McFarland warned the American people not to be "deceived by the current peace drive of the Kremlin." A State Department analysis indicated that the noncommunist western European press gave much more attention to Shvernik's response than to Truman's initial letter, noting that the former was "almost universally regarded . . . with suspicion." The executive council of the American Federation of Labor (AFL) called the five-power proposal a "Trojan horse."[46]

Yet others perceived the Soviet response more optimistically. Edward

Morgan of CBS cautioned against rejecting the proposal out of hand, even though it appeared phony. The *New York Times* agreed that Shvernik's response was a sham, but it lauded the publishing of an American message to the Soviet public. The *Washington Post* reported that the McMahon resolution had "paid off—with a dividend" because it gave the Soviets an opportunity to back up their peace rhetoric with action. Even Senator Harry P. Cain, who had once demanded a declaration of war against China, said the United States should be ready to come "more than half way" with the Soviets. Criticizing Shvernik for waiting a month before following the "usual Communist propaganda line with monotonous regularity," McMahon was nevertheless "delighted." He declared that the friendship resolution was the "biggest hole blasted in the Iron Curtain since it was first established more than thirty years ago."[47]

The administration and key congressional figures butted heads concerning how or even whether Truman should answer Shvernik. The U.S. embassy in Moscow advocated a speedy reply from the president to keep the peace issue alive and the Soviets on the defensive. However, three weeks later, when reporters asked the president about responding to Shvernik, he said there was "no hurry." Although at one point the State Department considered asking the Soviets to broadcast a speech by Truman live (calling it a "gimmick"), it dropped the idea in early October. Despite "working assiduously" on an answer to Shvernik, Acheson's group decided there was nothing meaningful to communicate and concluded it would be better for Truman not to respond at all than to reply "simply for the sake of replying." McMahon and Ribicoff strongly disagreed. McMahon pointed out that Winston Churchill, who was likely to be reelected prime minister, was planning to convene a conference with Truman and Stalin. Arguing that the United States "should not be in a position of following Churchill's lead," the senator advocated a forceful peace initiative by the president. McMahon noted that Soviet progress in producing atomic weaponry was another motivation to stop the war. Stating that he did not believe the American people "could be reconciled to another winter of indecision in Korea," he claimed that political pressure could force the administration to use nuclear weapons. This remark shocked everyone present, including Ribicoff. Nevertheless, the senator reasoned that as long as international tension and defense buildups continued, people would believe that war was inevitable, causing them to lose confidence in the administration's foreign policy. All this, according to McMahon, justified a push to end the war. Ribicoff suggested that Truman respond directly to Stalin. Also discussed was the possibility of Truman giving a major address on peace at an upcoming gathering of the UN General Assembly, but nothing was decided. In the end, Acheson addressed the General Assembly in December, and the dialogue on the friendship resolution withered.[48]

In the midst of all the hoopla over the McMahon-Ribicoff resolution, an innovative formula for peace in Korea emerged. Senator Ralph Flanders, described as a "peppery little man from Vermont," had spent the early months of the war marshaling spiritual resources for the UN cause. Making a speech on the Senate floor titled "Let's Try God," he had exhorted his colleagues to heed the command of Jesus Christ to "love thy neighbor as thyself" by applying it to the Russian people. The senator argued that the United States had to adhere to the moral law of the universe as well as to physical laws to prevail in Korea. Flanders then persuaded twenty-six of his Senate colleagues to join him in submitting a petition urging President Truman to wage a "psychological and spiritual offensive against the Kremlin." The senator later wrote, "Military forces . . . can bring victory only. Only moral forces can bring peace."[49]

Flanders's proposal to end the war went beyond moral exhortations. The Vermonter suggested a demilitarized zone (DMZ) 50 to 100 miles wide along the Yalu River, which formed much of the boundary between North Korea and China (see figure 1 in chapter 1). The UN would permanently supervise the DMZ. Flanders probably got this idea from a plan advocated briefly by the British and discussed at the State Department during the lull between China's initial entry and its second offensive in November 1950. The senator's plan recognized the importance of China's industrial complex along the Yalu and sought to allay communist concerns about the security of the key port cities of Rashin and Vladivostok. He also proposed that the UN negotiate an agreement with the "Korean government" to rebuild North and South Korea within three years.[50]

Flanders fleshed out his plan through the spring of 1952. He specified that Asiatic UN member nations would supervise the DMZ to eliminate suspicions that America and its allies were seeking to cement themselves into the region. Later, the senator stipulated that no capitalistic nations, nor any "white races," could participate in supervising the DMZ, reasoning that such restrictions would refute communist accusations of U.S. imperialism in Korea. Calling the entire peninsula an "abode of unimaginable misery," Flanders justified his plan to rebuild Korea by pointing out that the UN had "practically ruined the people we set out to save." With his DMZ positioned at the Chinese border, the Vermonter was one of few people in the government calling for a "Korean settlement of a Korean war." Flanders therefore proposed UN-supervised elections to unite Korea under one government after the second year of the three-year rebuilding plan. He believed that once the skeptical North Koreans saw the benefits of the reconstruction effort, they would be won over and could be persuaded to participate in reunification elections. The senator then made some startling concessions. Although he doubted that elections would produce a communist regime after two years of UN rebuilding efforts, such a result was not unthinkable. Declaring that South Korea certainly would have gone communist if left to its own devices in early 1951, Flanders suggested that even though reunification elections could result in a Marxist regime, the United States "must run that risk."[51]

The Vermont senator's proposal attracted little media attention at the time and received only lip service from the Truman administration. Flanders obtained an audience with Secretary Acheson and others in the State Department in December 1951, but Acheson's notes on the meeting indicate that he merely thanked the senator for his views and told him the proposal was "interesting." Although the secretary himself had proposed a buffer zone ten miles wide on each side of the Yalu in November 1950, he had apparently discarded the idea. Flanders recalled that, in response to his idea, Truman and Acheson simply replied that the "Russians don't understand anything but military force."[52]

Senator McCarthy apparently ignored the Flanders proposal as well, and he spent the summer and fall of 1951 continuing his war on the State Department. In August, after a well-orchestrated publicity blitz, he named twenty-six State Department officials who allegedly had communist ties. McCarthy also made a vociferous attempt to block Truman's nomination of Philip C. Jessup as a delegate to the UN General Assembly. Jessup had attracted McCarthy's ire as a contributor to Acheson's Far East policies. Because of the controversy, the Senate never voted on Jessup's nomination.[53]

Flanders finally attracted public attention in the run-up to the 1952 presidential election. Pitching his plan in Ottawa, Canada, to the Commonwealth Parliamentary Association, he suggested that since China had entered the war to protect its interests in Manchuria, his buffer-zone idea would work. Flanders blasted the effects of the UN armistice objectives on the North Korean people, declaring, "To destroy them endlessly without giving them acceptable peace terms is to plumb the depths of human iniquity." Pointing out that America's war costs amounted to $6 billion annually, Flanders argued that he would prefer to spend the money on construction rather than destruction. At least one portion of his speech proved prophetic. The senator asserted that the ongoing negotiations would not guarantee peace. Instead, he predicted, "Two hostile armed forces will continue to face each other for an indefinite period."[54]

Senator Flanders was the only member of Congress to put forth a peace plan for Korea after the armistice talks began. It had some strong points. The senator's proposal attempted to mitigate the war's effects on the Korean people and the UN threat to Manchuria in the eyes of the Chinese. Applying the logic of the Marshall Plan, he was banking on a similarly successful program in Korea. His willingness to accept a communist regime after reunification elections indicates that Flanders recognized the fallacy of the domino theory. All of East Asia would not inevitably fall into the Soviet sphere if Korea became communist. Yet in other respects, the senator's plan was unrealistic. As one historian pointed out, his scheme did not address the issue of POW repatriation (see chapter 5), which became the main roadblock to peace. Moreover, China perceived the United Nations as its enemy and never would have trusted it to maintain a DMZ on the Korea-China border. The UN, after all, had declared China the aggressor in the war after the bombing of bridges over the Yalu. Flanders also underestimated the determination of both Syngman Rhee and Kim Il Sung, presidents of South and North Korea, respectively, to unite the peninsula under their individual rule. A reconstructed Korea would not have softened either man's desire to govern the peninsula. Finally, by mid-1951, Chinese communists had decided to consider an armistice only at the thirty-eighth parallel. They stubbornly and successfully rejected an initial attempt by the UN to divide the peninsula *slightly* north of that parallel. Acheson later faulted himself for not seeing that his adversaries would have considered a division anywhere else as a loss of face. Unlike Flanders, the communists were not willing to risk losing Korea to the other side in reunification elections, giving the senator's plan little hope for success.[55]

A common element of these congressional attempts to end the Korean War is that individual lawmakers, rather than groups, pushed the proposals. None of these peace initiatives received any meaningful endorsement from influential panels such as the Senate Foreign Relations Committee or the House Committee on Foreign Affairs. In Congress, power comes from coalitions that can force the president to pay attention to them, and no such groups motivated the Truman administration to give these ideas more than token consideration. The most useful idea came from Senator Flanders. Although his proposal had its flaws, it could have provided a starting point for the armistice talks. However, Flanders did not serve on any foreign policy committees; nor did he have enough clout to alter administration policy in any meaningful way, particularly since he was a Republican. Edwin Johnson was a Democrat, but he too lacked influence in foreign affairs and was not a favorite of the president. The McMahon-Ribicoff measure had potential. Even though the resolution originated from only two members of Congress, it eventually earned the endorsement of both houses. Here, Truman can be faulted for failing to push the measure at the UN. Had the proposal originated from a powerful committee or bloc, the president might have been compelled to follow through more forcefully.

Another lesson of Korea is that foreign adversaries pay attention to the utterances of individual lawmakers, sometimes with negative consequences for the executive branch. Johnson's peace initiative, though well intentioned, clearly provided ammunition for communist propaganda, forcing the State Department to counter his remarks. The Russians had legitimate reasons to doubt the sincerity of American peace feelers issued while U.S. senators were openly proposing the massive bombing of the Soviet Union.

Most important, the array of congressional proposals for peace in Korea raises the question of the power of McCarthyism. Biographers of the Wisconsin senator, writing over several decades, have debated a number of issues: the validity of his charges, whether he was a populist or an elitist, and whether he was a true believer or a cynical political opportunist. However, the muscle McCarthy wielded is nearly unquestioned, for several reasons. Less than a month into the war, the FBI arrested Julius Rosenberg for sharing atomic secrets with the Soviets. Shortly thereafter, Congress ran roughshod over Truman to pass the McCarran Act. Many attributed Democratic losses in the 1950 elections to McCarthy. By 1951, his continued attacks on the State Department were apparently producing a "new reticence in the reporting from the field of Foreign Service officers, particularly those in the Far East." A courageous attempt by Democrat William Benton to expel his Wisconsin colleague from the Senate never got off the ground. As a result, one historian declared, "McCarthy, and no one else in Congress, ruled America's front pages for almost five years." Comparing McCarthy's rise in the Senate to Lyndon Johnson's, another noted, "McCarthy and Johnson made themselves their [Senate members'] equals—and in McCarthy's case, their fear." At McCarthy's peak, one biographer opined, nearly everyone in the Senate was "scared stiff of him."[56]

Despite the terror McCarthy allegedly struck into the hearts of his colleagues, they were not deterred from proposing peace negotiations with the communists. It is possible that conservatives' flip-flopping on Korea emboldened peace initiatives from both parties. After initially backing Truman's intervention as an overdue stand against communism, many conservatives reversed field when the war ground to a stalemate and American casualties mounted. By the spring of 1951, many hard-line anticommunists were criticizing the war. Days before Johnson announced his resolution, McCarthy himself advocated replacing American troops with Chinese Nationalists, writing off Korea as a betrayal by the Truman administration. Thus, it is possible that the lawmakers who were pushing for peace believed that McCarthy would not criticize their proposals to end the war.

A better explanation lies in an analysis of McCarthy's targets during the war. At the outset, he doggedly attacked the State Department, criticizing Dean Acheson for encouraging the North Korean invasion. After briefly calling for Truman's impeachment after General MacArthur's removal, the senator resumed his assault on Acheson, hoping to use the subsequent hearings to discredit him. When that failed, McCarthy went after George Marshall, Acheson's predecessor, and made headlines later in 1951 with his attempt to block the Jessup nomination (another State Department issue). Although the Wisconsin senator occasionally threatened Democrats who might stand in his way, his congressional adversaries were clearly not his prime targets. McCarthy was after the Department of State. Thus, it is not surprising that no evidence has emerged indicating that the lawmakers who pushed for peace were concerned that their proposals would draw McCarthy's ire. In the 1952 elections, all these legislators who were up for reelection won their races. Although McCarthy affected the Truman State Department, has his power over Congress been overrated? The story of congressional initiatives to end the Korean War answers that question affirmatively.

Senator Millard Tydings (D-MD). Tydings's poor handling of the McCarthy hearings divided and weakened the Democrats prior to the beginning of the war. (U.S. Senate Historical Office)

Senator Joseph McCarthy (R-WI). McCarthy was a constant concern for the Truman administration, particularly due to his attacks on the State Department. (Courtesy of Harry S. Truman Library)

First U.S. troops to Korea, July 1, 1950. (U.S. Army; courtesy of Harry S. Truman Library)

Truman and Secretary of State Dean Acheson. They were loyal to each other through thick and thin. (National Park Service, Abbie Rowe; courtesy of Harry S. Truman Library)

Truman and Senate majority leader Scott Lucas, June 19, 1950. Lucas did not push Truman to ask for congressional approval to go to war in Korea, and he lost his Senate seat in the 1950 elections. (Courtesy of Harry S. Truman Library)

Truman and the Big 4 congressional leaders, circa 1951. From left to right: House Speaker Sam Rayburn, Truman, Senate majority leader Ernest McFarland, House majority leader John McCormack, Vice President Alben Barkley. (Courtesy of Harry S. Truman Library)

Charles E. Wilson at his swearing in as director of the Office of Defense Management. Wilson would resign as head of the war mobilization bureaucracy in protest over the steel workers' wage dispute in 1952. From left to right: Wilson, Truman, Chief Justice Fred Vinson. (National Park Service, Abbie Rowe; courtesy of Harry S. Truman Library)

Senator Robert A. Taft (R-OH), leader of the GOP conservatives. (U.S. Senate Historical Office)

Chinese communist POWs, October 30, 1950. (U.S. Army; courtesy of Harry S. Truman Library)

Senator Edwin Johnson (D-CO). Johnson submitted a peace proposal that attracted some attention from the communist powers in 1951. (U.S. Senate Historical Office)

Senator Brien McMahon (D-CT). He led the peace initiative that the Soviet government eventually shared with its citizens in 1951. (U.S. Senate Historical Office)

Senator Ralph Flanders (R-VT). He proposed rebuilding the Koreas prior to reunification elections as a pathway to peace. (U.S. Senate Historical Office)

5

The Third War,
July 1951–December 1952

Stalemate marked the third and final phase of the Korean War during the Truman presidency. Both sides recognized that they could not conquer the entire peninsula without expanding the conflict beyond Korea, risking another world war. As a result, Korea became a war of attrition rather than strategy. The adversaries sought nothing more than to inflict as many casualties as possible on the opponent to create an advantage at the negotiating table. Against the backdrop of stalemate, the administration fought several difficult political battles. Particularly challenging was Truman's effort to extend his mobilization program, which he considered vital for the nation's long-term security. The president's determination on this issue led him to take the unprecedented step of nationalizing the steel industry, precipitating a constitutional battle. In an effort to reassemble a bipartisan foreign policy, Truman intensified his efforts to discredit the Republicans' China Bloc, a faction that he believed was the main obstacle to achieving his ideal. This period also encompassed the presidential election season, and Truman keenly desired to take the lead in choosing his successor as the Democratic Party's standard-bearer. To do so, he had to keep his party together. However, charges of corruption within the administration made the task of unifying the Democrats more challenging. This chapter explains how the stubborn stalemate in Korea, Harry Truman's inability to effectively counterpunch GOP criticism of his Far East policies, and the scandals rocking the last two years of his presidency set the stage for an uphill battle for the Democrats in 1952.

Stalemate in Korea

The armistice talks got off to a rocky start in Kaesong, North Korea, on July 10, 1951. The negotiators, led by Admiral C. Turner Joy representing the United Nations, General Nam Il of North Korea, and General Hsieh Fang of China, quickly clashed on issues ranging from the presence of the press to whether the thirty-eighth parallel would be a part of the discussions. The latter dispute proved exasperating for the United States, as the communists changed their minds twice before finally insisting on the thirty-eighth parallel as the line of demarcation, a location that UN commander Matthew Ridgway called "neither defensible nor strategically important." Similar quarrels continued for weeks, preventing any progress toward ending the war. As a result, Korea disappeared from the front pages of American newspapers, displaced by Senator Joseph McCarthy's latest accusations of communism in the government and by corruption scandals in the Truman administration. The Chinese and the Americans took turns accusing each other of violating the neutral perimeter around Kaesong until the former suspended negotiations on August 24, after blaming the United Nations for nearby bombings. Ridgway later wrote that the talks demanded "patience that even Job would have found all but unendurable."[1]

A ray of hope emerged in the fall of 1951. The armistice talks resumed at a new location, Panmunjom, on October 25 after the communists dropped (for the second time) their demand that the thirty-eighth parallel be the final dividing line between the Koreas. The UN thereupon accepted the current "line" of military contact as a demilitarized zone, and the parties agreed that it would remain as such for thirty days while negotiations continued. This agreement, made on November 27, produced a de facto cease-fire until the last week of December. Optimism dominated press coverage of the negotiations. The United Press (UP) reported that directives "possibly from the White House itself . . . brought the Korean ground fighting to a complete if temporary halt." Moreover, the UP proclaimed, "The communist infantry came out in the open, played ball games, and after dark lit glaring camp fires in full view of U.N. troops who held their fire."[2]

Thirty days later, optimism evaporated when the negotiators ended the cease-fire after making no meaningful progress. The Chinese and

North Koreans opposed capping the number of military personnel on the peninsula and adamantly asserted their right to build new airfields, conditions the UN refused to accept. More important, as Ridgway had feared, the communists used the cease-fire to bolster their defenses, including construction of a fourteen-mile trench network. With trenches deeper than those of World War I, the communists now had better protection for their troops. The ground war resumed in late December and, in a scenario similar to that of the Great War, bogged down into a stalemate for the remainder of the conflict. Making matters worse for the UN, China became a major airpower by the end of November, boasting some 1,400 planes. About half the Chinese air force consisted of Soviet MiG-15s, which could outrun and outclimb the American F-86s, the top U.S. aircraft in Korea at the time.[3]

On January 1, 1952, the Truman administration declared its opposition to the forcible repatriation of prisoners of war. The military did not like the president's position, believing that ending the war and bringing American POWs home should take precedence over protecting North Korean and Chinese prisoners. Even Secretary of State Acheson opposed the idea initially. Nevertheless, the president stuck to his guns for moral reasons, remembering the execution and imprisonment of Soviet POWs forced to return home from Nazi concentration camps after World War II. Truman also knew that many of those held in UN prison camps in Korea were former Chinese Nationalists or South Koreans pressed into service by the communists. The POW repatriation issue ultimately became the major stumbling block for the negotiators at Panmunjom, with the communists insisting that all prisoners be returned to their home countries. Digging in his heels, Truman declared, "We will not buy an armistice by turning over human beings for slaughter or slavery."[4]

The Korean situation brought nothing but bad news as the war continued in 1952. Operation Strangle, a UN bombing mission designed to cut the enemy's supply lines in the north, lost more than 600 aircraft between the summer of 1951 and January 1952 due to improvements in the communists' antiaircraft weaponry. In February the Soviet Union alleged that the United States was introducing smallpox, typhus, and lepers into North Korea as a means of biological warfare. The following month China condemned the UN for using rats, shellfish, and even chicken feathers to infect its troops. Problems in UN-run POW camps exploded. A riot on the island of Koje-do resulted in 77 POWs killed and 140 wounded. At another camp, POWs grabbed Brigadier General Francis T. Dodd as he spoke to them through a gate and held him hostage until their demands were met. (Both Dodd and Brigadier General Charles F. Colson, who agreed to the prisoners' demands, were demoted to colonel due to this incident.) During the six months preceding April 1952, communist troop strength grew from 502,000 to 866,000, versus only a slight increase in UN ground forces. By the spring of 1952, one out of every nine South Korean men, women, and children had perished as a result of the war. As General Ridgway departed for his new assignment as NATO commander in May, he told the Joint Chiefs of Staff that a UN offensive would be fruitless owing to the lack of resources. Peace talks remained stuck over one issue—POW repatriation. On October 8, 1952, the UN declared there would be no more negotiating until further notice.[5]

The Nation at Home

The beginning of the armistice talks in the summer of 1951 coincided with the debate at home over the renewal of the Defense Production Act (DPA). Central to this dispute was whether to extend the wage and price controls implemented after China's entry into the war. These controls would expire unless the DPA was renewed by June 30, 1951. Inflation was a key issue. Although inflation had leveled off at around 9 percent, the Truman administration feared it would resume its upward climb if Congress eliminated the controls. About $2 billion a month of the civilian economy was going for defense production at the time, and the government planned to order $58 billion of military equipment in the next year, most of it for defense buildups unrelated to Korea. Although both sides in the debate agreed that these necessary defense expenditures could fuel inflation, they had utterly different ideas about how to prevent price escalations. Truman's plan was to extend the DPA for two years and *increase* the scope of his authority to control the economy. Specifically, the chief executive wanted more power to control rents, bank lending practices, agricultural commodity prices, and credit limits for housing sales. In addition, he asked Congress to authorize the government to procure and operate manufacturing plants. Labor unions, consumer groups, academic and religious leaders, and the Americans for Democratic Action backed the president's approach. Business groups, realtors, lending institutions, and agricultural organizations such as the American Farm Bureau Federation rallied against Truman's proposal, enlisting support from their Republican and southern Democratic allies in Congress. These groups believed the best way to control inflation was to eliminate wage and price controls, continue credit restrictions, cut nondefense spending, and increase excise and income taxes (but not corporate taxes).[6]

Thus, in a sense, the debate over renewal of the DPA boiled down to philosophical differences over the fairest way to share the burden of continued mobilization. Truman's team felt very strongly about extending and expanding the DPA, and they launched a public relations blitz featuring members of the administration on radio and television programs such as *Meet the Press* and in announcements via the Ad Council. The U.S. Chamber of Commerce declared there was no need for wages to keep up with price increases. William H. Ruffin, head of the National Association of Manufacturers (NAM), said Truman's proposal would give the president of the United States "powers comparable to those exercised by foreign dictators." Truman lashed back, claiming that NAM was "giving us the same old song and dance: take off price controls and everything will be just dandy."[7]

Despite its considerable efforts, the Truman administration got little of what it wanted. Congress extended the DPA, but for only one year (rather than the two years Truman had requested). Moreover, the extension *decreased* the president's power to control wages, prices, and credit conditions. Ironically, the chief executive and Congress had reversed their positions from a year earlier, when conservatives had been screaming for mobilization and controls due to the outbreak of the Korean War, and Truman had been reluctant to use the economic powers granted to him. Despite the administration's significant campaign to obtain public support for expanded controls, it failed because most members of Congress could not see the need. Peace talks started in July 1951, leading to optimism that the war would end soon. With inflation leveling off and the nation enjoying low unemployment, Truman was unable to sell the idea of broadening the largely unpopular economic controls. A disappointed president called the bill extending the DPA "the worst I ever had to sign."[8]

Congress also rebuffed Truman's tax plan to fund his ongoing mobilization program, concluding a long budget fight initiated during the Great Debate. In February 1951 the White House had proposed boosting the fiscal year 1952 budget to $72 billion, even though it projected only $55 billion in revenue. Thus, to fund the desired defense increases for Korea and the Cold War without cutting existing domestic programs, the administration needed $17 billion in new revenue. Standing firm on his pay-as-you-go philosophy, Truman pursued what would have been the largest tax increase in U.S. history, asking Congress for an initial $10 billion tax bill. Truman proposed raising the additional revenue from a combination of (1) closing tax loopholes and increasing personal income taxes ($3.6 billion), (2) raising corporate income taxes ($3 billion), and (3) imposing excise taxes on a variety of consumer goods ($3 billion). Lawmakers on both sides of the aisle embraced the president's pay-as-you-go principle, but they agreed on little else and wrangled over the bill for eight months. Republicans and conservative Democrats believed there was rampant waste in the government's budget, primarily in foreign aid programs, and they argued that defense spending could rise with little or no tax increase. Conservatives such as House minority leader Joseph Martin (R-MA) railed against "sadistic taxation" of the wealthiest Americans, while Senator James Kem (R-MO) reminded his colleagues of what Lenin had said: "We must cause the Americans to spend themselves to destruction." Such comments reflected the belief that increased tax burdens would crush the free-enterprise system, leading to a communist takeover of the nation. Liberal Democrats, conversely, believed the tax boost was necessary to protect the nation from communist encroachment. Pointing to booming corporate profits and soaring business investment in the midst of higher wartime government spending, legislators such as Senator Herbert Lehman (D-NJ) dismissed the conservatives' arguments, noting, "Free enterprise has died a thousand deaths here in the Halls of Congress."[9]

Even though the Democrats controlled both houses of Congress, lawmakers gave Truman only $5.7 billion of the $10 billion he wanted, thanks to a coalition of Republicans and conservative southern Democrats. The Revenue Act of 1951, which passed in October, increased excise taxes on alcohol, tobacco, gasoline, and automobiles through March 1954 and upped corporate income tax rates to a new high of 30 percent. The measure also raised personal income taxes across the board, with Americans in the lowest tax brackets seeing an increase of slightly more than 2 percent; this brought the marginal rate to 22.2 percent, close to World War II levels. After reluctantly signing the bill, Truman criticized loopholes for family partnerships and capital gains taxes, calling these provisions "additional means by which wealthy individuals can escape paying their proper share in the national tax load." The president also hated the fact that the bill forced him into deficit spending to maintain the defense expenditures he believed were crucial to national security.[10]

Congress and the president also slugged it out over another issue related to mobilization: universal military training (UMT). In early 1951 Truman revived an idea he had pitched earlier in the Cold War to supplement the armed forces. UMT would require young American men to receive annual military training, providing a pool of potential soldiers waiting in the wings in the event of war. The UMT battle in Congress lasted a year. In its final form, the UMT program would train 800,000 men for six months each year. The trainees would remain classified as civilians, but they could be drafted into active duty by Congress for up to twenty-four months. The Senate rejected Truman's desire to extend conscription indefinitely and imposed a July 1, 1955, expiration date.

The president and supporters of UMT justified it as a cost-saving measure. Without UMT, they argued, the nation would need a standing army of 3.7 million men and 1 million reservists. With UMT, the army could be reduced to 2 million troops while creating a larger reserve of 2.5 million men, saving $13 billion per year. On at least two occasions, Speaker Rayburn stepped down from the chair to personally lobby for UMT from the House floor. Proponents saw UMT as reflecting a change in the notion of citizenship brought about by the heating up of the Cold War. Citizenship now included a duty to be ready to defend the nation through military service. Representative Franck Havenner (D-CA) declared that a "drastic departure from the anti-militaristic tradition of our peace-loving America is now necessary." One historian aptly described the views of UMT proponents: "The distinction between war and peace had dissolved in a view of the Cold War as a permanent state of national emergency."[11]

The UMT proposal aroused fierce opposition. Ironically, groups that had backed Truman on the issue of economic controls, such as labor unions and church groups, voiced their disapproval at the grassroots level. Farm organizations also lobbied against the measure. In Congress, various UMT bills passed easily in the Senate after the addition of restrictions, such as the duration of the draft, and the House became the major battleground. Leslie Arends (R-IL) led the opposition in the House with an argument based on military strategy, claiming that America was protected by two oceans and that airpower and atomic weapons had rendered manpower less critical for the nation's defense. Others saw UMT as a reprise of the militarized societies of Germany and Japan during the World War II era. Some took this garrison-state argument even further back in history. Representative Edgar A. Jonas (R-IL) railed that if UMT passed, American youths would find themselves "Hessianized and put on the auction block as was done in the days of George III with standing armies." Despite such opposition in the House, it appeared that UMT had a chance to pass the lower chamber in early 1952. However, a complex set of parliamentary moves effectively killed the bill for good. Senator Edwin Johnson summed up the weariness of the opposition, recommending that "no more time or thought should be wasted on this fool idea." He added, "Let us stop our unproductive flirtation with this fetish and be on with the job of defending America."[12]

Rebellion by organized labor created yet another challenge for Truman. In late 1951 a large copper smelter in Garfield, Utah, was shut down over a labor-management dispute. A strike at a large Aluminum Corporation of America plant in Cleveland threatened aircraft production. More than 100 wildcat strikes occurred in the auto industry between January 1951 and March 1952 over work speedups imposed by management. UAW members protested the pressure to produce more vehicles faster in the midst of relatively high unemployment in their industry. On factory floors, workers threatened any colleagues who accepted the speedups, warning, "Stool pigeons, beware!" The Wage Stabilization Board (WSB) responded by appointing a committee to study the autoworkers' concerns. When the committee recommended pay raises, the WSB rejected the idea, increasing the workers' ire.[13]

The labor issue dwarfing all others, however, was a crisis in the nation's steel industry. With the steelworkers' contract set to expire at the end of 1951, negotiations began early in the fall. The United Steelworkers announced it would seek a wage increase (excluding benefits) in the range of ten to fifteen cents an hour, which was considerably higher than the four-cent raise allowed by the guidelines imposed for wartime mobilization. Truman's Council of Economic Advisers believed the steel companies had made adequate profits to absorb the wage increase demanded by the union. The companies felt otherwise, maintaining that steel prices would have to be raised to accommodate any wage increase. Buying into the beliefs of his economic team, and mindful of the omnipresent specter of inflation, Truman rejected the notion of an automatic steel price increase tied to the wage increase in the new labor contract. On December 22, only nine days before the expiration of the contract, Truman referred the case to the WSB for arbitration. To give the agency time to work out a compromise, the president obtained an agreement from the union to delay a strike for 150 days. A few months later, the drama kicked into high gear.[14]

On March 22, 1952, the WSB proposed a hefty raise for steelworkers amounting to about twenty-six cents an hour (covering both wages and benefits). Moreover, the WSB agreed to the demand for a union shop provision in the contract (requiring union membership as a condition of employment at a given job site). All three business representatives on the WSB voted against the proposal, but Truman endorsed it. The steel companies insisted that this contract would increase the cost of steel production by $12 per ton. Much of the American public was outraged at such a generous offer to the workers, and the business community criticized it as inflationary. The media split on the issue, with major publications such as *Fortune, New Republic,* and *U.S. News* supporting the WSB.

Bureaucratic infighting soon began in earnest. According to rules laid down in the DPA, the Office of Price Stabilization (OPS) could authorize a steel price increase of $2 to $3 per ton. When the steel companies petitioned for $9 to $10 per ton beyond that, the OPS offered them zero! (Truman's economic team believed that, in light of the proposed wage increase, an increase of $1 or $2 per ton was warranted.) Charles Wilson, head of the Office of Defense Management and thereby the man running the mobilization effort, met with Truman and came away believing that the president would accept a $4 to $5 per ton price increase in exchange for the proposed wage hikes. Wilson attempted to pressure his subordinates in the OPS to accept the price increase, and when they balked, he tried to bring Truman in as an ally in the debate. However, the president had apparently changed his mind and refused to back the price increase. Wilson, believing Truman had reneged on their agreement, made a public spectacle of resigning his post, calling the Truman administration a patsy for the unions. With the steel companies refusing to ink labor contracts under the terms proposed by the OPS, the president made a momentous decision. On April 8, 1952, Truman announced that the federal government was seizing the nation's steel mills, owned by 86 companies and employing 600,000 workers.[15]

The president's speech to the nation came down hard on the steel companies. Calling their demands for such a hefty price increase "the most outrageous thing I ever heard of," Truman asserted that giving in "would scuttle our whole price control program." In the chief executive's eyes, the companies were the bad guys because they, unlike the unions, refused to abide by the decision of the Office of Defense Management, the agency governing them. (Of course, labor's offer from the WSB was much better than the companies' offer from the OPS.) A key issue was the legal basis of the president's action. Truman justified the seizure based on his constitutional powers as commander in chief during the current "national emergency." The president declared that if the steelworkers went on strike, troops in Korea would be jeopardized; therefore, as commander in chief, he was justified in taking over the steel industry. In Truman's message to Congress on the matter, he offered to work with lawmakers to craft legislation dealing specifically with the steel industry. However, some have suggested that because 1952 was an election year, the president did not expect Congress to act. Truman had other options to justify his action. The Selective Service Act of 1948 allowed the commander in chief to take over any manufacturer supplying material for the military or the Atomic Energy Commission if it failed to fill an order on time. However, Truman's team rejected this choice because it would have allowed him to seize only specific plants, making administration more complicated. Many in Congress thought Truman could have averted the takeover by using his powers under the Taft-Hartley Act of 1947, which gave him the authority to obtain a court injunction to delay strikes for up to 80 days, a provision designed to give both sides a "cooling-off period." But to Truman, utilizing Taft-Hartley would have been unfair to the union as a matter of principle. The steelworkers had already agreed to stay on the job for 100 days beyond the expiration of their contract on December 31, 1951, and the president could not ask them to do so for another two to three months.[16]

When Truman implemented the takeover, he changed nothing about the operation of the steel mills other than requiring the companies to keep an extra set of books for the government. The federal government did not immediately raise workers' wages, as the companies had expected. Nevertheless, the steel industry launched a major campaign to whip up public support for its cause. The companies wisely attempted to steer attention toward the constitutional and political aspects of the takeover rather than their desire to raise prices. (What most of the public did not know was that, unlike other major industries during the war, the steel industry enjoyed very favorable tax amortization arrangements.) The steel companies took out full-page ads in major newspapers and sent a detailed memo to newspaper editors throughout the nation, arguing their case. A speech by industry spokesman Clarence Randall was carried on national television and radio. The administration presented its arguments primarily through Commerce Secretary Charles Sawyer, who wrote letters to the editors of major newspapers. The companies' media blitz worked well on the media itself, which overwhelmingly criticized Truman's decision. At least one historian compared the outcry to that over the firing of General MacArthur a year earlier. Interestingly, many newspapers argued that in the absence of a formal declaration of war, the federal takeover was unjustified, yet another indication that the Korean conflict had become the "Forgotten War." Of the major newspapers in the country, only the *New York Post* supported the seizure of the steel plants, and the *New Republic* was the only national magazine to do so. At a press conference ten days after the announcement of the government takeover, a reporter asked Truman if he had the power to seize radio stations or newspapers. Truman did not help his cause when he responded bluntly, "The President of the United States has to act for whatever is for the best of the country." The *Nation* accused the president of distorting the inherent powers in Article II of the Constitution, while a *New York Daily News* headline blared, "Truman Does a Hitler."[17]

Media opinion notwithstanding, public opinion proved more sympathetic to Truman's seizure of the steel industry. Mail to the White House was evenly split on the issue, while a poll in fifty-three eastern and midwestern cities indicated that 51 percent of respondents supported the president's decision, versus 43 percent opposed. A survey by the *Minneapolis Sunday Tribune* indicated that 74 percent of Democrats supported Truman, with only 10 percent opposed; independents supported him by a margin of 41 to 37 percent; and Republicans disapproved, with only 22 percent supporting the president and 66 percent opposing the steel seizure. A national Gallup poll taken a few weeks after the president's action revealed that 35 percent of Americans supported Truman and 43 percent condemned him. For the White House, the good news was that Truman's job approval rating increased by 9 percent in the three-month period following the steel takeover. The bad news was that this raised the president's approval rating to only 32 percent, indicating the depths of Truman's unpopularity at the time.[18]

Congress engaged in rancorous debate over the steel crisis. Representative Donald O'Toole (D-NJ) complained that the media were misleading Americans with their attacks on the president. Senator Homer Ferguson (R-MI) whined about the lack of public outrage against Truman, suggesting that Americans were so accustomed to White House corruption that they accepted the obvious violation of the Constitution. The House generated a flurry of fourteen resolutions calling for the impeachment of the president; it then went into recess from April 10 to 22, leaving most of the meaningful debate to the Senate. In the upper chamber, Hubert Humphrey (D-MN) and Wayne Morse (R-OR) chastised their colleagues for voting down earlier legislation that would have given Truman the authority to take over the steel industry. Opponents defended their defeat of those bills and portrayed the president's takeover of steel as a blatant circumvention of Congress. Morse asserted that, behind closed doors, senators had admitted that the Taft-Hartley Act was inadequate for national emergencies, a view consistent with Truman's reasoning. For a month, Republicans attempted to maneuver the issue into committees chaired by their conservative southern Democratic allies, without success. Ultimately, Congress did nothing and, as one historian suggests, allowed Truman to take the heat, hoping the courts would overrule him.[19]

The drama now moved to the judiciary as the steel companies asked for an injunction to get their mills back. With the position of attorney general vacant (discussed later in this chapter), assistant attorney general Holmes Baldridge engaged in the following dramatic exchange with federal district judge David Pine:

> PINE: So, when the sovereign people adopted the Constitution, it enumerated the powers set up in the Constitution, but limited the

powers of the Congress and limited the powers of the judiciary, but it did not limit the powers of the Executive. Is that what you say?

BALDRIDGE: That is the way we read Article II of the Constitution.

Baldridge's assertion caused quite a stir. Harold Enarson, a presidential aide on labor relations, claimed that Baldridge's argument was "never dreamed of by anyone in the White House at any time" and called it the "legal blunder of the century." Senators who had previously supported the White House publicly rebuked Baldridge, as did the *New York Post*, which was normally a friend of the administration. On April 29, some three weeks after Truman took over the mills, Judge Pine imposed an injunction against the president's order, declaring that the power to seize private property was not an inherent power of the chief executive under the Constitution. The union immediately declared a strike, but it was called off when Truman asked the union to delay a walkout until the Supreme Court could rule on the case.[20]

Most of the media rejoiced at Pine's ruling. Arthur Krock of the *New York Times* said the decision contained the "firmest restraints on executive power that have been stated by a federal court in our history." The *Saturday Evening Post* likened the ruling to the "Hans Christian Andersen fairy tale when the child, watching the royal procession, said, 'The King has no clothes on.' . . . So it was when Pine declared that the President was not clothed with the authority so persuasively claimed for him." As the nation awaited the Supreme Court ruling, a crucial question arose: if a strike occurred, would there be a bona fide steel shortage? In a congressional committee hearing, OPS director Ellis Arnall said a strike would be disastrous. However, according to Senator Burnet Maybank (D-SC), sources in the Defense Production Administration claimed that the military was already turning steel back to civilian use. The press reported conflicting stories as well. The *Wall Street Journal* quoted Pentagon sources who said the nation had more ammunition in storage than had been used in the war to date, and it reported that there was a seventy-day supply of consumer steel. Others discussed shortages of certain types of steel. The question of actual steel supply would not be definitively answered until a few months later.[21]

Truman was sure the Supreme Court would rule in his favor. As the justices prepared to hear the case, the president's confidence was on display at one of his routine press conferences. When a reporter asked if Truman would like to see Congress pass legislation permitting him to seize the steel mills, he responded, "The President has the power and they can't take it away from him." In part, Truman's faith in the Court stemmed from the fact that he had appointed four of the nine justices, including Chief Justice Fred Vinson. Franklin D. Roosevelt had appointed the other five jurists. In 1949, when Justice Tom Clark (a Truman appointee) was the attorney general, he had written a memo to his boss asserting that inherent presidential powers included the power to seize facilities in the event of labor disputes. Truman had relied heavily on that memo when he decided to seize the steel mills. Moreover, Chief Justice Vinson, who routinely attended the president's poker games, had assured Truman before the fact that he could legally take over the mills. To the president's dismay, on June 5 the Court decided against him, upholding Judge Pine's injunction by a 6–3 vote. Vinson sided with Truman but was unable to convince a majority of the Court to do the same. Clark surprisingly voted with the majority in a devastating defeat for the president, who accepted the decision and ordered the steel plants returned to the companies. The United Steelworkers immediately went out on strike.[22]

The reaction to the Court's decision revolved around the curbing of presidential power and ignored the ramifications of the work stoppage. With the exception of the *New York Post,* most liberal newspapers lauded the decision, including the *New York Times* and the *Washington Post.* The *Pittsburg Press* praised the Court for fulfilling "its constitutional duty to check a headstrong President gone rampant." In the Senate, Truman ally Herbert Lehman called on lawmakers to pass legislation authorizing the president to take over the mills. However, most of the public responses by members of Congress mimicked that of the press. Senator Harry Cain (R-WA) declared the Constitution had been saved, while his GOP colleague Charles Tobey (NH) exclaimed, "Hurrah! Thank God for the Supreme Court."[23]

As the nation's steel plants sat idle, Congress attempted to resolve the situation. Lawmakers considered, then rejected, amendments to the DPA that would have legalized government seizure of the mills. Congress resorted to *requesting* (rather than ordering, which it could have done by law) the president to invoke the emergency provisions of the Taft-Hartley

Act; this would have ordered the strikers to return to work for eighty days while negotiators worked out a contract. Truman refused, as noted earlier, because the union had already delayed its strike. The president also felt that Congress had abdicated its responsibility to resolve the situation months earlier. With the executive and legislative branches at a standoff, the strike continued for fifty-three days after the Court's ruling.[24]

The shutdown of the steel industry began to be felt throughout the country about a month into the strike. Automakers were hit hard, and industry layoffs occurred. Steel reserves for defense purposes approached a critical level by early July. As a result, Truman got directly involved in the negotiations that finally ended the work stoppage on July 24. Both sides compromised, with the union getting a wage-benefit increase of 21.5 cents an hour (versus the 26 cents proposed by the WSB), and the companies getting a price increase of $5.20 per ton (versus the $12 they wanted and the zero offered by the OPS). However, the settlement clearly signaled a union victory, given the hefty wage increases awarded in the new contract.[25]

The decision to nationalize the steel industry turned out to be one of the worst decisions of Truman's presidency. Although he had political motives for siding with organized labor, an important Democratic Party constituent, there were other, more important reasons for his error. The president acted with complete confidence that if the decision went to the Supreme Court, it would rule in his favor. He had been assured by his good friend Chief Justice Vinson of the legality of his act, and he had relied on Justice Clark's 1949 memo supporting the constitutionality of commandeering an industry. As Truman had confided to Commerce Secretary Sawyer, he would be "terribly shocked, disappointed and disturbed" if the Court rebuked him. Another problem for the president was that most Americans did not believe a true national emergency existed by the spring of 1952. The war had settled into a stalemate and had disappeared from the front pages of newspapers. This made it impossible for Truman to whip up a solid majority of the public to support his seizure of the steel mills. Most disastrously for the president, there was no critical shortage of steel. As historian Maeva Marcus wrote, "The enormous inventory of steel on hand at the beginning of the strike became a source of amazement to the entire country." The economic and military disaster Truman had predicted in the event of a strike did not occur, further damaging his credibility with the American people. Moreover, the president's aggressive approach made the steel case the "ultimate litmus test" for his mobilization program. When Truman took over the steel industry, conservatives' fears of a garrison state became a reality. These fears manifested themselves in early 1953. When the lame-duck president pushed for a *standby* economic control program for future emergencies, the GOP and the business community crushed the idea.[26]

Although enthusiasm for economic controls waned during the third phase of the Korean War that began in the summer of 1951, zeal for defense spending did not. Despite the commencement of armistice talks, Truman wanted more money for the military. Congress agreed, approving a fiscal year 1952 defense budget of $57 billion, compared with $48 billion in 1951. Only a fraction of this appropriation was for Korea; most was for Cold War pursuits elsewhere. Among other things, this boost enabled the air force to grow from seventy combat wings to ninety-five. By the fourth quarter of 1952, production of military jets had quintupled since the start of the war, and aircraft plants were making 1,000 planes each month, up from 250 a month in mid-1950. Thus, the accelerated defense spending for Korea (leading to more Cold War expenditures) transformed the U.S. economy. Before the war, national security had constituted 6 percent of gross national product (GNP); by 1953, defense contributed 18 percent of GNP. The fiscal year 1953 budget totaled $85 billion, *three-quarters* of which was earmarked for defense. Thus, ongoing boosts in military spending were Truman's only major success in terms of extending his mobilization program.[27]

Attempts to Resuscitate a Bipartisan Foreign Policy

In the midst of the Truman administration's struggles to extend the mobilization program at home, it also tried to maintain a bipartisan foreign policy abroad. The truth of the matter was that General Douglas MacArthur's removal killed any meaningful possibility of the two parties presenting a unified front on foreign affairs. Truman's team, however, refused to give up. With the enthusiastic blessing of the White House and the State Department, Ken Hechler assembled a sixty-page history of bipartisan foreign policy consultations. In October 1951 the administration released it. *Review of Bipartisan Foreign Policy Consultations since*

World War II sometimes overstated its case, claiming, for example: "Since the outbreak of the Korean conflict, there has been bipartisan support for the United States policy toward Formosa." The paper also included the major details of the debate over sending troops to Europe, an event Truman would not have cited as an example of nonpartisanship at its finest. Overall, the report was a reasonably accurate and comprehensive summary. Despite the administration's considerable efforts, it attracted little national media attention, probably because the press was preoccupied with the fight over Philip Jessup's confirmation as a UN delegate. The project failed, but it seemingly demonstrated Truman's determination not to give up on promoting bipartisanship in foreign policy, even after the rancor of the MacArthur incident.[28]

Yet appearances were deceiving. While Hechler assembled his history of bipartisan cooperation, others in the administration planned an offensive against the opponents of Truman's Far East policies: the China Bloc and the China Lobby. The China Bloc—consisting of GOP senators Knowland, Taft, Wherry, McCarthy, Bridges, H. Alexander Smith, and Nixon, along with House Republicans Walter H. Judd and John Vorys—was determined to help Jiang Jieshi reverse the results of the Chinese civil war. Their media and business allies, known as the China Lobby, were led by publishers Henry Luce of *Time* and *Life* magazines and William Loeb of the *Manchester (NH) Union Leader,* along with importer Alfred Kohlberg. The administration believed that Chinese Nationalists were taking American aid money and funneling it to the China Bloc politicians, who then used the funds to attack the administration's foreign policy. (The *Washington Post* called the China Lobby the "chief nourisher of McCarthyism.") Another concern was that American and Chinese business interests in Formosa and China were pumping money into the hands of legislators for the same purpose.[29]

Presidential aide George Elsey recommended to Truman in March 1951 that Congress conduct a "vigorous investigation" of the China Bloc and China Lobby. Truman detested the members of the China Bloc, calling them men "who saw nothing wrong in plunging headlong into an Asian war but would raise no finger for the defense of Europe; who thought a British prime minister was never to be trusted, but Chiang Kai-shek (Jiang Jieshi) could do no wrong." Staffers in the DNC, State Department, and White House endorsed the probe, and Elsey believed it would be "highly embarrassing to a sizeable group of Republicans in and out of Congress" and reveal "interesting information" about the financial supporters of senators such as McCarthy and Knowland. The president agreed, noting at a meeting of the Americans for Democratic Action that a previous congressional probe had fallen short due to the failing health of Frank Buchanan (D-PA), chairman of the House Select Committee on Lobbying Activities. Despite Buchanan's lack of success, Undersecretary of State James E. Webb suggested that the House would be a more effective investigator than the Senate due to "senatorial courtesy," the unspoken law that discouraged senators from going after one another on ethical issues. Webb's optimism turned out to be unfounded.[30]

The administration's inquiries into the China Lobby remained under wraps until Dean Acheson's testimony near the end of the MacArthur hearings. Since the China Bloc staunchly backed the general, its activities came up for discussion. When Senator Wayne Morse (R-OR) announced his intention to question Acheson on the topic, one journalist reported, "You could have heard a pin drop." Following the stunned silence, Senator McMahon exclaimed, "Oh! Oh!" and Senator Wiley chirped, "What's that? What's that?" Once they got their wits about them, the senators quickly let everyone know whose side they were on. McMahon declared that "speculators, grafters and corruptionists" sympathetic to Jiang were enriching themselves, courtesy of the U.S. government. Senator Bridges countered that the "so-called China Lobby and influence is a very minor thing compared to the whole." As the questioning continued, Acheson told the panel that the president had instructed government agencies to gather information on the China Lobby and to work with any congressional inquiry "to the fullest extent."[31]

The secretary of state's testimony lit a fire under the administration's languishing inquiry into the China Lobby. According to Elsey, Truman aide Charles Murphy initiated numerous discussions on the topic between White House and State Department staffers within days of the end of the MacArthur hearings. Truman's staff complained that the State Department "dragged its heels" in collecting information about the China Lobby, even though the president had assigned the task months earlier, and it produced "only a watery 5-page memo" on June 5. In July, to rejuvenate the probe, Truman had Attorney General J. Howard McGrath form an investigatory committee that included representatives from the Bureau of Internal Revenue, the Federal Reserve Board, and the Departments of State, Justice, and Agriculture. The president wanted to investigate the China Lobby "from hell to breakfast."[32]

The White House worked on the China Lobby probe through the summer and fall of 1951. In addition to the cabinet agencies, the administration tapped nongovernmental resources, such as editors Alfred Friendly of the *Washington Post* and Ed Harris of the *St. Louis Post Dispatch.* They even approached a Columbia University graduate student writing a thesis about the China Lobby, but he was "rather reluctant" to turn his research over to the government. The most fruitful effort involved cooperation with *Reporter* magazine, which published a detailed story on the China Lobby in consecutive issues beginning in April 1952. The story described the China Lobby as a "vast tentacular thing" that "developed its power through an incredible combination of crookedness and idealism." Noting that parts of the Republican Party were "inextricably tied" to the alliance, the magazine also reported that, like other lobbyists, the China Lobby had garnered a "large measure of bipartisan support"—menacing words for the Democrats. Legislators from both parties greeted the *Reporter* story with silence.[33]

Truman's team uncovered suspicious information about the China Lobby but failed to find sufficient proof of wrongdoing to make a legal case against its political tormentors. Part of the problem was a lack of zeal for the project within the bureaucracy, particularly the Federal Reserve, the Justice Department, and the FBI. Another issue was the complexity and lack of formality of the Jiang backers' organization. An aide estimated that the Treasury Department would need a staff of fifty to seventy-five people working eight months to follow the money trail of aid to the Nationalists. The administration found that Alfred Kohlberg, a prominent businessman who traded in the Far East, had provided the funds used by two Republican congressmen to fight the Jessup nomination. The White House believed Kohlberg and his staff were writing Senator Bridges's speeches on the Far East. The investigators also found that an agent for the National Resources Commission of China had "entertained Members of Congress extensively." Such fragments, though failing to pass the smell test, did not prove any lawbreaking. By December 1951, the participating agencies decided they had done all they could do and threw in the towel. Asserting only that it had found indications of a "direct relationship between the money now being used for propaganda and political influence," the administration conceded that such information was not "sufficient in itself to establish this connection." In conclusion, "Since the passing of money, *if any* . . . has been skillfully conducted in very devious manners," it had no case. Although further investigation into the corruption of Chinese Nationalists operating in U.S. political circles *might* lead to proof of wrongdoing by legislators, such a congressional probe involved a "grave risking of failure."[34]

Meanwhile, Senators Morse and McMahon pushed for a congressional investigation. A couple of days after questioning Acheson about the China Lobby during the MacArthur hearings, McMahon communicated his desire for an inquiry to the White House. Morse told Michael Straight, editor of the *New Republic,* that he hoped for approval to "open up on the China Lobby," but only if it would not embarrass the administration. On July 6 the two senators sponsored a resolution requesting $50,000 ($400,000 in today's dollars) for the Foreign Relations Committee to conduct the investigation. Morse readily agreed to demands from Jiang supporters in the Senate that the probe be expanded to include improper communist Chinese influence over American policy. Henry Luce's *Time* claimed, "Just when cooler heads in the Administration had about decided to forget the whole thing," McMahon jumped up to "wave excitedly at an old dragon."[35]

Congress's probe into the China Lobby went nowhere. After months of inaction by the Senate Foreign Relations Committee, Morse tried to reenergize the investigation in April 1952. The Oregon Republican somehow got his hands on more than two dozen incriminating cables sent from the Nationalist Chinese embassy in the United States to Jiang Jieshi and presented them to the committee. One message discussed secret information Jiang had obtained from Representative Judd. Another related that a close associate of William Boyle had served as a lawyer for the Nationalists at a salary of $30,000 per year while Boyle was chairman of the DNC. With the exception of the *New York Times,* the major media ignored the story, and the Foreign Relations Committee apparently did the same. A similar House probe led by Frank Karsten (D-MO) of the Committee on Executive Expenditures in Executive Departments was equally fruitless.[36]

Senator Harry Cain's outburst in June 1952 may provide a clue to Congress's inaction. Entering seventy-three pages from various reports into the *Congressional Record* to make his point, Cain accused Truman's 1948 campaign of accepting $10,000 in small bills from representatives of the Chinese Nationalists, suggesting that they believed a "little moola doled out in administration circles might do them good." The senator also hinted about information implicating former secretary of defense Louis Johnson, explaining why the Morse-McMahon resolution "now gathers dust in the pigeon hole of Sen. Connally." Representative Fred Busbey (R-IL) piled on, demanding that Truman revive the investigation and accusing the administration of "running its own China lobby to cover up its treasonable acts." A couple of weeks later, Karsten and the White House had a dialogue about conducting hearings, but nothing came of it. The congressional inquiry into the China Lobby died a quiet death.[37]

Despite the failure of these investigations, we now know that the Chinese Nationalist government sought to influence the U.S. government by illegal and unethical means. Jiang's regime offered General Albert C. Wedemeyer a sizable sum to act as an adviser to the Nationalists while he was serving in the U.S. military. Wedemeyer, to his credit, turned the offer down. Although Senator H. Alexander Smith based his advocacy of the Nationalists on information gained from his frequent trips to China, other lawmakers had their speeches written by the Chinese embassy. Moreover, the Chinese Nationalist government received confidential information from John Foster Dulles of the State Department and from Representative Judd. Jiang also had a secret fund in the United States that was controlled by an official from the International Monetary Fund and used for "special purposes," such as financing a U.S. foreign legion for China. Although it was unsuccessful in proving such activities, the Truman administration had legitimate reasons to be suspicious of the China Bloc and the China Lobby.[38]

Amazingly, in the midst of the haranguing over the China Lobby, Truman got bipartisan support on a major issue associated with the Korean peace negotiations in 1952 without even asking for it. Democrats and Republicans agreed solidly with the president's stance on the POW repatriation issue, even though it became the stumbling block for peace in Korea. Editorials and the general public praised Truman's position. One letter to the editor came from such unlikely allies as Senator Paul Douglas, a New Deal liberal; conservative William F. Buckley Jr.; socialist Norman Thomas; and Representative Judd of the China Bloc. The most startling supporter was Senator William Jenner (R-IN), normally one of the president's most venomous adversaries. Jenner spearheaded a bipartisan resolution supported by sixty members of Congress proclaiming their opposition to forced repatriation. Equally remarkably, Secretary of Defense Robert A. Lovett and a group of senators managed to persuade the headstrong Indianan to keep his resolution under wraps to avoid upsetting the armistice talks. Nevertheless, negotiations came to a halt in early October when communist recalcitrance on the POW issue caused the UN to declare an indefinite recess. Even though this occurred during the heat of the 1952 campaign season, few Republicans second-guessed Truman's position on repatriation.[39]

Historians have debated whether the notion of a bipartisan foreign policy was worthwhile. Arthur Schlesinger Jr. called it a dangerous stifling of debate and an aid to presidential power. Cecil V. Crabb Jr., reflecting on the topic after his tenure in the Acheson State Department, took a more moderate approach. In Crabb's view, the disadvantages of nonpartisanship sometimes outweighed the advantages, and it had a mixed track record of effectiveness. In contrast, Gary W. Reichard has argued that a bipartisan foreign policy was the exception rather than the rule during the early Cold War, the only exceptions being the Truman Doctrine and Marshall Plan in 1947–1948 and the first year of the Eisenhower administration. Schlesinger's view is correct if the executive defines bipartisanship as the opposition party simply following the president's lead, no matter what. However, when a president includes the opposition party in policymaking, whether through appointments (the most effective method) or congressional consultations, Schlesinger's view is questionable. Crabb is more historically correct than Reichard; the latter ignores the bipartisan support at the outset of the Korean War and the Japanese peace treaty. The challenge in such analyses is that definitions of bipartisanship vary widely, and Korea is a prime example.[40]

The bipartisan foreign policy during the Korean War ebbed with the passing of Senator Arthur Vandenberg. In what had to be a painful irony for Truman, the Republican stalwart died the day before MacArthur gave his address to Congress. Truman professed a belief in nonpartisanship in international affairs through the end of his presidency and included it in his rhetoric, even after he fired the general. Although McCarthyism and war crises such as the Chinese intervention prodded him to try to shore up relations with the GOP, Truman never intended to allow the Republicans to influence his policies once Vandenberg was gone. The president defined bipartisanship as communication of *his* policies to the opposition; in return, he felt the Republicans should support and trust him. In contrast, the Republicans expected Truman to consult with them *before* making up his mind, and then to do what they wanted. With the firing of MacArthur, the GOP's last real chance to control Far East policy slipped away, and shortly thereafter the president tried long and hard to punish the China Bloc for opposing his policy. Yet, in his heart, Truman had to know that true bipartisanship disappeared once Vandenberg was no longer a force on Capitol Hill.

The president's leadership style was not conducive to a nonpartisan foreign policy. An anecdote from journalist Drew Pearson is illustrative. While attending the funeral for Harold Ickes, a member of Roosevelt's cabinet, Pearson noticed Truman sitting practically alone in a pew. A couple of rows behind him sat most of his and FDR's cabinet members. The journalist mused in his diary, "Almost as he sat alone in the church, Truman operates alone as a President. Roosevelt had strong men around him to take the share of the criticism. . . . Truman takes it all on his own shoulders." Indeed, Truman was famous for his slogan: "The buck stops here." He believed the president should lead, and to him, leadership meant making decisions in foreign policy. He considered it a waste of time to meet with congressional figures and listen to their opinions just to make them feel good.[41]

Truman's own doctrine exacerbated the irreconcilable differences between his Far East policy and the beliefs of many Republicans. "It must be the policy of the United States to support free peoples who are resisting attempted subjugation by armed minorities or by outside pressures," he had declared in 1947. How, then, could the president give up on Jiang Jieshi's quest to defeat the communists in 1949? Irritating the GOP hawks even further, the administration passed up a chance to punish the Chinese communist victors when it refused to commit the United States to total war with Mao in 1951 over Korean reunification. Truman and much of the Republican Party fundamentally disagreed on the scope of the containment policy. The president and Secretary Acheson believed that preventing communist expansion in Europe was the top priority due to its industrial power and historic ties to America; they correctly realized that the United States did not have the resources to confront communism everywhere in the world. This view, however, contradicted Truman Doctrine rhetoric. A substantial bloc of Republicans believed that the Far East was just as vital to American interests as Europe (and China's increasing economic might in the twenty-first century might prove them right). No amount of bipartisan consultation would have overcome this basic disagreement (even if Vandenberg had lived), which was a key political dynamic of the Korean War.[42]

Democratic Unity for 1952

In the midst of the stalemate in Korea, the 1952 presidential election loomed. As Truman toyed with the idea of seeking another term, corruption scandals in his administration, collectively dubbed the "mess in Washington," threatened to fracture his party. The mess began in May 1950, when Senator Estes Kefauver (D-TN) launched an inquiry into organized crime. The Tennessean's investigation got plenty of publicity, and some of the hearings were broadcast on the brand-new medium of television. The president never thought much of Kefauver, describing the senator as having "no reputation for anything in particular but his being unable to understand what was going on" in Congress, and he saw the inquiry as divisive to the Democratic Party.[43]

The Kefauver probe made for great television, attracting an estimated 20 million to 30 million viewers who were anxious to see notorious crime figures such as Greasy Thumb Guzik and Frank Costello (they saw only the latter's hands and heard his raspy voice). However, the closest the investigation got to Truman was through the testimony of William O'Dwyer, a former mayor of New York City who was currently serving as U.S. ambassador to Mexico. O'Dwyer admitted to appointing friends and relatives of known gangsters to political office during his stint as mayor, which was one of the reasons he had been forced to resign. The president steadfastly refused to recall the ex-mayor from his diplomatic post and gave him a ringing endorsement for being "a fighter, just like I am." Truman's backing of O'Dwyer sullied the administration only slightly, but it provided the first bit of ammunition for the president's political enemies as the 1952 campaign season approached.[44]

Influence peddling by members of his administration produced a more serious scandal for Truman. Federal officials were obtaining government contracts for businesses and, as compensation for their services, taking a 5 percent cut of the contract, a down payment, and a monthly retainer fee. Congress launched several investigations of the "5 percenters," including one headed by Senator William Fulbright (D-AR) that found questionable dealings with the Reconstruction Finance Corporation (RFC). Initially, the RFC had been created to make federal loans to help banks and industrial concerns recover from the Great Depression. However, in a case uncovered by the Fulbright committee, the RFC had made a multimillion-dollar loan to the Lustron Corporation to build prefabricated homes, in response to a housing shortage. After the RFC finalized the loan, its chief examiner, E. Merl Young, a fellow Missourian and Truman's former Senate aide, left the agency and went to work for Lustron. Young's new employer paid him handsomely—some two and a half times his RFC salary. The inquiry also discovered Young had given his wife, a White House stenographer, a $9,540 mink coat paid for by a Lustron lawyer. Lustron eventually went bankrupt and defaulted on its RFC loan. To the public, it looked like Truman's Missouri cronies were working for the federal government, taking bribes, and buying their spouses mink coats with the proceeds, an image the Republicans hammered on during the 1952 campaign.[45]

The Lustron case did not smell right to the investigating committee. When the panel discovered Young's activities, Fulbright and two other committee members took their findings to Truman to try to minimize the political damage, asking him to reform the RFC. The president, however, saw the investigation as a personal attack and later vented his anger, stating, "The real crooks and influence peddlers were members of this committee, as we might soon find out." He added, a "great many members of Congress had accepted fees for their influence in getting R.F.C. loans for their constituents." The president proceeded to dig up evidence of correspondence between members of Congress and the RFC, including the fact that Fulbright had obtained RFC loans for a resort hotel in his home state. Truman's reaction stemmed largely from his personal dislike for Fulbright and their previous political clashes; privately, Truman called Fulbright "Senator Halfbright" and "an overeducated Oxford s.o.b." The senator, concluding that the president did not intend to reform the RFC, submitted his committee's preliminary report in February 1951. Its title was short and devastating: "Favoritism and Influence."[46]

Although the Fulbright committee's probe dragged on for months and included testimony from a number of administration officials, the only high-level casualty was DNC chairman William Boyle Jr., who resigned in October 1951. Yet the RFC investigation was not the end of the corruption story. Improprieties in the Bureau of Internal Revenue (BIR) and the tax division of the Justice Department produced more headaches for Truman and his party. As Truman aide Ken Hechler wrote, "The situation with five per centers and the RFC was penny-ante stuff" compared with the tax agency scandals.[47]

A congressional investigation into the BIR produced some startling discoveries. Officials in the agency showed favoritism to gamblers who were under investigation for tax evasion and used the department to dole out political patronage. Ultimately, the government convicted a number of BIR employees of bribery, extortion, embezzlement, and, to the outrage of American taxpayers, tax evasion. The culprits included about ten tax collectors overseeing BIR activities in large cities throughout the nation. All of them were the products of political machines, casting an additional shadow over the Truman administration due to the president's longtime ties to the Pendergast machine based in Kansas City.[48]

Conditions within the tax division of the Justice Department were no better. A House probe learned that Theron Lamar Caudle, head of the division, had accepted gifts from tax lawyers and businesspeople who were under investigation for tax violations, including a new car, plane trips to Florida, and mink coats. Attorney general Howard McGrath did little as investigators began to close in on Caudle, forcing Truman to go around McGrath and terminate Caudle himself. Making matters worse, the attorney general refused to cooperate with an assistant hired to ferret out the problems uncovered by Congress. Truman ultimately asked McGrath for his resignation and fired him over the telephone during a staff meeting. Matt Connelly, Truman's appointments secretary, eventually served prison time for activities associated with the tax division scandal. Unlike the investigations into organized crime and the 5 percenters, the chief executive actually responded to these probes by proposing BIR reforms, probably because of the large number of people who lost their jobs and earned criminal convictions. The fact that the tax scandals were emerging as a hot-button issue in the 1952 elections contributed as well. However, Truman's response was too late to keep corruption charges out of the Republicans' arsenal.[49]

Of the corruption scandals uncovered by the Kefauver, RFC, and BIR probes, the last produced the loudest public outcry. The BIR and Justice Department scandals surfaced just as Truman was requesting multiple tax increases to support the Korean War and an overall defense buildup, and Americans were incensed when they learned that government officials were dodging their own taxes and helping their cronies do the same. Moreover, a Gallup poll reported that 82 percent of Americans knew about the BIR corruption probe, an exceptionally high level of awareness. "Indignation against any monkey business in the collection of income taxes," according to one assessment, was "bound to be as hot as a blow torch." This report noted that the administration had suffered "substantial damage" due to the public's perception of wrongdoing, and it predicted problems in the 1952 campaign unless the president "gets rid of the smoke and the smell by putting out some fires."[50]

Due to the fallout from these investigations and scandals, the Republicans found a third prong for their 1952 campaign strategy to go along with the Korean War and communism from two years earlier: corruption. The Republicans hoped their "K_1C_2" formula would help them regain control of the White House and Congress for the first time in decades. The corruption scandals, though not directly related to the war, had one key thing in common with Korea: both caused significant difficulties in the Democrats' quest to retain power once Truman left office. With the 1952 campaign looming, Truman, Korea, and corruption were typically mentioned in the same sentence.

The Democrats handed the GOP another weapon that was a hangover from the 1948 election: the southern wing's rebellion against the Truman liberals. Many southern Democrats had made it clear that they would not support Harry Truman in 1952 under any circumstances. At a Jefferson-Jackson Day dinner in June 1951, Senator Harry F. Byrd (VA) vowed to oppose any Fair Dealer, particularly the president. Calling on Democrats to restore a convention rule that would boost southern influence by requiring a two-thirds majority to select a candidate, Byrd, sounding like Truman's worst Republican enemies, accused the administration of "corruption," "irresponsibility," and "moral and ethical turpitude."[51]

Truman loyalists fought back. At New York's Democratic committee gathering a few days later, state chairman Paul Fitzpatrick counterattacked, lambasting the "infamous, reactionary Dixiecrats" for making their "unholy alliance" with Republicans to kill the Fair Deal. Friction between the Fair Dealers and their Dixiecrat opponents heated up in November 1951 at the Southern Governors Conference in Hot Springs, Arkansas. Ironically, this meeting had traditionally avoided political speechmaking, but the southerners broke this precedent in flamboyant fashion. The loyalists, led by Arkansas governor Sid McMath, maneuvered behind the scenes to arrange for House Speaker Sam Rayburn to speak, without bothering to seek the approval of states' righters such as Governor James Byrnes of South Carolina. Responding to criticism that he had broken the group's tradition of avoiding partisanship, McMath retorted that the key speaker at the 1949 conference had been Governor Byrnes, who had used the occasion to berate the Truman administration. Rayburn strongly admonished his audience to be loyal to the Democratic Party, defending its record since the New Deal era. The Speaker went on to remind the governors that southern Democrats controlled key committees in Congress, and electing a Republican president in 1952 would jeopardize their power. Harking back to 1948, he urged the former Dixiecrats in the audience to recall the futility of backing a third-party candidate, and he invoked patriotism as an incentive to back the president, regardless of whether they loved or hated Truman.[52]

Rayburn's speech brought the Democratic Party's internal strife into the open. "The best way to avoid a split in the party is for Mr. Truman not to be nominated," grumbled Georgia governor Herman Talmadge. Texas governor Allan Shivers added, "Some fellow once wrote, 'methinks thou protests thy virtue too loudly.'" Conveniently forgetting his own 1949 speech to the group, Byrnes accused Rayburn of being the one to break the conference's tradition of avoiding political discussion. Even though it exposed a rift in the party, Rayburn expressed no remorse about his speech, writing to a friend, "I do not think I enjoyed making a speech in my life more . . . especially to the Dixiecrat crowd of them. . . . I told some of them if they were tired of hearing that kind of speech they would get more tired between now and 1952." President Truman, of course, loved the Speaker's message, telling Rayburn it "hit some people in the raw in exactly the right place."[53]

Truman and Rayburn enjoyed getting in their digs against the former Dixiecrats, but this attack did not make political sense. These governors were not direct participants in the Democrats' intraparty clashes in Washington. Thus, it may have been easier to mend the party's fences through dialogue with the governors than with the Trumanites' Democratic adversaries in Congress. Despite Governor Byrnes's ongoing feud with the president, if Rayburn had taken a more conciliatory stance toward the others, this might have encouraged party unity. This confrontation was also a bad idea because it occurred only six months after Senator Russell had led the MacArthur hearings to a conclusion that proved very helpful to Truman. The president and his allies could have tried to build on that, but instead, they elected to go on the attack against the Dixiecrats, ensuring some entertaining fireworks at the party's 1952 convention in—where else?—Chicago.

6

The Fall of the Trumanites

The 1952 presidential election presented a host of issues for the Democratic Party. Would Harry Truman run for another term, given the beating the Korean War was inflicting on his approval rating? Despite the president's upset victory in 1948, the party still smarted from the bolt of the Dixiecrats, and many Democrats were determined to prevent another fracturing. Unlike the 1948 contest, foreign policy was now fair game for debate in presidential politics, thanks to the end of any meaningful semblance of bipartisanship in international affairs. Since the last election, mainland China had fallen to Mao Zedong, fueling Senator Joseph McCarthy's assault on the Truman administration for being soft on communism. Secretary of State Dean Acheson had become the chief whipping boy for the McCarthyites, yet Truman had stubbornly stood by him, much to the displeasure of many Democrats who lobbied, unsuccessfully, to jettison the secretary. Furthermore, McCarthy had terrified many Democrats in the 1950 midterm elections. Was he still a force to be reckoned with in 1952? How would the party's campaign rhetoric deal with a stalemated war in Korea?

Ultimately, from the Democrats' perspective, the 1952 election boiled down to Harry Truman and the Korean War. Throughout the process of choosing their eventual nominee, Adlai Stevenson, Truman's Fair Deal program and, in particular, his civil rights agenda emerged as the most prominent points of contention. Korea had stopped the momentum of the Fair Deal in a couple of ways. As discussed in chapter 2, the war was the main factor in the 1950 midterm elections, leading to the defeat of a number of Truman's allies. These losses robbed the president of liberal allies to push the Fair Deal. By the spring of 1951, the "new war" with China and escalation of the Cold War made economic mobilization the top priority, forcing Truman to put his domestic reforms on the back burner. Another area of conflict for Democrats was the stigma of the "mess in Washington" resulting from the Kefauver investigation. Once the president bowed out of the race, the dominant question became how much, if any, of Truman's Fair Deal would be carried on by the new standard-bearer. Surprisingly, despite all the dissension surrounding Acheson over the past four years, he was conspicuously absent from debates within the party, as was McCarthyism. The Korean War took center stage during the general election campaign as Stevenson dueled GOP nominee Dwight Eisenhower. While the Republicans hammered away on the Democrats' handling of the conflict, southerners in the president's party feuded over whether Stevenson was too Trumanesque for their liking on domestic issues. Thus, for the old Dixiecrats, Harry Truman remained the main issue, even though he was not the nominee. Ironically, it was the lame-duck president who gave a badly needed boost to Stevenson's faltering campaign late in the game, leaving the sidelines to attack Eisenhower as if he were just another presidential candidate rather than a World War II hero. In the end, Ike played a trump card on the Korean issue, bringing the curtain down on the Democrats' two-decade hold on the White House.

Democratic Primary Season

A few days after the Southern Governors Conference in November 1951, President Truman made a momentous announcement to his senior staff. Vacationing in Key West, the president read a memorandum he had written to himself in 1950, before the war erupted: he would not run for another term. Incredibly, to their credit, his staff kept a lid on this bombshell. Truman nonetheless strongly desired the role of kingmaker and immediately began to work behind the scenes to find a Democratic standard-bearer for 1952. His first choice was Fred Vinson, a good friend who happened to be chief justice of the Supreme Court. Vinson declined, forcing the chief executive to turn to his NATO commander, Dwight Eisenhower. When Ike announced in January 1952 that he would run—as a Republican—Truman approached Illinois governor Adlai Stevenson, who vacillated for six months.[1]

Meanwhile, Truman seemed to waffle on his decision not to run. The day after telling his staff he would not be a candidate, the president spoke to the National Women's Democratic Club. Calling the upcoming election a "matter of considerable interest to me," Truman did not disclose who the candidate would be but professed to "have some ideas on that subject." The *Dallas Morning News,* assuming the worst (from its conservative perspective), interpreted this as a statement of his clear intention to run. On February 18, 1952, the chief executive met with six of his closest advisers and discussed possible nominees, himself included. They disagreed over whether Truman should run. A few days later, in an address to fellow Masons, Truman coyly remarked about the job of being president, "Just between you and me and the gate post, I like it." In March Truman released a book of his presidential papers, *Mr. President.* Unusual because presidents typically do not release their personal papers while still in office, the book fueled rumors that the incumbent was considering another run.[2]

Other Democratic presidential hopefuls waited on the sidelines for "Give 'em Hell Harry" to announce his intentions—save one. Estes Kefauver jumped into the race first and emerged as the early leader, even though Truman turned down his request for an endorsement. A loner in the Senate, Kefauver's probe of organized crime had made him popular with the voters but unpopular with Democratic leaders, some of whom were smarting from the fallout over the investigation. Others worried about the presence of political mavericks such as Robert La Follette Jr. in the senator's organization. When the Tennessean announced he would enter the California primary, Florida's Democratic governor issued a press release calling Kefauver a "fabulous faker" and a "political phony," and he offered to debate this "cunning conniver."[3]

Kefauver affected the race in an important way: he helped nudge Truman out of the contest. Although the president did not campaign for the March 11 New Hampshire primary, he left his name on the ballot, probably due to a combination of his distaste for Kefauver and a desire to test the political waters. After stumping vigorously in the state, the senator soundly thrashed the president, 55 to 44 percent. Despite Truman's lack of campaigning, the results shocked the state chairman. After the primary, the president again discussed the possibility of running with his top advisers. This time, they unanimously agreed that he should step aside. With Truman's job approval rating bottoming out at 22 percent in February 1952, the corruption issue and the Korean War were taking their toll on his viability as a candidate. On March 29, at a Jefferson-Jackson Day dinner, the president announced once and for all that he would not actively campaign for another term, nor would he accept a draft at the convention, provoking cries of "Oh, my God!" and "Oh no!" among the party faithful in attendance. Still, he wielded considerable power in the selection of his successor as the party's standard-bearer.[4]

The South pinned its hopes on the candidacy of Richard Russell. The Georgia senator had enhanced his already solid credibility within the party during the MacArthur hearings. Truman thought highly of him, saying Russell had "all the qualifications as to ability and brains." Influential members of the Senate shared the president's sentiments, in spite of their ideological differences with Russell. Even though Senator Russell tried to portray himself as a moderate and emphasized his internationalist approach to foreign policy, he could not overcome the stigma of being a regional, anti–civil rights candidate. As Truman noted, the Georgian was "poison to Northern Democrats and honest Liberals."[5]

Southern Democrats made contingency plans in case the party's nominee did not appeal to them. One tactic was to change Electoral College rules to allow Democratic slates of electors to cast their votes for an opposition candidate, even if the Democratic ticket carried the state. Truman aide David D. Lloyd, recalling a Virginia law passed in 1948 that empowered the state's Democratic Committee to instruct Democratic electors, wisely pushed the administration to mount a legal opposition to such moves and tried to spur the DNC to commit resources to do the same. In Alabama a court battle ensued over an attempt to permit Democratic electors to vote for candidates from other parties. During the litigation, one witness declared under oath that he would be willing to steal votes to prevent Truman's nomination. The president's faithful successfully challenged this move, winning a U.S. Supreme Court decision requiring Alabama electors to support the party's candidate. However, Trumanites failed to stop Georgia from passing a law that omitted the names of the presidential candidates from the ballot, listing the names of the presidential electors instead. This freed electors from the moral and legal obligation to vote for any particular candidate, enabling them to vote as they pleased. Such activities emphasize why Truman should have tried to patch things up with the southern governors, who could have influenced state laws designed to circumvent the national party.[6]

In Texas, where the intensity of Democratic disharmony matched the state's size and its strength in the Electoral College, Governor Allan Shivers pursued a different strategy to undermine the Truman loyalists. After slapping the administration in the face by coordinating a speaking tour for General MacArthur in his state, the governor facilitated the first *Republican* primary in Texas history for the 1952 elections. Shivers was not planning to jump to the GOP, but he wanted to help Eisenhower get the Republican nomination in case a Trumanite became the Democratic candidate. By legalizing cross-filing, which permitted the names of local Democratic contenders to appear on both parties' slates, conservative Democrats could vote for Eisenhower as the Republican nominee and select Democratic candidates for state office in the Republican primary. A worried Truman supporter wrote to the president, "Something must be done or we real Democrats are blown up." The president, weary of the divisiveness within the party, responded that if Texas wanted to vote Republican, he could do little about it.[7]

Shivers's moves in Texas drew national interest and inspired Republican dreams of finally returning to power on Capitol Hill. Senator Karl Mundt (R-SD) jumped on the opportunity to woo anti-Truman Democrats, suggesting that Texas could "pull most of the South along on some effective program of political realignment." Mundt went on to make an unusual proposal: if southern Democrats helped Republicans win the House in 1952, they could retain their committee chairmanships and Rayburn could continue as Speaker.[8]

The few southern Democrats who responded to the Mundt plan did so cautiously, lulling the White House into a false sense of security about the upcoming elections. After meeting with a key Texan on the DNC, Truman adviser Clark Clifford dismissed the Shivers crusade, claiming, "The South cannot get anywhere by leaving the Democratic Party." Clifford failed to recognize the political realities. Shivers and company were not trying to engineer another Dixiecrat third-party revolt, like in 1948. The whole point of the cross-filing bill was to allow Democrats to oppose Truman or any other Fair Dealer for president *without* leaving the party.[9]

Governor Shivers's opposition to Truman, like that of other southern Democrats, had little to do with the Korean War. Southerners targeted the ongoing expansion of the federal government's power at the expense of the states, begun during the New Deal and continued by Truman through the Fair Deal. Thus, the South's main concern early in the primary season was halting federal programs such as the FEPC, a civil rights initiative, and the Brannan agricultural plan. Some southerners publicly endorsed the "principles of 1840," apparently waxing nostalgic for the days when white men reigned supreme. However, the war handed them a campaign weapon against the liberal wing of the party because it gave McCarthyism a new lease on life, reviving fears of communist infiltration at home. The South believed that red-baiting could help their cause against the Trumanites, leading Shivers to trumpet, "I'm tired of a lot of ultra-intellectual parlor pinks and so-called liberal crackpots running the Democratic Party." Such rhetoric gave credence to *Newsweek*'s report on the eve of the national convention that if the sitting president tried to nab the nomination, conservative southern Democrats would definitely "try to blow the Democratic Party to bits."[10]

An examination of party loyalty to Truman's foreign policy reveals some interesting trends. During the latter half of 1951, presidential aide Ken Hechler prepared a voting summary of Democratic committee chairs and other congressional leaders for the period January 1947–July 1951, revealing insights into the harmony between them and the administration's agenda. Of sixteen Democratic leaders in the Senate, six consistently backed the president (all westerners), and four (three westerners and one southerner) steadfastly opposed him. The remaining "middle" group of six southerners exhibited a drastic reduction in support for Truman beginning in 1949 and lasting through 1950. Yet this group's support of the president rebounded strongly in 1951. Analysis of the twenty-one Democratic leaders in the House showed that eleven (including two southerners) consistently backed Truman's programs. The remaining ten, all from the South, exhibited the same trend as the "middle" group in the Senate, with steeply declining support for Truman in 1949–1950 and a sharp rebound the following year. The UAW's report on Congress's performance in 1951 noted that a strong majority of Democrats backed the president on rearmament and foreign policy issues.[11]

What does this all mean? Surprisingly, it shows that in the Senate, most southern leaders did not consistently oppose Truman throughout his administration. Certainly, the erosion of support among southerners in 1949–1950 was a reaction to Truman's 1948 civil rights initiatives and the communist victory in China. As a result, the commander in chief's position within his party was very weak in June 1950 when the Korean War began. Lacking Democratic solidarity at the war's outset, the president found it increasingly difficult to rally support for the war as it descended into stalemate. An unexpected conclusion of the analysis is that, in the Senate, Truman's most consistent Democratic detractors came from the West, not the South. The Democrats' failure to rally around Acheson gave McCarthyism a boost following the 1950 elections, but it did not significantly affect Truman's conduct of the war. Finally, Hechler's report indicates that Democratic support of Truman survived the furor over China's intervention in Korea and the firing of MacArthur, rebounding in the first half of 1951. Thus, the blasting of the administration by Shivers and others during the campaign did not reflect deep dissension over foreign policy; the war was just a handy weapon to use against the president. Truman, however, was not content with party loyalty; he believed that in foreign policy, the opposition party should also rally around the president.

Democratic Convention

One historian called the 1952 Democratic Convention "relatively harmonious," while another called it a "free-for-all marked by confusion, uncertainty and near-chaos." They were both right. Compared with the 1948 convention, which had featured a Dixiecrat walkout and another faction splintering into Henry Wallace's Progressive Party, 1952's might have looked relatively tranquil. Yet the lack of a clear front-runner for the nomination and the upheaval caused by southern recalcitrance made the convention far more exciting than the staged coronations of recent decades.[12]

The Chicago convention focused almost exclusively on domestic issues, largely ignoring foreign affairs and the Korean War. Likewise, little debate occurred over a frequent source of division: the policies of Dean Acheson. Since this was the first time in twenty years that the Democrats would not be nominating an incumbent president, opponents of Franklin Roosevelt and his legacy saw this as a window of opportunity. Would the party maintain the trend begun by Roosevelt and continued by Truman, advocating an activist federal government in areas such as civil rights, or would southerners regain control of the party and rein in Washington? Determined to prevent a recurrence of the Dixiecrat walkout, DNC chairman Frank McKinney told the press that the main mission of the

Platform Committee would be to "remove the disunity that existed in 1948." Liberal Democrats therefore bent over backward to appease the southerners, diluting the party's civil rights plank, backing away from demands for loyalty to the national candidate, and accepting a compromise candidate who was opposed to much of the Fair Deal.[13]

A pair of southern states managed to disrupt party unity before the convention even got started. Mississippi's controversy was a carryover from its bolt to the Dixiecrat Party. The 1948 Democratic Convention had ended up seating the Mississippi delegation with limited credentials, giving the state organization the authority to oppose the presidential ticket and the party platform, even though its delegates had participated in the national convention. The Mississippi state convention selected its delegates in June 1952 with similar instructions, apparently expecting to get the same concessions as in 1948. Protesting this threat to party unanimity, a breakaway group of Mississippi Democrats who were loyal to the national party held a rump convention on July 5 and picked its own slate of delegates. Therefore, two Mississippi delegations showed up in Chicago, challenging the convention to decide which group to seat without provoking another Dixiecrat walkout. Presidential hopefuls Estes Kefauver and Averell Harriman immediately went to work on behalf of the loyalists, but to no avail. The convention seated the former Dixiecrats.[14]

Texas also produced two slates of delegates—one group elected by Truman loyalists, and the other elected by the Shivers Democrats opposed to the president (Truman referred to them as "Texas Bolsheviks"). The Shivers contingent, naturally, refused to promise their unconditional support for the party's nominee. Legally, they had a strong position and could threaten to bolt if the convention refused to seat them, possibly sparking a reprisal of the 1948 Dixiecrat exodus. Harriman and Kefauver again backed the loyalists. Although he sympathized with the Trumanites, convention chairman Sam Rayburn met privately with Governor Shivers and brokered an agreement that sent the pro-Truman delegates home. Rayburn believed he had agreed to seat the Shivers delegation in return for the governor's promise to support the party's nominee, no matter who it was. Later, the Speaker discovered that Shivers thought otherwise.[15]

The controversy over the seating of the Texas and Mississippi delegations precipitated a larger debate over the enforcement of party unity in the upcoming presidential contest. Senators Humphrey, Lehman, and

Blair Moody (MI) drafted a resolution stating, "No Delegate shall be seated unless he shall give assurance to the Credentials Committee that he will exert every honorable means available to him in any official capacity he may have" to ensure that the party's nominees appeared on his state's ballot. This could be accomplished by printing the candidates' names on the ballot or by listing the electors' names and specifying that they were committed to voting for the Democratic ticket. Moody explained that the resolution was intended merely to ensure that the convention's nominees appeared on state ballots. Although the newspapers termed the Moody resolution a loyalty "oath," this was an overstatement; it did not require delegates to swear that they would back the convention's nominee. The liberals in the party were asking the southerners to meet them in the middle, stopping short of mandating support for the convention's candidate but demanding that the delegates allow the Democratic nominee's name to appear on the ballot.[16]

Nevertheless, the resolution sent many southerners into an uproar, for it could have barred as many as six state delegations from participating in the proceedings, including such heavyweights as South Carolina governor James Byrnes and Senator Harry F. Byrd of Virginia. Byrnes "trembled with rage" at the prospect of being booted from the convention, and moderate southerners intentionally jockeyed to keep him off the podium, which could have jeopardized the negotiations on the Moody resolution. Texas agreed to take the pledge because, as Shivers pointed out, it did not require delegates to support the nominee personally. Mississippi and Georgia took a different approach, simply sending polite but noncommittal letters to the Credentials Committee, which seated their delegations. Louisiana, South Carolina, and Virginia, however, refused to make any such gesture. Their strategy, according to a defiant Byrd, was to "not communicate with the credentials committee, just remain in our seats and let them be the aggressors and let them read us out of the convention or throw us out bodily if they will." The loyalists blinked first. Even though the Louisiana, South Carolina, and Virginia delegations refused to sign the loyalty pledge, Rayburn seated them anyway, for the sake of party unity.[17]

Sectional divisions in the party came into play at the convention in other ways. Civil rights was the only issue that engendered significant debate over the party platform; in contrast, the delegates adopted a "stay the course" position on foreign policy. Party liberals and southern conservatives eventually compromised on the civil rights plank, as the liberals abandoned a proposal to ban Senate filibusters and avoided explicit endorsement of FEPC legislation. Instead, the platform advocated the "right to equal opportunity of employment" and a commitment to fight racial discrimination. This compromise represented a significant step back from the party's 1948 stand on civil rights. Yet one journalist called these provisions the "largest concessions that Southern Democrats have ever consented to." Reflecting the goal of preventing another southern exodus at all costs, Platform Committee chairman and House majority leader John McCormack congratulated a colleague for producing a "strong platform, and above all—maintaining unity in this Party." For some southerners, however, these conciliations were not enough. Eleanor Roosevelt provided the most stirring moment of the convention with a speech that electrified the attendees, yet the entire Texas delegation remained seated throughout. When the audience rose to cheer the former First Lady, Senator Byrd stalked out.[18]

The Democrats then turned to selecting a candidate. Coming into the convention, no one was close to having a majority of delegates, but a "draft Stevenson" committee hit the ground running once the proceedings began. On Thursday of convention week, Stevenson called Truman and asked if the president would be embarrassed if Stevenson allowed his name to be placed in nomination. In his memoirs, Truman wrote that he responded with a "show of exasperation and some rather vigorous words" and then gave his enthusiastic assent. After the first two ballots, Kefauver took the lead, with Stevenson running a close second and gaining ground. But the senator from Tennessee had little chance of winning, and not just because of the party leadership's animus. Kefauver had led the unsuccessful crusade to take a hard line against the southerners over the loyalty pledge issue, and delegates had labeled him an extremist. He and the other candidates eventually dropped out and endorsed Stevenson, giving the Illinois governor the nomination he had resisted for so long.[19]

A big reason for Stevenson's acceptability as a compromise candidate was his moderate approach to government activism. He believed that on the issue of civil rights, the federal government should not "put the South completely over a barrel" and should leave enforcement to the states. The irony of Stevenson's selection by a convention dominated by domestic issues was that he proved to be much more passionate about world affairs. His nomination amounted to a ringing endorsement of the administration's Korean policy. Later, on the campaign trail, Stevenson declared that if the president had not fought in Korea, "Munich would follow Munich."[20]

Governor Stevenson chose Alabama senator John Sparkman as his running mate. Despite this obvious move to appeal to the Dixiecrats, six southern delegations refused to endorse the ticket immediately. Sparkman had supported most of Truman's policies, with the exception of civil rights. The delegations of South Carolina, Louisiana, Mississippi, Georgia, Texas, and Virginia decided to hold follow-up state conventions after departing Chicago to decide whether they would support the nominee. State gatherings in Louisiana, Georgia, and Virginia endorsed Stevenson. Conventions in Texas, South Carolina, and Mississippi went in the opposite direction, deciding that, by law, their delegates did not have to support the national nominee.[21]

The results of these state conventions did not reflect the whole picture of southern sentiment toward the Stevenson-Sparkman ticket, however. Paradoxically, South Carolina's state convention voted to support the ticket but gave its delegates the freedom to support Eisenhower. Some key southerners got behind the nominees. Richard Russell pledged to deliver not only Georgia but also the entire South to Stevenson. Mississippi governor Hugh White, who had fought in Chicago for his delegation's right to refuse to endorse the national ticket, called Stevenson an "elegant gentleman and a very capable man" who would unite the party.[22]

General Election

Candidates Dwight Eisenhower and Adlai Stevenson shared similar views on most domestic issues, including the regulation of organized labor through the Taft-Hartley Act of 1947. This law, passed over Truman's veto by the Republican-controlled Congress, required union leaders to sign affidavits that they were not communists. Taft-Hartley also banned the closed union shop and secondary labor strikes designed to pressure companies other than the one to which the union was contracted. Under this law, the president received additional powers to stop labor strikes deemed dangerous to the health and safety of the nation. Eisenhower favored amending the Taft-Hartley Act, declaring, "America wants no law licensing union-busting. And neither do I." Ike suggested that if union leaders had to officially profess that they were not communists, employers should be required to do the same. Stevenson found the issue troubling. Despite organized labor's tradition of being a core constituent of the Democratic Party, the Illinois governor could not bring himself to endorse the repeal of Taft-Hartley, as the unions desired. For one thing, Stevenson did not care for the practices of some union leaders and believed that the perception of being in labor's pocket had hurt Truman politically. More important, Stevenson detested the idea of pandering to any special interest group such as labor. But because the governor believed that unions should be respected, he publicly criticized the Taft-Hartley provision that allowed injunctions against strikes related to national emergencies. After much vacillating, Stevenson decided to placate the unions by favoring repeal and *replacement* of the law, a circuitous way of saying that unions needed to be curbed. After the candidate spelled out his position in Detroit, the heart of unionism, a close friend noted that the audience had "no real fire" and called it a "defeated group." Like Eisenhower, Stevenson believed that Taft-Hartley just needed some revising.[23]

The presidential contenders also had similar views on civil rights. Both professed to support civil rights for blacks but believed that the states rather than the federal government should be in charge of ensuring racial equality. As governor, Stevenson had practiced what he preached, desegregating the Illinois National Guard and the state parks system. He had proposed an Illinois Fair Employment Practices Commission to protect African Americans from discrimination by employers but opposed a national FEPC. (The FEPC was a federal agency created during World War II to prevent discriminatory practices in the defense industries. Congress ended its funding in 1946, and Truman had tried unsuccessfully to revive it.) With Jim Crow firmly established in the South for decades, the governor admitted that the "problem is more serious" there, but he believed that federal attempts to fix the race issue would only exacerbate a sectional divide between North and South. Stevenson saw race as an individual rather than an institutional problem in America, and he questioned the value of federal legislation to assure civil rights. He therefore supported the filibuster, the main tool used by southern senators to fend off civil rights legislation. Like his opponent, Eisenhower opposed an

FEPC at the federal level. Ike confided to his campaign chairman, "I do not consider either race relations or labor relations to be issues"; nor did he believe that "problems arising within either of them can be ended by a punitive law or a statement made in a press conference." Stevenson easily could have made the same statements.[24]

Eisenhower and Stevenson agreed, for the most part, on the need to restrain the growth of federal government programs. Both opposed Truman's desire to create a national health insurance program. To the delight of the conservative Taft wing of the GOP, Ike came out for lower taxes and free trade via the removal of import tariffs, and he advocated the elimination of "artificial direct legislative controls," an allusion to the wage and price controls implemented after the Chinese intervention in Korea. Confusion reigned on the topic of wartime economic regulations. In June 1952 a coalition of Republicans and conservative Democrats voted to curb the mobilization program by trimming nearly 40 percent from the Economic Stabilization Agency's budget, forcing Truman to cut 1,700 jobs and thereby dampening his ability to administer price controls. Shortly after the overwhelming victory of Eisenhower, who had denounced price controls, 61 percent of Americans indicated they *favored* such controls. Despite virtually full employment in the nation, rising wages, strong farm prices, and low inflation during the 1952 campaign season, the public was unhappy about having to shoulder such a great tax burden to pay for a stalemated war. On the campaign trail, Eisenhower tapped into this frustration by doing things like holding an egg in his hand and announcing that there were sixty-eight taxes on it. Yet the GOP nominee also wanted to "improve and extend the federal program of Social Security," the popular New Deal program initiated by the Democrats. Although Stevenson told a reporter at one point that "foolish or irresponsible promises of substantial tax reduction can be very misleading," he conceded late in the campaign that there were few differences in the candidates' views on the federal budget and taxes.[25]

Eisenhower unified the Republican Party during the campaign. The general believed that the two-party system would end if the Democrats captured the White House for a sixth straight time in 1952. However, he strongly opposed the strident isolationism of Senator Taft, the darling of the conservative, Old Guard wing of the party and the initial favorite to be the nominee. After defeating Taft for the nomination, the general brought the Old Guard and internationalist wings of the party together by endorsing Taft's proposals for large spending and tax cuts. In the general election, Eisenhower planned to ignore Stevenson and run against the policies of Truman, whom the general described as "a fine man who, in the middle of a stormy lake, knows nothing of swimming."[26]

Stylistically, Eisenhower lacked Stevenson's oratorical skills. Yet the general proved to be more effective on the campaign stump because he stuck to his scripted "eight-point plans," whereas Stevenson tended to give more nuanced but lengthier discourses on the issues. For this reason, the Democrat failed to use television as well as he could have. With one-third of American households owning televisions, Stevenson's campaign staff recognized the importance of the new medium and bought advertising time for their candidate. The governor criticized Eisenhower's ads for "selling the presidency like cereal" and wondered how to "talk seriously about the issues on one-minute spots." As a result, Stevenson's advertisements often cut him off in midsentence because he did not adhere to his time limits, a habit that persisted until his very last paid TV spot on the eve of the election. Ironically, the governor came across well on television, but he failed to take the new medium seriously, and his ads seemed less professional than those of his opponent.[27]

Unsurprisingly, Democratic Party unity proved elusive in the general election, primarily because many southerners decided they liked Ike. "Democrats for Eisenhower" organizations developed in several states. Governor Byrnes blasted his party, even though South Carolina's state convention had endorsed the Stevenson-Sparkman ticket. He refused, however, to go so far as to approve of a scheme allowing Democratic presidential electors to cast their votes for Eisenhower. Instead, Byrnes approved a petition containing 53,000 signatures (only 10,000 were required) to list Eisenhower and his running mate Richard Nixon on the state's ballot as *independents*, apparently enabling the governor and other Democrats to support Ike without feeling the guilt of voting for the opposition party. Mississippi did the same thing. Byrnes subsequently came out publicly for Eisenhower, adding to the hard feelings between Truman and his former secretary of state.[28]

Virginia Democrats also produced a splinter faction for Eisenhower, even though Governor John Battle and the state's organization threw their weight behind Stevenson. The backing of the state's convention turned out to be worthless, however, because the Virginia Democrats were controlled by a bitter foe of the Truman administration: Senator Harry F. Byrd. The Virginia senator differed from most of his southern colleagues, in that he had been vehemently opposed to the New Deal from day one, fighting both the Social Security Act and the National Recovery Act. He also believed that the Marshall Plan had been a waste of money. Although Byrd was unwilling to campaign for Eisenhower, he made sure the Democratic machine did little to help Stevenson. Byrd called the main issues of the campaign "usurpation of power by the Executive" and "trends to socialism." In response, Vice President Barkley observed that the Democratic defectors were "like the woman who keeps her husband's name . . . but bestows her favors to the man across the street." Thanks in part to Byrd, in 1952 Eisenhower became the second Republican to carry Virginia since post–Civil War Reconstruction.[29]

Unlike in Virginia, the state organization in Texas repudiated the Democratic ticket, and its leadership actively campaigned for Eisenhower. Governor Allan Shivers concocted what became the top campaign issue in his state. Texans prided themselves on their oil, and they had been fighting with the federal government since the 1930s over revenue from offshore drilling lands—or the "tidelands," as the southerners deceptively called them. According to the Truman administration's estimates, some $40 billion of petroleum revenue was at stake for the coastal oil-producing states such as Texas, California, Louisiana, and Alabama. Furthermore, the Korean War had increased the demand for petroleum products, leading the U.S. Petroleum Administration for Defense to predict that world demand for oil would exceed supply by the end of 1951, increasing the stakes in the tidelands fight. The Department of the Interior quantified a deficit in domestic oil production of 276,000 barrels per day, along with a significant shortfall in natural gas. Shivers therefore decided to make the tidelands the litmus test for whether to support Stevenson.[30]

Key politicians alerted Stevenson to the sensitivity of the tidelands issue, suggesting that it could cost the Democrats Texas, Louisiana, and perhaps Alabama and California in the election. Even southern states without offshore oil saw the tidelands as a states' rights issue. Nevertheless, Stevenson told Shivers that he could not support Texas's claim to the tidelands, prompting Senate majority whip Lyndon Johnson (D-TX) to call him a "goddamned fool" for allowing the Texas governor to pin him down on the issue. Stevenson opposed transferring federal assets to the states, but he offered a compromise, saying that he would consider having the federal government send rebates from oil royalties to the tidelands states. Shivers rejected the offer, renounced his support for the Democratic ticket, and campaigned for Eisenhower, who supported state claims to tidelands oil. Believing that Shivers had reneged on his promise to back the party's nominee, Sam Rayburn fumed, "He lied to me. . . . You don't lie to me. I don't want the son of a bitch at my funeral."[31]

Governor Shivers did a masterful job in using the oil rights controversy against Stevenson. "Most people in Texas didn't give a damn about the Tidelands," a Shivers aide conceded. The key was: "We made them feel they were losing something." Representative Frank Boykin (D-AL) noted that during a visit to Texas, "a taxicab driver told us that we were trying to take the school children's lunch money away" by opposing the state's right to the tidelands. Indeed, the ballyhoo over offshore oil revenue was a smoke screen Shivers used to oppose any Democrat who endorsed an activist federal government in the Truman tradition. In a brass-knuckles campaign in which the Shivercrats ridiculed Rayburn as a "pinhead" and "peanut-brain" for backing Stevenson, they delivered Texas for Eisenhower.[32]

The tidelands issue had little effect elsewhere in the South. Although Louisiana and Alabama both stood to profit from gaining control of tax revenue from offshore mineral rights and had joined the Dixiecrat revolt in 1948, Stevenson carried them handily in the election. However, as far as other southerners were concerned, there was a more important reason to oppose Stevenson: Truman had endorsed him, which, in their eyes, was the ultimate curse.

In Mississippi, a faction of former Dixiecrats kept the spirit of 1948 alive. Even though Truman had decided to forgo another term, the Mississippians blasted the Truman wing of the party, railing against "active and dangerous minority and racial groups." The ex-Dixiecrats warned, "As long as this gang, with its pinks and punks, is in control of the National Democratic Party those who stand for Constitutional government and States' Rights can expect absolutely nothing." The states' rights Democrats also threatened to organize a splinter group, suggesting that a third party could prevent any candidate from gaining a majority in the Electoral College and throw the election into the House of Representatives, where, they believed (for reasons known only to them), Richard Russell could be elected. This faction harbored a striking hatred toward the Fair Dealers and adamantly refused to compromise with them. Nevertheless, thanks to Governor Hugh White's leadership, these Dixiecrats did not get their way in the general election; Stevenson carried Mississippi handily.[33]

Other influential southerners such as Senator Strom Thurmond of South Carolina and Louisiana governor Robert Kennon backed Eisenhower. Interestingly, Stevenson managed to carry these Deep South states anyway. However, with the help of disaffected leaders such as Governor Shivers, Eisenhower carried the traditionally Democratic states of Florida, Oklahoma, Tennessee, Texas, and Virginia, providing a final indicator of southern Democrats' disenchantment with the Truman wing of their party. In these five states, the president's backing of Stevenson was the kiss of death.

Stevenson faced another challenge in the campaign. Mindful of the Republicans' "K_1C_2" (Korea, communism, and corruption) strategy, the candidate wisely recognized the need to distance himself from the unpopular Truman and the recent corruption allegations against the administration. Confiding to a friend that "the line to emphasize is that I am *not* Truman's candidate," Stevenson moved his headquarters to Springfield and replaced DNC chairman Frank McKinney, a Truman man tainted by charges of financial improprieties, with Stephen Mitchell, a "reform-minded" Chicago lawyer who had recently served as counsel for the House's investigation of the Justice Department. Although Mitchell was relatively unknown in political circles, his appointment was designed to ease tensions within the party over the corruption issue. The president initially kept a stiff upper lip, inviting Stevenson and Sparkman to the White House to discuss campaign strategy, where they agreed that Truman would wait until October to hit the campaign trail. However, when a reporter baited Stevenson into conceding that there was a mess in Washington that needed cleaning up, Truman's resentment bubbled over. Venting his anger in an unsent letter, the president told the candidate to "take your crackpots, your high socialites with their noses in the air, run your campaign and win if you can," describing himself as a "bystander who has become disinterested." Regarding Stevenson, *Newsweek* reported, "Harry S. Truman was good and mad at him, and didn't care who knew it."[34]

The corruption issue proved to be a double-edged sword in the campaign—for both parties. As expected, the GOP, in the person of vice presidential candidate Richard Nixon, went on the attack first, calling Stevenson an alumnus of Secretary of State Dean Acheson's "Cowardly College of Communist Containment." Nixon continued to pound on the issue, declaring that the Illinois governor had been elected by "mobsters, gangsters and the remnants of the Capone gang." Then, on September 18, the press reported that a group of wealthy California businessmen had established a trust fund to help Nixon finance his Senate campaign. Even though the fund was relatively modest (about $18,000) and had been spent mostly on legitimate office expenses, the Democrats and the press blasted Nixon mercilessly, primarily due to *his* hounding of Truman and Stevenson over corruption and influence peddling. The cry to drop Nixon from the Republican ticket faded after he made his now-famous speech claiming he had done nothing wrong and asserting his right to keep the campaign gifts, among them his daughter's black cocker spaniel puppy named Checkers. The Democrats' attempt to embarrass the Republican ticket failed again when the press reported that Stevenson had benefited from a similar fund during his 1948 gubernatorial campaign. To the Democrats' chagrin, Stevenson's trust fund contained $500 more than Nixon's. Unsurprisingly, for the remainder of the campaign, both parties were less eager to use the corruption issue to bludgeon each other.[35]

Foreign policy emerged as a big issue in the campaign, distinguishing this contest from previous elections. The unwritten rule of presenting a unified front to the world on international issues was cast aside. The *New York Times* reported that the American people were "arguing it [foreign policy] hotly all over the place—grocers and taxi drivers, farmers and mechanics, high school students and old-age pensioners." The State Department was besieged with 5,000 letters and telegrams per week. Convincing the electorate of the virtues of the Korean effort was therefore a high priority, and the Democrats had their work cut out for them, given the apparent "uncertainty among the people as to our sense of direction and continuity of policy." Moreover, the Democrats believed the press was against them, and they were right. A subsequent analysis found that pro-Eisenhower newspapers controlled 80 percent of the national circulation.[36]

Nevertheless, the Trumanites did their best to defend the president's war policy, beginning with an "old reliable." A revised edition of *Our Foreign Policy,* the highly successful booklet first published in 1950, reap-

peared as 300,000 copies were sent out across the nation. The administration blanketed the media with this pamphlet. To reach rural America,
the State Department sent copies to 10,000 weekly and nonmetropolitan
newspapers. The combined readership of the newspapers and periodicals
receiving the booklet was an estimated 75 million, representing about 68
percent of the voting-age population.[37]

Our Foreign Policy 1952 made a good case for the Truman administration's war policy. However, it contained a few curiosities. Only five
pages dealt with Korea and the Far East, compared with nine pages dedicated to European affairs. The pamphlet mentioned China only once, and
it emphasized "Soviet aggression . . . in Korea," including a drawing of
a Stalinesque figure leaning over an Asian officer and examining a map
of eastern Asia. It also noted that the United States had gone to war in
Korea to stop aggression against "our particular interests in the Pacific,"
without explaining precisely what those interests were. These weaknesses
notwithstanding, the booklet pointed out that the UN's credibility was at
stake, if it were to avoid the fate of the League of Nations. The brochure
argued that America's enemies had not "pushed us into the sea," and they
had ended up at the thirty-eighth parallel, where they had started. The
State Department summed up its case for limited war perfectly: "The
U.N. forces have not destroyed all the power of China. That was not their
job, and to have attempted it might have precipitated World War III." UN
forces had, however, repelled aggression in Korea.[38]

The State Department booklet generated lots of attention, as it had in
1950. It was the subject of thirty editorials, eighty-one front-page stories,
and ninety-eight other news stories in the major metropolitan papers. The
Louisville Times called it "must reading for every citizen," while the *Philadelphia Bulletin* quipped, "If the cracker barrel experts take time to read it,
just possibly they might develop a better understanding" of foreign policy.
The State Department summed up press reaction as "widespread and on
the whole very favorable."[39]

The administration had to play defense to sell its war policy during the
1952 campaign. In response to ten questions posed by columnist David
Lawrence, the DNC published a ten-page rebuttal, including counterpoint
questions for Republicans. For example, Lawrence asked, "Why was a
'stalemate war' and a 'stalemate peace' advocated by the Truman-Acheson
administration?" The DNC accurately replied that the North Korean

army had been "all but demolished" and that heavy casualties had been inflicted on the Chinese. Democrats reminded the public that the UN had driven the communists to the armistice table. However, the DNC also responded that whereas the UN had gone to war to "repel the armed attack" and to "restore international peace and security to the area," it "did not set out to take over North Korea by force." This, of course, did not explain why UN forces had advanced so deeply into the north before the Chinese intervention, underscoring the challenge the war posed for the Democrats in the campaign.[40]

Truman did everything he could to convince the American public of the virtues of intervention in Korea, seeking to educate them on the reasons for the war while simultaneously convincing them it was not a prelude to World War III. Nevertheless, his war salesmanship had its flaws. The president's oratory skills left much to be desired, particularly when compared with those of his predecessor. Truman made some tactical errors as well, getting off to a slow start in communicating with the public at the war's outset and uttering vague public statements about the momentous decision to carry the fighting north of the thirty-eighth parallel. Most important, he made his job much harder by changing the war's objective several times, and the concept of limited war proved inscrutable to many Americans, coming so soon after the Allies' unconditional victory in World War II.[41]

So how does history judge the president's attempt to sell the Korean War to Americans? In one sense, it appears that Truman failed because the war helped him attain the lowest presidential approval rating in U.S. history to that point (22 percent) and facilitated the 1952 election of Republican Dwight Eisenhower. For all his unpopularity, however, Truman managed to keep the nation on board with his policies. Eisenhower essentially continued his predecessor's Korean strategy, concluding the war just six months after the Missourian left office, and under the same terms Truman had insisted on throughout the latter stages of the conflict. Many Americans had called for policy changes ranging from expansion of the war into mainland China to a complete pullout of American troops, but these alternatives never generated enough support to force Truman to redirect his course. After a significant drop in popular support when China entered the war, backing for U.S. involvement held steady for the remainder of Truman's term. Events such as the firing of

MacArthur, the stalemated peace talks, and several Chinese offensives did not steadily erode public support for the war, as one might have expected them to. The commander in chief sold the war well enough to carry it out as he saw fit.[42]

Republicans thought the other "C" in their K_1C_2 formula—communism—could be useful, given their belief in the success of Joseph McCarthy's antics in the 1950 elections. However, this created a ticklish problem due to McCarthy's attacks on George Marshall, Eisenhower's mentor during his military career. As army chief of staff during World War II, Marshall had helped Ike leapfrog others and attain promotion from lieutenant colonel to major general in less than two years. McCarthy had started to target Marshall in 1951, viciously condemning his policies while serving as secretary of state early in the Truman administration. He accused Marshall of enabling the communist triumph in China's civil war and called him a "front man for traitors" and a "living lie." Eisenhower therefore faced the unsavory task of having to publicly support McCarthy (and, by extension, the notion that the Democrats were soft on communism), in spite of the senator's irresponsible attacks on a friend. This issue came to a head when Eisenhower made a campaign swing through McCarthy's home state of Wisconsin. The Republican candidate had planned to defend Marshall's reputation and to chide McCarthy's reckless methods in a speech in Milwaukee, but at the last minute, he decided to do neither. The press, which had advance access to the text of the speech, let the public know about the omissions, causing Ike significant embarrassment. This incident illustrated the importance of anticommunism to the GOP. The Republicans believed that McCarthy was a necessary weapon in the campaign, and Eisenhower squelched his loyalty to Marshall to avoid a confrontation with the junior senator from Wisconsin.[43]

Eisenhower's refusal to publicly defend Marshall from McCarthy's venom energized Stevenson, who stood firm with Truman against McCarthyism. Most notably, the Illinois governor refused to abandon Acheson. The secretary of state delivered two major speeches during the campaign attacking the Soviet Union, and Stevenson defended him by reminding voters that both Eisenhower and MacArthur had recommended pulling American troops out of Korea prior to 1950. Although he allowed a key backer to predict that his administration would have a new head of the State Department, Stevenson refused pleas by DNC chairman

Mitchell and India Edwards, the top woman in the party organization, to announce that Acheson would retire after the election.[44]

Stevenson faced the additional challenge of supporting Truman's foreign policies while avoiding political damage from the president's abysmal approval rating. (The president's poll numbers actually climbed a bit once he dropped out of the race, improving from 25 percent approval early in 1952 to 32 percent during the campaign. This was probably no coincidence, since some 80 percent of Democratic county chairpersons were pleased that Truman had dropped out of the race. Nevertheless, 32 percent was a dismal number and presented an obstacle to Stevenson.) Moreover, the candidate was in the awkward situation of trying to manage an incumbent president who wanted to mix it up with Republicans on the campaign trail. During the final month of the campaign, Korea became the most prominent element of the Republicans' K_1C_2 formula. Interestingly, this occurred due to Truman's success on the campaign trail and his failure to produce an armistice.[45]

By late September, Republican attacks on the president's record had him so riled up that he had to enter the fray, whether Stevenson invited him to or not. After Eisenhower criticized his foreign policy, Truman said, "I nearly choked to hear him," since the general had been heavily involved in developing the administration's international approach. The president made a difference in the campaign, despite his lame-duck status. Over the next several weeks, Truman threw himself into a whistle-stop trip covering 19,000 miles, and he made 211 speeches. Truman energized voters with his freewheeling attacks on the Republicans, in contrast to Stevenson, who sometimes talked over their heads. As one historian wrote, "Truman's most valuable contribution to Stevenson's cause was to take on Eisenhower personally, and thus end the pretense that the General stood above partisan politics." Among other things, the president hammered on the fact that Eisenhower had recommended withdrawing troops from Korea in 1947. Truman recalled years later that he "took the hide off" Eisenhower and "skinned him from the crown of his head to the heel of his foot." These tactics started to work by early October. One poll showed that the gap between Stevenson and Eisenhower had shrunk to four percentage points, prompting a Republican research service to report there was "little doubt that Truman is responsible for this alarming shift of public opinion." An analysis for the Democratic campaign called Truman the "only threat to the whole farm vote falling into Ike's lap . . . and it is a real threat."[46]

The Republicans responded by making the war the top issue for the rest of the campaign. Polling data indicated that Korea was the number-one concern of independent voters, who were weary of armistice negotiations that had gone on for more than a year with seemingly little progress. A Gallup poll produced the most dramatic numbers, indicating that two-thirds of potential voters thought Eisenhower was the best man to handle Korea, versus 9 percent for Stevenson. Shortly thereafter, events in the war intervened. Following a July–August UN bombing campaign designed to induce communist concessions at the peace talks, the negotiations broke down on October 8 over the repatriation of POWs. The Truman administration refused to force North Korean and Chinese prisoners to return home, recalling Russian POWs who had been executed or sent to Siberia after World War II, and those who had committed suicide rather than accept such fates. With the fifteen-month-old armistice talks stalled, the war escalated, producing some 1,000 American casualties per week.[47]

The war presented a tough problem for Stevenson. Some Democrats had been optimistically predicting the end of the war since the summer of 1951, creating disillusionment among the electorate. He nonetheless stuck by Truman's policies, backing the armistice talks even though they were at a temporary halt. Stevenson mused, "Many wars have been avoided by patience and many have been precipitated by reckless haste." He was right, but the public was in no mood for such an analysis. Stevenson also affirmed Truman's decision to go into Korea, making Wilsonian statements such as, "God has set for us an awesome mission: nothing less than leadership of the free world."[48]

The Democrats also countered the Republicans' emphasis on Korea by attacking Eisenhower, attempting to use his war-hero image against him. The DNC reminded the public of Ike's January 1951 statement that military draftees should receive little, if any, pay because they were simply fulfilling their obligation to their country. Stevenson's team attempted to undermine the general's credibility by citing a 1948 quote of his: "The necessary and wise subordination of the military to civil power will be best sustained . . . when life-long professional soldiers . . . abstain from seeking high political office." In addition, the Democrats referred to Eisenhower's previous statements supporting Truman's actions in Korea, such as his

November 1951 assertion that there was "no recourse but to do what President Truman said and did." Democrats reminded the electorate that in June 1952 the general had supported the armistice talks, saying it was not "possible for our forces to carry through a decisive attack" and that the best option was to "try to get a decent armistice out of it." Truman dared Ike and his "snollygoster foreign state advisers" to tell the public how he proposed to end the war.[49]

Eisenhower did not help himself much early in the campaign. In August he cited the "really terrible blunders that led up to the Korean War" but added, "I do not see how these conditions, having occurred and having been created, how you could stay out of the thing. I don't know." Later, in an October speech foreshadowing the Vietnamization crusade of America's next limited war, the general said of the Korean conflict, "If there must be a war there, let it be Asians against Asians, with our support on the side of freedom." Although it played well with his Republican base, Eisenhower's comment seemed racist to several international observers. On October 8, the same day the armistice negotiations collapsed, the GOP candidate criticized Truman for entering the peace talks because it allowed the enemy forces to regroup.[50]

Ike's best move, however, came on October 24. Speaking in Detroit, Eisenhower responded to the president's challenge to tell the nation how to end the Korean War, delivering the knockout punch of the election. He began by railing that the current administration "cannot be expected to repair what it failed to prevent." Then he made a dramatic announcement: "The job requires a personal trip to Korea. I shall make that trip. Only in that way could I learn how best to serve the American people in the cause of peace. I shall go to Korea." Even though Eisenhower failed to mention what he would do in Korea, the media immediately declared him the victor, with Election Day still two weeks away. Reporters told one of the general's aides, "That does it—Ike is in." *Newsweek* trumpeted that the Eisenhower campaign had "hit its peak in a single sentence." Even the editors of the liberal *New Republic* agreed, admitting, "twelve million parents found it hard to turn down a five-star General who assured them he would protect their sons from enemy fire."[51]

Election night proved decisive. By midnight, one Democratic state boss moaned, "They're murdering us; it's a total disaster." He was right. Eisenhower defeated the Illinois governor in a landslide, taking 55 percent of the popular vote and carrying thirty-nine states, including the home states of both Stevenson and Truman. Americans showed much more interest than they had in the previous presidential race, with 13 million more people casting ballots in 1952 than in 1948. Ironically, Stevenson garnered 2.5 million more votes in a losing cause than the victorious Truman had four years earlier. However, a quarter of the people who said they voted for Truman in 1948 voted for Eisenhower in 1952. Thus, the contest rejected the conventional wisdom that higher voter turnout favored the Democrats because they had more registered voters than the Republicans.[52]

The election results surprised most Democrats. Hoping for a repeat of 1948, they were apparently counting on an Election Day switch to Stevenson that never materialized. Some took it hard. A New York grocer turned in five false fire alarms on the day of the election; he was arrested by police as he tried for a sixth. A Democratic renter who was upset by the "triumphant smirks" of his Republican landlord took out his frustrations by setting her house ablaze. "I just didn't like her attitude," he explained to firefighters. Others took the defeat more gracefully as they paid off losing bets to Republicans. In Alabama a girl had to eat the front page of the pro-Eisenhower *Montgomery Advisor,* but not before burning it and dunking it in her coffee. A Lowell, Massachusetts, Democrat allowed a victorious friend to pelt him with custard pies. Perhaps the taste of defeat was not so bad, after all.[53]

Democratic politicos had a more bitter taste in their mouths. Senator Guy Gillette (IA) confided to a colleague that he had expected to lose the White House and the House, but not the Senate, and he lamented the second consecutive loss of the Democrats' majority leader there. This time, Ernest McFarland (AZ) bit the dust, losing to Republican Barry Goldwater. McFarland's defeat was particularly surprising, given that he was a two-term incumbent defending his seat in an overwhelmingly Democratic state. Goldwater's strategy was to attract members of the mine workers' union by blaming recent mine closures on the New Dealers' support for tariff reductions. Goldwater also argued that entitlement programs from the New Deal legacy were cutting into workers' paychecks. Since McFarland, as majority leader, was linked inextricably to Truman's policies, Goldwater kept the incumbent on the defensive while portraying himself as a Jeffersonian advocate of limited government. Like Eisenhower, Goldwater won narrowly. Senator Clinton Anderson consoled his fallen colleague, "My guess is that every person who was cussing President Truman voted against you."[54]

Senator McCarthy ultimately campaigned for Republican incumbents in thirteen states in 1952. Some historians argue that McCarthy was instrumental in the unseating of a personal nemesis, Senator William Benton (D-CT)—a feat the GOP had been unable to accomplish in a special election two years earlier. Another view is that Eisenhower had a greater effect on Benton's defeat than McCarthy did, due to the large number of internationalist liberal Republicans in the Connecticut electorate. In the end, Benton garnered more votes than Stevenson in a losing effort, showing the limited effects of red-baiting in a race McCarthy treated as his second-highest priority (after his own reelection, of course). This trend held true in every state where McCarthy specifically targeted Democratic senatorial candidates. Moreover, in his own reelection bid, McCarthy ran seven points behind Eisenhower in Wisconsin and lagged behind all other candidates for statewide office. In the end, McCarthy wielded little influence in the 1952 campaign, and the issue of communism was not as important as the Republicans initially expected.[55]

Eisenhower's victory clearly contributed to at least two additional defeats of Democratic incumbents in the Senate. The Michigan race pitted incumbent Blair Moody against GOP challenger Charles E. Potter. Moody, appointed to fill the vacancy caused by the death of Senator Vandenberg, had been in office only a little over a year. Potter, who served on the House Un-American Activities Committee, accused Moody of "appeasement of communism, which is an anti-God philosophy and, hence, immoral." Ike, Potter, and every Republican candidate for statewide office won big in Michigan. The more surprising defeat of Joseph O'Mahoney in Wyoming was a dramatic example of the Eisenhower effect. O'Mahoney had served in the Senate since 1933, yet he lost to Republican Frank Barrett, the reigning governor. The large uptick in voter turnout caused by Ike's candidacy did O'Mahoney in, as most of the "new" voters in 1952 cast their ballots for Barrett to express their desire for change. The Republican message that Eisenhower needed a GOP-controlled Senate apparently resonated with Wyoming voters. Tellingly, O'Mahoney's swift return to the Senate in 1954 was another indicator of the Eisenhower coattail effect in Wyoming.[56]

As discussed earlier, Ike's decision to reach out to the Taft wing of the GOP and the party's determination to use McCarthyism as a campaign weapon helped unify the Republicans. However, in several Senate races, these strategies were insufficient to save right-wing GOP incumbents. In Missouri Eisenhower endorsed and campaigned for incumbent James P. Kem, even though Kem had opposed troops for NATO during the general's tenure as the organization's military head. Ike's help was not enough, and Kem lost to Stuart Symington, who had left the Truman administration to run for Kem's seat. Another GOP isolationist, Zales Ecton, lost in the Montana contest. Ecton's opponent was Mike Mansfield, who had a solid track record of service in the House of Representatives. Ecton played the anticommunism card, producing articles from the communist publication the *Daily Worker* that spoke favorably of Mansfield. Even though McCarthy and Taft both campaigned in the state on Ecton's behalf, neither their efforts nor Eisenhower's nineteen-point margin of victory in Montana were enough to stop Mansfield from capturing the seat. In Washington State, Republican incumbent Harry Cain lost to Henry "Scoop" Jackson, a three-term Democratic member of the House. Like Kem and Ecton, Cain had been in the Senate for only one term and was closely associated with the Old Guard wing of the party, as evidenced by the support of McCarthy and Taft. Senator Cain was one of the more strident isolationists in the party, sharply criticizing the Korean War. Like Mansfield, Jackson had built a solid reputation as a competent public servant in the House. Even though Eisenhower won the Washington popular vote by nearly a ten-point margin, and Republicans won most of the statewide offices, Jackson defeated Cain by the largest margin of any race in the state.[57]

Eisenhower's efforts to unify his party alienated a key internationalist Republican in the Senate, affecting the outcome of the 1952 elections—sort of. Just weeks before the election, Senator Wayne Morse (OR) announced that he was "leaving" the Republican Party. Morse was disturbed by Ike's rapprochement with Taft and his appearance at campaign stops with McCarthy, leading the Oregonian to question Eisenhower's ethics. Morse, who was not up for reelection in 1952, felt that liberalism was being driven from a party "dominated by reactionaries running a captive general for the Presidency." As a statement of protest, when the Eighty-Third Congress opened for business in January 1953, Morse brought his own metal chair and positioned it between the two aisles in the Senate chamber. Had Morse truly decided to become an independent, the Senate would have been deadlocked between the two major parties. However, Morse generally voted with the Republicans, probably to avoid giving Vice President Nixon the tie-breaking vote. Soon afterward, Morse's perception that Eisenhower was compromising liberal principles drove the Oregonian from the GOP completely. In 1956 Morse was reelected to the Senate—as a Democrat.[58]

Overall, Eisenhower had short coattails in the 1952 congressional elections. The GOP gained twenty-two seats in the House, leaving them with a meager eight-vote majority. The Republicans picked up only one seat in the Senate, but it was enough to give them a single-seat majority (counting Morse). Moreover, eighteen of the twenty-three Democrats running for the Senate performed better in their states than Stevenson did against Ike, another indication that most of the crossover vote went to Eisenhower but not to Republicans in general. Nevertheless, for the first time since the Hoover administration, the GOP had control of the White House and both houses of Congress.

Analysis of the issues affecting the election results yielded some surprises. One pollster found that only 3 percent of voters brought up negative views about the Truman administration's "softness on communism" or communist infiltration as factors in their voting decisions. As noted earlier, Senators Kem, Ecton, and Cain—all staunch McCarthy allies—lost their seats to Democrats. Another McCarthy supporter, William Jenner (IN), nearly met the same fate and just managed to eke out enough votes to win reelection. McCarthyism thus mattered little in the election. Southern voting produced some interesting patterns. Although Stevenson won back the four southern states the Democrats had lost to the Dixiecrats in 1948, the popular vote throughout the region told a more complete story. In the eleven states of the former Confederacy, Stevenson collected 51 percent of the vote, compared with Truman's 53 percent and Dixiecrat Strom Thurmond's 17 percent in 1948. Thus, even without a Dixiecrat Party to siphon away white Democratic votes, the governor did not do as well as the president had four years earlier. Among blacks throughout the nation, Stevenson matched Truman's results in 1948. Why, then, did a large chunk of the white South vote for Eisenhower? According to pollster Louis Harris, southern whites who voted for Eisenhower did so out of concern about economic issues, the Korean War, and the "mess in Washington," rather than Stevenson's views on civil rights. One regional economic concern was tidelands oil, the main factor in Texas going Republican, and probably a contributing factor in California as well. The tidelands matter was also a psychological issue symbolizing the president's perceived attack on states' rights.[59]

Ultimately, just about everyone agreed that the Korean War was most prominent in voters' minds. Did Truman deliver victory to Eisenhower by suspending the peace talks in October rather than compromising with the communists on the POW repatriation issue and possibly ending the war before Election Day? The answer is no. The Pentagon and the American public backed the president's stand, and the perception of capitulating to the enemy would have made things even tougher on Stevenson. Nevertheless, as political scientists have noted, "Foreign policy became a dynamic component of total public motivation in 1952 in a manner which contrasted sharply with the 'bipartisan' era of 1948." The war accounted for the big increase in voter turnout in 1952 because, unlike in 1948, debates on foreign affairs were no longer unmentionable. Secretary of the Interior Oscar Chapman, a key Truman political operative, said the Democrats lost the election due to "Korea, more than anything else." Virtually all the media agreed with him, and so did Stevenson. Political analysts noted that the ability to handle the war was the most frequently mentioned positive quality voters saw in Eisenhower. Scholars James MacGregor Burns and Philip Hastings summed up the election well, noting parallels with Franklin Roosevelt's popularity in the 1930s. Just as FDR represented economic stability, Eisenhower "served as a symbol of national security" during the uncertainty of the Korean War.[60]

Conclusion

Harry Truman faced many challenges from both sides of the aisle in Congress as he led the nation through the fluctuations and frustrations of the Korean War. Truman's party gave him poor advice concerning congressional involvement in the decision to take the nation to war. Moreover, a number of individuals allowed their personal dislike of Secretary of State Dean Acheson to poison their support for the administration whenever U.S. fortunes in the war soured. The partisan rancor over war policy therefore cannot be blamed solely on the Republicans. For his part, the president did not devote adequate attention to congressional relations early in his term and was slow to react to charges of corruption within his administration, weakening his party politically. Thus, Truman and the congressional Democrats failed each other in important ways during the war.

The struggles between the Democrats and their president in the early 1950s underscore the importance of this relationship. Although the president of the modern era clearly functions as the party's leader, the party needs to guide the chief executive at times. A recent example illustrates this dynamic. In 2003 President George W. Bush led a preemptive strike into Iraq, triggering an intervention that continued beyond his presidency. At the time, Bush's Republican Party controlled both houses of Congress. To his credit, unlike Truman, Bush secured a congressional resolution before going to war. However, the Republican congressional leadership forgot the lessons of Vietnam and failed to require Bush to explain exactly how regime change would be implemented, resulting in a long and increasingly unpopular war. The lesson, then, from Truman and the Democrats is that a president and his or her party in Congress must act as a critical check and balance against each other.

The other major point of this study is that the influence of Joseph McCarthy on the American political scene has been overrated. At first glance, this may seem to be a foolhardy suggestion. McCarthy's quest to root out communist subversion led to wholesale purges of Far Eastern experts from the State Department, robbing it of valuable expertise. Hundreds in the entertainment industry were blacklisted for their alleged connections to the Communist Party. When the Republican victory in 1952 gave McCarthy the chairmanship of the Permanent Subcommittee on Investigations, he ruined the reputations of dozens of people by hauling them before his panel and accusing them of communist insurgency, based on flimsy evidence. Dissent earned severe punishment during this era. For example, John W. Powell, editor of the *China Monthly Review,* received a $130,000 fine and 260 years in prison for criticizing the U.S. intervention in Korea. However, McCarthy demonstrated only a limited ability to ruin his fellow lawmakers. With the exception of the defeat of Millard Tydings, he made only a marginal difference in the 1950 and 1952 elections. The terror McCarthy inspired in his colleagues was largely unfounded, for the State Department was the senator's primary target during the war. Even there, he failed to oust his chief scapegoat, Dean Acheson. Furthermore, as the war stalemated, a number of legislators advanced proposals to end the fighting in Korea short of unconditional surrender of the enemy. None were branded as being soft on communism, nor did they express any fears about McCarthyite attacks for their efforts to end the war.[1]

Another theme involves partisanship. Truman and Acheson's definition of a bipartisan foreign policy was substantially different from that of the Republicans. To the president, bipartisanship simply meant communicating his intentions to GOP leaders on Capitol Hill before publicizing his policies to the nation. To him, nonpartisanship meant that he should take the Republicans into his confidence, and they should trust his judgment and refrain from publicly criticizing his policies. The GOP believed it should be consulted, not just informed. Truman largely manipulated the idea of bipartisanship for political advantage. Despite all his talk about conducting a bipartisan foreign policy, the president sought little input from Republicans once Senator Vandenberg fell ill with cancer. Ironically, had he taken the advice of John Foster Dulles early in the war, he could have mitigated the GOP explosion over the firing of MacArthur. For the most part, the clash between the administration and Congress was not an institutional struggle between the executive and legislative branches of government. It was personal and political. Secretary Acheson regarded the GOP opposition as Neanderthals; they detested his arrogance and his pin-striped suits. Republicans and conservative Democrats loathed Truman's domestic liberalism and attempted to use the war to rid the country of the vestiges of the New Deal. Despite these battles, the commander in chief managed to conduct the war as he chose.

Although Truman and the Republicans defined bipartisanship differently, the president practiced what he preached when it came to the importance of trust. The following anecdote is illustrative. After Truman's December 1950 meeting with a bipartisan group of congressmen to discuss the declaration of a national emergency, a White House usher brought presidential aide Charles Murphy a memo that had been found under the table, apparently having been dropped accidentally. In this note, the Senate Minority Policy Committee advised GOP attendees Robert Taft and Kenneth Wherry that if the president asked for a pledge of bipartisan support for his continuing conduct of the war, they should resist "at all costs." The reason: the war could turn bad by the Easter recess, and Republicans "might wish to accuse Truman of treason and should be free to do so." Murphy's lieutenants "fell upon it with whoops of joy," crying, "get it copied . . . show it to the President . . . leak it to the press." Murphy, however, simply smiled, placed the memo in an envelope, and had it hand-delivered to Senator Taft. In the Truman administration, the maxim "What's said in the White House stays in the White House" applied even to his bitterest enemies.[2]

The Korean War marked the end of a brief period of bipartisanship in foreign policy begun during World War II. One lesson of Korea is that it is not feasible for Congress to share management of international affairs with the executive branch. Therefore, the only realistic way to ensure bipartisan input into foreign policy is to appoint members of the opposing party to significant positions in the administration. Even though Truman did not use Dulles as well as he could have, his appointment of the Republican was a good move. The lack of bipartisanship in Congress is even more apparent today than it was in the 1950s. The 2014 gridlock over immigration reform highlights how difficult it is for the legislature to come together on big policy issues.

Truman nevertheless helped create one bipartisan tradition that continues today. Perhaps recalling his own lack of knowledge of the international situation when FDR died, the president took pains to ensure that Eisenhower would have few surprises when he became commander in chief. Immediately after the election, Truman offered to work with Ike's appointees and to let them observe the preparation of a budget and the affairs of the major departments. Eisenhower dispatched his future budget director, Joseph M. Dodge, along with Senator Henry Cabot Lodge, destined to be the new ambassador to the UN, to work with the outgoing administration. Truman also made his top aide, John Steelman, available to consult with Sherman Adams, who would become Ike's chief of staff. Thus the first transition team was born.[3]

In conclusion, the Truman administration traversed a host of problems as it managed the Korean intervention. The Republican opposition generated some of the challenges, and the lack of Democratic unity created others. The administration's indecision regarding war objectives before finally settling on a new concept—limited war—added to the headaches. Even though the war drove Truman's approval rating to such depths that it ruined his chances for reelection in 1952, Eisenhower validated his predecessor's stance by ending the conflict on the terms Truman had established. Nevertheless, as someone in the Truman White House wrote, "Korea is one place where we have had to learn hard."[4]

Acknowledgments

I have many people and organizations to thank for their help with this project. The Harry S. Truman Library Foundation awarded me a generous grant in 2005–2006 that enabled me to get started on this work. Randy Sowell was immensely helpful with my research at the Truman Library, both while I was there and from afar, as he unfailingly found the materials I needed. I also owe a word of thanks to the College of Liberal Arts and the Glasscock Humanities Center and Texas A&M University, which provided funding for my research at the Library of Congress, Princeton University, and Syracuse University.

This book would not have been possible without the encouragement and support of a number of mentors and colleagues who encouraged a forty-something graduate student to make the transition from laboratory manager to historian. Dr. Leslie Hunter at Texas A&M University–Kingsville was the first person to participate in that process, to whom I will be forever grateful. I owe a huge debt of gratitude to the Department of History at Texas A&M University, which gave me the opportunity to pursue a doctoral degree and taught me what research was all about. I must also thank my grad school colleagues, particularly Dr. Phil Smith and Dr. Derek Mallett, for putting up with me as I bounced ideas off them in the early stages of this process. Dr. Terry H. Anderson has been a constant source of advice and encouragement, going well beyond the call of duty as my dissertation adviser. Seven years after my graduation, he has been kind enough to stay in touch with me, giving me valuable pointers and motivating me to stay the course while writing this book.

Most important, I must thank my family. My wife, Colleen, and my younger children, Elizabeth and Alex, allowed me to uproot them so that I could pursue my dream of making a contribution to the history profession. My older children, T. J. and Candice, have been blessings and inspirations to me in countless ways. To all of you, my heartfelt thanks.

Appendix A

Excerpts from the United Nations Charter

Article 39

The Security Council shall determine the existence of any threat to the peace, breach of the peace, or act of aggression and shall make recommendations, or decide what measures shall be taken in accordance with Articles 41 and 42, to maintain or restore international peace and security.

Article 40

In order to prevent an aggravation of the situation, the Security Council may, before making the recommendations or deciding upon the measures provided for in Article 39, call upon the parties concerned to comply with such provisional measures as it deems necessary or desirable. Such provisional measures shall be without prejudice to the rights, claims, or position of the parties concerned. The Security Council shall duly take account of failure to comply with such provisional measures.

Article 41

The Security Council may decide what measures not involving the use of armed force are to be employed to give effect to its decisions, and it may call upon the Members of the United Nations to apply such measures. These may include complete or partial interruption of economic relations and of rail, sea, air, postal, telegraphic, radio, and other means of communication, and the severance of diplomatic relations.

Article 42

Should the Security Council consider that measures provided for in Article 41 would be inadequate or have proved to be inadequate, it may take such action by air, sea, or land forces as may be necessary to maintain or restore international peace and security. Such action may include demonstrations, blockade, and other operations by air, sea, or land forces of Members of the United Nations.

Article 43

All Members of the United Nations, in order to contribute to the maintenance of international peace and security, undertake to make available to the Security Council, on its call and in accordance with a special agreement or agreements, armed forces, assistance, and facilities, including rights of passage, necessary for the purpose of maintaining international peace and security.

Such agreement or agreements shall govern the numbers and types of forces, their degree of readiness and general location, and the nature of the facilities and assistance to be provided.

The agreement or agreements shall be negotiated as soon as possible on the initiative of the Security Council. They shall be concluded between the Security Council and Members or between the Security Council and groups of Members and shall be subject to ratification by the signatory states in accordance with their respective constitutional processes.

Appendix B

United Nations Participation Act of 1945

Section 6

The President is authorized to negotiate a special agreement or agreements with the Security Council which shall be subject to the approval of the Congress by appropriate Act or joint resolution providing for the numbers and types of armed forces, their degree of readiness and general location, and the nature of facilities and assistance, including rights of passage, to be made available to the Security Council on its call for the purpose of maintaining international peace and security in accordance with article 43 of said Charter. The President shall not be deemed to require the authorization of the Congress to make available to the Security Council on its call in order to take action under article 42 of said Charter and pursuant to such special agreement or agreements the armed forces, facilities, or assistance provided for therein: Provided, That nothing herein contained shall be construed as an authorization to the President by the Congress to make available to the Security Council for such purpose armed forces, facilities, or assistance in addition to the forces, facilities, and assistance provided for in such special agreement or agreements.

Notes

Abbreviations

CR	*Congressional Record*
FRUS	*Foreign Relations of the United States*
HSTL	Harry S. Truman Library, Independence, MO
MDLOC	Manuscript Division, Library of Congress, Washington, DC
NYT	*New York Times*
PP	*Public Papers of Presidents of the United States: Harry S. Truman 1945–1953,* http://www.trumanlibrary.org/publicpapers/
PPF	President's Personal File
PSF	President's Secretary's File
SMOF	Staff Member and Office Files
WHCF	White House Central File

Preface

1. *Public Papers of Presidents of the United States: Harry S. Truman, 1950* (Washington, DC: U.S. Government Printing Office, 1965), 513; Robert H. Ferrell, *Harry S. Truman: A Life* (Columbia: University of Missouri Press, 1994), 324.

2. MacArthur quoted in David McCullough, *Truman* (New York: Simon & Schuster, 1992), 797; Halsey quoted in Burton Ira Kaufman, *The Korean War: Challenges in Crisis, Credibility and Command,* 2nd ed. (New York: McGraw-Hill, 1997), 54.

3. "Resolution 376 (V), Adopted by the United Nations General Assembly, October 7, 1950," in *FRUS, 1950,* vol. 7, *Korea* (Washington, DC: U.S. Government Printing Office, 1976), 904 (emphasis added); Connally quoted in Alfred Steinberg, *Sam Rayburn: A Biography* (New York: Hawthorn Books, 1975), 263; David Rees, *Korea: The Limited War* (New York: St. Martin's Press, 1964), 129; Gary R. Hess, *Presidential Decisions for War: Korea, Vietnam, and the Persian Gulf* (Baltimore: Johns Hopkins University Press, 2001), 63; McCullough, *Truman,* 818; Brian Catchpole, *The Korean War, 1950–53* (New York: Carroll & Graf, 2000), 159–60; MacArthur quoted in Office of the Chief of Military History, U.S. Army, "The Korean War, 1950–1953," in *American Military History,* 560, http://www.army.mil/cmh-pg/books/AMH/AMH-25.htm (accessed November 2, 2005).

4. Eric Goldman, *The Crucial Decade and After: America, 1945–1960* (New York: Vintage Books, 1962), 246–47; Office of the Chief of Military History, "The Korean War, 1950–1953," 570.

5. For an example of the contemporary view of Korea as the "Forgotten War," see Matthew B. Ridgway, *The Korean War* (New York: Doubleday, 1961), 103.

6. William S. White, "Congress Cautious in Korean Comment," *NYT,* July 28, 1953, 1; Hanson W. Baldwin, "Not Victory, Not Defeat: But Another War, Marked by Shining Deeds as Well as Misery, Passes into History," *NYT,* July 28, 1953, 6.

Introduction

1. Truman quoted in Kari A. Frederickson, *The Dixiecrat Revolt and the End of the Solid South, 1932–1968* (Chapel Hill: University of North Carolina Press, 2001), 52; Executive Order 9981, "Desegregation of the Armed Forces," http://www .trumanlibrary.org/whistlestop/study_collections/desegregation/large/index.php#1948.

2. Poll numbers from Alonzo L. Hamby, *Man of the People: A Life of Harry S. Truman* (New York: Oxford University Press, 1995), 435; woman quoted in Frederickson, *Dixiecrat Revolt,* 77; Truman quoted in Robert H. Ferrell, ed., *Truman in the White House: The Diary of Eben A. Ayers* (Columbia: University of Missouri Press, 1991), 283.

3. Sean J. Savage, *Truman and the Democratic Party* (Lexington: University Press of Kentucky, 1997), 67–68; Clinton P. Anderson with Milton Viorst, *Outsider in the Senate: Senator Clinton Anderson's Memoirs* (New York: World Publishing, 1970), 96; Tom Connally to George H. Crank, August 17, 1948, box 104, Thomas Connally Papers, MDLOC. Ferrell faults Truman for insufficient punishment of the Dixiecrats in *Harry S. Truman,* 291. The top Democrats in Congress at the time, House Speaker Sam Rayburn (TX) and Senate majority leader Scott Lucas (IL), were staunch Truman allies and probably would have ousted the Dixiecrats from leadership positions had the president urged them to do so.

4. "Annual Message to Congress on the State of the Union, January 5, 1949," *PP,* http://www.trumanlibrary.org/publicpapers/index.php?pid=1013&st=fair+deal &st1= (accessed July 16, 2010). For southern views of the Brannan Plan, see Savage, *Truman and the Democratic Party,* 158, and Hamby, *Man of the People,* 496. Eastland quoted in Ferrell, *Harry S. Truman,* 297.

5. Savage, *Truman and the Democratic Party,* 24; George M. Elsey, memorandum for file, January 17, 1950, Ken Hechler folder, George Elsey Papers, HSTL; James E. Webb to Truman, memorandum for the president, February 15,1950, PSF: Korean War file, General Data folder, Harry S. Truman Papers, HSTL.

6. Charles S. Murphy to Truman, January 16, 1950, Truman—memos to and from the president, 1947–53, folder 5 of 5, Charles S. Murphy Papers, HSTL; John Fisher, "Knock Out New Deal Power to Railroad Bills," *Chicago Tribune,* January 4, 1951, 3.

7. Memo from Truman to Senator Elbert D. Thomas, June 14, 1950, PSF

Subject File 124: Congress—Miscellaneous, Truman Papers; "President's Conference with ADA Leaders—5/21/51," David D. Lloyd folder, Murphy Papers. Winthrop Griffith, *Humphrey: A Candid Biography* (New York: Morrow Publishing, 1964), 188, discusses one-party rule in the South.

8. "Memorandum of Conversation with President and Judge Kee," May 4, 1950, Memoranda of Conversation file, May–June 1950 folder, Dean Acheson Papers, HSTL.

9. Ken Hechler, *Working with Truman* (Columbia: University of Missouri Press, 1982), 152–55, 162, 174; Savage, *Truman and the Democratic Party*, 59.

10. For Benton's and Acheson's views, see "Confidential," March 16, 1951, Memoranda of Conversations file, 1949–1953, March 1951 folder, Acheson Papers; for Davies's complaints, see memorandum, January 5, 1951, Kenneth W. Hechler folder, Murphy Papers.

11. Truman did not designate a chief of staff per se. He gave his staffers generic titles such as assistant to the president or special assistant to the president, and their duties often overlapped. John R. Steelman, Truman's de facto chief of staff, carried the title *the* assistant to the president. For Truman's management style, see Francis H. Heller, ed., *The Truman White House: The Administration of the Presidency 1945–1953* (Lawrence: Regents Press of Kansas, 1980), 229–30. For Truman's meetings with small groups, see Charles Murphy to Truman, May 19, 1951, PSF: General File, Meetings: White House, Special folder, Truman Papers, and "Suggested Items for Discussion with the Big Four, Monday, May 21, 1951," Memos—Big 4 Meetings folder, Murphy Papers.

12. For White House concerns about Byrnes, see Frederickson, *Dixiecrat Revolt*, 197, 204; Truman quoted in *PP*, http://www.trumanlibrary.org/publicpapers/index.php?pid=585&st=byrnes&st1= (accessed May 16, 2013); Charles Murphy to Truman, January 25, 1950, Truman—memos to and from the president, 1947–53, folder 5 of 5, Murphy Papers; Hechler, *Working with Truman*, 133–34, 138–39, 144.

13. Savage, *Truman and the Democratic Party*, 171–75. Pepper's move toward Truman's hard line against communism is discussed in Thomas G. Paterson, "The Dissent of Senator Claude Pepper," in *Cold War Critics: Alternatives to American Foreign Policy in the Truman Years*, ed. Thomas G. Paterson (Chicago: Quadrangle Books, 1971), 115–17, 126, 131–33. Pepper's motivations were the Soviet invasion of Czechoslovakia, the communist victory in the Chinese civil war, and the Korean War. Truman quoted in Savage, *Truman and the Democratic Party*, 172.

14. Savage, *Truman and the Democratic Party*, 175–80; Boddy quoted in ibid., 176; attacks on Douglas described in memo from Glenn M. Anderson, chairman of the California Democratic Committee, to Clinton P. Anderson, November 28, 1950, box 1052, Clinton Anderson Papers, MDLOC; Monaghan quoted in Savage, *Truman and the Democratic Party*, 178.

15. Clinton Anderson to William Boyle, March 15, 1950; Frank Keenan and James H. Hawley to Anderson, March 1, 1950; telegram from Gilbert Larsen to Senator Clinton P. Anderson, September 9, 1950, all in box 1052, Anderson Papers.

16. Cecil V. Crabb Jr., *Bipartisan Foreign Policy: Myth or Reality?* (Evanston, IL: Row, Peterson, 1957), 33, 46–47; Tom Connally, *My Name Is Tom Connally* (New York: Thomas Y. Crowell, 1954), 265.

17. Crabb, *Bipartisan Foreign Policy,* 56–60; James Reston, "Vandenberg Acts to Restore Bipartisan Policy," *NYT,* March 26, 1950, 141; Robert J. Donovan, *Tumultuous Years: The Presidency of Harry Truman, 1949–1953* (New York: W. W. Norton, 1982), 27. According to Acheson, there were "endless consultations" with Republicans on Far East policy, but they wanted to deny this because things did not turn out so well in Asia. Dean Acheson *Present at the Creation: My Years in the State Department* (New York: New American Library, 1969), 96.

18. Harry S. Truman, *Memoirs,* vol. 2, *Years of Trial and Hope* (Garden City, NY: Doubleday, 1956), 430–31; Acheson, *Present at the Creation,* 95–97; Thomas G. Paterson, "Presidential Foreign Policy, Public Opinion and Congress: The Truman Years," *Diplomatic History* 3, no. 1 (1979): 17.

19. See, for example, Vandenberg to Truman, March 29, 1950, and Truman to Vandenberg, March 31, 1950, PSF: General File, V folder, Truman Papers; "Substance of Conversation with Senator Vandenberg," January 21, 1951, Memoranda of Conversations file, January 1950 folder, Acheson Papers; Truman, *Memoirs,* 2:103. Connally quoted in Lawrence John Letellier, "Departure of a Statesman: Senator Tom Connally" (master's thesis, University of Maryland, 1993), 11. For descriptions of Connally, see McCullough, *Truman,* 529–30; David S. McLellan, *Dean Acheson: The State Department Years* (New York: Dodd, Mead, 1976), 236; Donald A. Ritchie, "Oral History Interview with Francis O. Wilcox, February 10, 1984," 78–81, http://trumanlibrary.org/oralhist/wilcox2.htm#74 (accessed April 6, 2007); Ferrell, *Truman in the White House,* 295–96; Arthur H. Vandenberg Jr. and Joe Alex Morris, eds., *The Private Papers of Senator Vandenberg* (Boston: Houghton Mifflin, 1952), 505–6.

20. David R. Kepley, *The Collapse of the Middle Way: Senate Republicans and the Bipartisan Foreign Policy, 1948–52* (Westport, CT: Greenwood Press, 1988), 53–74; Ritchie, "Oral History Interview with Francis O. Wilcox," 81–83.

21. The Open Door policy refers to the American assertion that trade with China should be available to all nations, especially the United States, initiated by Secretary of State John Hay in 1899. Roots of the China Bloc are discussed in Foster Rhea Dulles, *American Policy toward Communist China, 1949–1969* (New York: Thomas Crowell, 1972), 71–72. Senate China Bloc members are discussed in Kepley, *Collapse of the Middle Way,* 38–39. For the backgrounds and beliefs of Judd and Vorys, see Dulles, *American Policy,* 74, and Nancy Bernkopf Tucker, *Patterns in the Dust: Chinese-American Relations and the Recognition Controversy, 1949–1950* (New York: Columbia University Press, 1983), 89–90.

22. "Connally Pledges New European Aid," *NYT,* January 3, 1949, 3; "Democrats Get 8–5 Rule of Key Senate Groups," *Chicago Daily Tribune,* January 5, 1949, 7.

23. Donovan, *Tumultuous Years,* 78–83; Melvyn Leffler, *A Preponderance of Power: National Security, the Truman Administration, and the Cold War* (Stanford, CA: Stanford University Press, 1992), 325–27.

24. Lislie Rose, *The Cold War Comes to Main Street: America in 1950* (Lawrence: University Press of Kansas, 1999), 169, 172; "NSC 48/2, a Report to the President by the National Security Council, December 30, 1949," in *FRUS, 1949*, vol. 7, pt. 2, *The Far East and Australasia* (Washington, DC: U.S. Government Printing Office, 1976), 1215–20; Arnold A. Offner, *Another Such Victory: President Truman and the Cold War, 1945–1953* (Stanford, CA: Stanford University Press, 2002), 365–67; Hamby, *Man of the People*, 528. For George's background, see Kepley, *Collapse of the Middle Way*, 35, 108; George's view of NSC-68 is discussed in Raymond P. Ojserkis, *Beginnings of the Cold War Arms Race: The Truman Administration and the U.S. Arms Build-up* (Westport, CT: Praeger Publishing, 2003), 78. Truman had instituted a limited draft in 1948.

25. John W. Spanier, *The Truman-MacArthur Controversy* (New York: W. W. Norton, 1965), 155; Hamby, *Man of the People*, 511; Acheson, *Present at the Creation*, 101.

26. William S. White, "Senate Will Query Military Leaders on Formosa Policy," *NYT*, January 14, 1950, 1.

27. For the Truman Doctrine, see "Special Message to the Congress on Greece and Turkey," March 12, 1947, in *Public Papers of Presidents of the United States: Harry S. Truman, 1945–1953* (Washington, DC: U.S. Government Printing Office, 1966); for Acheson's Press Club speech, see Walter H. Waggoner, "Four Areas Listed," *NYT*, January 13, 1950, 1; William S. White, "Democrats Unite in Senate on China," *NYT*, January 18, 1950, 3.

28. Robert L. Beisner, *Dean Acheson: A Life in the Cold War* (New York: Oxford University Press, 2006), 329–30. The administration originally intended to end aid to Jiang Jieshi in February 1950.

29. "Acheson Renews Defense of Hiss," *NYT*, January 26, 1950, 14; Nixon, Arends, and Davis quoted in "I Do Not Intend to Turn My Back," *Time*, February 6, 1950, 12; Eastland quoted in "Acheson under Fire in Senate and House," *NYT*, February 1, 1950, 20. Hiss continued to deny that he was a Soviet spy until his death, and his guilt is still debated. In the mid-1990s the release of the VENONA files, a secret program of the U.S. Army Signal Intelligence Service to decode Soviet diplomatic messages, appeared to implicate Hiss. See, for example, G. Edward White, *Alger Hiss's Looking-Glass Wars: The Covert Life of a Soviet Spy* (New York: Oxford University Press, 2004). For a discussion of the ongoing controversy, see Eduard Mark, "In Re Alger Hiss," *Journal of Cold War Studies* 11, no. 3 (2009): 26–67.

30. See David Oshinsky, *A Conspiracy So Immense: The World of Joe McCarthy* (New York: Free Press, 1983), 106.

31. Allan Nevins, *Herbert H. Lehman and His Era* (New York: Charles Scribner's Sons, 1963), 336.

32. "Tydings Promises 'Fair' Jobholder Probe," *Washington Post*, February 26, 1950, M4; Hamby, *Man of the People*, 530–31; Oshinsky, *Conspiracy So Immense*, 119–20.

33. For a description of the proceedings, see Oshinsky, *Conspiracy So Immense*,

120; for discussions between Tydings and the State Department, see L. D. Battle, memoranda to file, April 3 and 17, 1950, Memoranda of Conversations file, April 1950 folder, Acheson Papers.

34. Bridges quoted in "G.O.P. Bloc Drives to Oust Acheson," *Dallas Morning News,* March 28, 1950, 1; Benton, Young, and Magnuson quoted in Robert C. Albright, "Democrats about Ready to Rake in GOP's," *Washington Post,* March 26, 1950, B3; William S. White, "President Implies It Is Not Possible to Libel McCarthy," *NYT,* April 14, 1950, 1; William S. White, "Political Stake Is High in M'Carthy Inquiry," *NYT,* April 16, 1950, E3.

35. Memorandum from Charles Murphy to Truman, March 27, 1950, Memos—Big Four Meetings folder, Murphy Papers; Joseph A. Loftus, "A.D.A. Is 'Revolted' by Acheson Attack," *NYT,* April 4, 1950, 7.

36. McLellan, *Dean Acheson,* 235; "The President's News Conference at Key West," March 30, 1950, *PP,* http://www.trumanlibrary.org/publicpapers/index.php?pid=703&st=bipartisan&st1= (accessed March 31, 2007).

37. "Statement by the President on the Importance of Maintaining a Bipartisan Foreign Policy," April 18, 1950, *PP,* http://www.trumanlibrary.org/publicpapers/index.php?pid=712&st=bridges&st1= (accessed March 31, 2007); Kepley, *Collapse of the Middle Way,* 82; Connally quoted in Drew Pearson, "Mixed Signals Scuttle GOP Parley," *Washington Post,* April 29, 1950, B13; Hamby, *Man of the People,* 524.

38. "Memorandum of Conversation—The President, Secretary Acheson, and Senator Tom Connally," April 27, 1950, Memoranda of Conversations file, April 1950 folder, Acheson Papers.

39. Dean Acheson, "Visit of Congressman Brooks Hays," April 4, 1950, and L. D. Battle, "Memorandum of Conversation (with Governor Dewey)," April 10, 1950, Memoranda of Conversations file, April 1950 folder, Acheson Papers; Anthony Leviero, "Truman Applauds Hoover on Speech," *NYT,* April 29, 1950, 5.

40. Truman quoted in Donovan, *Tumultuous Years,* 168; "Memorandum of Conversation, Dean Acheson and Herbert Lehman," April 5, 1950, and "Memorandum of Conversation, Acheson and John Foster Dulles," April 6, 1950, Memoranda of Conversations file, April 1950 folder, Acheson Papers; James Reston, "Dulles Named U.S. Adviser to Renew Bipartisan Policy," *NYT,* April 7, 1950, 1.

41. "President Praises Plan by Connally," *NYT,* April 28, 1950, 22; "Senate Foreign Relations Committee—Suggested Subcommittees for Consultative Purposes," April 10, 1950, box 586, Theodore F. Green Papers, MDLOC; H. Smith Horace, "Reorganization—Senate Style," *American Foreign Service Journal,* June 1950, 18–19, 50–52; Jerry N. Hess, "Oral History Interview with Jack K. McFall," June 24, 1970, 68–71, http://www.trumanlibrary.org/oralhist/mcfallj.htm (accessed April 4, 2007). According to McFall, the House later adopted a similar system but named its subcommittees differently. This apparently did not occur until sometime after 1950, based on a check of the *New York Times.* Donald A. Ritchie, "Oral History Interview with Francis O. Wilcox," March 21, 1984, 158, http://www.trumanlibrary.org/oralhist/wilcox3.htm#99 (accessed April 4, 2007).

42. Telegram from H. A. Smith to Tom Connally, April 17, 1950, box 101, H. Alexander Smith Papers, Seeley G. Mudd Manuscript Library, Princeton University (all citations to this source used by permission of Princeton University); Kepley, *Collapse of the Middle Way,* 94–95; Vandenberg and Morris, *Private Papers of Senator Vandenberg,* 543.

43. "Supplementary Days: More Washington Press Comment," n.d., box 1107, Green Papers; this source contains newspaper opinion from March 16 to April 1, 1950. Caroline H. Keith, *For Hell and a Brown Mule: The Biography of Millard E. Tydings* (New York: Madison Books, 1991), 75, also notes press coverage of the hearings. For the opinion poll, see Glenn Paige, *The Korean Decision: June 24–30, 1950* (New York: Free Press, 1968), 46; Truman quoted in Ferrell, *Truman in the White House,* 348–50; Harvey Klehr and Ronald Radosh, *The Amerasia Spy Case: Prelude to McCarthyism* (Chapel Hill: University of North Carolina Press, 1996), 196–97; journalist quoted in Constantine Brown, "This Changing World," *Washington Star,* July 19, 1950, A7.

44. Senators quoted in Albert Friendly, "Senate Bloc Seeks to Tag McCarthy as Liar on Floor," *Washington Post,* May 4, 1950, 1; Acheson to H. H. Fisher, May 3, 1950, Alphabetical File, F (2 of 2) folder, Acheson Papers.

1. Into Korea

1. Paige, *Korean Decision,* 79–81, 93, 100.

2. "Washington Holds Russia to Account," *NYT,* June 25, 1950, 20; "North Korea Forces Drive into South, Seoul Hears," *Washington Post,* June 25, 1950, M1. All subsequent references to the time of day are eastern daylight time unless otherwise noted.

3. Paige, *Korean Decision,* 102–10. Gross had recently been elevated to acting ambassador to fill in for Warren Austin, who was on a leave of absence. Prior to Austin's temporary departure, Gross had served as the deputy ambassador to the UN. The USSR had been boycotting the Security Council over its refusal to recognize the communist Chinese government.

4. Truman, *Memoirs,* 2:324–27, 332; Donovan, *Tumultuous Years,* 195–96. Blair House normally served as the official guesthouse for visiting dignitaries.

5. Donovan, *Tumultuous Years,* 195–96.

6. Paige, *Korean Decision,* 116–22.

7. Ibid., 125; Donovan, *Tumultuous Years,* 197–99; Dean Acheson, "Memorandum of Conversation—'Korean Situation,'" June 25, 1950, Memoranda of Conversations file, May–June 1950 folder, Acheson Papers.

8. Paige, *Korean Decision,* 150–54; Knowland, Connally, and Millikin quoted in Harold B. Hinton, "Connally Says U.S. Is Firm on Korea," *NYT,* June 27, 1950, 12.

9. Acheson quoted in memorandum of telephone conversation, June 26, 1950, and untitled memorandum, June 26, 1950, Memoranda of Conversations file, May–

June 1950 folder, Acheson Papers; Roosevelt quoted in Matthew J. Connelly, memorandum for the president, June 26, 1950, PSF: President's Appointment File, Daily Appointment Sheets, June 1950 folder, Truman Papers; Connally, *My Name Is Tom Connally,* 346.

10. Paige, *Korean Decision,* 162–63, 165; memorandum of conversation, "Korean Situation," June 26, 1950, Memoranda of Conversations file, May–June 1950 folder, Acheson Papers; *FRUS, 1950,* 7:179; John D. Hickerson, oral history interview by Richard D. McKinzie, June 5, 1973, http://trumanlibrary.org/oralhist/hickrson.htm#subjects (accessed June 29, 2007); Acheson, *Present at the Creation,* 407–8.

11. Hickerson oral history interview (emphasis in original).

12. *FRUS, 1950,* 7:200–202; Connally, *My Name Is Tom Connally,* 347–48; Acheson, *Present at the Creation,* 409.

13. John E. Wiltz, "The Korean War and American Society," in *The Korean War: A 25-Year Perspective,* ed. F. H. Heller (Lawrence: Regents Press of Kansas, 1977), 113; "Statement by the President on the Violation of the 38th Parallel in Korea—June 26, 1950," *PP,* http://www.trumanlibrary.org/publicpapers/index.php?pid=799&st=&st1= (accessed December 14, 2006); "Statement by the President on the Situation in Korea," June 27, 1950, *PP,* http://trumanlibrary.org/publicpapers/index.php?pid=800&st=&st1= (accessed July 2, 2007); for Truman's change in rhetoric, see Halford R. Ryan, *Harry S. Truman: Presidential Rhetoric* (Westport, CT: Greenwood Press, 1993), 46–48; Marcantonio quoted in Harold B. Hinton, "Legislators Hail Action by Truman," *NYT,* June 28, 1950, 1.

14. "Resolution Adopted by the United Nations Security Council," June 27, 1950, and "Resolution Adopted by the United Nations Security Council," June 25, 1950, in *FRUS, 1950,* 7:211, 155–56; Kim Il Sung quoted in Paige, *Korean Decision,* 207.

15. Michael S. Twedt, "The War Rhetoric of Harry S. Truman during the Korean Conflict" (PhD diss., University of Kansas, 1969), 75.

16. Lodge quoted in Hinton, "Legislators Hail Action by Truman," 1; "House Votes Draft Extension, Power to Call Reserves, Guard," *Washington Post,* June 28, 1950, 1; "House Votes 315–4 to Prolong Draft," *NYT,* June 28, 1950, 1; "Draft Extension Sent to President," *NYT,* June 29, 1950, 6; "Selective Service," *NYT,* June 28, 1950, 26; "Democracy in Action," *NYT,* June 29, 1950, 28. In the 1950 elections, voters punished only one of the four House members who opposed the draft extension: Vito Marcantonio. There is no indication that any of the legislators abstained from voting as a matter of protest. See Matthew E. Mantell, "Opposition to the Korean War: A Study in American Dissent" (PhD diss., New York University, 1973).

17. Harold B. Hinton, "Taft Says Truman Bypasses Congress," *NYT,* June 29, 1950, 4; Walter Trohan, "Taft Demands Acheson Quit in War Fiasco," *Chicago Tribune,* June 29, 1950, 1; Avalon Project at Yale Law School, "United Nations Participation Act, December 20, 1945," http://www.yale.edu/lawweb/avalon/decade/decad031.htm (accessed July 24, 2007). For other details of Taft's speech, see *CR,* 81st Cong., 2nd sess., June 28, 1950, 96, pt. 7, 9323.

18. Robert C. Albright, "Taft Sees Acheson Reversed and Calls for Resignation," *Washington Post,* June 29, 1950, 1; "Illegality over Korea," *Washington Post,* July 4, 1950, 8; Acheson, *Present at the Creation,* 410.

19. Paige, *Korean Decision,* 239–41, 245–46; Omar N. Bradley and Clay Baird, *A General's Life: An Autobiography by General of the Army Omar N. Bradley* (New York: Simon & Schuster, 1983), 538; Beisner, *Dean Acheson,* 345; George Elsey, "Meeting Notes," June 29, 1950, Project File, Korea—June 29, 1950, White House, State, Defense Meeting folder, Elsey Papers.

20. "The President's News Conference—June 29, 1950," *PP,* http://www.trumanlibrary.org/publicpapers/index.php?pid=806&st=&st1= (accessed December 14, 2006); Ryan, *Harry S. Truman,* 50–51.

21. Bradley and Baird, *General's Life,* 538–39; Acheson, *Present at the Creation,* 412–13; Beisner, *Dean Acheson,* 346–47; Truman, *Memoirs,* 2:342–44.

22. "White House Statement Following a Meeting between the President and Top Congressional and Military Leaders to Review the Situation in Korea," *PP,* http://trumanlibrary.org/publicpapers/index.php?pid=811&st=&st1= (accessed July 10, 2007); George Elsey, meeting notes, June 30, 1950, 11 o'clock, Subject File, Korea—June 30, 1950, Congressional Leaders' Meeting folder, Elsey Papers; Connally, *My Name Is Tom Connally,* 349.

23. Elsey meeting notes, June 30, 1950.

24. H. Alexander Smith diary entries, June 28–29, 1950, box 282, Smith Papers; H. Alexander Smith, "The U.N. Participation Act," n.d., box 100, Smith Papers; Acheson, *Present at the Creation,* 413. Interestingly, Elsey's notes of the meeting do not mention Smith's proposal.

25. Acheson, *Present at the Creation,* 413; Connally, *My Name Is Tom Connally,* 349.

26. "Congressional Action," July 1950, Subject File, Korea—July 1950 folder, Elsey Papers; "Memorandum of Telephone Conversation—Secretary of Defense Johnson and Secretary Acheson," July 3, 1950, PSF: President's Appointment File, July 1950 folder, Truman Papers; two drafts, dated July 3, 1950, of a possible resolution of Congress proposed by the Department of Defense are in Elsey Papers, http://www.trumanlibrary.org/whistelstopstudy_collections/korea/large/week2/kw_74_1.htm (accessed July 12, 2007).

27. "Meeting at Blair House," July 3, 1950, Memoranda of Conversations file, July 1950 folder, Acheson Papers. After leaving the June 30 briefing, Wherry still believed that Truman should have consulted Congress beforehand. However, he couched it in more conciliatory language, saying, "I think Congress should be required to share the responsibility of whatever acts the President takes." See Harold B. Hinton, "Sea Blockade Set," *NYT,* July 1, 1950, 1.

28. "Meeting at Blair House," July 3, 1950.

29. Ibid.; Acheson, *Present at the Creation,* 414.

30. "Memorandum of Conversation with the President—Item No. 6, Message to Congress," July 10, 1950, Memoranda of Conversations file, July 1950 folder,

Acheson Papers; Wiley quoted in William S. White, "Bigger G.O.P. Role in Crisis Proposed," *NYT,* July 11, 1950, 21, and Willard Edwards, "Truman Calls Lawmakers to Korea Parley," *Chicago Tribune,* July 11, 1950, 6; "Congressional Action," July 1950, Elsey Papers; George M. Elsey, *An Unplanned Life: A Memoir by George McKee Elsey* (Columbia: University of Missouri Press, 2005), 195.

31. Beisner, *Dean Acheson,* 349; Ridgway, *Korean War,* 25–26; "The President's News Conference—July 6, 1950," *PP,* http://www.trumanlibrary.org/publicpapers/index.php?pid=814&st=&st1= (accessed December 15, 2006); "The President's News Conference—July 13, 1950," *PP,* http://www.trumanlibrary.org/publicpapers/index.php?pid=820&st=&st1= (accessed December 15, 2006).

32. "Truman's Stand Electrifies Nation," *Newsweek,* July 10, 1950, 24; "The Nation," *NYT,* July 2, 1950, E2; "Report from the Nation: All Eyes on Korea," *NYT,* July 2, 1950, E8; Harsch quoted in Goldman, *Crucial Decade,* 158–59; Lawrence Wittner, *The Struggle against the Bomb,* vol. 1, *One World or None: A History of the Nuclear Disarmament Movement through 1953* (Stanford, CA: Stanford University Press, 1993), 316; "New Support for Truman," *NYT,* June 30, 1950, 4; E. Timothy Smith, *Opposition beyond the Water's Edge: Liberal Internationalists, Pacifists, and Containment, 1945–1953* (Westport, CT: Greenwood Press, 1999), 122–24; Goldman, *Crucial Decade,* 173.

33. Theodore Green to Gurney Edwards, August 5, 1950, box 600, Green Papers; Green to William Greenlees, January 12, 1951, and Green to Mrs. Otis Rylander, June 18, 1951, box 634, Green Papers.

34. "Truman Act Is Held Legal by Douglas," *Washington Post,* July 6, 1950, 8; Paul H. Douglas, *In the Fullness of Time: The Memoirs of Paul H. Douglas* (New York: Harcourt Brace Jovanovich, 1971), 496–97.

35. *CR,* 79th Cong., 1st sess., November 28, 1945, 91, pt. 13, 11085.

36. "Truman Act Held Legal by Douglas."

37. Gilbert C. Fite, *Richard B. Russell, Jr., Senator from Georgia* (Chapel Hill: University of North Carolina Press, 1991), 253–54; Charles A. Lofgren, "Congress and the Korean Conflict" (PhD diss., Stanford University, 1966), 72; "U.N. Participation Act of 1945," http://www.yale.edu/lawweb/avalon/decade/decad031.htm (accessed July 16, 2007).

38. Memorandum from Charles Maylon to Matt Connelly, August 24, 1950, PSF: General File, Charles Maylon folder, Truman Papers.

39. Vandenberg and Morris, *Private Papers of Senator Vandenberg,* 543; Ralph E. Flanders, "Broadcast for Vermont Stations, Week of July 2, 1950," box 138, Ralph E. Flanders Papers, Special Collections Research Center, Syracuse University Library, Syracuse, NY; *CR,* 81st Cong., 2nd sess., June 28, 1950, 96, pt. 7, 9315; Robert C. Albright, "Taft Sees Acheson Reversed and Calls for Resignation," *Washington Post,* June 29, 1950, 1; Ronald J. Caridi, *The Korean War and American Politics: The Republican Party as a Case Study* (Philadelphia: University of Pennsylvania Press, 1969), 45; H. Alexander Smith diary entry, June 28, 1950, box 282, Smith Papers; Bridges quoted in "Time for Unity," *Time,* July 10, 1950, http://www.time.com/time/

magazine/article/0,9171,805447,00.html (accessed April 12, 2007); Eaton quoted in William S. White, "Congress Adheres Swiftly to Action," *NYT,* July 1, 1950, 1; Ross quoted in Hechler, *Working with Truman,* 151. GOP senators James P. Kem (MO) and Arthur V. Watkins (UT) briefly questioned Truman's bypassing of Congress when they reacted to the commitment of naval and air forces on June 27; see Hinton, "Legislators Hail Action by Truman."

40. "Memorandum of Conversation with Sen. Wiley," June 26, 1950, Memoranda of Conversations file, May–June 1950 folder, Acheson Papers; Acheson quoted in L. D. Battle, "Memorandum for Sec. of State," July 12, 1950, Memoranda of Conversations file, July 1950 folder, Acheson Papers; Truman to Arthur Vandenberg, July 6, 1950, PSF: General File, V folder, Truman Papers.

41. "GOP Group Forms 'Progressive' Bloc," *NYT,* July 2, 1950, 1; "Press Release, July 1, 1950 (from Sen. Ralph Flanders)," box 110, Politics: "Declaration of Republican Principles"—released July 1, 1950, folder, Flanders Papers. For GOP views, see "Republican Advance Finds Old Guard Cold," *NYT,* July 6, 1950, 24; "The Nation," *NYT,* July 9, 1950, E2.

42. Rees, *Korea,* 442–45; Hamby, *Man of the People,* 534–37; Arthur Schlesinger Jr., "Introduction to the Transaction Edition," in Richard Halworth Rovere and Arthur Meier Schlesinger, *General MacArthur & President Truman: The Struggle for Control of American Foreign Policy* (New Brunswick, NJ: Transaction Publishers, 1997), xi–xv.

43. Joyce Kolko and Gabriel Kolko, *The Limits of Power: The World and United States Foreign Policy, 1945–1954* (New York: Harper & Row, 1972), 1–8, 565–67; Bruce Cumings, *The Origins of the Korean War,* vol. 2, *The Roaring of the Cataract* (1990; reprint, Seoul, South Korea: Yuksabipyungsa, 2002), 757–74; Stephen Pelz, "U.S. Decisions on Korean Policy," in *Child of Conflict: The Korean-American Relationship, 1943–1953,* ed. Bruce Cumings (Seattle: University of Washington Press, 1983), 101, 112–13, 132.

44. Barton J. Bernstein, "The Truman Administration and the Korean War," in *The Truman Presidency,* ed. Michael J. Lacey (New York: Cambridge University Press, 1989), 410–44.

45. Acheson, *Present at the Creation,* 415; Truman quoted in Offner, *Another Such Victory,* 371; Truman, *Memoirs,* 2:339; Acheson quoted in Beisner, *Dean Acheson,* 333.

46. Walter LaFeber, *America, Russia, and the Cold War, 1945–2002,* 9th ed. (New York: McGraw-Hill, 2002), 42, describes the American reaction to Stalin's speech; Offner, *Another Such Victory,* 355–56 explains the challenges the United States faced in controlling Rhee.

47. Truman to McKeller in Ruth B. Russell, *A History of the United Nations Charter: The Role of the United States 1940–1945* (Washington, DC: Brookings Institution, 1958), 945.

48. See "To Make the Charter Work," *NYT,* November 27, 1945, 22; Anthony Leviero, "Senate Today Gets U.S. Plan for UNO," *NYT,* November 26, 1945, 1; C. P. Trussell, "UNO Bill in Senate Sparks a Debate," *NYT,* November 27, 1945, 8; C.

P. Trussell, "Senate Beats Plan to Hobble US in UNO," *NYT,* December 4, 1945, 1; C. P. Trussell, "UNO Bill Approved by Senate, 65 to 7, with One Change," *NYT,* December 5, 1945, 1; "The Big Four Dozen," *NYT,* December 2, 1945, E8; "House for UNO Bill; Colombian Is Irked," *NYT,* December 18, 1945, 8; Charles A. Lofgren, "Mr. Truman's War: A Debate and Its Aftermath," *Review of Politics* 31, no. 2 (April 1969): 228–29.

49. General Assembly quoted in Leland M. Goodrich, Edward Hambro, and Anne Patricia Simons, *Charter of the United Nations: Commentary and Documents* (New York: Columbia University Press, 1969), 319; committee report in William R. Kintner, "The United Nations Record of Handling Major Disputes," in *The United States and the United Nations,* ed. Franz B. Gross (Norman: Oklahoma University Press, 1964), 71.

50. Goodrich et al., *Charter of the United Nations,* 315, 325–26.

51. Caridi, *Korean War and American Politics,* 46–48; "U.N. Participation Act of 1945," http://www.yale.edu/lawweb/avalon/decade/decad031.htm (accessed July 16, 2007), emphasis added; "Charter of the United Nations, Chapter VII," www.unhchr.ch/htm./menu3/b/ch-chp7.htm (accessed July 28, 2007). Political scientist Louis Fisher gives an excellent explanation of the UNPA in "The Korean War: On What Legal Basis Did Truman Act?" *American Journal of International Law* 89, no. 1 (January 1995): 29–32.

52. Edward Keynes, *Undeclared War: Twilight Zone of Constitutional Power* (University Park: Pennsylvania State University Press, 1982), 111.

53. Fisher, "Korean War," 30–32; Schlesinger, "Introduction to the Transaction Edition," xi–xv; Arthur M. Schlesinger Jr., *The Imperial Presidency* (Boston: Houghton Mifflin, 1973), 131–35; Offner, *Another Such Victory,* 368–77.

54. Jerry N. Hess, "Oral History Interview with Frank Pace, Jr.," February 17, 1972, 79, http://trumanlibrary.org/oralhist/pacefj3.htm#76 (accessed July 24, 2007); Acheson quoted in Paterson, "Presidential Foreign Policy, Public Opinion and Congress," 18.

55. Lofgren, "Mr. Truman's War," 234.

56. Offner, *Another Such Victory,* 376, describes Truman's directive to Acheson about the historical research; U.S. Department of State, "Authority of the President to Repel the Attack in Korea," *Department of State Bulletin* 23, no. 578 (July 31, 1950): 178; Shanghai intervention described in "Text of White House Statement," *NYT,* February 1, 1932, 1.

57. Truman quoted in memorandum of conversation, meeting at Blair House, July 3, 1950, Acheson Papers; George M. Elsey, memorandum for Mr. Smith, July 16, 1951, Subject File, Korea—July 1950 folder, Elsey Papers.

58. Memorandum of conversation, meeting at Blair House, July 3, 1950; Jerry N. Ness, "Oral History Interview with Charles S. Murphy," June 24, 1969, http://www.trumanlibrary.org/oralhist/murphy5.htm (accessed July 12, 2007).

59. Lofgren, "Mr. Truman's War," 225, 228–29; Arthur V. Watkins, "War by Executive Order," *Western Political Quarterly* 4, no. 4 (December 1951): 539–49.

60. Acheson, *Present at the Creation,* 415.

61. Connally, *My Name Is Tom Connally,* 351; Elsey, memorandum for Mr. Smith, July 16, 1951.

62. Hamby, *Man of the People,* 537–39; Offner, *Another Such Victory,* 368–77.

63. Stennis quoted in *CR,* 81st Cong., 2nd sess., June 30, 1950, 96, pt. 7, 9540; James MacGregor Burns, "Is the Presidency Too Powerful?" *NYT,* July 16, 1950, SM7; Elsey, *Unplanned Life,* 194–95; Hechler, *Working with Truman,* 150–51. Elsey and Hechler both note Averell Harriman's failed attempt to persuade Truman to get a war resolution.

64. Elsey, *Unplanned Life,* 195; Ferrell, *Truman in the White House,* 357.

2. The First War, July–October 1950

1. J. A. Livingston, "It's 1940 Again in Washington; City's a Beehive of Indecision," *Washington Post,* July 19, 1950, B8; Anthony Leviero, "President Sees U.S. Holding in Korea for Counter-Attack," *NYT,* July 14, 1950, 1; Joseph Alsop and Stewart Alsop, "Matter of Fact," *Washington Post,* July 10, 1950, 6; Smith quoted in George Gallup, "Sugar-Coated War News Not Popular in America," *Dallas Morning News,* July 19, 1950, sec. 1, 10; Brewster, Johnson, and Graham quoted in "National Affairs," *Time,* July 24, 1950, 11.

2. Truman's request to the NSC is in "Memorandum by the Executive Secretary of the National Security Council (Lay) to the National Security Council," July 17, 1950, in *FRUS, 1950,* 7:410; see also Beisner, *Dean Acheson,* 395. State Department discussions on proceeding north of the thirty-eighth parallel are in *FRUS, 1950,* 7:272, 386–87, 410, 449–54, 458–61, 469–73, 486–87, 502–9; Allison quoted in "Memorandum by the Director of the Office of Northeast Asian Affairs (Allison) to the Assistant Secretary of State for Far Eastern Affairs (Rusk)," July 1, 1950, ibid., 272.

3. Clifford quoted in Ryan, *Harry S. Truman,* 8; "The Days Ahead," *Time,* September 11, 1950, 22; Ryan, *Harry S. Truman,* 11.

4. Steven Casey, *Selling the Korean War: Propaganda, Politics, and Public Opinion in the United States, 1950–1953* (New York: Oxford University Press, 2008), 69; "Radio and Television Address to the American People on the Situation in Korea—July 19, 1950," *PP,* http://www.trumanlibrary.org/publicpapers/index. php?pid=823&st=&st1= (accessed December 26, 2006); Twedt, "War Rhetoric of Truman," 148–49.

5. Twedt, "War Rhetoric of Truman," 93–95; "Radio and Television Address on Korea—July 19, 1950" (emphasis added).

6. "The Fabric of Peace," *Time,* July 31, 1950, 10; Drew Pearson, "President Needs All Help in Crisis," *Washington Post,* July 24, 1950, B9; "National Affairs," *Time,* August 14, 1950, 7; Ken Hechler, memorandum for Mr. Elsey, August 2, 1950, Subject File, Establishment of a Research Comm. folder, Kenneth Hechler Papers, HSTL; Marquis Childs, "President's Message," *Washington Post,* July 20, 1950,

11; Edward T. Folliard, "No Further Aggression, Notice Given World Reds," *Washington Post,* July 20, 1950, 1. Jack Gould, "Radio and TV in Review," *NYT,* July 20, 1950, 32, also gave Truman's speech a favorable review.

7. Truman's budgetary priorities are discussed in Michael J. Hogan, *A Cross of Iron: Harry S. Truman and the Origins of the National Security State* (New York: Cambridge University Press, 1998), 294; struggles with postwar demobilization are noted in Donovan, *Tumultuous Years,* 320; the railroad issue is discussed in Paul G. Pierpaoli, *Truman and Korea: The Political Culture of the Early Cold War* (Columbia: University of Missouri Press, 1999), 33; Truman's concerns about full mobilization are in Hogan, *Cross of Iron,* 300, 310.

8. Rayburn quoted in Richard E. Neustadt, *Presidential Power: The Politics of Leadership* (New York: John Wiley & Sons, 1960), 104; for criticism of Truman's initial decision not to request the authority to control prices, see Ferrell, *Harry S. Truman,* 325; inflation data from Coinnews Media Group, "US Inflation Calculator," http://www.usinflationcalculator.com/inflation/historical-inflation-rates/ (accessed December 31, 2013).

9. "Radio and Television Address on Korea—July 19, 1950"; Edwin E. Willis to Truman, July 30, 1950, WHCF: Official File 571B, box 1305, Korean emergency (June–July 1950) folder, Truman Papers; Goldman, *Crucial Decade,* 187; Pierpaoli, *Truman and Korea,* 30–31; Neustadt, *Presidential Power,* 105; Hamby, *Man of the People,* 549.

10. Rose, *Cold War Comes to Main Street,* 197; Hogan, *Cross of Iron,* 307. At the time, the federal government's fiscal year ran from July 1 through June 30; fiscal year 1951 therefore ended in June 1951. Military appropriations and budget information are from Ojserkis, *Beginnings of the Cold War Arms Race,* 93, 95, 100–103.

11. "G.I.'s Curse Lack of Tanks, Planes," *NYT,* July 9, 1950; Hickenlooper and Capehart quoted in Anthony Leviero, "Truman Preparing Messages on War," *NYT,* July 15, 1950, 1.

12. Harold B. Hinton, "Taft Says Truman Bypasses Congress," *NYT,* June 29, 1950, 4; McCarthy quoted in "M'Carthy Assails Acheson on Korea," *NYT,* July 3, 1950, 2; Walter H. Waggoner, "Four Areas Listed," *NYT,* January 13, 1950, 1; Anne O'Hare McCormick, "Abroad: The Search for a New Policy in the East," *NYT,* January 14, 1950, 11; "Democrats and G.O.P. Feud over Blame in Korea," *Chicago Daily Tribune,* July 28, 1950, 4.

13. "M'Arthur Pledges Defense of Japan," *NYT,* March 29, 1949, 22; McLellan, *Dean Acheson,* 209–10; Beisner, *Dean Acheson,* 328. The Stalin-Kim meetings are described in Evgeniy P. Bajanov and Natalia Bajanova, "The Korean Conflict, 1950–1953" (unpublished ms., North Korean International Documentation Project, Wilson Center, Princeton University), 41. For arguments that Acheson's speech invited the war, see Elizabeth A. Stanley, *Paths to Peace: Domestic Coalition Shifts, War Termination and the Korean War* (Stanford, CA: Stanford University Press, 2009), 98; Kathryn Weathersby, "The Soviet Role in the Korean War: The State of Historical Knowledge," in *The Korean War in World History,* ed. William W. Stueck (Lexington:

University Press of Kentucky, 2004), 68–69; Chen Jian, "In the Name of Revolution: China's Road to the Korean War Revisited," ibid., 104. For arguments to the contrary, see Cumings, *Origins of the Korean War*, 2:408–38; Lloyd C. Gardner, "Korean Borderlands: Imaginary Frontiers of the Cold War," in Stueck, *Korean War in World History*, 134–36.

14. "M'Carthy Assails Acheson on Korea," *NYT*, July 3, 1950, 2.

15. William S. White, "Bigger G.O.P. Role in Crisis Proposed," July 11, 1950, 21; David M. Kennedy, *Freedom from Fear: The American People in Depression and in War, 1929–1945* (New York: Oxford University Press, 1999), 457–58.

16. White, "Bigger G.O.P. Role in Crisis Proposed," 21.

17. Dulles and Taft quoted in Robert C. Albright, "Dulles Helps Senators Plan Part in Policy," *Washington Post*, July 12, 1950, 2; Kepley, *Collapse of the Middle Way*, 80, 89; John M. Redding to Michael J. Kirwan, July 26, 1950, box 1052, Anderson Papers, notes the use of the "Mr. Truman's War" moniker by the Republican National Committee; "'Blame' for Korea to Be Polls Issue," *NYT*, July 16, 1950, 51; Taft letter quoted in James T. Patterson, *Mr. Republican: A Biography of Robert A. Taft* (Boston: Houghton Mifflin, 1972), 455.

18. Oshinsky, *Conspiracy So Immense*, 168–71; Constantine Brown, "This Changing World," *Washington Star*, July 19, 1950, A7; Richard Fried, *Nightmare in Red: The McCarthy Era in Perspective* (New York: Oxford University Press, 1990), 128; William S. White, "Red Charges by M'Arthy Ruled False," *NYT*, July 18, 1950, 1.

19. Wherry and Morgan quoted in Oshinsky, *Conspiracy So Immense*, 169–70; Jenner quoted in Robert Griffith, *The Politics of Fear: Joseph R. McCarthy and the Senate* (Lexington: University Press of Kentucky, 1970), 101. Griffith, *Politics of Fear*, 105–6, notes that the Tydings vote was the last display of Democratic unity until December 1954.

20. Donovan, *Tumultuous Years*, 253; Neustadt, *Presidential Power*, 105; public opinion data from "Speed of U.S. Advances in Korea Came as Big Surprise to U.S. Public," October 4, 1950, and "Truman Popularity Turns Upward after Summer Slump," September 25, 1950, 1950 folder, Records of American Institute of Public Opinion, HSTL; "National Affairs," *Time*, August 14, 1950, 7.

21. Charles E. Bennett to Truman, August 7, 1950, and Truman to Bennett, August 12, 1950, PSF: General File, Ba–Bl folder, Truman Papers; H. A. Smith, "Memo re Conference H.A.S. & Averell Harriman," box 101, Foreign Relations 1950 Averell Harriman folder, Smith Papers.

22. Wherry and Sikes quoted in William S. White, "Truman Terms Contemptible Wherry's Attack on Acheson," *NYT*, August 18, 1950, 1; Priest's concerns noted in Edward T. Folliard, "President Enters Disputes; Defends Johnson and Acheson," *Washington Post*, August 4, 1950, 1. Although Bennett was pushing for peace, he also had concerns about Acheson, which he relayed to Truman. See Truman to Bennett, August 12, 1950; Bennett to Truman, August 8, 1950; Truman to Bennett, August 5, 1950; and Bennett to Truman, July 31, 1950, PSF: General File, Ba–Bl folder, Truman Papers. Douglas quoted in Griffith, *Politics of Fear*, 105.

23. For the importance of anticommunism to McCarran's career, see Fried, *Nightmare in Red,* 3. Savage, *Truman and the Democratic Party,* 171, discusses McCarran's divisiveness within the party.

24. Truman quoted in Hechler, *Working with Truman,* 190; Truman's veto message quoted in Hamby, *Man of the People,* 549, and Donovan, *Tumultuous Years,* 296. Hamby, *Man of the People,* 548–49, analyzes why Truman vetoed the McCarran Act.

25. Oshinsky, *Conspiracy So Immense,* 173; Edward Folliard, "Vote of 286 to 48 Polled within Hour after Truman Calls Measure 'Mistake,'" *Washington Post,* September 23, 1950, 1; "How Senate Voted on Anti-Red Bill Veto," *Washington Post,* September 24, 1950, M8; press release, Sunday, October 1, 1950, from the offices of Senator Paul H. Douglas and other Democrats voting with Truman, box 603, Green Papers. The two losers in 1950, John Carroll (CO) and Helen Gahagan Douglas (CA), were House members who ran unsuccessfully for the Senate.

26. See Richard Fried, "Electoral Politics and McCarthyism: The 1950 Campaign," in *The Specter: Original Essays on the Cold War and the Origins of McCarthyism,* ed. Robert Griffith and Athan Theoharis (New York: New Viewpoints, 1974), 221.

27. MacArthur's message in Rovere and Schlesinger, *General MacArthur & President Truman,* 131; Matthews quoted in "Instituting a War," *Time,* September 4, 1950, 12.

28. "Radio and Television Report to the American People on the Situation in Korea—September 1, 1950," *PP,* http://www.trumanlibrary.org/publicpapers/index.php?pid=861&st=&st1= (accessed December 27, 2006), emphasis added; Austin quoted in "Verbatim Record of Yesterday's Session of the United Nations Security Council," *NYT,* August 18, 1950, 8; "National Affairs," *Time,* September 11, 1950, 21. For examples of media support of Truman's speech, see Anthony Leviero, "Manpower Goal Up," *NYT,* September 2, 1950, 1; "Fireside Chat," *Washington Post,* September 4, 1950, 6; "Policy on Formosa," *NYT,* September 3, 1950, 67. For internal discussions in July 1950 about reunifying the Koreas, see Donovan, *Tumultuous Years,* 268–72, and William W. Stueck, *The Korean War: An International History* (Princeton, NJ: Princeton University Press, 1995), 61, 76. Truman followed up his September 1 speech with another on September 9, which dealt with the Defense Production Act and domestic economic controls.

29. Pierpaoli, *Truman and Korea,* 34, 59, describes public demands for more controls; poll data from Hugh G. Wood, "American Reaction to Limited War in Asia: Korea and Vietnam, 1950–1968" (PhD diss. University of Colorado, 1974), 75–76; Gallup quoted in Casey, *Selling the Korean War,* 75; employment data from Goldman, *Crucial Decade,* 182. The journalist quoted is Thomas L. Stokes, "Congress Faces the Crisis—and the Voters," *NYT,* September 3, 1950, 87.

30. For the debate and compromise over the Defense Production Act, see Neustadt, *Presidential Power,* 104, and Casey, *Selling the Korean War,* 76–78.

31. "Radio and Television Address to the American People Following the Signing of the Defense Production Act—September 9, 1950," *PP,* http://www.trumanlibrary.org/publicpapers/index.php?pid=872&st=&st1= (accessed January 13, 2007); for public reaction, see Rose, *Cold War Comes to Main Street,* 198.

32. Pierpaoli, *Truman and Korea*, 67, 103, 106.

33. Seth Wigderson, "The Wages of Anticommunism: U.S. Labor and the Korean War," in *Labor's Cold War: Local Politics in a Global Context*, ed. Shelton Stromquist (Urbana: University of Illinois Press, 208), 231–32, 229. Wigderson asserts that some in the Truman administration saw the Ford and Chrysler contracts as unpatriotic, but he gives no primary source for this information. Pierpaoli, *Truman and Korea*, 87, 106–7, discusses the Truman administration's approach to labor and mobilization.

34. Hamby, *Man of the People*, 549; U.S. Department of State, Office of the Historian, "NSC-68, 1950," http://history.state.gov/milestones/1945–1952/NSC68 (accessed May 21, 2014).

35. Kepley, *Collapse of the Middle Way*, 92–95; "Text of G.O.P. Senators' Statement Charging Foreign Policy Bungling in Europe, Asia," *NYT*, August 14, 1950, 10. Senator Vandenberg did not sign the GOP statement due to his illness; however, the drafters kept in touch with the senator by phone, and he stated his agreement in principle when it was released.

36. Kepley, *Collapse of the Middle Way*, 95; William S. White, "Truman Is Blamed," *NYT*, August 14, 1950, 1; Senator Eugene Millikin quoted in "Upsets & Switches," *Time*, August 21, 1950, http://www.time.com/time/magazine/article/0,9171,812978,00.html (accessed April 12, 2007).

37. Connally quoted in William S. White, "Connally Decries Foreign Policy Rift," *NYT*, August 15, 1950, 1; "Press Statement of Senator Tom Connally (Dem., Texas)," August 14, 1951, box 7, Addresses & Releases, Aug. 1950 folder, Brien McMahon Papers, MDLOC; McMahon quoted in "Blood on Whose Hands?" *Time*, August 28, 1950, http://www.timecom/time/magazine/article/0,9171,813054,00.html (accessed April 12, 2007); Truman to Clinton P. Anderson, August 5, 1950, PSF: Chronological Name File, Clinton P. Anderson folder, Truman Papers. Although it was not Dulles's idea for the Republicans to issue a statement on foreign policy, the authors did enlist his support. See William M. Leary, "Smith of New Jersey: A Biography of H. Alexander Smith, United States Senator from New Jersey, 1944–1959" (PhD diss., Princeton University, 1966), 161.

38. William S. White, "Bipartisan Policy Now a Campaign Casualty," *NYT*, August 20, 1950, 119.

39. Arthur Krock, "Truman Appointments Rise above Politics," *NYT*, October 1, 1950, 151; "New Appointments," *Washington Post*, September 29, 1950, 22.

40. Republican National Committee, *Background to Korea* (Washington, DC: Republican National Committee, 1950), 3, 45, 49–50.

41. Henry Cabot Lodge Jr., "Lodge Defines the Minority Role," *NYT*, September 17, 1950, 176; Kepley, *Collapse of the Middle Way*, 96–98.

42. "Situation Fluid," *Time*, October 2, 1950, http://www.time.com/time/printout/0,8816,813404,00.html (accessed April 12, 2007); "Truman Backs Harriman, Says Taft Views Aid Reds," *NYT*, September 22, 1950, 35.

43. Memorandum from Charlie Markham to Senator Anderson, October 13, 1950, box 1052, Anderson Papers.

44. "Address in Kiel Auditorium, St. Louis," November 4, 1950, *PP,* http://
www.trumanlibrary.org/publicpapers/index.php?pid=909&st=republicans&st1=
attack (accessed April 10, 2007).

45. "Korea to Be Issue in November Vote," *NYT,* August 8, 1950, 20; Lofgren,
"Congress and the Korean Conflict," 58, 60–61.

46. John D. Morris, "Democrats Assail G.O.P. on Korea," *NYT,* July 28, 1950,
3; Myers quoted in "Korea to Be Issue"; "Korean Aid Defeat Blamed for Attack,"
Dallas Morning News, July 28, 1950, 3; Redding to Kirwan, July 26, 1950.

47. Carter to Rayburn, September 5, 1950, and Rayburn to Carter, September
13, 1950, 1950 Political*Texas and District folder, Sam Rayburn Papers, Center for
American History, University of Texas at Austin.

48. Griffith, *Politics of Fear,* 104–5, quantifies the support for Acheson among
Senate Democrats.

49. Truman to Bill Boyle, August 22, 1950, and attached memorandum from
Henri Warren to Truman, PSF: Political File, Truman Papers. "The President's
Day—January 25, 1950," President's Daily Appointment Calendar, n.d., http://www
.trumanlibrary.org/calendar/main.php?curYear=1950&currMonth=1&currDay=24
(accessed February 11, 2006), indicates Warren's relationship with Truman; Warren's
several visits to the White House during 1949–1950 are also documented in WHCF:
PPF 774 (Henri Warren), Truman Papers.

50. Requests for fact sheets are in Ed Downs to Democratic Senatorial Campaign Committee, August 1, 1950, Senator Anderson to A. S. Mike Monroney,
October 26, 1950, and M. P. Hogan to Senator Clinton Anderson, August 25,
1950, box 1052, Anderson Papers; Democrats' defensiveness about Korea as a campaign issue is described in Ken Hechler, memorandum to Charles Van Devander,
September 6, 1950, Subject File, General Research—Truman White House folder,
Hechler Papers; Clinton P. Anderson to Democratic Speakers, September 20, 1950,
with attachment, "The Truth about Korea," PSF: Political File, Washington folder,
Truman Papers.

51. Democratic National Committee, "Questions and Answers on Foreign Policy," 1950, Subject File, General Research—Truman White House folder, Hechler
Papers (emphasis in original). Although the DNC published this document, Ken
Hechler and the State Department put it together. U.S. Department of State, Office
of Public Affairs, "Building the Peace," *Foreign Affairs Outlines,* Far Eastern Series
37, Pub. 3971, No. 24 (Autumn 1950), 8; "Information Objectives for the Rest of
1950," August 3, 1950, PSF: General File, Speech: Instructions for Public Statements
folder, Truman Papers; Korean fact sheet in Kenneth Hechler, memorandum, "State
Department Campaign Materials on Foreign Policy," August 31, 1950, Subject File,
General Research—Truman White House folder, Hechler Papers; Acheson quoted
in "North Atlantic Union and Related Matters," August 14, 1950, Memoranda of
Conversations file, Aug. 1950 folder, Acheson Papers.

52. Elsey, *Unplanned Life,* 187–88; Ken Hechler to George Elsey, "State Department's 'Popular' Account of Foreign Policy," September 9, 1950, Subject File, For-

eign Policy—State Department Pamphlet, "Our Foreign Policy" folder, Elsey Papers; Ken Hechler, interview with the author, January 16, 2007.

53. U.S. Department of State, Office of Public Affairs, *Our Foreign Policy*, Pub. 3972 (Washington, DC: U.S. Government Printing Office, 1950), 7–10, 15, 27, 58, 91–92.

54. Hechler to Elsey, "State Department's 'Popular' Account of Foreign Policy," September 9, 1950; Hechler, *Working with Truman*, 230; Francis Russell to George Elsey, October 27, 1950, PSF: General File, George Elsey folder, Truman Papers; "How the U.S. Works toward Peace in a Tense World," *Washington Post*, October 15, 1950, B1; Arthur Sears Henning, "Truman Thrown on Defensive by G.O.P. Blasts," *Chicago Daily Tribune*, October 9, 1950, 3; Godwin quoted in memorandum, "Our Foreign Policy," author unknown, n.d., Foreign Policy—State Department Pamphlet folder, Elsey Papers.

55. Savage, *Truman and the Democratic Party*, 177, 180–83; Hamby, *Man of the People*, 550; Truman quoted in Savage, *Truman and the Democratic Party*, 177; Hechler, *Working with Truman*, 147.

56. "Tydings in Trouble," *Newsweek*, October 23, 1950, 35; Oshinsky, *Conspiracy So Immense*, 174; Griffith, *Politics of Fear*, 125. Fried, "Electoral Politics and McCarthyism," 216, 218, describes the limits of McCarthy's influence in the 1950 congressional elections. McCarthy's control of Butler's campaign is detailed in Oshinsky, *Conspiracy So Immense*, 175–76; Griffith, *Politics of Fear*, 126–28; and Savage, *Truman and the Democratic Party*, 180.

57. See William F. Boyle Jr. to Fellow Democrats, August 25, 1950, box 584, Green Papers; Edwin C. Johnson to Clinton Anderson, September 2, 1950, box 1052, Anderson Papers, criticizing the attacks on McCarthy.

58. For examples of Democratic optimism, see Clinton P. Anderson to Carl V. Rice, September 18, 1950, and Senator William Benton to Galen Van Meter, October 9, 1950, box 1052, Anderson Papers. For examples of GOP accusations, see "Press Release from Headquarters of Senator Brien McMahon," October 1950, and Brien McMahon to Edward W. Barrett (State Department), October 17, 1950, box 8, McMahon Papers; Clinton Anderson to Thomas H. Gunter, October 10, 1950, and Gunter to Anderson, October 5, 1950, box 38, Anderson Papers.

59. Stanley, *Paths to Peace*, 135–40, discusses the reasons for advancing north of the thirty-eighth parallel. The British role is analyzed in William W. Stueck, *Rethinking the Korean War: A New Diplomatic and Strategic History* (Princeton, NJ: Princeton University Press, 2002), 98–100. Direct quotes are from *FRUS, 1950*, 7:763–64, 768–73, 826–28, 903–5.

60. Troop allocation information is from Rees, *Korea*, 32–33; U.S. strength in the General Assembly is discussed in Stueck, *Korean War*, 77–93.

61. Poll data from Beisner, *Dean Acheson*, 400; support by the press and the public noted in Stanley, *Paths to Peace*, 140, and Leffler, *Preponderance of Power*, 378–79; "But What Comes Next?" *Life*, October 9, 1950, 38; O'Mahoney and Scott quoted in Donovan, *Tumultuous Years*, 277; Truman, "Address in San Francisco at the War

Memorial Opera House—October 17, 1950," *PP,* http://www.trumanlibrary.org/
publicpapers/index.php?pid=899&st=&st1= (accessed January 9, 2007).

62. Hamby, *Man of the People,* 541–42; Leffler, *Preponderance of Power,* 377–80;
Ryan, *Harry S. Truman,* 60–61.

63. Clinton Anderson to Francis J. Meyers, October 12, 1950, box 1052, Anderson Papers; "U.S. Units Retreat 50 Miles in Korea," *Dallas Morning News,* November 3, 1950, 1; "Another Acheson Betrayal," *Chicago Daily Tribune,* November
4, 1950, 10; "Red Counterblows Again Throw Allies Back in Furious No. Korea
Clashes," *Washington Post,* November 4, 1950, 1; Republican National Committee,
"News Release," November 6, 1950, box 100, unlabeled folder in front of "Twitchell
Report" folder, Smith Papers; Bolling quoted in Hamby, *Man of the People,* 550.

64. Savage, *Truman and the Democratic Party,* 183; Helen Dunphy to Edward J.
Higgins, November 20, 1950, box 595, Green Papers; Hamby, *Man of the People,* 551.

65. Congressman quoted in Savage, *Truman and the Democratic Party,* 71; Savage, *Truman and the Democratic Party,* 69–77, and Hechler, *Working with Truman,*
132, describe complaints about Boyle and the lack of a research division; for Anderson's role, see William Benton, statement to campaign supporters, December 13,
1950, box 1052, Anderson Papers. The Democrats reinstated a research division in
the 1952 presidential campaign.

66. Schlesinger quoted in Hamby, *Man of the People,* 551; McCarran Act data
from Fried, "Electoral Politics and McCarthyism," 221.

67. See Anderson, *Outsider in the Senate,* 106–7; Fried, "Electoral Politics and
McCarthyism," 216; various letters between Anderson and Lucas, box 1052, Anderson Papers. For Truman's view of Lucas's defeat, see Robert H. Ferrell, ed., *Off the
Record: The Private Papers of Harry S. Truman* (New York: Harper & Row, 1980),
282–83.

68. Clinton Anderson to Irving Dilliard (of the *St. Louis Post-Dispatch*), January
10, 1951, box 519, Anderson Papers; Savage, *Truman and the Democratic Party,* 180;
McMahon quoted in Drew Pearson, "Campaign Photo Rouses Ire," *Washington Post,*
January 9, 1951, B13; Drew Pearson, "McCarthy Ouster Move Detailed," *Washing-
ton Post,* August 11, 1951, B13; Democratic senator quoted in Oshinsky, *Conspiracy
So Immense,* 218.

69. Ojserkis, *Beginnings of the Cold War Arms Race,* 116; "Democrats Fume at
McCarthy, But He Has Them Terrorized," *Newsweek,* August 20, 1951, 19.

70. J. J. Perling to Anderson, "What Voters Are Discussing," August 10, 1950,
box 1056, Anderson Papers; Anderson to Senator William Benton, October 18,
1950, box 1052, Anderson Papers; George Gallup, "Survey Finds GOP Stock on
Upgrade," *Los Angeles Times,* September 20, 1950, 12.

71. Richard Bolling to Truman, December 18, 1950, WHCF: PPF, File PPF
4379 "Richard Bolling," Truman Papers; Hechler, *Working with Truman,* 166.

72. Truman diary entry, November 30, 1950, PSF: Longhand Notes File, November 30, 1950 folder, Truman Papers; Charles Murphy to Truman, May 19, 1951,
PSF: General File, Meetings: White House, Special folder, Truman Papers.

73. Charlie Markham to Ken Hechler, "Analysis Shows Bi-Partisan Foreign Policy Will Have Majority Support in the 82nd Congress Despite Republican Gains," n.d., Bipartisan Foreign Policy—Study by Hechler folder, Hechler Papers.

74. Charles Maylon to Matthew Connelly, January 4, 1951, PSF: General File, Charles Maylon folder, Truman Papers; David D. Lloyd to Charles Murphy, January 20, 1951, Chronological File, January 1949–May 1953 folder 1, David D. Lloyd Papers, HSTL; McCormack quoted in "The Coalition Reigns," *New Republic,* January 15, 1951, 7.

3. The Second War, November 1950–July 1951

1. Casualty figures from David Halberstam, *The Coldest Winter: America during the Korean War* (New York: Hyperion, 2007), 469.

2. Lofgren, "Congress and the Korean Conflict," 106–7; November poll in Wiltz, "The Korean War and American Society," 127; "Public Favors Withdrawing Troops from Korean Front," January 20, 1951, 1951 folder, Records of American Institute of Public Opinion, HSTL; "55 Per Cent in Survey See United States Already in Third World War," December 6, 1950, 1950 folder, ibid.

3. "The President's News Conference—November 16, 1950," *PP,* http://www.trumanlibrary.org/publicpapers/index.php?pid=977&st=&st1= (accessed January 14, 2007); "The President's News Conference—November 30, 1950," *PP,* http://www.trumanlibrary.org/publicpapers/index.php?pid=985&st=&st1= (accessed January 14, 2007).

4. Twedt, "War Rhetoric of Truman," 80–81; Harry S. Truman, *Memoirs,* vol. 1, *Years of Decisions* (Garden City, NY: Doubleday, 1955), 48; Elmer E. Cornwell Jr., *Presidential Leadership of Public Opinion* (Bloomington: Indiana University Press, 1965), 162–63, 330n66; McCullough, *Truman,* 818–20.

5. Donovan, *Tumultuous Years,* 277–79; Hamby, *Man of the People,* 542–43, 546.

6. Webb to Truman, December 11, 1950, PSF: Political File, S folder, Truman Papers; Truman quoted in Ferrell, *Harry S. Truman,* 291; Fite, *Richard B. Russell,* 251.

7. Cannon's problems described in Charles S. Murphy to Truman, February 3, 1951, Truman—memos to and from the president, 1947–53, folder 4 of 5, Murphy Papers. For background on Cannon, see Edward F. Ryan, "Cannon's Face Winning Fame on TV Screen," *Washington Post,* July 26, 1952, 3. Committee of 78 described in "What's Happening in Taxation and Government," *What's Happening in Washington,* September 4, 1950, 1950 Congressmen III folder, Rayburn Papers.

8. Memorandum (author unknown), "Republican-Dixiecrat Coalition," April 30, 1951, PSF: General File, William Boyle folder, Truman Papers.

9. James Reston, "Democrats' Election Losses Weaken Acheson's Position," *NYT,* November 9, 1950, 28; James Webb to Charles Murphy, "Action by the Senate Republican Conference," December 7, 1950, Department of State folder, Murphy Papers; "Republicans," *Time,* December 18, 1950, 17.

10. Richard Bolling to Truman, December 18, 1950, PPF 4379, Truman Papers.

11. Truman diary entry, November 30, 1950, PSF: Longhand Notes File, November 30, 1950 folder, Truman Papers.

12. John Hersey, *Aspects of the Presidency* (New Haven, CT: Ticknor & Fields, 1980), 30; memorandum from Ken Hechler to George Elsey, April 4, 1951, and Appendix B, Selected List of White House Appointments with Republican Congressmen and Other Leading Republicans, box 57, Foreign Relations—Hechler Study on Bipartisan Foreign Policy folder, Elsey Papers.

13. Acheson, Millikin, and Connally quoted in "Connally Says 'To Hell with All That' in Reply to GOP Moves for More Policy Say," *Washington Post,* November 28, 1950, 6; "The Greeks Had a Word," *Time,* December 11, 1950, http://www.time.com/time/magazine/article/0,9171,814035,00.html (accessed May 11, 2007).

14. Acheson quoted in George Elsey, notes from cabinet meeting—4:20 p.m. on 11/28/50, Subject File, Korea—November 1950 folder, Elsey Papers; Elsey, notes from congressional leaders meeting, 11:00 a.m., December 1, 1950, Subject File, Korea, Elsey Papers; Wherry quoted in William S. White, "President in Plea," *NYT,* December 2, 1950, 1; Vorys quoted in Robert Young, "Senate, House Chiefs Confer at State Department," *Chicago Daily Tribune,* December 4, 1950, 1; letter from eight congressmen to Truman, December 5, 1950, WHCF: Official File 571B, Korean emergency (Dec. 1950–Aug. 1951) folder, Truman Papers. In this letter, the congressmen also urged Truman to allow 500,000 Nationalist Chinese troops to attack communist China.

15. Frank W. Boykin to Admiral Sidney W. Souers, December 5, 1950, and Truman to Boykin, December 8, 1950, PSF: General File, Bo–Bz folder, Truman Papers; telegram from Francis Case to President Truman, December 8, 1950, WHCF: Official File 471B, Korean emergency (Dec. 1950–Mar. 1951) folder, Truman Papers. By early 1952, Case had reversed his conciliatory view toward China, opposing its admission to the UN. See Richard Chenoweth, "Francis Case: A Political Biography," *South Dakota Historical Collections* 39 (1978): 367–68. Interestingly, around the time of the Boykin and Case proposals, the Chinese government indirectly approached the State Department about starting armistice talks. To verify the seriousness of the Chinese offer, the United States asked them to free an American who had been jailed in Shanghai on spy charges. Unfortunately, the prisoner had already been shot, ending the tenuous negotiations. See Joseph C. Goulden, *Korea: The Untold Story of the War* (New York: New York Times Books, 1982), 548–49. Chinese troops entered the conflict in late October 1950 and then withdrew on November 7; they launched their second offensive on November 25 in response to a UN counteroffensive.

16. "The President's News Conference," November 30, 1950, *PP,* http://www.trumanlibrary.org/publicpapers/index.php?pid=985&st=&st1= (accessed May 7, 2007). The Joint Chiefs of Staff were considering the use of atomic weapons in Korea but had not made a recommendation to the president at the time of his news conference.

17. Stueck, *Korean War,* 131–32. Kaufman, *Korean War,* 70, and Catchpole, *Ko-*

rean War, 96–97, discuss western European pressure on Attlee to meet with Truman quickly. Jiang Jieshi's Nationalist Chinese government had fled to Taiwan following the 1949 communist victory in the Chinese civil war. The communist regime claimed ownership of Taiwan but was being blocked from taking control of it by the U.S. Navy's Seventh Fleet, which Truman had sent to the Formosa Strait at the outset of the Korean War.

18. Acheson, *Present at the Creation,* 481; Knowland quoted in William S. White, "Knowland Prods Attlee on Stand," *NYT,* December 5, 1950, 11; Taft quoted in "Taft Bids Truman Tell Public More," *NYT,* December 6, 1950, 11; Malone quoted in "Taft Demands That Truman Give Nation More Information on Affairs in Asia, Europe," *Washington Post,* December 6, 1950, 2.

19. Resolution and Douglas quoted in Robert C. Albright, "GOP Seeks Senate Consent on Deal," *Washington Post,* December 7, 1950, 3; William S. White, "24 in GOP Demand Truman Submit Attlee Pacts to Senate," *NYT,* December 7, 1950, 1. The Republican push for Acheson's removal produced resolutions from the House and Senate on December 15. See Robert C. Albright, "Congress GOP Asks Ouster of Acheson," *Washington Post,* December 16, 1950, 1.

20. Truman, *Memoirs,* 2:409; Acheson, *Present at the Creation,* 484; "Joint Statement Following Discussions with the Prime Minister of Great Britain," December 8, 1950, *PP,* http://www.trumanlibrary.org/publicpapers/index.php?pid=991&st =&st1= (accessed May 10, 2007).

21. Wiley quoted in Drew Pearson, "Legislators Spurred by Korea Report," *Washington Post,* December 11, 1950, B13; "Taft Demands That Truman Give Nation More Information on Affairs in Asia, Europe," *Washington Post,* December 6, 1950, 2; Brewster quoted in "Senators Disagree on Result of Talks," *NYT,* December 9, 1950, 4; "Statement for the Press by Senator Tom Connally and Senator Alexander Wiley," December 9, 1950, box 101, Miscellaneous—1950 folder, Smith Papers.

22. Charles S. Murphy, memorandum for the president, December 9, 1950, PSF: General File, Charles S. Murphy folder, Truman Papers.

23. List of Meetings at White House with Republican Leaders, April 17, 1945–March 1, 1951, box 59, Foreign Relations—Hechler Study in Bipartisan Foreign Policy folder, Elsey Papers.

24. Ferrell, *Harry S. Truman,* 371; Ojserkis, *Beginnings of the Cold War Arms Race,* 131; Hamby, *Man of the People,* 415–18; Donovan, *Tumultuous Years,* 320; Leffler, *Preponderance of Power,* 403; Pierpaoli, *Truman and Korea,* 118; Jack McFall, memorandum for the president, November 29, 1950, box 14, Truman—memos to and from the president, 1947–1953, folder 5 of 5, Murphy Papers.

25. "Duty Done," *Time,* December 25, 1950, http://www.time.com/time/ printout/0,8816,859059,00.html (accessed May 14, 2007); List of Meetings at White House with Republican Leaders, April 17, 1945–March 1, 1951, Elsey Papers; Alfred Friendly, "Bi-Partisan Group to Discuss Crisis before Address on Defense Plans," *Washington Post,* December 13, 1950, 1; Anthony Leviero, "President Defers Decision on Curbs as Advisers Meet," *NYT,* December 12, 1950, 1.

26. "Duty Done," *Time,* December 25, 1950.

27. George Elsey, "Meeting of the President with Congressional Leaders in the Cabinet Room, 10:00 a.m., Wednesday, December 13, 1950," Subject File, Korea—Congressional leaders meeting, 10:00 a.m., Dec. 13, 1950 folder, Elsey Papers; Drew Pearson, "Truman-GOP Talk Described," *Washington Post,* December 18, 1950, B11.

28. Elsey, "Meeting of the President with Congressional Leaders," December 13, 1950.

29. Ibid.

30. Pearson, "Truman-GOP Talk Described"; Taft's statement quoted in C. P. Trussell, "Congress Chieftains Agree on Rapid Military Build-up," *NYT,* December 14, 1950, 1; "White House Statement Concerning a Meeting with Congressional Leaders to Discuss the National Emergency," December 13, 1950, *PP,* http://www.trumanlibrary.org/publicpapers/index.php?pid=992&st=&st1= (accessed May 14, 2007).

31. Marshall Andrews, "Emergency Plan Finds GOP Doubtful," *Washington Post,* December 14, 1950, 1; Trussell, "Congress Chieftains."

32. "Radio and Television Report to the American People on the National Emergency— December 15, 1950," *PP,* http://www.trumanlibrary.org/publicpapers/index.php?pid=993&st=&st1= (accessed January 14, 2007); Pierpaoli, *Truman and Korea,* 44.

33. "National Affairs," *Time,* December 25, 1950, 7; "Report from the Nation: Facing the Crisis," *NYT,* December 17, 1950, E3; Pierpaoli, *Truman and Korea,* 43.

34. Robert L. Ivie, "Declaring a National Emergency: Truman's Rhetorical Crisis and the Great Debate of 1951," in *The Modern Presidency and Crisis Rhetoric,* ed. Amos Kiewe (Westport, CT: Praeger Publishers, 1994), 6; Twedt, "War Rhetoric of Truman," 70; Rosemary Foot, *The Wrong War: American Policy and the Dimensions of the Korean Conflict, 1950–1953* (Ithaca, NY: Cornell University Press, 1985), 108.

35. "Radio and Television Report to the American People on the National Emergency—December 15, 1950"; Ivie, "Declaring a National Emergency," 3.

36. Rees, *Korea,* 176–77; Kaufman, *Korean War,* 73.

37. Stueck, *Korean War,* 152, 157–58, 162–63.

38. William S. White, "Acheson Ouster Demanded by Congress Republicans," *NYT,* December 16, 1950, 1. Senators Irving Ives (NY) and Leverett Saltonstall (MA), who were normally supportive of Truman's foreign policy, voted with the majority. Truman quoted in "The President's News Conference," December 19, 1950, *PP,* http://trumanlibrary.org/publicpapers/index.php?pid=999&st=&st1= (accessed May 28, 2013); leaks discussed in note to Senator Smith from WI, December 21, 1950, box 101, Smith Papers.

39. Ferrell, *Harry S. Truman,* 323; Ted Galen Carpenter, "United States' NATO Policy at the Crossroads: The 'Great Debate' of 1950–1951," *International History Review* 8, no. 3 (August 1986): 390–91, 394–95, 398–99.

40. Hoover quoted in Kepley, *Collapse of the Middle Way,* 104.

41. Resolutions quoted in Carpenter, "United States' NATO Policy at the Cross-

roads," 405 (emphasis added); Patterson, *Mr. Republican,* 477; Caridi, *Korean War and American Politics,* 134; Taft quoted in Hogan, *Cross of Iron,* 329.

42. Schlesinger, *Imperial Presidency,* 136–37; Carpenter, "United States' NATO Policy at the Crossroads," 405; Vandenberg and Morris, *Private Papers of Senator Vandenberg,* 566–73; Caridi, *Korean War and American Politics,* 132–33; Francis Wilcox diary entry, January 24, 1951, Diary, 1951–1952 folder, Francis O. Wilcox Papers, HSTL; H. Alexander Smith diary entries, January 7 and 15, 1951, box 282, Smith Papers; "Bipartisan Unity Urged," *NYT,* February 13, 1951, 24; "Jenner Blames Korean Crisis on Democrats," *Chicago Tribune,* July 1, 1950, 4; Connally quoted in "The Fin of the Shark," *Time,* January 22, 1951, http://time.com/time/magazine/article/0,9171,888874,00.htm (accessed June 20, 2007).

43. "Memorandum of Telephone Conversation (Dean Acheson and Henry Cabot Lodge), January 16, 1951," box 68, January 1951 folder, Acheson Papers; McMahon speech, March 30, 1951, box 8, Addresses and Releases, March 1951 folder, McMahon Papers; Taft quoted in Caridi, *Korean War and American Politics,* 128.

44. Caridi, *Korean War and American Politics,* 138–39; Hogan, *Cross of Iron,* 326–28.

45. Patterson, *Mr. Republican,* 478; Beisner, *Dean Acheson,* 451; Humphrey quoted in Hogan, *Cross of Iron,* 330.

46. Rees, *Korea,* 33; Patterson, *Mr. Republican,* 479; Beisner, *Dean Acheson,* 451; "Crisis in Korea," *NYT,* November 29, 1950, 16; Department of State memo, "Importance of Increasing Britain's Defense Effort, December 6, 1950," PSF: General File, Clement Attlee folder, Truman Papers.

47. "The President's News Conference, January 11, 1951," *PP,* http://www.trumanlibrary.org/publicpapers/index.php?pid=206&st=&st1= (accessed June 26, 2013); Taft quoted in Richard H. Parke, "Ohioan Call on Congress to Reassert Rights to Pass on Foreign Policy," *NYT,* January 16, 1951, 1.

48. Robert David Johnson, *Congress and the Cold War* (New York: Cambridge University Press, 2006), 51; Beisner, *Dean Acheson,* 451–52; Acheson, *Present at the Creation,* 285; Carpenter, "United States' NATO Policy at the Crossroads," 414.

49. The House decided not to participate in the resolution, effectively washing its hands of the debate. Carpenter, "United States' NATO Policy at the Crossroads," 413–14.

50. "The President's Press Conference—December 19, 1950," *PP,* http://www.trumanlibrary.org/publicpapers/index.php?pid=999&st=&st1= (accessed May 7, 2007); H. Alexander Smith diary entry, January 17, 1951, box 282, Smith Papers; Representative Thomas E. Martin (R-IA) to Truman, January 13, 1951, and Matt Connelly to Martin, January 20, 1951, WHCF: Official File 571B, Korean emergency (Dec. 1950–Mar. 1951) folder, Truman Papers; Dean Acheson, memorandum of conversation with Sen. William Knowland, n.d., Memorandum of Conversations file, Jan. '51 folder, Acheson Papers; Hechler, *Working with Truman,* 156–57; Ken Hechler to George Elsey, April 4, 1951, and Hechler to Elsey, March 20, 1951, Subject File, Bipartisan Foreign Policy Study by Hechler folder, Hechler Papers; "Demo-

bilize, Lift Curtain, Barkley Advises Stalin," *Washington Post,* February 25, 1951, M2. Neither the *New York Times* nor *Time* mentioned Barkley's speech.

51. For a summary of Taft's anti-bipartisanship rhetoric, see Beisner, *Dean Acheson,* 305. For one example of it, see "Truman Charges False, Says Taft," *NYT,* November 6, 1950, 19.

52. Ferrell, *Truman in the White House,* 359–60; all direct quotes from Townsend Hoopes, *The Devil and John Foster Dulles* (Boston: Little, Brown, 1973), 98–103.

53. Truman, *Memoirs,* 2:342–43; MacArthur quoted in Caridi, *Korean War and American Politics,* 62. Dennis Wainstock, *Truman, MacArthur and the Korean War* (Westport, CT: Greenwood Press, 1999), 42, describes MacArthur's efforts to get his remarks publicized.

54. For descriptions of the planned peace overture, see Acheson, *Present at the Creation,* 518–19; *FRUS, 1951,* 7:252–64; William Manchester, *American Caesar: Douglas MacArthur, 1880–1964* (Boston: Little, Brown, 1978), 634; "Text of MacArthur Statement on Korea," *NYT,* March 8, 1951, 3. For internal discussions of MacArthur's statement, see *FRUS, 1951,* 7:265–66. The journalist quoted is Marquis Childs, "Korean Stalemate," *Washington Post,* March 29, 1951, 11.

55. Truman, *Memoirs,* 2:442–46; MacArthur's letter to Martin quoted in Rovere and Schlesinger, *General MacArthur & President Truman,* 171; Truman, *Memoirs,* 2:446; Hanson W. Baldwin, "MacArthur—I," *NYT,* March 28, 1951, 4. Acheson believed that Truman made the decision to fire MacArthur prior to the revelation of the Martin letter; see Acheson, *Present at the Creation,* 519. Truman held the press conference announcing the firing at the unusual time of 1:00 a.m. because he feared that MacArthur might resign if he thought the president was going to relieve him. Truman told Omar Bradley, "The son of a bitch isn't going to resign on me, I want him fired." Quoted in Hamby, *Man of the People,* 556. MacArthur's remarks sparked outrage among UN allies when the peace initiative had to be shelved. For foreign reaction to MacArthur, see *FRUS, 1951,* 7:275; "Nehru Scores MacArthur Move," *NYT,* March 29, 1951, 3; and telegram from Charles Bohlen to Secretary of State, March 26, 1951; memorandum of conversation, Mr. Campbell (Canadian Embassy) and Mr. W. A. Johnson, "President's Statement on Korea," March 24, 1951; telegram no. 1727, Moscow to Secretary of State, March 27, 1951; telegram no. 1327, New York to Secretary of State, March 26, 1951; memorandum of conversation, "Norwegian Inquiry re MacArthur Statement," March 27, 1951, all in SMOF: Dept. of State Topical Subseries, folder 36, Truman Papers.

56. Twedt, "War Rhetoric of Truman," 180, 187; "Radio Report to the American People on Korea and on U.S. Policy in the Far East," April 11, 1951, *PP,* http://www.trumanlibrary.org/publicpapers/index.php?pid=290&st=&st1= (accessed January 21, 2007).

57. "Impeach Truman," *Chicago Tribune,* April 12, 1951, 1; William J. Hopkins, memorandum for the president, May 8, 1951, in *The Korean War: President Truman's Dismissal of General Douglas MacArthur,* vol. 20 of *Documentary History of the Truman Presidency,* ed. Dennis Merrill (Bethesda, MD: University Publications of

America, 1997), 227; "National Affairs: Action on M-Day," *Time,* April 23, 1951, http://www.time.com/time/magazine/article/0,9171,821513,00.html (accessed May 24, 2010); McCarthy quoted in Spanier, *Truman-MacArthur Controversy,* 212; Truman diary quoted in Hamby, *Man of the People,* 557.

58. Kepley, *Collapse of the Middle Way,* 123–24; Brien McMahon, speech transcript, April 14, 1951, and press release, April 16, 1951, box 8, Addresses and Releases, Feb. 1951 folder, McMahon Papers; Farwell Rhodes Jr., "1,500 Democrats Hear McMahon Defend Truman's Firing of Mac," *Indianapolis Star,* April 15, 1951, 1.

59. MacArthur quoted in Rovere and Schlesinger, *General MacArthur & President Truman,* 275–77; Short quoted in Rees, *Korea,* 227; Truman quoted in David Halberstam, *The Fifties* (New York: Villard Books, 1993), 115.

60. Hamby, *Man of the People,* 564; Spanier, *Truman-MacArthur Controversy,* 212–13; William S. White, "M'Arthur Inquiry May Begin Monday," *NYT,* April 24, 1951, 4; "Cabinet Meeting, Monday, April 23, 1951," box 2, April 1951 folder, Matthew Connelly Papers, HSTL; "Sens. Capehart, Humphrey, Lehman Scuffle," *Washington Post,* April 21, 1951, 1; Wherry quoted in "M'Arthur Due Back in U.S. Next Week," *NYT,* April 13, 1951, 1.

61. Wainstock, *Truman, MacArthur and the Korean War,* 130; Kaufman, *Korean War,* 103; H. Alexander Smith, memorandum, "Possible Aggressive Policy for the Far East," April 28, 1951, box 105, Special File— Acheson ouster folder, Smith Papers; Caridi, *Korean War and American Politics,* 153–54; W. H. Lawrence, "M'Arthur as Asset Stirs G.O.P. Doubts," *NYT,* April 18, 1951, 5.

62. Burleson to Acheson, May 7, 1951, Personal Correspondence File, A–B folder, Acheson Papers; "Acheson Won't Resign till Truman Asks, He Repeats," *Washington Post,* May 17, 1951, 5; "Acheson Is 'Liability,' Senator Douglas Says," *NYT,* May 27, 1951, 1; Stewart Alsop, "Acheson: Not Whether But When," *Washington Post,* June 2, 1951, 7. Anderson responded to Alsop's article with a letter to the editor of the *Washington Post,* denying his participation in the meeting; see Clinton Anderson to Editor, *Washington Post,* June 6, 1951, box 38, Anderson Papers. Francis Wilcox, the key congressional aide mentioned, was chief of staff of the Senate Foreign Relations Committee from 1947 to 1955, serving under both Democrats and Republicans. He therefore had no political ax to grind and likely gave a fair assessment of Acheson's treatment in the hearings. See Francis O. Wilcox diary entry, June 1, 1951, Diary, 1951–1952 folder, Wilcox Papers. Sam Rayburn to George Nokes, July 28, 1951, and Nokes to Rayburn, July 19, 1951, 1951 Politicals—National folder, Rayburn Papers, indicates the political pressure caused by Acheson even at the local level.

63. Rusk quoted in Russell Porter, "Rusk Hints U.S. Aid to Revolt in China," *NYT,* May 19, 1951, 1; telegram from Maury Maverick to Truman, May 22, 1951, PSF: General File, M (1 of 2—Ma–Me) folder, Truman Papers. For examples of the media attention Rusk generated, see Marquis Childs, "Another China Policy," *Washington Post,* May 23, 1951, 15; Editorial, "Our Changing China Policy," *NYT,* May 19, 1951, 11; "Policy Change on China War Denied Here," *Washington Post,* May 22, 1951, 1.

64. The quotes attributed to Van Devander are from Kenneth W. Hechler, memorandum, April 12, 1951, Subject File, DNC—Establishment of a Research Comm. folder, Hechler Papers, in which Hechler summarizes their conversations. Thus, these are Hechler's words describing what Van Devander said, with the exception of the last statement, which is a direct quote from Van Devander.

65. Benton to Truman, April 30, 1951, PSF: General File, William Benton—U.S. Senate folder, Truman Papers; Rayburn to Garner, May 19, 1951, Correspondence: Presidents, Vice Presidents, and Others, 1951–1952 folder, Rayburn Papers; John A. Carroll to Truman, "Suggestions for This Evening's Meeting," July 10, 1951, Truman—memos to and from the president, 1947–52 folder, Murphy Papers.

66. Congressman Francis E. Walter (D-PA) quoted in Harry H. Vaughan, memorandum for the president, July 5, 1951, WHCF: Official File 471B, Korean emergency (Apr. 1951–1953) folder, Truman Papers; Goldman, *Crucial Decade,* 199; Clark M. Clifford to Charles S. Murphy, May 10, 1951, and Chester Bowles to Clifford, May 2, 1951, Clark Clifford folder, Murphy Papers.

67. H. Alexander Smith diary entries, April 23 and 28, May 1–31, June 1, 1951, box 282; Smith to Phillip Marshall Brown, May 2, 1951, and other correspondence, box 105, Special File—Acheson ouster, Smith Papers.

68. Fite, *Richard B. Russell,* 255–64; Phillip Dodd, "M'Arthur Firing Probe to Start May 3 in Senate," *Chicago Tribune,* April 25, 1951, 7; "The M'Arthur Hearings," *NYT,* April 29, 1951, E8; Caridi, *Korean War and American Politics,* 152–53. Staffer Francis O. Wilcox, who worked under committee chairs of both parties and was probably as unbiased an observer as one could find, supported Russell's logic; see Wilcox diary entries, April 30 and May 2, 1951, Diary, 1951–1952 folder, Wilcox Papers. Ritchie quoted in "Oral History Interview with Francis O. Wilcox," March 21, 1984, 121–22, http://www.trumanlibrary.org/oralhist/wilcox3.html#117 (accessed June 2, 2007).

69. McMahon-MacArthur dialogue quoted in William S. White, "Senate Inquiry On," *NYT,* May 4, 1951, 1; "The Course Ahead," *Time,* May 14, 1951, http://www.time.com/time/magazine/article/0,9171,935205,00.html (accessed June 8, 2007); "Oral History Interview with Wilcox," 119.

70. Marshall's testimony in Kepley, *Collapse of the Middle Way,* 126–27; Bradley's testimony quoted in Rovere and Schlesinger, *General MacArthur & President Truman,* 285, 287.

71. "Political Squall," *Time,* May 28, 1951; Kaufman, *Korean War,* 108.

72. Fite, *Richard B. Russell,* 263; H. Alexander Smith diary entry, July 29, 1951, box 282, Smith Papers; Harold B. Hinton, "8 G.O.P. Senators Find 'Catastrophe' in Far East Policy," *NYT,* August 20, 1951, 1; W. H. Lawrence, "Both Sides Now Claim M'Arthur Case Victory," *NYT,* August 26, 1951, B3.

73. Rooney quoted in "Needling Acheson," *Newsweek,* August 6, 1951, 17.

74. Fite, *Richard B. Russell,* 255–64; Halberstam, *Coldest Winter,* 612; Sidney Hyman, *The Lives of William Benton* (Chicago: University of Chicago Press, 1969), 448.

75. Bill Max to Truman, April 26, 1951, PSF: General File, M folder, Truman Papers.

76. Pierpaoli, *Truman and Korea*, 225–26, 229–30.

77. Ibid., 84–85, 150–53, 227; Offner, *Another Such Victory*, 383, 422.

78. Casey, *Selling the Korean War*, 176–77; Wigderson, "Wages of Anticommunism," 233–34.

79. Wigderson, "Wages of Anticommunism," 233.

80. Casey, *Selling the Korean War*, 202.

81. Wigderson, "Wages of Anticommunism," 236; Truman quoted in Hamby, *Man of the People*, 578.

82. The railroad workers' union signed an agreement to end its strike in December 1950, only to have the switchmen go out on strike the following month. Truman was enraged, but a new agreement was finally worked out in March 1951. See Hamby, *Man of the People*, 578.

83. For an analysis of inflation, see Pierpaoli, *Truman and Korea*, 100.

84. Ibid., 116; Goldman, *Crucial Decade*, 182.

85. Pierpaoli, *Truman and Korea*, 111–13, 114.

86. Elsey, *Unplanned Life*, 203.

87. Hamby, *Man of the People*, 576–77; Pierpaoli, *Truman and Korea*, 105–6; Kaufman, *Korean War*, 95; Rose, *Cold War Comes to Main Street*, 313; James Reston, "U.S. Is Now Running a Marathon, Not a Sprint," *NYT*, March 11, 1951, 143.

88. NCAC discussed in Pierpaoli, *Truman and Korea*, 201–5; Truman quoted in Hamby, *Man of the People*, 577.

89. William S. White, "M'Arthur Due Back in U.S. Next Week," *NYT*, April 13, 1951, 1; Congressman Edward H. Jenison to Truman, February 19, 1951, WHCF: Official File 471B, Korean emergency folder, Truman Papers; George Gallup, "Poll Favors Split Korea to End War," *NYT*, March 28, 1951, 7; other polling data from Wood, "American Reaction to Limited War in Asia," 141.

4. The Forgotten Attempts to End the Forgotten War

1. Representative Albert Gore Sr. (D-TN) quoted in "'Cataclysmic' U.S. Weapon Reported," *Los Angeles Times*, April 16, 1951, 1.

2. For examples of historians arguing that the political atmosphere was not conducive to dissent, see Fried, *Nightmare in Red*, 102, 129, 142; Smith, *Opposition beyond the Water's Edge*, 122–23; James T. Patterson, *Grand Expectations: The U.S., 1945–1974* (New York: Oxford University Press, 1997), 261–63; Lawrence S. Wittner, *Rebels against War: The American Peace Movement, 1933–1983* (Philadelphia: Temple University Press, 1984), 225–27. Foot's *Substitute for Victory* discusses the effects of American domestic politics on the armistice negotiations once they got under way.

3. "Atomic Death Belt Urged for Korea," *NYT*, April 17, 1951, 3; "A Radioactive Belt across Korea?" *NYT*, April 22, 1951, 157; "'Cataclysmic' U.S. Weapon

Reported," 1; Douglas MacArthur, *Reminiscences* (New York: McGraw-Hill, 1964), 384; Wainstock, *Truman, MacArthur and the Korean War,* 118–19. It is unknown whether Gore's idea came from MacArthur.

4. "'Cataclysmic' U.S. Weapon Reported"; McMahon, the army, and Gore quoted in "Atomic Belt Plan Held Not Feasible," *NYT,* April 18, 1951, 16. For other press coverage, see Frank Carey, "Radioactive Zone across Korea Urged," *Washington Post,* April 17, 1951, 7; Drew Pearson, "Atomic Super-Weapons Reported," *Washington Post,* April 24, 1951, B15; and *NYT* articles cited in note 3.

5. George M. Elsey, "Memorandum for Mr. Murphy," April 24, 1951, Subject File, Korea—New Peace Proposal, 1951 folder, Elsey Papers. Plans for the communist offensive are described in Kathryn Weathersby, "Stalin, Mao, and the End of the Korean War," in *Brothers in Arms: The Rise and Fall of the Sino-Soviet Alliance,* ed. Odd Arne Westad (Washington, DC: Woodrow Wilson Center Press, 1998), 95, and Shu Guand Zhang, *Mao's Military Romanticism: China and the Korean War, 1950–1953* (Lawrence: University Press of Kansas, 1995), 144–34. The April 22–29, 1951, Chinese offensive employed 250,000 soldiers in twenty-seven divisions fighting five U.S. Army divisions. See U.S. Department of Defense, "Commemoration of 50th Anniversary of the Korean War," http://korea50.army.mil/history/chronology/timeline_1951.shtml (accessed September 12, 2007). Discussions of the initiative and China's reaction are in *FRUS, 1951,* 7:370, 375, 379.

6. McFarland's proposal and Acheson quoted in L. D. Battle, untitled note to file, May 14, 1951, Memoranda of Conversations File, May 1951 folder, Acheson Papers. For additional discussion, see James E. McMillan Jr., ed., *The Ernest W. McFarland Papers: The United States Senate Years, 1940–1952* (Prescott, AZ: Sharlot Hall Museum Press, 1995), 285.

7. "Can We Keep the Peace?" *Cosmopolitan,* August 1951, 32–35, 120–21 (emphasis added).

8. S. Res. 140, May 17, 1951, SMOF: Dept. of State Topical Subseries, Negotiations for an Armistice, Dec. 1950–June 1951 folder, Truman Papers; "Sen. Johnson Believes Cease-Fire Order Will Be Issued June 25 to End Conflict," *Pueblo Star Journal and Chieftain,* May 28, 1951, 6; for Johnson's speech, see *CR,* 82nd Cong., 1st sess., pt. 4, May 17, 1951, 5424.

9. Barnet Nover, "Big Ed Disappointed by Truman's Action," *Denver Post,* April 11, 1951, 2; "Big Ed Demands U.S. Use New Arms in Korea," *Denver Post,* September 9, 1951, 14A; "Use of Atomic Arms in Korea Is Urged by Senator Johnson," *Washington Evening Star,* November 5, 1951, A3.

10. "United States Objectives, Politics and Courses of Action in Asia," May 17, 1951, NSC 48/5, Digital National Security Archive, document no. PD00141, 4–5.

11. Press coverage is discussed in Rees, *Korea,* 261. Examples of the scant coverage include "For Halt in Korean War," *NYT,* May 18, 1951, 3; "Back in the Sand with Big Ed," *Denver Post,* May 18, 1951, 18. The *Washington Post* did not mention Johnson's proposal in its May 18, 1951, issue.

12. Telegram, Dept. of State to USUN, Circular #728, May 22, 1951, SMOF:

Dept. of State Topical File Subseries, Negotiations for an Armistice, Dec. 1951–June 1951 folder, Truman Papers; Stewart Alsop, "Our Korean Objectives Decided," *Washington Post,* May 27, 1951, p. B5; *Pravda* quoted in "Russians Play up Johnson Peace Bid," *NYT,* May 21, 1951, 6; "Pravda Prints Peace Bid by Senator of Colorado," *NYT,* May 20, 1951, 8; "Reds' Interest in Korea Armistice Plan Heartens Sen. Ed Johnson," *Rocky Mountain News,* May 28, 1951, 3.

13. "Big Ed and Russia Start Peace Rumors Flying in West Europe," *Rocky Mountain News,* May 21, 1951, 3; Ferdinand Kuhn, "Safeguards against New Attack Asked," *Washington Post,* June 24, 1951, M1; "Acheson to U.S. Representatives to U.N., 22 May 1951," SMOF: Dept. of State Topical File Subseries, Negotiations for an Armistice, Dec. 1950–June 1951 folder, Truman Papers; "Russians Play up Johnson Peace Bid"; William R. Frye, "Rau Asks UN Peace Offer with Partition of Korea," *Christian Science Monitor,* May 19, 1951, 1; Austin proposal in *FRUS, 1951,* 7:451; Alsop, "Our Korean Objectives."

14. Ralph Flanders, "Broadcast for Vermont Stations—Week of June 16, 1951," box 152, Flanders Papers; "Harriman Questioned on Big Ed's Peace Plan," *Denver Post,* May 25, 1951, 3; "Union Backs Big Ed in Peace Program," *Rocky Mountain News,* May 30, 1951, 12.

15. "Reds' Interest in Korea Armistice Plan," *Rocky Mountain News,* May 28, 1951, 3; Barnet Nover, "Big Ed Claims Wide Support for Peace Plan," *Denver Post,* May 26, 1951, 1; "Korean Envoy Calls Johnson 'Daydreamer,'" *Rocky Mountain News,* May 31, 1951, 11. Johnson made a valid point about coverage in the American press. Major publications such as the *New York Times, Chicago Tribune, Washington Post, Time,* and *Newsweek* ignored his May 26, 1951, address; the *Los Angeles Times* mentioned it briefly. See "Senator Pushes War Anniversary Armistice Plan," *Los Angeles Times,* May 28, 1951, 4.

16. Oshinsky, *Conspiracy So Immense,* 195; "McCarthy Sees Acheson Ouster within 3 Weeks," *NYT,* May 13, 1951, 13.

17. Among the sources that fail to mention Johnson's resolution are Weathersby, "Stalin, Mao, and the End of the Korean War"; Kathryn Weathersby, "New Russian Documents on the Korean War," *Cold War International History Bulletin* 6/7 (Winter 1995): 30–59, http://www.wilsoncenter.org/topics/pubs/ACF1A6.pdf (accessed May 30, 2009); Zhang, *Mao's Military Romanticism;* Robert C. Tucker, "The Cold War in Stalin's Time: What the New Sources Reveal," *Diplomatic History* 21, no. 2 (1997): 273–81; Chen Jian (the foremost authority on Chinese sources regarding the Korean War), *Mao's China and the Cold War* (Chapel Hill: University of North Carolina Press, 2001); Pingchao Zhu, "The Road to an Armistice: An Examination of the Chinese and American Diplomacy during the Korean War" (PhD diss., University of Miami at Ohio, 1998); Andrei Gromyko, *Memoirs* (New York: Doubleday, 1989); Andrei Gromyko, *History of Soviet Foreign Policy, 1945–1970,* ed. B. Ponomaryov and V. Khvostov, trans. David Skvirsky (Moscow: Progress Publishers, 1973); Dehuai Peng (Mao's military commander in Korea), *Memoirs of a Chinese Marshal: The Autobiographical Notes of Peng Dehuai* (Beijing: Foreign Language Press, 1984).

18. *FRUS, 1951,* 7:401–10, 421–22; John D. Hickerson, memorandum for files, May 16, 1951, SMOF: Dept. of State Topical File Subseries, Negotiations for Armistice, Dec. 1950–June 1951 folder, Truman Papers.

19. Thomas J. Hamilton, "Soviet Proposal to Discuss Truce in Korea Is Revealed," *NYT,* May 24, 1951, 1; Thomas J. Hamilton, "Soviet Denies Move for Peace in Korea," *NYT,* May 29, 1951, 1; Pearson and Lie cited in Rees, *Korea,* 261–62; Anthony Leviero, "Acheson Unaware of Talks," *NYT,* June 3, 1951; Acheson, *Present at the Creation,* 532; Charles Burton Marshall, State Department policy planning staff, quoted in Goulden, *Korea,* 550.

20. *FRUS, 1951,* 7:507–11, 536–38.

21. Truman, note to self, June 21, 1951, PSF: Longhand Notes File, June 21, 1951 folder, Truman Papers; H. Maier, "Rumors of Peace in Korea," June 6, 1951, WHCF: Official File 471B, Korean emergency (Apr. 1951–1953) folder, Truman Papers (emphasis in original). The open letter's author is unknown, but it originated in the State Department. White House press secretary Joseph Short requested a copy of the open letter to Malik a month later but apparently never released it. See Edward W. Barrett, memorandum for Joseph Short, July 9, 1951, WHCF: Official File 471B, Korean emergency (Apr. 1951–1953) folder, Truman Papers.

22. Foot, *Substitute for Victory,* 37; Rees, *Korea,* 263. See *FRUS, 1951,* 7:548–83, for U.S. foreign policy leaders' responses to the Malik speech.

23. Jenner quoted in Michael Paul Poder, "The Senatorial Career of William E. Jenner" (PhD diss., University of Notre Dame, 1976), 91; George and Millikin quoted in Kuhn, "Safeguards against New Attack"; "Cain Demands that U.N. Forces Hit Enemy 'with Everything,'" *Washington Post,* June 25, 1951, 3.

24. Kuhn, "Safeguards against New Attack."

25. Ibid.

26. McMahon quoted in ibid; telegram from Sidney Wilkinson to Senator Theodore F. Green and news release, June 25, 1951, box 620, Green Papers; memorandum of telephone conversation between Senator Tom Connally and Mr. Acheson, June 29, 1951, Memoranda of Conversations File, June 1951 folder, Acheson Papers; Representative John A. Blatnik to Truman, June 29, 1951, WHCF: Official File 471B, Cease-Fire Truce—Pro folder, Truman Papers.

27. Harold Hinton, "Now G.O.P. Senators Shy from McCarthy," *NYT,* June 20, 1951, 3; Drew Pearson, "Diplomats Call Peace Bid 'Smart,'" *Washington Post,* June 28, 1951, B15; Fried, *Nightmare in Red,* 131; McCarthy quoted in John H. Fenton, "M'Carthy Brands Korea a 'Betrayal,'" *NYT,* June 29, 1951, 2. Kuhn, "Safeguards against New Attack," reported the reactions of eleven members of Congress to the Malik speech; more than half of them, like McCarthy, were not members of foreign affairs committees.

28. Department of State, "Statement Concerning Malik Broadcast of June 23," No. 553, June 23, 1951; telegram from Kirk to Acheson, June 25, 1951; Truman, speech at Tullahoma, Tennessee, June 25, 1951, all in SMOF: Dept. of State Topical Subseries, Negotiations for an Armistice, Dec. 1950–June 1951 folder, Truman

Papers; Edward T. Folliard, "Malik Cease-Fire Proposal Delayed Release of Text," *Washington Post,* June 25, 1951, 1; George M. Elsey, memorandum for file, June 30, 1951, Subject File, Korean War folder, Elsey Papers.

29. Memoranda of telephone conversations, Dean Acheson and Senator Wiley, Acheson and Senator Connally, Acheson and Representative Charles Eaton, June 29, 1951, Memoranda of Conversations File, June 1951 folder, Acheson Papers; James Reston, "Ridgway in Offer," *NYT,* June 30, 1951, 1; "The President's News Conference," June 28, 1951, *PP,* http://trumanlibrary.org/publicpapers/index.php?pid=354&st=&st1= (accessed September 21, 2007).

30. Ralph E. Flanders, (Radio) Broadcast for Vermont Stations, July 5, 1951, box 152, Vermont broadcasts—week of July 1, 1951 folder, Flanders Papers; "Draft UC Statement," June 14, 1951, SMOF: Dept. of State Topical Subseries, folder 36, Truman Papers.

31. Foot, *Substitute for Victory,* 37.

32. Connally, Wherry, and Rayburn quoted in Walter Trohan, "Reds Accept Bid to Parley," *Chicago Tribune,* July 2, 1951, 1; Taft, McCarran, and Mundt quoted in "No Whistles Blew," *Time,* July 9, 1951, http://www.time.com/time/magazine/article/0,9171,806084,00.html (accessed September 29, 2007).

33. "The President's Press Conference—July 12, 1951," *PP,* http://www.trumanlibrary.org/publicpapers/index.php?pid=367&st=sabotage&st1= (accessed January 25, 2007); Weathersby, "New Russian Documents," 34; "Korean War Costs Not Included," *Wall Street Journal,* June 8, 1951, 3; "Taft Counsels $70 Billion Budget Limit," *Washington Post,* June 11, 1951, 2; defense spending data from "Government Spending Chart," USGovernmentspending.com, www.usgovernmentspending.com/spending_chart_1950_1960USb_14s21i011mcn_30f##view (accessed July 23, 2013); Peng quoted in Zhang, *Mao's Military Romanticism,* 221.

34. Halberstam, *The Fifties,* 36; Peter Pringle and James Spigelman, *The Nuclear Barons* (New York: Holt, Rinehart & Winston, 1981), 88, 93; Brien McMahon, "We *Can* Get through the Iron Curtain," *NYT,* June 24, 1951, 150.

35. Allen Taylor, "Story of the Stockholm Petition," *NYT,* August 13, 1950, E6; Cabell Phillips, "What Russians Say about Korean War," *NYT,* July 30, 1950, E4; McMahon, "We *Can* Get through the Iron Curtain."

36. Senate Concurrent Resolution 11 and accompanying statement of Brien McMahon, February 8, 1951, box 3, 82nd Congress, 1st Session folder, McMahon Papers; Francis O. Wilcox diary entry, February 2, 1951, Diary, 1951–1952 folder, Wilcox Papers.

37. Ribicoff quoted in William A. Garrett, "M'Mahon, Ribicoff to Call for Peace," *Hartford Times,* February 6, 1951, 19.

38. "Memorandum of the Press and Radio News Conference, Wednesday, February 14, 1951," SMOF: Dept. of State Topical File Subseries, Restudy of the Question of the 38th Parallel folder, Truman Papers; "The McMahon-Ribicoff Resolution (H. Con. Res. 57)," March 15, 1951, Memoranda of Conversations File, March 1951 folder, Acheson Papers; "Acheson Letter on U.S. Relations," *NYT,* March 22, 1951, 36.

39. For the timeline of the bill's passage, see *FRUS, 1951,* 4:1607; Francis O. Wilcox diary entry, June 7, 1951, Diary, 1951–1952 folder, Wilcox Papers; Democrat quoted in "House Adopts Friendship Bid to Russians; Members Say Slim 36–7 Vote Ruins Effect," *NYT,* June 5, 1951, 18.

40. House changes to the bill are in *CR,* 82nd Cong., 1st sess., pt. 6, June 4, 1951, 6095; *FRUS, 1951,* 4:1607–8; Thomas J. Hamilton, "Malik, Sailing, Says Bid Was Censored," *NYT,* July 7, 1951, 3.

41. Truman and aide quoted in George M. Elsey, memorandum for file, July 5, 1951, Truman Presidency Subject File, Korean War folder, Elsey Papers; James Reston, "Korea Truce Issue Heading for '52 Political Cauldron," *NYT,* July 5, 1951, 9.

42. Brien McMahon to Theodore Francis Green, February 1, 1951, box 613, Green Papers; Marshall Andrews, "Truman Urges Soviet Chief to Publish U.S. Peace Aims," *Washington Post,* July 8, 1951, M1; Truman's letter quoted in *FRUS, 1951,* 4:1610–11.

43. Rusk speech in telegram from Dean Acheson to USUN, New York, May 22, 1951, SMOF: Dept. of State topical File Subseries, Negotiations for an Armistice, Dec. 1950–June 1951 folder, Truman Papers; Russell Porter, "Rusk Hints U.S. Aid to Revolt in China," *NYT,* May 19, 1951, 1; "To the Russian People," *NYT,* July 8, 1951, 112; McMillan, *McFarland Papers,* 295, 301; Brien McMahon, speech to International Federation of War Veterans Organizations, July 18, 1951, box 9, Addresses and Releases, July 1951 folder, McMahon Papers; "Exchange of Visits of U.S., Russian Veterans Urged," *Los Angeles Times,* July 19, 1951, 28; "Address of Senator Brien McMahon in the Senate," August 2, 1951, box 9, Addresses and Releases, July 1951 folder, McMahon Papers; "Freedoms of U.S. Scored by Pravda," *NYT,* August 3, 1951, 3.

44. Shvernik statement quoted in Department of State Press Release No. 705, August 6, 1951, Russian Peace Offer folder, Lloyd Papers; Harrison E. Salisbury, "Moscow Also Broadcasts McMahon Resolution on Nation-Wide Hook-up," *NYT,* August 8, 1951, 1. The Presidium was a small group within the Kremlin authorized to act in behalf of the Soviet Parliament when the latter was not in session.

45. *FRUS, 1951,* 4:1635–36; "State Department Calls It 'Propaganda Trap'—Cites Obligations Ignored," *NYT,* August 8, 1951, 1; Truman quoted in "Man at Work," *Time,* August 20, 1951, http://www.time.com/time/printout/ 0,8816,859245,00.html (accessed November 2, 2007).

46. Ribicoff quoted in "State Department Calls It 'Propaganda Trap'"; Wherry quoted in Alfred Friendly, "U.S., Britain, France Shrug Off Latest Soviet 'Propaganda' Bid," *Washington Post,* August 8, 1951, 3; McMillan, *McFarland Papers,* 309; "World-Wide Reaction to the Friendship Resolutions Exchanged between the US and the USSR, July and August 1951," September 10, 1951, and "Meeting Notes—Mutual Security Programs," August 8, 1951, Foreign Relations—Russia (1949–1951) folder, Elsey Papers; AFL quoted in "Meeting Notes," ibid.

47. "Meeting Notes—Mutual Security Programs," August 8, 1951; "On the Limb," *Washington Post,* August 8, 1951, 14; Cain quoted in "U.S., Britain, France

Shrug Off Latest Soviet 'Propaganda' Bid"; "State Department Calls It 'Propaganda Trap'"; "Senate Address by Senator Brien McMahon," August 20, 1951, box 9, Addresses and Speeches—Aug. 1951 folder, McMahon Papers.

48. *FRUS, 1951,* 4:1640, 1658–60; "The President's Press Conference," August 30, 1951, *PP,* http://www.trumanlibrary.org/publicpapers/index.php?pid=425&st=&st1= (accessed November 7, 2007); David D. Lloyd, memorandum for Mr. Murphy, September 5, 1951, David D. Lloyd folder, Murphy Papers; Lloyd to Charles Murphy, "McMahon Luncheon Concerning Reply to Shvernik," October 4, 1951, Foreign Relations—Truman-Shvernik folder, Elsey Papers; Howland H. Sargeant to Lloyd, December 4, 1951, Files of David D. Lloyd, Truman Papers.

49. Acheson, *Present at the Creation,* 370; Flanders to John Foster Dulles, February 5, 1951, box 105, Paul Hoffman folder, Flanders Papers; W. McNeil Lowry, "The Senator Who Would Call on God," box 139, October 1950 "The Senator Who Would Call on God" folder, Flanders Papers.

50. "Address by Senator Ralph E. Flanders—Vermont Press Association," June 30, 1951, box 140, June 30, 1951 Vt. Press Ass'n Bellows Falls Speech folder, Flanders Papers; Peter N. Farrar, "Britain's Proposal for a Buffer Zone South of the Yalu in November 1950: Was It a Neglected Opportunity to End the Fighting in Korea?" *Journal of Contemporary History* 18, no. 2 (April 1983): 331–34. The British proposal was covered by the major newspapers. See "South Korean Bars North Buffer Strip," *NYT,* November 18, 1950, 2; "Guns—and Talks," *NYT,* November 26, 1950, E1; "Capital Cautious in Truce Comment," *NYT,* July 10, 1951, 4.

51. Ralph Flanders, "A New Peace Plan for Korea," December 1951, and "Proposals for a Positive Policy in Korea," March 1, 1952, both in box 141, Flanders Papers.

52. Dean Acheson, "A Possible Line for US Action in Korea," December 19, 1951, Memoranda of Conversations File, November–December 1951 folder, Acheson Papers; Farrar, "Britain's Proposal for a Buffer Zone," 333; Flanders quoted in *FRUS, 1952–1954,* 15:816. Searches of the *New York Times, Washington Post, Chicago Tribune,* and *Time* magazine yielded no coverage of Flanders's proposal.

53. The twenty-six officials McCarthy named were among those he had accused (*without* naming them) in his February 20, 1950, speech on the Senate floor, which propelled him to fame. See Griffith, *Politics of Fear,* 133. Although Jessup was eventually seated in the UN as a recess appointment by Truman, this was widely considered a political victory for McCarthy against the president.

54. P. J. Philips, "Truce Advocated at Ottawa Parley," *NYT,* September 13, 1952, 2; Eugene Griffin, "Neutral Zone in N. Korea Urged by U.S. Senator," *Chicago Tribune,* September 13, 1952, 12; Ralph E. Flanders, "Peace Terms for Korea," September 12–13, 1952, box 142, Peace Terms for Korea—Ottawa, Canada folder, Flanders Papers.

55. Foot, *Substitute for Victory,* 141; Acheson, *Present at the Creation,* 536.

56. "Pulling the Punches," *NYT,* June 30, 1951, 14; Oshinsky, *Conspiracy So Immense,* 185; Arthur Herman, *Joseph McCarthy: Reexamining the Life and Legacy of*

America's Most Hated Senator (New York: Free Press, 2000), 4; Richard H. Rovere, *Senator Joe McCarthy* (New York: Harcourt, Brace, 1959), 35. For a sampling of other McCarthy biographies, see Griffith, *Politics of Fear;* Fred J. Cook, *The Nightmare Decade: The Life and Times of Senator Joe McCarthy* (New York: Random House, 1971); Mark Landis, *Joseph McCarthy: The Politics of Chaos* (London: Associated University Presses, 1987); Ellen Schrecker, *Many Are the Crimes: McCarthyism in America* (Boston: Little, Brown, 1998).

5. The Third War, July 1951–December 1952

1. Ridgway, *Korean War,* 116, 198.

2. Quoted in Casey, *Selling the Korean War,* 278–79.

3. Kaufman, *Korean War,* 128–31.

4. Beisner, *Dean Acheson,* 437–38; "Statement by the President on General Ridgway's Korean Armistice Proposal—May 7, 1952," *PP,* http://www.trumanlibrary.org/publicpapers/index.php?pid=1288&st=&st1= (accessed May 31, 2014).

5. Kaufman, *Korean War,* 131, 145, 157–58, 161.

6. See Hogan, *Cross of Iron,* 350–51.

7. Pierpaoli, *Truman and Korea,* 199; Ruffin quoted in Hogan, *Cross of Iron,* 351; Truman quoted in Donovan, *Tumultuous Years,* 368.

8. Truman quoted in Hamby, *Man of the People,* 580.

9. Martin, Kem, and Lehman quoted in Hogan, *Cross of Iron,* 338, 339. For a discussion of the congressional debate, see ibid., 338–41.

10. Donald C. Miller, "The Revenue Act of 1951: A General Survey," *National Tax Journal* 5 (1952): 41; "Statement by the President upon Signing the Revenue Act of 1951—October 20, 1951," *PP,* http://www.trumanlibrary.org/publicpapers/index.php?pid=523&st=tax&st1= (accessed May 31, 2014). The marginal tax rate is the actual rate assessed and does not take deductions into account.

11. Hogan, *Cross of Iron,* 319. For an excellent discussion of the congressional politics of UMT, see James Richard Riggs, "Congress and the Conduct of the Korean War" (PhD diss., Purdue University, 1972), 170–73, 258–63.

12. Jonas quoted in Hogan, *Cross of Iron,* 320; Johnson quoted in Riggs, "Congress and the Conduct of the Korean War," 262. For grassroots opposition and how opponents killed the bill, see ibid., 259–61.

13. Wigderson, "Wages of Anticommunism," 242.

14. Pierpaoli, *Truman and Korea,* 162–63; Ferrell, *Harry S. Truman,* 371.

15. Pierpaoli, *Truman and Korea,* 165, 166; Maeva Marcus, *Truman and the Steel Seizure Case: The Limits of Presidential Power* (New York: Columbia University Press, 1977), 67, 71–72; Hamby, *Man of the People,* 594; Ferrell, *Harry S. Truman,* 373.

16. "Radio and Television Address to the American People on the Need for Government Operation of the Steel Mills—April 8, 1952," *PP,* http://www.trumanlibrary.org/publicpapers/index.php?pid=965&st=&st1= (accessed June 4, 2014); Marcus, *Truman and the Steel Seizure,* 75–77, 94–95.

17. Ferrell, *Harry S. Truman*, 371; "The President's News Conference—April 17, 1952," *PP*, http://www.trumanlibrary.org/publicpapers/index.php?pid=1263&st=seize&st1=radio (accessed June 5, 2014); Marcus, *Truman and the Steel Seizure*, 83, 89–90, 91, 93, 293; McCullough, *Truman*, 899.

18. Marcus, *Truman and the Steel Seizure*, 91–92.

19. Ibid., 91, 95–96, 98–99; Ferrell, *Harry S. Truman*, 373.

20. Marcus, *Truman and the Steel Seizure*, 124–25.

21. Ibid., 131, 133, 174–75.

22. "The President's News Conference—May 22, 1952," *PP*, http://www.trumanlibrary.org/publicpapers/index.php?pid=1303&st=&st1= (accessed June 6, 2014); Donovan, *Tumultuous Years*, 386.

23. *Pittsburg Press* quoted in Marcus, *Truman and the Steel Seizure*, 213; Cain and Tobey quoted in Duane Tananbaum, *The Bricker Amendment Controversy: A Test of Eisenhower's Political Leadership* (Ithaca, NY: Cornell University Press, 1988), 51.

24. Marcus, *Truman and the Steel Seizure*, 251.

25. Pierpaoli, *Truman and Korea*, 170–71.

26. Truman quoted in Donovan, *Tumultuous Years*, 389; Marcus, *Truman and the Steel Seizure*, 251–52; Pierpaoli, *Truman and Korea*, 162. For a discussion on the actual steel inventory situation, see Ferrell, *Harry S. Truman*, 372–73, and Marcus, *Truman and the Steel Seizure*, 251–52, 356; for the fate of standby control for 1953, see Pierpaoli, *Truman and Korea*, 218–19.

27. Ojserkis, *Beginnings of the Cold War Arms Race*, 105–6; Pierpaoli, *Truman and Korea*, 228, 187.

28. U.S. Senate, *Review of Bipartisan Foreign Policy Consultations since World War II*, 82nd Cong., 1st sess., 1952, S. Doc. 87. Hechler, *Working with Truman*, 156–57, describes the project. For White House and State Department endorsements, see Roger Tubby to Joseph Short, July 24, 1951; Short to Charles S. Murphy, July 25, 1951; George Elsey, memorandum for Lucius Battle, August 1, 1951; and Hechler to Elsey, August 14, 1951, all in Foreign Relations—Hechler Study on Bipartisan Foreign Policy folder, Elsey Papers. A search of the *New York Times, Washington Post, Chicago Tribune,* and *Time* revealed no coverage of the report. McCarthy vilified Jessup, a former Far East adviser in the State Department, as a communist sympathizer, killing his nomination.

29. "Draft, China Lobby," n.d., David D. Lloyd Files, folder 2, Truman Papers; Ross Y. Koen, *The China Lobby in American Politics* (1960; reprint, New York: Octagon Books, 1974), 27–29, 33–55; "That China Lobby," *Washington Post*, June 26, 1951, 10.

30. George M. Elsey, memorandum for the president, March 28, 1951, Foreign Relations—China Lobby folder, Elsey Papers; Truman, *Memoirs*, 2:410; "President's Conference with ADA Leaders," May 21, 1951, David D. Lloyd folder, Murphy Papers; Webb quoted in George Elsey, memorandum to Mr. Tannenwald, April 30, 1951, Correspondence and General File A–G, China Lobby folder, Lloyd Papers. Buchanan died on April 27, 1951.

31. Drew Pearson, "The Washington Merry-Go-Round," *Washington Post,* June 9, 1951, B13; McMahon and Wiley quoted in Doris Fleeson, "Way Open to Probe China Lobby," *Washington Evening Star,* June 5, 1951, A13; "'China Lobby' Study Pledged by Acheson," *Washington Post,* June 8, 1951, 1; Bridges and Acheson quoted in Ferdinand Kuhn, "Acheson Informs Senate Hearing Chiang Propaganda Is Being Sifted," *Washington Post,* June 10, 1951, M1. The investigation covered the activities of both the China Bloc and the China Lobby. Truman used the term "China Lobby" to refer to both, a convention I follow throughout this discussion.

32. Truman to Attorney General, June 11, 1951, PSF: General File, China Lobby folder, Truman Papers; Robert Accinelli, *Crisis and Commitment: United States Policy toward Taiwan, 1950–1955* (Chapel Hill: University of North Carolina Press, 1996), 77; George M. Elsey, memorandum on China Lobby, June 8, 1951, Subject File, China Lobby folder, Theodore Tannenwald Papers, HSTL.

33. Theodore Tannenwald Jr. to George Elsey, "Notes on China Lobby Investigation," July 9, 1951, Subject File, Foreign Relations—China Lobby folder, Elsey Papers; J. S. Lanigan to W. A. Harriman, October 4, 1951, PSF: Subject File, China Lobby—General folder, Truman Papers; Elsey to Charles Murphy, "China Lobby," July 6, 1951, Subject File, Foreign Relations, China Lobby folder, Elsey Papers; "The Reporter's Notes," *Reporter,* April 1, 1952, 1. The other articles in the *Reporter* series were Charles Wertenbaker, "The China Lobby," *Reporter,* April 15, 1952, 4–24, and Max Ascoli, Phillip Horton, and Charles Wertenbaker, "The China Lobby," *Reporter,* April 29, 1952, 5–24. I found no congressional comment on the *Reporter* series in the *New York Times, Washington Post,* or *Time.* One *Post* reporter commented on the story; see Marquis Childs, "Chinese in U.S. Politics," *Washington Post,* April 15, 1951, 10, and "China Lobby II," *Washington Post,* April 17, 1951, 16.

34. Tannenwald to Elsey, "Notes on China Lobby Investigation," July 9, 1951, Elsey Papers; Kenneth Hechler, memorandum, July 18, 1951; "Summary of State Department Files," n.d.; "Miscellaneous Information," n.d.; and J. S. Lanigan to W. A. Harriman, October 4, 1951, all in PSF: Subject File, China Lobby—General folder, Truman Papers; Matthew S. Flynn, "Reconsidering the China Lobby: Senator William F. Knowland and US-China Policy, 1945–1958" (PhD diss., Ohio University, 2004), 69–70 (emphasis added).

35. Edwin O'Brien to Brien McMahon, June 10, 1951, PSF: Subject File, China Lobby—General folder, Truman Papers; Michael Straight to George Elsey, June 5, 1951, Subject File, China Lobby folder, Elsey Papers; Robert Albright, "Proposed Chiang Lobby Quiz Would Cover Red China, Too," *Washington Post,* July 7, 1951, 3; "Probe of Foreign Lobbies Asked," *Washington Post,* July 6, 1951, 8; "The 'China Lobby,'" *Time,* July 16, 1951, http://www.time.com/time/printout/0,8816,889064,00.html (accessed June 18, 2007).

36. Mason Drukman, *Wayne Morse: A Political Biography* (Portland: Oregon Historical Society Press, 1997), 180; Paul P. Kennedy, "Senate Gets 'Files' on Secret Activity in U.S. to Aid Chiang," *NYT,* April 11, 1952, 1; "Investigation of China Lobby," July 10, 1951, Memoranda of Conversations File, July 1951 folder, Acheson Papers.

37. Cain quoted in Willard Edwards, "Report Truman Kick-in in 1948 by China Lobby," *Chicago Tribune,* June 10, 1952, 7; Busbey quoted in Willard Edwards, "Dares Truman Revive Probe of China Lobby," *Chicago Tribune,* June 15, 1952, 10; David D. Lloyd, memorandum for the president, June 26, 1952, PSF: General File, China Lobby—General folder, Truman Papers; "China Lobby," *Washington Sunday Star,* April 20, 1951, C4; Drew Pearson, "China Lobby Quiz Seems Stalled," *Washington Post,* May 23, 1952, B15. Pearson claimed that Johnson once offered him $10,000 to make a favorable reference in his column to Dr. H. H. Kung, the brother-in-law of Jiang Jieshi. See Tyler Abell, ed., *Drew Pearson Diaries, 1949–1959* (New York: Holt, Rinehart & Winston, 1974), 212.

38. Tucker, *Patterns in the Dust,* 76–77, 95. One of Tucker's key sources was V. K. Wellington Koo, the Chinese Nationalist ambassador to the United States at the time.

39. Foot, *Wrong War,* 191–92; William F. Buckley Jr. et al., "POW's Must Be Protected," *NYT,* April 21, 1952, 8; Barton J. Bernstein, "Struggle over the Korean Armistice," in *Child of Conflict: The Korean-American Relationship, 1943–1953,* ed. Bruce Cumings (Seattle: University of Washington Press, 1983), 280, 296–97; Acheson, *Present at the Creation,* 653. A *New York Times* search indicated that the only Republican criticizing the president's position on repatriation following the October 9 recess was Senator Homer Capehart of Indiana. See "Truce Held Scuttled," *NYT,* October 11, 1952, 73.

40. Schlesinger, *Imperial Presidency,* 129–30; Crabb, *Bipartisan Foreign Policy,* 2–4; Gary W. Reichard, "The Domestic Politics of National Security," in *The National Security: Its Theory and Practices, 1945–1960,* ed. Norman A. Graebner (New York: Oxford University Press, 1986), 243–74.

41. Abell, *Pearson Diaries,* 200.

42. "Special Message to the Congress on Greece and Turkey: The Truman Doctrine," March 12, 1947, *PP,* http://trumanlibrary.org/publicpapers/index .php?pid=2189&st=greece&st1= (accessed June 19, 2007).

43. Truman quoted in Ferrell, *Off the Record,* 260–61.

44. Savage, *Truman and the Democratic Party,* 168–69; Hamby, *Man of the People,* 585–88. The Kefauver hearings caught the public's fancy. For example, Senator Theodore Green's papers include ten to twenty letters from constituents supporting an extension of the hearings, with no letters opposed. See box 2, Misc. Legislation #2 folder, Green Papers.

45. Ferrell, *Harry S. Truman,* 359–63; Savage, *Truman and the Democratic Party,* 186.

46. Truman quoted in Ferrell, *Harry S. Truman,* 363. Andrew J. Dunar, *The Truman Scandals and the Politics of Morality* (Columbia: University of Missouri Press, 1984), 89, notes that Fulbright had previously spoken out against RFC loans to build hotels, making him sensitive to Truman's charges.

47. Hechler, *Working with Truman,* 197.

48. Hamby, *Man of the People,* 588–89; Ferrell, *Harry S. Truman,* 364. Through-

out his political career, Truman defended himself against charges of having ties to political machines through his association with the Pendergasts. The president had friendly relations with the Pendergast organization but otherwise kept his hands clean.

49. Savage, *Truman and the Democratic Party,* 188; Ferrell, *Harry S. Truman,* 368.

50. Poll data from Frank McKinney to Democratic National Committee, "Opinion Surveys on Issues," February 8, 1952, box 666, Green Papers; UAW report from Paul Sifton to Abraham A. Ribicoff, January 7, 1952, xiii–xiv, box 5, Abraham A. Ribicoff Papers, MDLOC.

51. "Democrats Afraid Truman Will Run," *Newsweek,* July 9, 1951, 22.

52. Fitzpatrick quoted in ibid.; Allen Duckworth, "Byrnes Backing Shivers to Run South's Revolt," *Dallas Morning News,* November 15, 1951, 1; Allen Duckworth, "Maryland's Chief Snubs Texan's Talk," *Dallas Morning News,* November 13, 1951, 1.

53. Talmadge quoted in John N. Popham, "Rayburn Delivers Warning to South," *NYT,* November 13, 1951, 25; Shivers quoted in Duckworth, "Maryland's Chief Snubs Texan's Talk," 1; Byrnes's accusation in Duckworth, "Byrnes Backing Shivers to Run South's Revolt," 1; Byrnes's 1949 speech in "Byrnes Blasts Administration for Spending," *Dallas Morning News,* November 22, 1949, 1; Rayburn to William J. Holloway, November 20, 1951, and Truman to Rayburn, November 16, 1951, Correspondence: Presidents, Vice Presidents and Others, 1951–1952 folder, Rayburn Papers.

6. The Fall of the Trumanites

1. Truman, note to self, April 16, 1950, PSF: Longhand Notes File, April 16, 1950 folder, Truman Papers. Jerry N. Hess, "Oral History Interview with Admiral Robert L. Dennison," November 2, 1971, 193–96, http://www.trumanlibrary.org/oralhist/dennisn3.htm#193 (accessed March 1, 2007), describes how the staff kept Truman's intentions confidential. For Truman's kingmaking activities, see Hamby, *Man of the People,* 600–603.

2. "Address before the Women's Democratic Club, November 20, 1951," *PP,* http://www.trumanlibrary.org/publicpapers/index.php?pid=560&st=&st1= (accessed March 3, 2007); "Candidate Truman Forgets One Issue," *Dallas Morning News,* November 22, 1951, pt. 3, 2; Hechler, *Working with Truman,* 246–47; "People: President Likes Job; On Drafting Doctors," *Dallas Morning News,* February 22, 1952, pt. 1, 6; Anthony Leviero, "President's Papers Printed; His Charges Stir Disputes," *NYT,* March 18, 1952, 1; Orville Prescott, "Books of the Times," *NYT,* March 18, 1952, 25; "Mr. President," *NYT,* March 19, 1952, 28.

3. Hamby, *Man of the People,* 602; Robert A. Divine, *Foreign Policy and U.S. Presidential Elections, 1952–1960* (New York: New Viewpoints, 1974), 19; Clinton P. Anderson to Sheldon F. Sackett, July 29,1952, box 38, Anderson Papers; "Statement of Fuller Warren, Governor of Florida," December 4, 1951, box 5, Ribicoff Papers.

4. Hamby, *Man of the People*, 603–4; John H. Fenton, "Eisenhower Defeats Taft, Kefauver Wins over Truman in New Hampshire's Primary," *NYT,* March 12, 1952, 1; University of Connecticut, "Roper Center Public Opinion Archives," http://webapps.ropercenter.uconn.edu/CFIDE/roper/presidential/webroot/presidential_rating.cfm#comparison (accessed May 17, 2012); George Gallup, "Popularity of Truman Rising from November All-Time Low," *Washington Post,* February 8, 1952, B6 (citing a 23 percent approval rating in November 1951 and 25 percent in January 1952); Savage, *Truman and the Democratic Party,* 192; Divine, *Foreign Policy,* 19.

5. Truman quoted in Ferrell, *Off the Record,* 260; Edwin Johnson to Theodore F. Green, June 4, 1952, and Green to Johnson, June 11, 1952, box 675, Green Papers; Clinton P. Anderson to A. H. Sarrett Jr., April 1, 1952, box 38, Anderson Papers; Savage, *Truman and the Democratic Party,* 194.

6. Memorandum from David D. Lloyd to Charles Murphy, November 27, 1951, David D. Lloyd folder, Murphy Papers; Frederickson, *Dixiecrat Revolt,* 223–25; "Southern Democrats' Strategy: Pick President, Control Party," *Newsweek,* March 3, 1952, 21.

7. Ricky Dobbs, *Yellow Dogs and Republicans: Allan Shivers and Texas Two-Party Politics* (College Station: Texas A&M University Press, 2005); 66–71; Truman to Maury Maverick, June 27, 1951, and Maverick to Truman, June 23, 1951, PSF: General File, M (1 of 2: Ma–Me) folder, Truman Papers.

8. Walter C. Hornaday, "Texas Called Key State for Beat-Truman Tie-up," *Dallas Morning News,* July 31, 1951, sec. 1, 3.

9. Walter C. Hornaday, "Capitol Hill Cool toward Mundt Plan," *Dallas Morning News,* August 1, 1951, sec. 1, 13; "Party Alliance Backed," *NYT,* August 1, 1951, 47; Dobbs, *Yellow Dogs,* 87–88.

10. Jon Ford, "Resolutions Pin Truman's Ears," *San Antonio Evening News,* May 28, 1952, 1; "Remarks of Governor Allan Shivers—State Democratic Executive Committee Meeting—New Braunfels, Texas," April 18, 1952, Democratic National Committee folder, Murphy Papers; Truman to Maverick, June 2, 1952, and Maverick to Truman, May 29, 1952, PSF: Political File, Texas folder, Truman Papers; Shivers quoted in Dobbs, *Yellow Dogs,* 83; "Southern Democrats' Strategy: Pick President, Control Party," *Newsweek,* March 3, 1952, 21.

11. Hechler to Truman, "Report on Congressional Voting Records as of 8/1/51, tables I and VI," Subject File, Congressional Voting Records folder, Hechler Papers; UAW report from Paul Sifton to Rep. Abraham A. Ribicoff, January 7, 1952, box 5, Ribicoff Papers.

12. Herbert S. Parmet, *The Democrats: The Years after FDR* (New York: Macmillan, 1976), 100; Divine, *Foreign Policy,* 17–18.

13. McKinney quoted in John Bartlow Martin, *Adlai Stevenson of Illinois: The Life of Adlai E. Stevenson* (Garden City, NY: Doubleday, 1976), 579.

14. Paul T. David, Malcolm Moos, and Ralph M. Goldman, *Presidential Nominating Politics in 1952,* vol. 1, *The National Story* (Baltimore: Johns Hopkins Press, 1954), 103–5, 113.

15. Truman quoted in "Confidential—The Texas Situation," July 12, 1952, Democratic Platform July 1952 folder, Murphy Papers; David et al., *Presidential Nominating Politics,* 112; Dobbs, *Yellow Dogs,* 86–87.

16. David et al., *Presidential Nominating Politics,* 125; Drew Pearson, "Byrnes Enraged by Loyalty Oath," *Washington Post,* July 26, 1952, 25.

17. David et al., *Presidential Nominating Politics,* 111–12, 133–34; Arthur Krock, "A Big Wind Dies Down," *NYT,* July 25, 1952, 10; Pearson, "Byrnes Enraged by Loyalty Oath," 25; Felix Belair Jr., "Russell Declares He Won't Quit Race," *NYT,* July 23, 1952, 12; Frederickson, *Dixiecrat Revolt,* 227–28; Kyle Palmer, "Stevenson Heads Field as South Bolt Reversed," *Los Angeles Times,* July 24, 1952, 1.

18. David et al., *Presidential Nominating Politics,* 111–12, 128, 131–32; Ernest K. Lindley, "Consequences of the Democratic Convention," *Newsweek,* August 4, 1952, 25; Theodore Green to McCormack, August 18, 1952, and McCormack to Green, August 12, 1952, box 663, Green Papers; John Frederick Martin, *Civil Rights and the Crisis of Liberalism: The Democratic Party, 1945–1976* (Boulder, CO: Westview Press, 1979), 108; Divine, *Foreign Policy,* 38–39.

19. Hamby, *Man of the People,* 608–9; Truman, *Memoirs,* 2:496; David et al., *Presidential Nominating Politics,* 150.

20. Martin, *Adlai Stevenson,* 540; Divine, *Foreign Policy,* 21.

21. Frederickson, *Dixiecrat Revolt,* 229–32; "Georgia Endorses Democrats' Ticket," *NYT,* August 5, 1952, 10; William H. Smith, "Va. Party Gives Adlai Lukewarm Support," *Washington Post,* August 29, 1952, 8.

22. Frederickson, *Dixiecrat Revolt,* 226–27; White quoted in "Democrats Together," *Newsweek,* August 18, 1952, 21.

23. Eisenhower quoted in Stephen E. Ambrose, *Eisenhower: Soldier, General of the Army, President-Elect, 1890–1952* (New York: Simon & Schuster, 1983), 568; Martin, *Adlai Stevenson,* 610, 637, 643, 661–62; Porter McKeever, *Adlai Stevenson: His Life and Legacy* (New York: William Morrow, 1989), 281.

24. McKeever, *Adlai Stevenson,* 221; Stevenson quoted in Martin, *Adlai Stevenson,* 656; Eisenhower quoted in Ambrose, *Eisenhower,* 527.

25. Eisenhower quoted in Ambrose, *Eisenhower,* 530, 568; budget and polling data from Pierpaoli, *Truman and Korea,* 198–99, 219; Divine, *Foreign Policy,* 57; Hamby, *Man of the People,* 615; Stevenson quoted in Martin, *Adlai Stevenson,* 610.

26. Divine, *Foreign Policy,* 43–45, 59; Ambrose, *Eisenhower,* 497–98, 527.

27. Stevenson quoted in Halberstam, *The Fifties,* 232; John Robert Greene, *The Crusade: The Presidential Election of 1952* (Lanham, MD: University Press of America, 1985), 1; Martin, *Adlai Stevenson,* 614; Halberstam, *The Fifties,* 225.

28. Frederickson, *Dixiecrat Revolt,* 229–30.

29. Parmet, *Democrats,* 100; Byrd and Barkley quoted in "Against Trumanism," *Time,* October 27, 1952, 27. Herbert Hoover (1928) was the other Republican who carried Virginia.

30. In general, the tidelands referred to the area constituting the difference in a coastline between high and low tides. Coastal states claimed the tidelands for oil reve-

nue rights. Eventually, the federal government defined the tidelands as a band within about two and a half miles of the coastline. Texas's claim to the tidelands extending ten miles out derived from its history as part of Mexico. When Texas was under Mexican rule in the 1820s–1830s, the Mexican government defined its offshore property as extending three Spanish leagues (approximately ten miles) into the Gulf of Mexico. Texas claimed that this definition was carried over in the treaty annexing Texas to the United States in 1845. This history is discussed in Martin, *Adlai Stevenson,* 650. For the administration's oil volume estimates, see "President Assails Offshore Oil Bill," *NYT,* May 18, 1952, 1. For an example of the president's blunt opposition to state control of tidelands oil, see Truman to Amon Carter, June 3, 1952, Correspondence: Presidents, Vice Presidents and Others, 1951–1952 folder, Rayburn Papers. The importance of the tidelands issue to Texas is expressed in Rayburn to O. O. Touchstone, June 22, 1950, and Touchstone to Rayburn, June 14, 1950, 1950 Political*National folder, Rayburn Papers. The domestic oil deficit is discussed in Anderson, *Outsider in the Senate,* 113; Daniel Yergin, *The Prize: The Epic Quest for Oil, Money and Power* (New York: Simon & Schuster, 1993), 464, also notes that the ongoing British embargo on Iranian oil was contributing to the stress on oil supplies. For Shivers's plan to use the tidelands issue, see Dobbs, *Yellow Dogs,* 76–77.

31. Philip B. Perlman to Adlai E. Stevenson, August 19, 1952, Clinton P. Anderson to Stevenson, August 18, 1952, and Anderson to William C. Blair, August 28, 1952, all in box 1056, Anderson Papers; Sam Rayburn to Boykin, August 21, 1952, and Boykin to Stevenson, August 19, 1952, 1952 Congressmen folder, Rayburn Papers; Parmet, *Democrats,* 99; Johnson quoted in Dobbs, *Yellow Dogs,* 90; "Press Release from Governor Adlai Stevenson, August 23, 1952," box 6, Anderson Papers; Martin, *Adlai Stevenson,* 650–51; Rayburn quoted in Dobbs, *Yellow Dogs,* 86. Dobbs (ibid., 86–90) analyzes whether Shivers double-crossed Rayburn.

32. Aide quoted in Dobbs, *Yellow Dogs,* 91; Parmet, *Democrats,* 99; Congressman John E. Lyle (D-TX) to Sam Rayburn, n.d., 1952 Congressmen K–O folder, Rayburn Papers; Frank Boykin to Steve Mitchell, October 9, 1952, and Boykin to Rayburn, November 11, 1952, 1952 Congressmen folder, Rayburn Papers; Dobbs, *Yellow Dogs,* 96, 94, 93. Unlike Rayburn, Johnson campaigned halfheartedly for Stevenson, probably anticipating Eisenhower's triumph. He became the Senate's minority leader in January 1953. See Parmet, *Democrats,* 98–99.

33. "Mississippi States' Rights Democrats," n.d., PSF: Political File, Mississippi folder, Truman Papers; Frederickson, *Dixiecrat Revolt,* 230.

34. Stevenson quoted in Martin, *Adlai Stevenson,* 608 (emphasis in original); "Press Release—Democratic National Committee Publicity Division," May 19, 1952, box 666, Green Papers; Divine, *Foreign Policy,* 47; Ferrell, *Harry S. Truman,* 376–77; Ferrell, *Off the Record,* 268–69; "Everybody's Huffy," *Newsweek,* September 1, 1952, 19.

35. Ambrose, *Eisenhower,* 553; McKeever, *Adlai Stevenson,* 224, 225–26.

36. Anne O'Hare McCormick, "Abroad," *NYT,* March 24, 1952, 24; "Policy Stems Reds, Truman Declares," *NYT,* March 24, 1952, 3; Ken Hechler, memoran-

dum, "Mayflower Dinner Meeting of National Committee Research Group," January 23, 1951, DNC Establishment of a Research Comm. folder, Hechler Papers; Dean Acheson to Harry Truman, "Suggested Quarterly Report Prepared by the Dept. of State on the Progress of Our Foreign Policy," March 28, 1952, PSF: Chronological Name File, Dean Acheson folder, Truman Papers; "Final Report of Frank E. McKinney Submitted to the Democratic National Committee," August 20, 1952, 29, Democratic National Committee folder, Murphy Papers; Wood, "American Reaction to Limited War in Asia," 203.

37. Robert Thompson to George Elsey, April 23, 1952, and Madeline W. Harrington to Thompson, "Our Foreign Policy, 1952," n.d., Foreign Policy—State Dept. Pamphlet "Our Foreign Policy" folder, Elsey Papers. According to the 1950 census, the voting-age population of the United States was approximately 110 million. See Geospacial and Statistical Data Center, University of Virginia Library, http://fisher. lib.virginia.edu/collections/stats/histcensus/php/state.php (accessed January 28, 2007).

38. U.S. Department of State, *Our Foreign Policy 1952* (Washington, DC: U.S. Government Printing Office, 1952), 10, 11, 42–44.

39. Harrington to Thompson, "Our Foreign Policy, 1952," quotes the *Louisville Times* and the *Philadelphia Bulletin* without giving dates. It also summarizes media treatment of the pamphlet.

40. Democratic National Committee Research Division, "Answers to Questions on Peace and War," April 2, 1952, Political 1952 folder, Rayburn papers.

41. See Marcus, *Truman and the Steel Seizure*, 33.

42. Roper Center for Public Opinion Research, 2006, http://137.99.36.203/ CFIDE/roper/presidential/webroot/presidential_rating_detail.cfm?allRate=False (accessed December 9, 2006). Truman's 22 percent approval rating was statistically equivalent to Richard Nixon's lowest rating before his resignation. In 2008 George W. Bush's approval rating bottomed out at 19 percent. For trends in public support for the war after the Chinese intervention, see John E. Mueller, *War, Presidents, and Public Opinion* (New York: John Wiley & Sons, 1973), 45–52.

43. McCarthy quoted in McKeever, *Adlai Stevenson*, 234; Ambrose, *Eisenhower*, 561–67.

44. McKeever, *Adlai Stevenson*, 230; Divine, *Foreign Policy*, 67, 72.

45. George Gallup, "Popularity of Truman Rising from November All-Time Low," *Washington Post*, February 8, 1952, B6; George Gallup, *The Gallup Poll: Public Opinion, 1935–1971*, vol. 2, *1949–1958* (New York: Random House, 1972), 1071, 1102.

46. Donovan, *Tumultuous Years*, 398; Ferrell, *Harry S. Truman*, 377–78; Divine, *Foreign Policy*, 69; "Editorial Material—The Campaign," n.d., box 1056, Anderson Papers; Divine, *Foreign Policy*, 68, 79.

47. Divine, *Foreign Policy*, 69–70, 79.

48. Stevenson quoted in Divine, *Foreign Policy*, 67, 74. For examples of Democrats' premature predictions of the war's end, see Senator Blair Moody, speech be-

fore Indiana Young Democrats, July 21, 1951, box 634, and "Research Institute of America Recommendations," July 26, 1952, box 663, Green Papers.

49. Democratic National Committee, "Does Eisenhower Really Expect Veterans to Vote for Him?" n.d., and Democratic National Committee Research Division, "Report RD-60—Eisenhower Quotes," August 23, 1952, box 666, Green Papers; Truman quoted in Divine, *Foreign Policy,* 74.

50. "Report RD-60—Eisenhower Quotes"; Divine, *Foreign Policy,* 71.

51. Divine, *Foreign Policy,* 75; Charles Brown and Norman Nicholson, "Eisenhower: 'I Shall Go to Korea,'" *Newsweek,* November 3, 1952, 26; "Has Eisenhower Delayed Peace in Korea?" *New Republic,* November 10, 1952, 5–6. Ironically, Stevenson had decided in August 1952 that *he* would visit Korea if elected. Although he briefly considered mentioning it during the campaign, his advisers nixed the idea. See Martin, *Adlai Stevenson,* 705.

52. Connecticut Democratic Party chief John Bailey quoted in Greene, *Crusade,* 2. For comparisons with the 1948 election, see Angus Campbell, Gerald Gurin, and Warren E. Miller, *The Voter Decides* (Evanston, IL: Row, Peterson, 1954), 16.

53. "The Election," *Time,* November 17, 1952, 23–24.

54. Guy Gillette to Lister Hill, November 6, 1952, box 675, Green Papers; Elizabeth Tandy Shermer, "Origins of the Conservative Ascendancy: Barry Goldwater's Early Senate Career and the De-legitimization of Organized Labor," *Journal of American History* 95, no. 3 (December 2008): 689–91; Clinton Anderson to Ernest W. McFarland, November 28, 1952, box 1056, Anderson Papers. Recall that majority leader Scott Lucas lost in the 1950 midterm elections.

55. Oshinsky, *Conspiracy So Immense,* 238–39, 242–45; Hyman, *Lives of William Benton,* 478; Leroy C. Ferguson and Ralph H. Smuckler, *Politics in the Press: An Analysis of Press Content in 1952 Senatorial Campaigns* (East Lansing: Government Research Bureau, Michigan State College, 1954), 20–27. Connecticut's governor had appointed Benton to the Senate to fill a vacancy shortly before the 1950 election. In 1950 he had to stand for election to complete the six-year term expiring in 1952.

56. M. J. Heale, "The Triumph of Liberalism? Red Scare Politics in Michigan, 1938–1954," *Proceedings of the American Philosophical Society* 139, no. 1 (March 1995): 62; John T. Hinckley, "The 1952 Elections in Wyoming," *Western Political Quarterly* 6, no. 1 (March 1953): 135–38. O'Mahoney was elected in 1954 to fill the other Wyoming Senate seat vacated upon the death of Lester Hunt. O'Mahoney completed Hunt's term and served another full term.

57. Vincent P. DeSantis, "The Presidential Election of 1952," *Review of Politics* 15, no. 2 (April 1953): 137; Jules A. Karlin, "The 1952 Elections in Montana," *Western Political Quarterly* 6, no. 1 (March 1953): 113, 115–16; Daniel M. Ogden Jr., "The 1952 Elections in Washington," *Western Political Quarterly* 6, no. 1 (March 1953): 133–34.

58. G. Q. Unruh, "Republican Apostate: Senator Wayne L. Morse and His Quest for Independent Liberalism," *Pacific Northwest Quarterly* 82, no. 3 (July 1991): 89–90.

59. Campbell et al., *Voter Decides,* 52; Oshinsky, *Conspiracy So Immense,* 244–45; Casey, *Selling the Korean War,* 336; Savage, *Truman and the Democratic Party,* 200.

60. Foot, *Substitute for Victory,* 135–40; Campbell et al., *Voter Decides,* 175; Divine, *Foreign Policy,* 82; Caridi, *Korean War and American Politics,* 210–11; Campbell et al., *Voter Decides,* 56–58, 176; Chapman and Burns and Hastings quoted in Divine, *Foreign Policy,* 83; Martin, *Adlai Stevenson,* 762.

Conclusion

1. For the case against Powell, see Douglas Miller and Marion Nowak, *The Fifties: The Way We Really Were* (Garden City, NY: Doubleday, 1977), 37–38.

2. The anecdote is from Richard E. Neustadt, "The Constraining of the President: The Presidency after Watergate," *British Journal of Political Science* 4, no. 4 (October 1974): 383.

3. See Donovan, *Tumultuous Years,* 402–3.

4. "Some Notes on Republican Campaign Statements Regarding Korea," n.d., White House file, Eisenhower—Korea troops folder, Lloyd Papers.

Bibliography

Manuscript Collections and Oral Histories

Acheson, Dean, Papers. Harry S. Truman Library.

Anderson, Clinton, Papers. Manuscript Division, Library of Congress.

Connally, Thomas, Papers. Manuscript Division, Library of Congress.

Connelly, Matthew, Papers. Harry S. Truman Library.

Dennison, Robert L., Oral History. Harry S. Truman Library.

Elsey, George, Papers. Harry S. Truman Library.

Flanders, Ralph, Papers. Special Collections Research Center, Syracuse University Library, Syracuse, NY.

Green, Theodore F., Papers. Manuscript Division, Library of Congress.

Hechler, Kenneth, Papers. Harry S. Truman Library.

Hickerson, John D., Oral History. Harry S. Truman Library.

Lloyd, David D., Papers. Harry S. Truman Library.

McFall, Jack K., Oral History. Harry S. Truman Library.

McMahon, Brien, Papers. Manuscript Division, Library of Congress.

Murphy, Charles S., Oral History. Harry S. Truman Library.

Murphy, Charles S., Papers. Harry S. Truman Library.

Pace, Frank, Jr., Oral History. Harry S. Truman Library.

Rayburn, Sam, Papers. Center for American History, University of Texas at Austin.

Ribicoff, Abraham A., Papers. Manuscript Division, Library of Congress.

Smith, H. Alexander, Papers. Seeley G. Mudd Manuscript Library, Princeton University.

Tannenwald, Theodore, Papers. Harry S. Truman Library.

Truman, Harry S., Papers. Harry S. Truman Library.

Wilcox, Francis O., Oral History. Harry S. Truman Library.

Wilcox, Francis O., Papers. Harry S. Truman Library.

Books, Articles, Dissertations, and Theses

Abell, Tyler, ed. *Drew Pearson Diaries, 1949–1959.* New York: Holt, Rinehart & Winston, 1974.

Abramson, Rudy. *Spanning the Century: The Life of W. Averell Harriman, 1891–1986.* New York: William Morrow, 1992.

Accinelli, Robert. *Crisis and Commitment: United States Policy toward Taiwan, 1950–1955.* Chapel Hill: University of North Carolina Press, 1996.

Acheson, Dean. *A Democrat Looks at His Party.* New York: Harper & Brothers, 1955.
————. *Present at the Creation: My Years in the State Department.* New York: New American Library, 1969.
Alexander, Bevin. *Korea: The First War We Lost.* New York: Hippocrene Books, 2000.
Ambrose, Stephen E. *Eisenhower: Soldier, General of the Army, President-Elect, 1890–1952.* New York: Simon & Schuster, 1983.
Ambrose, Stephen E., and Douglas G. Brinkley. *Rise to Globalism: American Foreign Policy since 1938.* 8th ed. New York: Penguin Books, 1997.
Anderson, Clinton P., with Milton Viorst. *Outsider in the Senate: Senator Clinton Anderson's Memoirs.* New York: World Publishing, 1970.
Ascoli, Max, Phillip Horton, and Charles Wertenbaker. "The China Lobby." *Reporter,* April 29, 1952, 5–24.
Astor, Gerald. *Presidents at War: From Truman to Bush, the Gathering of Military Power to Our Commanders in Chief.* Hoboken, NJ: John Wiley & Sons, 2006.
Avalon Project at Yale Law School. "U.N. Participation Act of 1945." http://www.yale.edu/lawweb/avalon/decade/decad031.htm.
Bajanov, Evgeniy P., and Natalia Bajanova. "The Korean Conflict, 1950–1953." Unpublished ms. North Korean International Documentation Project, Wilson Center, Princeton University.
Ball, George W. "With AES in War and Politics." In *As We Knew Adlai: The Stevenson Story by Twenty-Two Friends,* edited by Edward P. Doyle, 138–53. New York: Harper & Row, 1966.
Bartel, Ronald F. "Attitudes toward Limited War: An Analysis of Elite and Public Opinion during the Korean Conflict." PhD diss., University of Illinois, 1970.
Beisner, Robert L. *Dean Acheson: A Life in the Cold War.* New York: Oxford University Press, 2006.
Bell, Jonathan. *The Liberal State on Trial: The Cold War and American Politics in the Truman Years.* New York: Columbia University Press, 2004.
Berger, Henry W. "Bipartisanship, Senator Taft, and the Truman Administration." *Political Science Quarterly* 90, no. 2 (Summer 1975): 221–37.
Bernstein, Barton J. "The Ambiguous Legacy: Civil Rights." In *Politics and Policies of the Truman Administration,* edited by Barton J. Bernstein, 269–314. Chicago: Quadrangle Books, 1970.
————. "Struggle over the Korean Armistice." In *Child of Conflict: The Korean-American Relationship, 1943–1953,* edited by Bruce Cumings, 261–308. Seattle: University of Washington Press, 1983.
————. "The Truman Administration and the Korean War." In *The Truman Presidency,* edited by Michael Lacey, 410–44. New York: Cambridge University Press, 1989.
————, ed. *Politics and Policies of the Truman Administration.* Chicago: Quadrangle Books, 1970.
Bernstein, Barton, and Allen J. Matusow, eds. *The Truman Administration: A Documentary History.* New York: Harper & Row, 1966.

Biles, Roger. *Crusading Liberal: Paul H. Douglas of Illinois.* De Kalb: Northern Illinois University Press, 2002.

Biographical Directory of the United States Congress. http://bioguide.congress.gov.

Birtle, Andrew J. "The Korean War: Years of Stalemate." U.S. Army Center of Military History, October 3, 2003. http://www.army.mil/cmh-pg/brochures/ kw-stale/stale.htm.

Blanton, Thomas. "The World's Right to Know." *Foreign Policy* 131 (July–August 2002): 50–58.

Bond, Jon R., and Richard Fleisher. *The President in the Legislative Arena.* Chicago: University of Chicago Press, 1990.

Bradley, Omar N., and Clay Baird. *A General's Life: An Autobiography by General of the Army Omar N. Bradley.* New York: Simon & Schuster, 1983.

Brands, H. W. *The Devil We Knew: Americans and the Cold War.* New York: Oxford University Press, 1993.

Brown, Seyom. *The Faces of Power: United States Foreign Policy from Truman to Clinton.* 2nd ed. New York: Columbia University Press, 1994.

Brune, Lester H., ed. *The Korean War: Handbook of the Literature and Research.* Westport, CT: Greenwood Press, 1996.

Burns, Richard Dean, ed. *Harry S. Truman: A Bibliography of His Times and Presidency.* Wilmington, DE: Scholarly Resources, 1984.

Caine, Philip D. "The United States in Korea and Vietnam: A Study in Public Opinion." *Air University Quarterly Review* 20, no. 1 (1968): 49–58.

Calkins, Fay. *The CIO and the Democratic Party.* Chicago: University of Chicago Press, 1952.

Campbell, Angus, Gerald Gurin, and Warren E. Miller. *The Voter Decides.* Evanston, IL: Row, Peterson, 1954.

Caridi, Ronald J. *The Korean War and American Politics: The Republican Party as a Case Study.* Philadelphia: University of Pennsylvania Press, 1969.

Carpenter, Ted Galen. "United States' NATO Policy at the Crossroads: The 'Great Debate' of 1950–1951." *International History Review* 8, no. 3 (August 1986): 345–516.

Casey, Steven. *Selling the Korean War: Propaganda, Politics, and Public Opinion in the United States, 1950–1953.* New York: Oxford University Press, 2008.

Catchpole, Brian. *The Korean War, 1950–53.* New York: Carroll & Graf, 2000.

Caute, David. *The Great Fear: The Anti-Communist Purge under Truman and Eisenhower.* New York: Simon & Schuster, 1978.

Chao, Ena. "The China Bloc: Congress and the Making of Foreign Policy, 1947–1952." PhD diss., University of North Carolina, 1970.

Chenoweth, Richard. "Francis Case: A Political Biography." *South Dakota Historical Collections* 39 (1978): 288–433.

Christianson, Stephen G. *Facts about Congress.* New York: H. W. Wilson, 1996.

Clubb, O. Edmund. "McCarthyism and Our Asian Policy." *Bulletin of Concerned Asian Scholars* 4 (May 1969): 23–26.

———. *The Witness and I.* New York: Columbia University Press, 1974.

Coinnews Media Group. "US Inflation Calculator." http://www.usinflationcalculator .com/inflation/historical-inflation-rates/.

Congressional Quarterly's Guide to U.S. Elections. 3rd ed. Washington, DC: Congressional Quarterly Publishing, 1994.

Connally, Tom. *My Name Is Tom Connally.* New York: Thomas Y. Crowell, 1954.

Cook, Fred J. *The Nightmare Decade: The Life and Times of Senator Joe McCarthy.* New York: Random House, 1971.

Cornwell, Elmer E., Jr. *Presidential Leadership of Public Opinion.* Bloomington: Indiana University Press, 1965.

Cotton, James, and Ian Neary, eds. *The Korean War in History.* Manchester, UK: Manchester University Press, 1989.

Crabb, Cecil V., Jr. *Bipartisan Foreign Policy: Myth or Reality?* Evanston, IL: Row, Peterson, 1957.

Crabb, Cecil V., Jr., and Pat M. Holt. *Invitation to Struggle: Congress, the President and Foreign Policy.* 2nd ed. Washington, DC: CQ Press, 1984.

Cumings, Bruce. *The Origins of the Korean War.* Vol. 2, *The Roaring of the Cataract.* 1990. Reprint, Seoul, South Korea: Yuksabipyungsa, 2002.

———, ed. *Child of Conflict: The Korean-American Relationship, 1943–1953.* Seattle: University of Washington Press, 1983.

Dalfiume, Richard M. *Desegregation of the Armed Forces: Fighting on Two Fronts, 1939–1953.* Columbia: University of Missouri Press, 1969.

Dallek, Robert. *Lone Star Rising: Lyndon Johnson and His Times, 1908–1960.* New York: Oxford University Press, 1991.

David, Paul T., Malcolm Moos, and Ralph M. Goldman. *Presidential Nominating Politics in 1952.* Vol. 1, *The National Story.* Baltimore: Johns Hopkins Press, 1954.

Davidson, Roger H., Donald Bacon, and Morton Keller. *Encyclopedia of the United States Congress.* 4 vols. New York: Simon & Schuster, 1995.

Deason, Brian S. "Eye of the Storm: A Political Biography of U.S. Senator Scott W. Lucas of Illinois." PhD diss., Southern Illinois University, 2000.

DeConde, Alexander. *Presidential Machismo: Executive Authority, Military Intervention, and Foreign Relations.* Boston: Northeastern University Press, 2000.

Democratic National Committee. *How to Win in '52: The Facts about the Democratic Road to Prosperity, Peace and Freedom.* Washington, DC: Democratic National Committee, 1952.

DeSantis, Vincent P. "The Presidential Election of 1952." *Review of Politics* 15, no. 2 (April 1953): 131–50.

Deutsch, Benjamin P. "Conviction and Ambition: Senator Brien McMahon and the Politics of Atomic Energy." Master's thesis, University of Wisconsin–Madison, 1989.

Diggins, John R. *The Proud Decades: America in War and in Peace, 1941–1960.* New York: W. W. Norton, 1988.

Divine, Robert A. *Foreign Policy and U.S. Presidential Elections, 1952–1960.* New York: New Viewpoints, 1974.

Dobbs, Ricky F. *Yellow Dogs and Republicans: Allan Shivers and Texas Two-Party Politics.* College Station: Texas A&M University Press, 2005.

Donaldson, Gary. *America at War since 1945: Politics and Diplomacy in Korea, Vietnam, and the Gulf War.* Westport, CT: Praeger Publishing, 1996.

Donovan, Robert J. *Tumultuous Years: The Presidency of Harry Truman, 1949–1953.* New York: W. W. Norton, 1982.

Douglas, Paul H. *In the Fullness of Time: The Memoirs of Paul H. Douglas.* New York: Harcourt Brace Jovanovich, 1971.

Doyle, Edward P., ed. *As We Knew Adlai: The Stevenson Story by Twenty-Two Friends.* New York: Harper & Row, 1966.

Drukman, Mason. *Wayne Morse: A Political Biography.* Portland: Oregon Historical Society Press, 1997.

Dulles, Foster Rhea. *American Policy toward Communist China, 1949–1969.* New York: Thomas Y. Crowell, 1972.

Dunar, Andrew J. *The Truman Scandals and the Politics of Morality.* Columbia: University of Missouri Press, 1984.

Eagleton, Thomas F. *War and Presidential Power: A Chronicle of Congressional Surrender.* New York: Liveright, 1974.

Elowitz, Larry, and John W. Spanier. "Korea and Vietnam: Limited War and the American Political System." *Orbis* 18, no. 2 (1974): 510–34.

Elsey, George M. *An Unplanned Life: A Memoir by George McKee Elsey.* Columbia: University of Missouri Press, 2005.

Farrar, Peter N. "Britain's Proposal for a Buffer Zone South of the Yalu in November 1950: Was It a Neglected Opportunity to End the Fighting in Korea?" *Journal of Contemporary History* 18, no. 2 (April 1983): 327–51.

———. "A Pause for Peace Negotiations: The British Buffer Zone Plan of November 1950." In *The Korean War in History,* edited by James Cotton and Ian Neary, 66–79. Manchester, UK: Manchester University Press, 1989.

Ferguson, Leroy C., and Ralph H. Smuckler. *Politics in the Press: An Analysis of Press Content in 1952 Senatorial Campaigns.* East Lansing: Governmental Research Bureau, Michigan State College, 1954.

Ferrell, Robert H. *Harry S. Truman: A Life.* Columbia: University of Missouri Press, 1994.

———. *Off the Record: The Private Papers of Harry S. Truman.* New York: Harper & Row, 1980.

———. "Truman's Place in History." *Reviews in American History* 18, no. 1 (March 1990): 1–9.

———, ed. *The Autobiography of Harry S. Truman.* Boulder: Colorado Associated University Press, 1980.

———. *Dear Bess: The Letters from Harry to Bess Truman, 1910–1959.* New York: W. W. Norton, 1983.

————. *Truman in the White House: The Diary of Eben A. Ayers.* Columbia: University of Missouri Press, 1991.

Fisher, Louis. "The Korean War: On What Legal Basis Did Truman Act?" *American Journal of International Law* 89, no. 1 (January 1995): 21–39.

Fite, Gilbert C. *Richard B. Russell, Jr., Senator from Georgia.* Chapel Hill: University of North Carolina Press, 1991.

Flanders, Ralph E. *Letter to a Generation.* Boston: Beacon Press, 1956.

————. *Senator from Vermont.* Boston: Little, Brown, 1961.

Flynn, George A. *Lewis B. Hershey, Mr. Selective Service.* Chapel Hill: University of North Carolina Press, 1985.

Flynn, George Q. "Conscription and Equity in Western Democracies, 1940–1975." *Journal of Contemporary History* 33, no. 1 (January 1998): 5–20.

Flynn, Matthew S. "Reconsidering the China Lobby: Senator William F. Knowland and US-China Policy, 1945–1958." PhD diss., Ohio University, 2004.

Foot, Rosemary. *A Substitute for Victory: The Politics of Peacemaking at the Korean Armistice Talks.* Ithaca, NY: Cornell University Press, 1990.

————. *The Wrong War: American Policy and the Dimensions of the Korean Conflict, 1950–1953.* Ithaca, NY: Cornell University Press, 1985.

Foreign Relations of the United States, 1949. Vol. 7, pt. 2, *The Far East and Australasia.* Washington, DC: U.S. Government Printing Office, 1976.

Foreign Relations of the United States, 1950. Vol. 7, *Korea.* Washington, DC: U.S. Government Printing Office, 1976.

Foreign Relations of the United States, 1951. Vol. 4, *Europe.* Washington, DC: U.S. Government Printing Office, 1985.

Foreign Relations of the United States, 1951. Vol. 7, *Korea and China.* Washington, DC: U.S. Government Printing Office, 1983.

Foreign Relations of the United States, 1952–1954. Vol. 15, *Korea.* Washington, DC: U.S. Government Printing Office, 1984.

Franck, Thomas M., and Faiza Patel. "UN Police Action in Lieu of War: 'The Old Order Changeth.'" *American Journal of International Law* 85, no. 1 (January 1991): 63–74.

Frederickson, Kari A. *The Dixiecrat Revolt and the End of the Solid South, 1932–1968.* Chapel Hill: University of North Carolina Press, 2001.

Fried, Richard M. "Electoral Politics and McCarthyism: The 1950 Campaign." In *The Specter: Original Essays on the Cold War and the Origins of McCarthyism,* edited by Robert Griffith and Athan Theoharis, 190–223. New York: New Viewpoints, 1974.

————. *Men against McCarthy.* New York: Columbia University Press, 1976.

————. *Nightmare in Red: The McCarthy Era in Perspective.* New York: Oxford University Press, 1990.

Gaddis, John L. "The Insecurities of Victory: The United States and the Perception of the Soviet Threat after World War II." In *The Truman Presidency,* edited by Michael Lacy, 235–72. New York: Cambridge University Press, 1989.

Gallup, George. *The Gallup Poll: Public Opinion, 1935–1971.* Vol. 2. New York: Random House, 1972.

———. "The Gallup Poll and the 1950 Election." *Public Opinion Quarterly* 15, no. 1 (Spring 1951): 16–22.

Gardner, Lloyd C. "Korean Borderlands: Imaginary Frontiers of the Cold War." In *The Korean War in World History,* edited by William W. Stueck, 126–44. Lexington: University Press of Kentucky, 2004.

Gartner, Scott Sigmund, and Marissa Edson Myers. "Body Counts and 'Success' in the Vietnam and Korean Wars." *Journal of Interdisciplinary History* 25, no. 3 (Winter 1995): 377–95.

Geospacial and Statistical Data Center, University of Virginia Library. http://fisher.lib.virginia.edu/collections/stats/histcensus/php/state.php.

Glad, Betty, ed. *Psychological Dimensions of War.* Newbury Park, CA: Sage Publications, 1990.

Goldman, Eric. *The Crucial Decade and After: America, 1945–1960.* New York: Vintage Books, 1962.

Goldman, Ralph M. *Search for Consensus: The Story of the Democratic Party.* Philadelphia: Temple University Press, 1979.

Goodman, Allan E., ed. *Negotiating while Fighting: The Diary of Admiral C. Turner Joy at the Korean Armistice Conference.* Stanford, CA: Hoover Institution Press, 1978.

Goodman, Walter. *The Committee.* New York: Farrar, Straus & Giroux, 1968.

Goodrich, Leland M., Edward Hambro, and Anne Patricia Simons. *Charter of the United Nations: Commentary and Documents.* New York: Columbia University Press, 1969.

Goulden, Joseph C. *Korea: The Untold Story of the War.* New York: New York Times Books, 1982.

Graebner, Norman A., ed. *The National Security: Its Theory and Practices, 1945–1960.* New York: Oxford University Press, 1986.

Graham, Thomas E. "Getting Right with China: Membership, Scandal, and Weaknesses of the China Lobby." PhD diss., Northern Illinois University, 1994.

Greene, John Robert. *The Crusade: The Presidential Election of 1952.* Lanham, MD: University Press of America, 1985.

Griffith, Robert. "Old Progressives and the Cold War." *Journal of American History* 66, no. 2 (September 1995): 334–47.

———. *The Politics of Fear: Joseph R. McCarthy and the Senate.* Lexington: University Press of Kentucky, 1970.

Griffith, Robert, and Athan Theoharis, eds. *The Specter: Original Essays on the Cold War and the Origins of McCarthyism.* New York: New Viewpoints, 1974.

Griffith, Winthrop. *Humphrey: A Candid Biography.* New York: Morrow Publishing, 1964.

Grimmett, Richard. "The Politics of Containment: The President, the Senate and American Foreign Policy, 1947–1956." PhD diss., Kent State University, 1973.

Gromyko, Andrei. *History of Soviet Foreign Policy, 1945–1970.* Edited by B. Ponomaryov and V. Khvostov. Translated by David Skvirsky. Moscow: Progress Publishers, 1973.

———. *Memoirs.* New York: Doubleday, 1989.

Gross, Franz B., ed. *The United States and the United Nations.* Norman: Oklahoma
University Press, 1964.

Gustafson, Merlin. "Harry Truman as a Man of Faith." *Christian Century* 90 (January
17, 1973): 75–77.

Halberstam, David. *The Coldest Winter: America and the Korean War.* New York: Hyperion, 2007.

———. *The Fifties.* New York: Villard Books, 1993.

Hamby, Alonzo L. *Beyond the New Deal: Harry S. Truman and American Liberalism.*
New York: Columbia University Press, 1973.

———. *Man of the People: A Life of Harry S. Truman.* New York: Oxford University
Press, 1995.

Harris, Merne A. "The MacArthur Dismissal: A Study in Political Mail." PhD diss.,
University of Iowa, 1966.

Haynes, John Earl, and Harvey Klehr. *Venona: Soviet Espionage in America.* New
Haven, CT: Yale University Press, 1999.

Heale, M. J. "The Triumph of Liberalism? Red Scare Politics in Michigan, 1938–
1954." *Proceedings of the American Philosophical Society* 139, no. 1 (March 1995):
44–66.

Hechler, Ken. *Working with Truman.* Columbia: University of Missouri Press, 1982.

Heller, Francis H., ed. *The Truman White House: The Administration of the Presidency,
1945–1953.* Lawrence: Regents Press of Kansas, 1980.

Hellman, Lillian. *Scoundrel Time.* Boston: Little, Brown, 1976.

Herken, Gregg. *The Winning Weapon: The Atomic Bomb in the Cold War.* New York:
Knopf, 1981.

Herman, Arthur. *Joseph McCarthy: Reexamining the Life and Legacy of America's Most
Hated Senator.* New York: Free Press, 2000.

Hersey, John. *Aspects of the Presidency.* New Haven, CT: Ticknor & Fields, 1980.

Herzon, Frederick D., John Kincaid, and Verne Dalton. "Personality and Public
Opinion: The Case of Authoritarianism, Prejudice and Support for the Korean
and Vietnam Wars." *Polity* 1 (1978): 92–113.

Herzstein, Robert E. *Henry L. Luce, Time, and the American Crusade in Asia.* Cambridge: Cambridge University Press, 2005.

Hess, Gary R. *Presidential Decisions for War: Korea, Vietnam, and the Persian Gulf.*
Baltimore: Johns Hopkins University Press, 2001.

Higgins, Trumbull. *Korea and the Fall of MacArthur: A Precis in Limited War.* New
York: Oxford University Press, 1960.

Hildebrand, Regan C. "The Week That Was: The Truman Administration, the United Nations and Public Opinion Confront the Korean War, June 25–30, 1950."
Master's thesis, Ohio University, 1999.

Hill, Forest L. "Congressional Reaction to the Korean Conflict, 1950–1953." Master's thesis, Southwest Texas State University, 1971.

Hinckley, John T. "The 1952 Elections in Wyoming." *Western Political Quarterly* 6, no. 1 (March 1953): 135–38.

Hogan, Michael J. *A Cross of Iron: Harry S. Truman and the Origins of the National Security State.* New York: Cambridge University Press, 1998.

Hood, Charles Eugene, Jr. "'China Mike' Mansfield: The Making of a Congressional Authority on the Far East." PhD diss., Washington State University, 1980.

Hoopes, Townsend. *The Devil and John Foster Dulles.* Boston: Little, Brown, 1973.

Horace, H. Smith. "Reorganization—Senate Style." *American Foreign Service Journal,* June 1950, 18–52.

Hyman, Sidney. *The Lives of William Benton.* Chicago: University of Chicago Press, 1969.

Ickes, Harold. "Diplomacy with an Ax." *New Republic,* December 3, 1951, 17.

Ivie, Robert L. "Declaring a National Emergency: Truman's Rhetorical Crisis and the Great Debate of 1951." In *The Modern Presidency and Crisis Rhetoric,* edited by Amos Kiewe, 1–18. Westport, CT: Praeger Publishers, 1994.

Jewell, Malcolm E. *Senatorial Politics and Foreign Policy.* Westport, CT: Greenwood Press, 1962.

Jian, Chen. "In the Name of Revolution: China's Road to the Korean War Revisited." In *The Korean War in World History,* edited by William W. Stueck, 93–125. Lexington: University Press of Kentucky, 2004.

———. *Mao's China and the Cold War.* Chapel Hill: University of North Carolina Press, 2001.

Johnson, Robert David. *Congress and the Cold War.* New York: Cambridge University Press, 2006.

Karlin, Jules A. "The 1952 Elections in Montana." *Western Political Quarterly* 6, no. 1 (March 1953): 113–17.

Kaufman, Burton Ira. *The Korean War: Challenges in Crisis, Credibility and Command.* 2nd ed. New York: McGraw-Hill, 1997.

Keeley, Joseph. *The China Lobby Man: The Story of Alfred Kohlberg.* New Rochelle, NY: Arlington House, 1969.

Keith, Caroline H. *For Hell and a Brown Mule: The Biography of Millard E. Tydings.* New York: Madison Books, 1991.

Kennan, George F. *Memoirs.* Vol. 2, *1950–1963.* Boston: Little, Brown, 1972.

Kennedy, David M. *Freedom from Fear: The American People in Depression and War, 1929–1945.* New York: Oxford University Press, 1999.

Kepley, David R. *The Collapse of the Middle Way: Senate Republicans and the Bipartisan Foreign Policy, 1948–52.* Westport, CT: Greenwood Press, 1988.

Keynes, Edward. *Undeclared War: Twilight Zone of Constitutional Power.* University Park: Pennsylvania State University Press, 1982.

Kiewe, Amos, ed. *The Modern Presidency and Crisis Rhetoric.* Westport, CT: Praeger Publishers, 1994.

Kintner, William R. "The United Nations Record of Handling Major Disputes." In *The United States and the United Nations,* edited by Franz B. Gross, 87–124. Norman: Oklahoma University Press, 1964.

Klehr, Harvey, John Earl Haynes, and Fridrikh Igorevich Firsov, eds. *The Secret World of American Communism.* New Haven, CT: Yale University Press, 1995.

Klehr, Harvey, and Ronald Radosh. *The Amerasia Spy Case: Prelude to McCarthyism.* Chapel Hill: University of North Carolina Press, 1996.

Klepper, James J. *Styles Bridges: Yankee Senator.* Sugar Hill, NH: Phoenix Publishing, 2001.

Koen, Ross Y. *The China Lobby in American Politics.* 1960. Reprint, New York: Octagon Books, 1974.

Kolko, Joyce, and Gabriel Kolko. *The Limits of Power: The World and United States Foreign Policy, 1945–1954.* New York: Harper & Row, 1972.

Lacey, Michael, ed. *The Truman Presidency.* New York: Cambridge University Press, 1989.

LaFeber, Walter. *America, Russia, and the Cold War, 1945–2002.* 9th ed. New York: McGraw-Hill, 2002.

———. "Crossing the 38th: The Cold War in Microcosm." In *Reflections on the Cold War,* edited by Lynn H. Miller and Ronald W. Pruessen, 71–90. Philadelphia: Temple University Press, 1974.

Landis, Mark. *Joseph McCarthy: The Politics of Chaos.* London: Associated University Presses, 1987.

LaPalombra, Joseph G. "Pressure Propaganda, and Political Action in the Elections of 1950." *Journal of Politics* 14, no. 2 (1952): 300–325.

Larson, Eric V. *Casualties and Consensus: The Historical Role of Casualties in Domestic Support for U.S. Military Operations.* Santa Monica, CA: Rand Corporation, 1996.

Leary, William M. "Smith of New Jersey: A Biography of H. Alexander Smith, United States Senator from New Jersey, 1944–1959." PhD diss., Princeton University, 1966.

Leffler, Melvyn. *A Preponderance of Power: National Security, the Truman Administration, and the Cold War.* Stanford, CA: Stanford University Press, 1992.

Letellier, Lawrence John. "Departure of a Statesman: Senator Tom Connally." Master's thesis, University of Maryland, 1993.

Levine, Erwin L. *Theodore Francis Green: The Washington Years, 1937–1960.* Providence, RI: Brown University Press, 1971.

Lofgren, Charles A. "Congress and the Korean Conflict." PhD diss., Stanford University, 1966.

———. "Mr. Truman's War: A Debate and Its Aftermath." *Review of Politics* 31, no. 2 (April 1969): 223–41.

Longley, Kyle. *Senator Albert Gore, Sr.: Tennessee Maverick.* Baton Rouge: Louisiana State University Press, 2004.

MacArthur, Douglas. *Reminiscences.* New York: McGraw-Hill, 1964.

MacDonald, Callum A. *Korea: The War before Vietnam.* New York: Free Press, 1986.

Manchester, William. *American Caesar: Douglas MacArthur, 1880–1964.* Boston: Little, Brown, 1978.

Mantell, Matthew E. "Opposition to the Korean War: A Study in American Dissent." PhD diss., New York University, 1973.

Marcus, Maeva. *Truman and the Steel Seizure Case: The Limits of Presidential Power.* New York: Columbia University Press, 1977.

Mark, Eduard. "In Re Alger Hiss." *Journal of Cold War Studies* 11, no. 3 (2009): 26–67.

Martin, John Bartlow. *Adlai Stevenson of Illinois: The Life of Adlai E. Stevenson.* Garden City, NY: Doubleday, 1976.

Martin, John Frederick. *Civil Rights and the Crisis of Liberalism: The Democratic Party, 1945–1976.* Boulder, CO: Westview Press, 1979.

Marwell, Gerald. "Party, Region, and the Dimensions of Conflict in the House of Representatives, 1949–1954." *American Political Science Review* 61, no. 2 (June 1967): 380–99.

Matray, James. *The Reluctant Crusade: American Foreign Policy in Korea, 1941–1950.* Honolulu: University of Hawaii Press, 1985.

———. "Truman's Plan for Victory: National Self-Determination and the Thirty-Eighth Parallel Decision in Korea." *Journal of American History* 66 (September 1979): 314–33.

McAuliffe, Mary Sperling. *Crisis on the Left: Cold War Politics and American Liberals, 1947–1954.* Amherst: University of Massachusetts Press, 1978.

McCarthy, William T. "Horse Sense: The Divided Politics of Edwin C. Johnson, 1923–1954." Master's thesis, University of Northern Colorado, 1996.

McCarty, Patrick Fargo. "Big Ed Johnson: A Political Portrait." Masters' thesis, University of Colorado, 1958.

McCrackin, Justin Matthew. "Truman's Undeclared War: The Path to War in Korea, Why Truman Intervened without Congress, and the Legalities of His Actions." Master's thesis, University of Tulsa, 2003.

McCullough, David. *Truman.* New York: Simon & Schuster, 1992.

McKeever, Porter. *Adlai Stevenson: His Life and Legacy.* New York: William Morrow, 1989.

McKerrow, Ray E. "Truman and Korea: Rhetoric in the Pursuit of Victory." *Central States Speech Journal* 28 (1997): 1–12.

McLellan, David S. *Dean Acheson: The State Department Years.* New York: Dodd, Mead, 1976.

McMillan, James E., Jr. *Ernest W. McFarland: Majority Leader of the United States Senate and Chief Justice of the State of Arizona.* Prescott, AZ: Sharlot Hall Museum Press, 2004.

———, ed. *The Ernest W. McFarland Papers: The United States Senate Years, 1940–1952.* Prescott, AZ: Sharlot Hall Museum Press, 1995.

Medhurst, Martin, Jr., Robert L. Ivie, Philip Wonder, and Robert L. Scott. *Cold War*

Rhetoric: Strategy, Metaphor and Ideology. East Lansing: Michigan State University Press, 1997.

Merrill, Dennis, ed. *Documentary History of the Truman Presidency.* Vol. 20, *The Korean War: President Truman's Dismissal of General Douglas MacArthur.* Bethesda, MD: University Publications of America, 1997.

Miller, Cynthia Pease. *Guide to Research Collections of Former Members of the United States House of Representatives, 1789–1987.* Washington, DC: Office of the Bicentennial of the House of Representatives, 1988.

Miller, Donald C. "The Revenue Act of 1951: A General Survey." *National Tax Journal* 5 (1952): 40–52.

Miller, Douglas, and Marion Nowak. *The Fifties: The Way We Really Were.* Garden City, NY: Doubleday, 1977.

Millett, Allan R. "The Korean War: A 50-Year Critical Historiography." *Journal of Strategic Studies* 24, no. 1 (March 2001): 188–224.

Milliken, Jennifer. *The Social Construction of the Korean War: Conflict and Its Possibilities.* New York: Manchester University Press, 2001.

Morgan, Anne Hodges. *Robert S. Kerr: The Senate Years, 1977.* Norman: University of Oklahoma Press, 1977.

Mueller, John E. *War, Presidents, and Public Opinion.* New York: John Wiley & Sons, 1973.

National Security Council. "United States Objectives, Politics and Courses of Action in Asia." NSC 48/5, May 17, 1951. Digital National Security Archive Document No. PD00141.

Nelson, Garrison. *Committees in the U.S. Congress, 1947–1992.* Washington, DC: Congressional Quarterly, 1993.

Neustadt, Richard E. "The Constraining of the President: The Presidency after Watergate." *British Journal of Political Science* 4, no. 4 (October 1974): 383–97.

———. *Presidential Power: The Politics of Leadership.* New York: John Wiley & Sons, 1960.

Nevins, Allan. *Herbert H. Lehman and His Era.* New York: Charles Scribner's Sons, 1963.

O'Neill, William L. *American High: The Years of Confidence, 1945–1960.* New York: Free Press, 1986.

Office of the Chief of Military History, U.S. Army. *American Military History.* http://www.army.mil/cmh-pg/books/AMH.

Offner, Arnold A. *Another Such Victory: President Truman and the Cold War, 1945–1953.* Stanford, CA: Stanford University Press, 2002.

Ogden, Daniel M., Jr. "The 1952 Elections in Washington." *Western Political Quarterly* 6, no. 1 (March 1953): 131–35.

Ojserkis, Raymond P. *Beginnings of the Cold War Arms Race: The Truman Administration and the U.S. Arms Build-up.* Westport, CT: Praeger Publishing, 2003.

Oshinsky, David M. *A Conspiracy So Immense: The World of Joe McCarthy.* New York: Free Press, 1983.

Paige, Glenn. *The Korean Decision: June 24–30, 1950.* New York: Free Press, 1968.

Parmet, Herbert S. *The Democrats: The Years after FDR.* New York: Macmillan, 1976.

Parry-Giles, Shawn S. *The Rhetorical Presidency, Propaganda and the Cold War, 1945–1955.* Westport, CT: Praeger Press, 2002.

Paterson, Thomas G. "The Dissent of Senator Claude Pepper." In *Cold War Critics: Alternatives to American Foreign Policy in the Truman Years,* edited by Thomas G. Paterson, 114–39. Chicago: Quadrangle Books, 1971.

———. "Presidential Foreign Policy, Public Opinion and Congress: The Truman Years." *Diplomatic History* 3, no. 1 (1979): 1–18.

Patterson, James T. *Grand Expectations: The U.S., 1945–1974.* New York: Oxford University Press, 1997.

———. *Mr. Republican: A Biography of Robert A. Taft.* Boston: Houghton Mifflin, 1972.

Pearlman, Michael D. *Truman & MacArthur: Policy, Politics, and the Hunger for Honor and Renown.* Bloomington: Indiana University Press, 2008.

Pelz, Stephen. "U.S. Decisions on Korean Policy." In *Child of Conflict: The Korean-American Relationship, 1943–1953,* edited by Bruce Cumings, 88–91. Seattle: University of Washington Press, 1983.

Pemberton, William E. *Harry S. Truman: Fair Dealer and Cold Warrior.* Boston: Twayne Publishers, 1989.

Peng, Dehuai. *Memoirs of a Chinese Marshal: The Autobiographical Notes of Peng Dehuai.* Beijing: Foreign Language Press, 1984.

Pepper, Claude Denson, with Hays Gorey. *Pepper: Eyewitness to a Century.* New York: Harcourt Brace Jovanovich, 1987.

Phillips, Cabell. *The Truman Presidency: The History of a Triumphant Succession.* New York: Macmillan, 1966.

Pierpaoli, Paul G. *Truman and Korea: The Political Culture of the Early Cold War.* Columbia: University of Missouri Press, 1999.

Poder, Michael Paul. "The Senatorial Career of William E. Jenner." PhD diss., University of Notre Dame, 1976.

Poole, Walter S. *The History of the Joint Chiefs of Staff: The Joint Chiefs of Staff and National Policy.* Vol. 4, *1950–52.* Wilmington, DE: Michael Glazier, 1980.

Powell, Colin, with Joseph E. Persiro. *My American Journey.* New York: Random House, 1995.

Powell, Lee Riley. *J. William Fulbright and His Time: A Political Biography.* Memphis, TN: Guild Bindery Press, 1995.

Pratt, William C. "Senator Glen H. Taylor: Questioning American Unilateralism." In *Cold War Critics: Alternatives to American Foreign Policy in the Truman Years,* edited by Thomas G. Paterson, 140–66. Chicago: Quadrangle Books, 1971.

Preston, Thomas. *The President and His Inner Circle: Leadership Style and the Advisory Process in Foreign Affairs.* New York: Columbia University Press, 2001.

Pringle, Peter, and James Spigelman. *The Nuclear Barons.* New York: Holt, Rinehart & Winston, 1981.

Public Papers of Presidents of the United States: Harry S. Truman, 1945–1953. Washington, DC: U.S. Government Printing Office, 1966. http://www.trumanlibrary
.org/publicpapers/index.php.

Public Papers of Presidents of the United States: Harry S. Truman, 1947. Washington,
DC: U.S. Government Printing Office, 1966.

Public Papers of Presidents of the United States: Harry S. Truman, 1950. Washington,
DC: U.S. Government Printing Office, 1965.

Public Papers of the Presidents of the United States. Vol. 2, *George H. W. Bush.* http://
frwebgate.access.gpo.gov.

Purifoy, Lewis McCarroll. *Harry Truman's China Policy: McCarthyism and the Diplomacy of Hysteria, 1947–1951.* New York: New Viewpoints, 1976.

Record, Jeffrey. *Making War, Thinking History: Munich, Vietnam, and Presidential
Uses of Force from Korea to Kosovo.* Annapolis, MD: Naval Institute Press, 2002.

Rees, David. *Korea: The Limited War.* New York: St. Martin's Press, 1964.

Reichard, Gary W. "The Domestic Politics of National Security." In *The National
Security: Its Theory and Practices, 1945–1960,* edited by Norman A. Graebner,
243–74. New York: Oxford University Press, 1986.

Relyea, Harold, and L. Elaine Halchin. *Informing Congress: The Role of the Executive
Branch in Times of War.* New York: Novinka Books, 2003.

"The Reporter Notes." *Reporter,* April 1, 1952, 1.

Republican National Committee. *Background to Korea.* Washington, DC: Republican National Committee, 1950.

Reston, James. *Deadline: A Memoir.* New York: Random House, 1981.

Ridgway, Matthew B. *The Korean War.* New York: Doubleday, 1967.

Riggs, James Richard. "Congress and the Conduct of the Korean War." PhD diss.,
Purdue University, 1972.

Robin, Ron Theodore. *The Making of the Cold War Enemy: Culture and Politics in
the Military-Intellectual Complex.* Princeton, NJ: Princeton University Press,
2001.

Roper Center for Public Opinion Research. 2006. http://137.99.36.203/CFIDE/
roper/presidential/webroot/presidential_rating_detail.cfm?allrate=False.

Rose, Lislie. *The Cold War Comes to Main Street: America in 1950.* Lawrence: University Press of Kansas, 1999.

Rovere, Richard H. *Senator Joe McCarthy.* New York: Harcourt, Brace, 1959.

Rovere, Richard Halworth, and Arthur Meier Schlesinger. *General MacArthur
& President Truman: The Struggle for Control of American Foreign Policy.* New
Brunswick, NJ: Transaction Publishers, 1997.

Rozell, Mark J. *Executive Privilege: The Dilemma of Secrecy and Democratic Account-
ability.* Baltimore: Johns Hopkins University Press, 1994.

Rusk, Dean, as told to Richard Rusk. *As I Saw It.* Edited by Daniel S. Papp. New
York: W. W. Norton, 1990.

Russell, Ruth B. *A History of the United Nations Charter: The Role of the United States,
1940–1945.* Washington, DC: Brookings Institution, 1958.

Ryan, Halford R. *Harry S. Truman: Presidential Rhetoric.* Westport, CT: Greenwood Press, 1993.

Savage, Sean J. *Truman and the Democratic Party.* Lexington: University Press of Kentucky, 1997.

Schappsmeier, Edward L., and Frederick H. Schappsmeier. "Scott W. Lucas of Havana: His Rise and Fall as Majority Leader in the U.S. Senate." *Journal of the Illinois State Historical Society* 70, no. 4 (November 1977): 302–20.

Schlesinger, Arthur M., Jr. *The Imperial Presidency.* Boston: Houghton Mifflin, 1973.

Schnabel, James F., and Robert J. Watson. *The History of the Joint Chiefs of Staff: The Joint Chiefs of Staff and National Policy.* Vol. 3, *The Korean War.* Wilmington, DE: Michael Glazier, 1979.

Schrecker, Ellen. *Many Are the Crimes: McCarthyism in America.* Boston: Little, Brown, 1998.

Shermer, Elizabeth Tandy. "Origins of the Conservative Ascendancy: Barry Goldwater's Early Senate Career and the De-legitimization of Organized Labor." *Journal of American History* 95, no. 3 (December 2008): 678–709.

Smith, E. Timothy. *Opposition beyond the Water's Edge: Liberal Internationalists, Pacifists, and Containment, 1945–1953.* Westport, CT: Greenwood Press, 1999.

Smith, Glenn H. *Langer of North Dakota: A Study in Isolationism.* New York: Garland Publishing, 1979.

Spalding, Elizabeth Edwards. *The First Cold Warrior: Harry Truman, Containment, and the Remaking of Liberal Internationalism.* Lexington: University Press of Kentucky, 2006.

Spanier, John W. *The Truman-MacArthur Controversy.* New York: W. W. Norton, 1965.

Stanley, Elizabeth A. *Paths to Peace: Domestic Coalition Shifts, War Termination and the Korean War.* Stanford, CA: Stanford University Press, 2009.

Stassen, Glen H. "Individual Preference versus Role-Constraint in Policy-Making: Senatorial Response to Secretaries Acheson and Dulles." *World Politics* 25, no. 1 (October 1972): 96–119.

Steinberg, Alfred. *Sam Rayburn: A Biography.* New York: Hawthorn Books, 1975.

Stone, I. F. *The Hidden History of the Korean War, 1950–1951.* Boston: Little, Brown, 1952.

Stueck, William W. *The Korean War: An International History.* Princeton, NJ: Princeton University Press, 1995.

———. *Rethinking the Korean War: A New Diplomatic and Strategic History.* Princeton, NJ: Princeton University Press, 2002.

———, ed. *The Korean War in World History.* Lexington: University Press of Kentucky, 2004.

Summers, Harry G., Jr. *Korean War Almanac.* New York: Facts on File, 1990.

Sundquist, James L. *The Decline and Resurgence of Congress.* Washington, DC: Brookings Institution, 1981.

Tananbaum, Duane. *The Bricker Amendment Controversy: A Test of Eisenhower's Political Leadership.* Ithaca, NY: Cornell University Press, 1988.

Theoharis, Athan. "The Threat to Civil Liberties." In *Cold War Critics: Alternatives* to American Foreign Policy in the Truman Years, edited by Thomas G. Paterson, 266–98. Chicago: Quadrangle Books, 1971.

Treese, Joel D., ed. Biographical Dictionary of the American Congress, 1774–1996. Alexandria, VA: CQ Staff Directories, 1997.

Truman, David B. The Congressional Party: A Case Study. New York: John Wiley & Sons, 1959.

Truman, Harry S. Memoirs. Vol. 1, Years of Decisions. Garden City, NY: Doubleday, 1955.

———. Memoirs. Vol. 2, Years of Trial and Hope. Garden City, NY: Doubleday, 1956.

Tucker, Nancy Bernkopf. Patterns in the Dust: Chinese-American Relations and the Recognition Controversy, 1949–1950. New York: Columbia University Press, 1983.

Tucker, Robert C. "The Cold War in Stalin's Time: What the New Sources Reveal." Diplomatic History 21, no. 2 (1997): 273–81.

Tucker, Spencer C., ed. Encyclopedia of the Korean War: A Political, Social, and Military History. New York: Checkmark Books, 2002.

Twedt, Michael S. "The War Rhetoric of Harry S. Truman during the Korean Conflict." PhD diss., University of Kansas, 1969.

Underhill, Robert. The Truman Persuasions. Ames: Iowa State University Press, 1981.

United Nations Human Rights Website. "Charter of the United Nations, Chapter VII." www.unhchr.ch/htm./menu3/b/ch-chp7.htm.

Unruh, G. Q. "Republican Apostate: Senator Wayne L. Morse and His Quest for Independent Liberalism." Pacific Northwest Quarterly 82, no. 3 (July 1991): 82–91.

U.S. Army Center of Military History. "The Korean War: Years of Stalemate." http://www.army.mil/cmh-pg/brochures/kw-stale/stale.htm.

U.S. Department of Defense. "Commemoration of 50th Anniversary of the Korean War." http://korea50.army.mil.history/chronology/timeline_1951.shtml.

U.S. Department of State. "Authority of the President to Repel the Attack on Korea." Department of State Bulletin 23, no. 578 (July 31, 1950): 173–77.

U.S. Department of State, Office of Public Affairs. "Building the Peace." Foreign Affairs Outlines. Far Eastern Series 37, Pub. 3971, No. 24 (Autumn 1950).

———. Our Foreign Policy. Pub. 3972. Washington, DC: U.S. Government Printing Office, 1950.

———. Our Foreign Policy 1952. Pub. 4466. Washington, DC: U.S. Government Printing Office, 1952.

U.S. Senate. Review of Bipartisan Foreign Policy Consultations since World War II. 82nd Cong., 1st sess., 1952. S. Doc. 87.

U.S. Senate Committee on Foreign Relations. The United States and the Korean Problem: Documents 1943–1953. 83rd Cong., 1st sess., 1953. S. Doc. 74.

Vandenberg, Arthur H., Jr., and Joe Alex Morris, eds. The Private Papers of Senator Vandenberg. Boston: Houghton Mifflin, 1952.

Wainstock, Dennis. Truman, MacArthur and the Korean War. Westport, CT: Greenwood Press, 1999.

Watkins, Arthur V. "War by Executive Order." Western Political Quarterly 4, no. 4 (December 1951): 539–49.

Weathersby, Kathryn. "New Russian Documents on the Korean War." *Cold War International History Bulletin* 6/7 (Winter 1995): 30–59. http://www.wilsoncenter.org/topics/pubs/ACF1A6.pdf.

———. "The Soviet Role in the Korean War: The State of Historical Knowledge." In *The Korean War in World History*, edited by William W. Stueck, 61–92. Lexington: University Press of Kentucky, 2004.

———. "Stalin, Mao, and the End of the Korean War." In *Brothers in Arms: The Rise and Fall of the Sino-Soviet Alliance*, edited by Odd Arne Westad, 90–116. Washington, DC: Woodrow Wilson Center Press, 1998.

Wertenbaker, Charles. "The China Lobby." *Reporter*, April 15, 1952, 4–24.

Westerfield, H. Bradford. *Foreign Policy and Party Politics: Pearl Harbor to Korea.* New Haven, CT: Yale University Press, 1955.

White, G. Edward. *Alger Hiss's Looking-Glass Wars: The Covert Life of a Soviet Spy.* New York: Oxford University Press, 2004.

Whitfield, Stephen. *The Culture of the Cold War.* Baltimore: Johns Hopkins University Press, 1991.

Wigderson, Seth. "The Wages of Anticommunism: U.S. Labor and the Korean War." In *Labor's Cold War: Local Politics in a Global Context*, edited by Shelton Stromquist, 226–57. Urbana: University of Illinois Press, 2008.

Williams, Jeannette Lea. "Citizen Responses to the Image of Savagery in Harry S. Truman's Korean War Rhetoric." Master's thesis, Texas A&M University, 1992.

Wiltz, John E. "The Korean War and American Society." In *The Korean War: A 25-Year Perspective*, edited by F. H. Heller, 112–58. Lawrence: Regents Press of Kansas, 1977.

Wittner, Lawrence S. *Rebels against War: The American Peace Movement, 1933–1983.* Philadelphia: Temple University Press, 1984.

———. *The Struggle against the Bomb.* Vol. 1, *One World or None: A History of the Nuclear Disarmament Movement through 1953.* Stanford, CA: Stanford University Press, 1993.

Wood, Hugh G. "American Reaction to Limited War in Asia: Korea and Vietnam, 1950–1968." PhD diss., University of Colorado, 1974.

Woods, Randall Bennett. *Fulbright: A Biography.* New York: University of Cambridge Press, 1995.

Wormuth, Francis D., and Edwin B. Firmage. *To Chain the Dog of War: The War Power of Congress in History and Law.* Urbana: University of Illinois Press, 1986.

Yergin, Daniel. *The Prize: The Epic Quest for Oil, Money and Power.* New York: Simon & Schuster, 1993.

Zhang, Shu Guand. *Mao's Military Romanticism: China and the Korean War, 1950–1953.* Lawrence: University Press of Kansas, 1995.

Zhu, Pingchao. "The Road to an Armistice: An Examination of the Chinese and American Diplomacy during the Korean War." PhD diss., University of Miami at Ohio, 1998.

Index

Acheson, Dean, 30, 58, 86, 208, 211–12; bipartisan foreign policy, definition, 10–11, 222; bipartisan foreign policy, implementation, 19–20, 41, 64, 74–75, 99–100, 104, 106, 118, 125, 182–83; China policy "white paper," 13–14, 123; defense of Alger Hiss, 15–16; Great Debate, 111, 114–16; initial intervention in Korea, 24–27, 29, 33, 37, 44; Pacific defense perimeter speech, 15, 62–63, 77–78, 80; relations with Congress, 5–6, 11, 14, 17–19, 22, 67, 78–79, 97–98, 103, 108, 111, 117, 124, 127, 141, 159, 191–92, 197, 221–22; responses to peace proposals, 137, 139, 142–43, 145–46, 150, 153–57; testimony in MacArthur hearings, 121–23, 178, 180; United Nations Participation Act (UNPA) and, 48; views on congressional approval for war, 32, 35–37, 48–49, 51; views on prisoner of war repatriation, 163
Adams, Sherman, 224
Allison, Emery W., 82
Allison, John M., 56
Almond, Edward M., 93
Alsop, Stewart, 140
Anderson, Clinton P., 3, 87–88, 123, 216
Arends, Les, 16, 168
Arnall, Ellis, 173

Attlee, Clement, 102–5
Attlee summit, 102–5
Austin, Warren, 70, 84, 140, 148

Baldridge, Holmes, 172–73
Barkley, Alben, 2, 6, 18, 22, 107, 117, 204
Bennett, Charles E., 66–67
Benton, William: clashes with McCarthyism, 76–77, 159; critical of Truman's congressional relations, 6; defends Dean Acheson, 18, 124; election of 1950 and, 83, 97; election of 1952 and, 216; responds to Tydings committee report, 88
Bernstein, Barton J., 43
bipartisan foreign policy, 1; attacks on Dean Acheson and, 19; election of 1950 and, 74–76; failures of Truman administration to pursue, 42; origins, xv, 10–11; promotion of, 94, 98, 117, 161, 176–78, 222; Republican attacks upon, 63–64, 118; setbacks to, 12, 111; studies of, xiv, 182
Blatnik, John A., 145
Boddy, Manchester, 8
Bolling, Richard, 86, 89, 98
Boykin, Frank W., 101, 206
Boyle, William, Jr., 87, 180, 186
Bradley, Omar, 28, 32, 36, 111, 126–27
Brannan Plan, 4, 91
Brewster, Owen, 56, 104
Bricker, John, 114

Bridges, Styles: attacks Dean Acheson, 14–15; member of China Bloc, 12, 177–78; supports intervention in Korea, 41; Truman's relations with, 18–19; Tydings committee hearings and, 17

Browder, Earl, 82

Buchanan, Frank, 178

Buckley, William F., 181

Bureau of Internal Revenue (BIR), 186–87

Burleson, Omar, 122

Burns, James MacGregor, 219

Busbey, Fred, 181

Bush, George W., 221

Butler, John Marshall, 82, 88

Byrd, Harry F., 90, 113, 187, 199–200, 205

Byrnes, James, 7, 188–89, 197, 204

Cain, Harry P., 144, 154, 174, 180–81, 217–18

Cannon, Clarence, 96

Capehart, Homer, 61, 121

Caridi, Ronald J., xiv, 47

Carroll, John A., 124

Carter, Jack, 78–79

Case, Francis, 101

Caudle, Theron Lamar, 186

Celler, Emmanuel, 78

Chiang Kai-shek. See Jiang Jieshi

China, 33, 110, 122, 144, 184, 211; civil war, 12–13, 21, 30, 44, 84–85, 114, 191; intervention in Korea, xi–xii, 23, 56, 59–60, 85–86, 93–103, 121, 124, 132, 155, 164, 191–92, 197, 210; Korean armistice talks, 137, 142, 147–49, 157, 162–63; seating of communist government in United Nations, 102, 139, 141–43

China Bloc, 12, 20, 30, 161, 177–78, 181, 183

China Lobby, 177–81

Churchill, Winston, 154

Clark, D. Worth, 9

Clark, Tom, 174–75

Clifford, Clark, 56–57, 195

Colmer, William G., 96

Colson, Charles F., 164

Congress: aid to Korea, 15; bipartisanship in foreign policy, 98–101, 104–8, 181–82, 223–24; commitment to Korean War, xi–xii, xiii, 26–35; constitutional authority to declare war, 35–42, 45–54; Great Debate over troops to Europe, 111–17; investigation of China Bloc/China Lobby, 177–81; investigations of corruption in Truman administration, 185–87; McCarran Act passed by, 68–69; mobilization for war, xi, 61, 71–73, 132, 164–70, 176; peace proposals, 135–52, 155–60; relations with Dean Acheson, 14, 97–100, 111, 122, 222–23; response to China entry into Korean War, 94, 101, 105–8; response to firing of MacArthur, 121, 124; response to steel crisis, 172–74; views on repatriation of POWs, 181–82

Congress, Eightieth, 5, 99

Congress, Eighty-first, xi, 4

Congress, Eighty-second, 90–91, 152

Connally, Tom: attempts to oust Dean Acheson, 123; bipartisanship, 10–12, 19–21, 74, 100–104, 107; China Lobby probe and, 181; congressional approval for war and, 28–29, 32, 49–53; decision to advance north of thirty-eighth parallel and, xii; Great Debate and, 113; peace initiatives and, 145, 147, 150; supports Truman regarding Korean intervention, 3, 27, 35,

61; supports Truman in Tydings committee hearings, 18; United Nations Participation Act (UNPA) and, 46, 52

Cooper, John Sherman, 20, 64, 75, 77

Costello, Frank, 184

Coudert, Frederic, 112, 121

Cox, Eugene E., 90, 97

Crabb, Cecil V., Jr., 182

Cumings, Bruce, 43

Davies, John C., 6

Davis, James C., 16

Defense Production Act (DPA) of 1950, 71–72, 117

Defense Production Act (DPA) of 1951, 164–65, 169, 174

Democratic National Committee (DNC): China Lobby probe and, 177, 180; communication with Truman administration, 6; election of 1950 and, 78, 83, 87; election of 1952 and, 194–95, 197, 207, 209–10, 213; purged of Dixiecrats by Truman, 3; response to firing of MacArthur, 123–24

Democratic Party, xv, 1, 89, 140; divisions after China's entry into Korean War, 94–98; divisions in late 1940s, 2–9; election of 1952 and, 161, 184–89, 192–206; organized labor and, 130, 175; unity, 66

Dewey, Thomas, 3, 20

Dixiecrats, 9; allied with congressional Republicans, 96–97; at 1951 Southern Governors Conference, 187–89; bolt from Democratic Party in 1948, 3–4, 191; election of 1952 and, 192, 195, 197–98, 201, 206–7

Dodd, Francis T., 164

Dodge, Joseph M., 224

Donnell, Forrest C., 82

Donovan, Robert J., xiv

Douglas, Helen Gahagan, 8, 82

Douglas, Paul H., 38–39, 67, 103, 122, 138, 181

Duff, James H., 122

Dulles, John Foster: appointed State Department advisor, Truman administration, 20–21; bipartisan foreign policy and, 64, 74–77, 222–23; China Lobby involvement, 181; preparation for MacArthur hearings, 121; secretary of state under Eisenhower, xv; supports limited war in Korea, 43; UN representative, 10; views on Douglas MacArthur, 118

Eastland, James, 4, 16

Eaton, Charles, 41, 107, 146

Economic Stabilization Agency, 130, 203

Ecton, Zales M., 144, 217–18

Eisenhower, Dwight: appointed supreme NATO commander, 111–12; attacked by Truman during 1952 election, 192, 212; bipartisanship during presidency of, 182; carries several southern states in 1952 election, 207; characteristics of victory in 1952 election, 214–19; effectiveness as campaigner, 204; influence on MacArthur hearings, 122, 127; Korean War as 1952 election issue, 213–14; Korean War policy as president, 210; McCarthyism and campaign of 1952, 211, 216; positions on domestic issues in 1952 election, 201; presidential transition from Truman in 1953, 223–24; pushes for arms to Europe, 129; supported by southern Democrats in 1952

Eisenhower, Dwight *(cont.)*
    election, 195, 201–6; support from
    media in 1952 election, 208; unifies
    Republican Party, 203–4
Elsey, George, 37, 80–81, 133, 177–78

Fair Deal: election of 1952 and, 191–
    92, 196, 198; opposed by southern
    Democrats, 4–5, 7–8, 79, 187–88;
    spending affected by Korean War,
    58; twenty-one-day rule and, 91
Fair Employment Practices Committee
    (FEPC), 4, 196, 200, 202–3
Ferguson, Homer, 75, 172
Fisher, Louis, 48
Fitzpatrick, Paul, 187
Flanders, Ralph: peace proposal,
    155–58; views on intervention in
    Korea, 32, 40–41; views on peace
    resolutions, 140, 146
Foot, Rosemary, xv
Formosa: American policy regarding,
    13, 15, 30, 44, 62, 69, 73, 75,
    101, 177; China Lobby and, 177;
    MacArthur's views on, 69, 119, 126;
    peace proposals and, 113; protection
    of by American Seventh Fleet,
    27, 29, 119; refuge for Chinese
    Nationalists, 14
Friendly, Alfred, 179
Fuchs, Klaus, 16
Fulbright, William, 185–86

Gallup, George, 70
George, Walter, 14, 107, 113, 144
Gillette, Guy, 40, 215
Godwin, Earl, 81
Goldman, Eric, 38, 132
Gore, Albert, Sr., 136–37
Graham, Billy, 56
Graham, Frank, 8
Graham, Wallace H., 26
Great Debate, 111–17

Green, Theodore, 17, 38, 145
Gromyko, Andrei, 139
Gross, Ernest A., 24, 237n3
Guzik, "Greasy Thumb," 184

Hamby, Alonzo, 42, 52, 85
Hamilton, Thomas J., 142
Harriman, Averell, 66, 76, 140, 198
Harsch, Joseph C., 38
Hastings, Philip, 219
Havenner, Franck, 167
Hayden, Carl, 97
Hays, Brooks, 19
Hechler, Ken: bipartisan foreign policy
    research, 176–77, 196; reaction
    to MacArthur firing, 123; views
    on 1950 elections, 82, 89; views
    on bipartisan foreign policy, 117;
    views on Truman administration
    scandals, 186; views on Truman
    congressional relations, 6
Hendrickson, Robert C., 121
Hickenlooper, Bourke, 17, 61, 116, 144
Hickerson, John, 28
Hill, Lister, 97
Hiss, Alger, 16
Holifield, Chet, 144
Hoover, Herbert, 20, 112, 114–15, 218
Hsieh Fang, 162
Hull, Cordell, 10
Humphrey, Hubert H., 115, 122, 172,
    198

Ickes, Harold, 183
Internal Security Act of 1959. *See*
    McCarran Act

Jenner, William, 65–66, 113, 144, 182
Jessup, Philip, 24, 156, 159, 177, 179
Jiang Jieshi: China Lobby and, 177–83;
    Chinese civil war and, 12–15;
    congressional views on usefulness
    in Korea, 122; loses support of

Truman administration, 75, 96; offers Chinese Nationalist troops to fight North Korea, 33, 118–19

Johnson, Edwin C., 39, 138–42, 147, 158–59, 168

Johnson, Louis, 64, 67, 181

Johnson, Lyndon B., 40, 56, 123, 144, 159, 205

Johnston, Victor, 7

Joint Chiefs of Staff (JCS): decision to intervene in Korea and, 27–29, 32; declaration of national emergency and, 100; and Douglas MacArthur, 110, 119, 125; and Matthew Ridgway, 164; support firing of General MacArthur, 126; views on invading North Korea, 83

Joliot-Curie, Frederic, 149

Jonas, Edgar A., 168

Joy, C. Turner, 162

Judd, Walter, 12, 19–20, 42, 75, 177, 180–81

Karsten, Frank, 180–81

Kee, John, 5, 26–27

Kefauver, Estes, 87–88, 138, 184, 187, 192–93, 198, 200

Kem, James, 144, 166, 217–18

Kennan, George, 142–43

Kepley, David R., xiv

Keynes, Edward, 47–48

Kilgore, Harley, 97

Kim Il Sung: alliance with Soviet Union, 26, 57; determination for total victory, 66; discussed in Democratic Party propaganda, 79; interpretation of Acheson Pacific defense perimeter speech, 62; invades South Korea, xi, 24; permitted by Stalin to initiate attack, 43, 45; response to UN resolution on withdrawal of North Korean troops, 30; thwarted by UN, xiii; underestimated in Flanders peace proposal, 157

Kirk, Alan G., 145

Kirwan, Michael J., 78

Knowland, William, 11–12, 27, 41, 63–64, 102, 115

Knox, Frank, 63

Kohlberg, Alfred, 177, 179

Koje-do prisoner of war riot, 163–64

Kolko, Gabriel, 43

Kolko, Joyce, 43

Krock, Arthur, 173

La Follette, Robert, Jr., 193

Langer, William, 68

Lattimore, Owen, 22

Leffler, Melvyn, 85

Lehman, Herbert, 17, 20, 97, 122, 166, 174, 198

Lie, Trygve, 24, 142

Lincoln, Abraham, 2, 39, 111

Lloyd, David D., 194

Lodge, Henry Cabot, Jr.: bipartisanship and, 19, 76; election of 1950 and, 73–74; Great Debate and, 113, 115; nomination as ambassador to the UN, 224; serves on Tydings committee, 17, 22, 65; supports firing of MacArthur, 122; supports intervention in Korea, 30; views on peace proposals, 138

Loeb, William, 177

Lovett, Robert A., 75, 77, 182

Lucas, Scott: Attlee summit and, 102; declaration of national emergency over Korean War and, 108; defends Dean Acheson, 111; defends Korean War policy, 61; elections of 1950 and, 86–88; opposes need for congressional approval of Korean intervention, 32, 35–37, 51–52; in Tydings Committee hearings, 17, 22

Luce, Henry, 177, 180

MacArthur, Douglas, 110, 182; criticism of, 67, 103; decision to advance north of thirty-eighth parallel and, 83–85, 93; firing of, 51, 117–23, 138, 142, 159, 171, 176–77, 183, 197, 210–11, 222; freedom to use atomic weapons, 95, 101; Inchon attack by, xii–xiii, 56, 83; initial intervention in Korea and, 28, 32–33, 48; line of defense in Pacific defined, 62–63; plan to use radioactive waste in Korea, 136; presidential candidate in 1952, 195; scuttles peace initiative, 137, 151

MacArthur hearings, 124–28, 141, 146, 178, 180, 189, 194

Magnuson, Warren, 18, 77

Malik, Jacob, 141–47, 151

Malone, George, 102

Mansfield, Mike, 78, 144, 217

Mao Zedong, 12, 70, 84, 191

Marcantonio, Vito, 8, 30–31

Marcus, Maeva, 175

Marshall, George: attacked by Republicans, 75, 159, 211; consulted regarding Malik peace proposal, 143–45; mobilization for Korea and, 71, 132; named Secretary of Defense, 67; testifies at MacArthur hearings, 126

Marshall Plan: basis for Flanders peace plan, 157; bipartisanship and, 10, 86, 117, 182; contrasted with Far East foreign policy, 89; opposition to, 205

Martin, Joseph, 107–8, 119, 144, 166

Martin, William, 130

Matthews, Francis P., 69

Max, Bill, 128

Maybank, Burnet, 173

McCarran, Pat, 67, 147

McCarran Act, 68–69, 87, 159

McCarthy, Joseph, 1, 55, 74, 79,
135; analysis of influence on politics, 221–22; attacks on Dean Acheson and State Department, 62, 67, 98, 141, 162; attacks on George Marshall, 145, 211; blocks nomination of Philip Jessup to UN, 156; Great Debate and, 113; influence on decision to intervene in Korea, 44; member of China Bloc, 177–78; peace initiatives and, 141, 145, 156, 158–60; response to Attlee summit, 103; response to firing of MacArthur, 120–21; role in 1950 elections, 82–83, 87–89; role in 1952 elections, 191, 216–18; Tydings committee investigation, 9, 17–18, 21–22, 63, 65; Wheeling, WV, speech, 16. See also McCarthyism

McCarthyism, xv, 1, 61; China Lobby and, 177; effects on bipartisanship, 20, 99, 182; effects on peace proposals, 136, 142, 158; election of 1952 and, 192, 196–97, 211, 217–18; influence on congressional declaration of war, 55; influence on decision to intervene in Korea, 44; McCarran Act and, 68–69. See also McCarthy, Joseph

McClellan, John, 116

McCormack, John, 5, 90–91, 123, 200

McFall, Jack, 21, 105

McFarland, Ernest, 123, 137–38, 152–53, 215

McGrath, J. Howard, 178, 186

McKellar, Kenneth, 46

McKinney, Frank, 197, 207

McMahon, Brien: China Lobby probe and, 178, 180–81; defends decision to fire MacArthur, 121; defends Truman foreign policy, 74; election of 1950 and, 83, 88, 97; Great Debate and, 114; MacArthur

hearings and, 126; peace proposals and, 136, 145, 148–55; Tydings committee hearings and, 17
McMahon-Ribicoff resolution, 150–53, 155
McMath, Sid, 188
Meyer, John, 8–9
Millikin, Eugene D., 27, 100, 107, 144
Monaghan, Hugh, II, 8–9
Moody, Blair, 199, 216
Morgan, Edward, 65
Morgan, Edward P., 153–54
Morse, Wayne, 12, 172, 178, 180–81, 217–18
Muccio, John J., 24
Mundt, Karl E., 51, 147, 195
Murphy, Charles, 7, 18, 50, 104–5, 178, 223
Murrow, Edward R., 81
Myers, Francis J., 22, 78, 86

National Consumer Advisory Committee (NCAC), 134
National Security Council (NSC): considers UN troops north of thirty-eighth parallel, 56; initial response to Korean crisis, 27–29, 32–33; proposes armistice conditions, 138–39; recommends defense spending boosts, 13–14; recommends ending American support for Nationalist China, 13
Nixon, Richard, 40, 218; anticommunism of, 16; election of 1950 and, 8, 82; election of 1952 and, 204, 208; member of China Bloc, 177
North Atlantic Treaty Organization (NATO), 8, 10, 111–16
North Korea, 55, 118, 142; advance into South Korea halted, 66; American decision not to declare war upon, 40; American public

opinion and war against, 98; analyses of American intervention against, 43–49; armistice talks and, 162–63; attacks South Korea, 24; causes change in American policy toward Formosa, 30; China as war ally, 93–94; commitment to offensive prior to MacArthur's removal, 137; congressional perceptions of, 40, 77–78, 140; demands for withdrawal from South Korea, xii, 26, 29; discussions on invasion of, 41, 56, 70, 85; invasion of by UN forces, 84, 86; land acquired via armistice, xiii; military failures, 209–10; military successes, xii, 30; peace proposals and, 155–57; reaction to Acheson defense perimeter speech, 62, 159; requests to bomb by American generals, 32; Truman authorizes attacks upon, 33, 38; Truman's perceptions about attack on South Korea, 23, 26, 29, 33, 57–58, 74, 111; UN offensives into, xiii
NSC-68, 14, 58, 71–72, 129, 133

O'Dwyer, William, 184
Office of Price Stabilization (OPS), 71, 169–70, 173, 175
Offner, Arnold, 48, 52
O'Mahoney, Joseph, 85, 216
O'Toole, Donald, 172

Pace, Frank, xii, 48
Pearson, Drew, 58, 88, 183
Pearson, Lester, 142
Pelz, Stephen, 43
Pendergast machine, 4, 186
Peng Dehuai, 148
Pepper, Claude, 8, 77
Pierpaoli, Paul, 105
Pine, David, 172–74

Pleven, Rene, 101
Potsdam Conference, 46
Priest, J. Percy, 67

Randall, Clarence, 171
Rau, Benegal N., 140
Rayburn, Sam, 78; asks for Dean
    Acheson's resignation, 123–24;
    Democratic party unity and, 5, 18,
    97; election of 1952 and, 188–89,
    195, 198–99, 206; input regarding
    declaration of national emergency,
    107; McCarran Act and, 68;
    mobilization policy and, 59, 167;
    support for twenty-one-day rule,
    91; views on start of armistice talks,
    147
Reconstruction Finance Corporation
    (RFC), 185–87
Rees, David, 42
Reichard, Gary W., 182
Republican Party, xiv; bipartisanship in
    foreign policy and, 11, 183; China
    Lobby probe and, 179; conservative
    wing of, 15, 55; during George W.
    Bush administration, 221; election
    of 1952 and, 203, 217; Great Debate
    and, 113; support for Douglas
    MacArthur, 118
Republic of Korea (ROK): army in
    retreat, 29, 110, 118; assisted by
    United Nations, 30, 81, 140;
    government flees Seoul, 27–28;
    justifications for assistance by
    United States, 41, 57; Stalin's
    permission to invade, 62; troop
    commitments, 84. See also South
    Korea
Reston, James, 97
Reuther, Victor, 72
Reuther, Walter, 130
Revenue Act of 1951, 166
Ribicoff, Abraham, 150–55

Ridgway, Matthew, 110, 140, 146–47,
    162–64
Ritchie, Donald, 125
Rooney, John J., 127
Roosevelt, Eleanor, 124, 200
Roosevelt, Franklin D.: bipartisan
    foreign policy of, 63; congressional
    relations, 6; New Deal program,
    3–4, 197; oratorical skills, 57–58;
    popularity, 219; relations with
    the press, 95; Supreme Court
    appointments, 174; use of advisors,
    183
Roosevelt, Franklin D., Jr., 28
Ross, Charlie, 41, 95
Ruffin, William H., 165
Rusk, Dean, 117, 123, 152
Russell, Richard, 3, 96, 125, 127–28,
    189, 194, 201, 206
Ryan, Halford R., 85

Sabath, Adolf J., 90–91
Saltonstall, Leverett, 18, 122
Sawyer, Charles, 171, 175
Schlesinger, Arthur, Jr., 43, 48, 81, 87,
    182
Schuman, Robert, 101
Scott, Hugh D., Jr., 85
Selective Service Act of 1948, 170
Senate Foreign Relations Committee:
    approves Marshall Plan, 10; China
    Lobby probe and, 180; consulted by
    Dean Acheson, 19, 104; Democratic
    members and election of 1950,
    103; election of 1948 and, 12;
    inaction regarding congressional
    approval for Korean intervention,
    37; lacking information justifying
    Korean War, 113; leaks from, 111;
    MacArthur hearings and, 124;
    peace initiatives and, 139, 149–
    50, 158; reorganization of, 11, 21;
    Republican members and election

of 1950, 73–74; reviews proposed
UN Charter, 10
Seward, William, 12, 111
Shafer, Paul W., 27
Shivers, Allan, 188, 195–99, 205–7
Short, Dewey, 34, 107, 121
Shvernik, Nikolay, 152–54
Sikes, Robert, 67, 78
Smathers, George, 8
Smith, H. Alexander: Great Debate
participation, 113; MacArthur
hearings, 125; member of China
Bloc, 12, 177, 181; peace proposals,
66, 149; role in bipartisan foreign
policy, 42, 64, 73–74, 117,
122; Senate Foreign Relations
Committee member, 21; views
on congressional approval for
war, 34–35; views on Korean
intervention, 27, 41
Smith, Margaret Chase, 56, 113
South Korea, 45, 66, 101; assessed
security of, 26–27, 41, 62, 118;
invaded by communist China,
86, 110; invaded by North Korea,
xi, 24; invasion of blamed on
isolationists, 78; peace proposals
and, 140–42, 144, 155–56; receives
assistance from UN, xi, 70; refuses
to sign war armistice, xiii; territorial
changes from armistice settlement,
xiii; Truman commits to defending,
29, 43, 47, 57; UN reestablishes
control of, xii, 119; UN troop
commitments to, 115. See also
Republic of Korea (ROK)
Soviet Union, 121, 126, 211; alleges
American use of chemical weapons,
163; beginning of Cold War and,
1; boycott of UN Security Council,
26, 84; Great Debate and, 111,
115; peace proposals and, 137–38,
145, 149, 151–53; preemptive war

against, 80, 158; spies for, 16;
Truman's view of, 23, 44, 81
Sparkman, John, 201, 204, 207
Stalin, Joseph: advises armistice talks
in Korea, 148; discussed in Senate,
8–9, 76; Great Debate and, 111,
115; McMahon-Ribicoff peace
initiative and, 152, 154–55; mocked
by Truman administration, 143;
role in start of Korean War, 43, 45,
62–63; Truman's beliefs about, 23,
45, 90
Stevenson, Adlai, 191; attacks
McCarthyism, 211; campaign
assisted by Truman, 192, 212;
chooses 1952 running mate,
201; corruption issue in 1952
and, 208; Democratic nominee
for president in 1952, 192, 200;
distances candidacy from Truman
in 1952, 207–8; and Korean War
as 1952 campaign issue, 213; and
results of 1952 election, 215–16,
218–19; skills as campaigner, 204;
struggles for support from southern
Democrats in 1952, 204–5, 207;
tidelands issue and, 205–6; views
on domestic issues, 200–203
Stimson, Henry, 63
Stueck, William, 101
Sundquist, James L., xiv

Taft, Robert A.: attacks Dean
Acheson, 62, 73; Attlee summit
and, 102–5; China Bloc and, 177;
congressional approval for Korean
War and, 31–32, 34–36, 38, 40, 51;
consulted on declaration of national
emergency, 106–8; criticized by
internationalist Republicans, 76;
election of 1952 and, 127, 203–
4, 217; isolationism, 11; opposes
deployment of troops to Europe,

Taft, Robert A. *(cont.)*
  112–16; rejects bipartisan foreign policy, 42, 64–65, 99, 117–18, 223; suggested for inclusion in bipartisan consultations, 104–5; supports intervention in Korea, 41, 49; Truman's views of, 74; views on peace proposals, 147
Taft-Hartley Act, 170, 172, 174, 201–2
Talmadge, Herman, 188
Taylor, Glen H., 9, 77
Thomas, Elbert, 41, 86
Thomas, Norman, 38
Thurmond, Strom, 207, 218
Tobey, Charles, 174
Truman, Harry S.: approval rating, 66, 172, 193, 210; Atlee summit and, 101–4; bipartisan foreign policy, 64, 74–77, 94, 98–101, 104–8, 111–13, 117, 127, 161, 176–77, 182–84, 222–23; China Bloc/China Lobby investigation, 177–80; civil rights agenda, 2–4, 96, 191, 196–97, 200; communication with Congress, 5–6; congressional approval for war and, xii, 33–37, 48–53; corruption scandals, 184–87; decision to move north of thirty-eighth parallel, 56, 69–70, 83–86; election of 1950 and, 81–82, 86–87; election of 1952 and, 192–94, 200, 207–9, 212–13, 219; fires Douglas MacArthur, 117–21, 127–28; Great Debate and, 111–17; initial intervention in Korea and, xi–xii, 24–35, 44–45; mobilization for war and, 57–61, 71–73, 105–10, 114–15, 128–34, 161, 164–68, 176; nationalizes steel mills, 168–76; promotion of war to the public, 56–60, 80–81, 84–85, 94–96, 108–10, 133, 210–11; relations with Democratic Party, 94–95, 122–23, 196–97, 221;

relations with Southern Democrats/Dixiecrats, 5, 89–90, 96–97, 187–89, 194–201; repatriation of prisoners of war and, 163, 181–82, 213; response to peace proposals, 136–37, 143–46, 150–56; support of Dean Acheson, 14, 67, 79; veto of McCarran Act, 68–69
Tydings, Millard: advice on declaration of national emergency regarding Korea, 107; chairs committee investigating McCarthyism, 17–22, 55, 65, 126; defends Dean Acheson, 63; election of 1950 and, 8–9, 78, 82–83, 88

United Automobile Workers (UAW), 72, 130–31, 168, 196
United Labor Policy Committee (ULPC), 130–31
United Nations (UN), xii–xiii, 55, 70, 118, 134; authorizes troop advancement north of thirty-eighth parallel, xii, 84; calls for military intervention in Korea, 30, 32–35, 47–51; calls for North Korean withdrawal from the south, 26, 29; considers armistice proposals, 119, 142; debates naming China aggressor in Korea, 110; decision to fight limited war, 120, 124, 210; military setbacks, 56, 66; reacts to potential use of nuclear weapons in Korea, 101; reoccupies Seoul, 116; troops advance into North Korea, 83–84
United Nations Participation Act (UNPA), xv, 31, 34, 39–40, 46–52
United Nations Security Council: beginning of Korean crisis and, 24, 26, 29–30, 32–33, 44, 49–51; powers defined in UN charter, 40, 45–48; proposal to abolish, 101;

United Nations Participation Act (UNPA) and, 31
universal military training (UMT), 70, 167–68

Vandenberg, Arthur: death of, 99, 182–83; supports bipartisanship in foreign policy, 10–11, 73; supports Korean intervention, 40; Truman's reliance on, 10, 18–20, 41–42, 65, 184, 222; views on composition of Foreign Relations Committee, 12, 21
Van Devander, Charlie, 123–24
Vinson, Fred, 174–75, 192
Voice of America, 61, 150, 152
Vorys, John, 12, 100, 177

Wage Stabilization Board (WSB), 130–32, 168–70, 175
Walker, Walton, xii, 93, 110
Wallace, Henry, 3, 9, 38, 197
Walsh, John, 40
Warren, Henri, 79
Watkins, Arthur V., 51
Webb, James E., 4, 96–97, 100, 102, 178
Wedemeyer, Albert C., 181
Welker, Herman, 9
Wherry, Kenneth: at Atlee summit, 104; attacks Dean Acheson, 67, 73, 99; calls Korea "Truman's War," 122; debate on Tydings committee findings and, 65; Great Debate resolution, 112–13, 116; McCarthyism and, 18, 77, 103; member of China Bloc, 177; reaction to peace resolutions, 153; Truman's opinion of, 74; views on armistice negotiations, 147; views on congressional approval for war, 34, 49, 51; views on declaration of national emergency, 100, 106–8, 223; views on Korean intervention, 27, 36
White, Hugh, 201, 207
Wilcox, Francis, 21, 113
Wiley, Alexander: Attlee summit and, 104; bipartisanship of, 19, 41; China Lobby and, 178; declaration of national emergency and, 107; election of 1950 and, 73–74; supports congressional approval for Korean War, 37; views on peace resolutions, 149
Wilson, Charles E., 130–31, 169
Wilson, Woodrow, 9, 94

Yalta (conference), 20, 73, 144
Young, E. Merl, 185

Studies in Conflict, Diplomacy, and Peace

Series Editors: George C. Herring, Andrew L. Johns, and Kathryn C. Statler

This series focuses on key moments of conflict, diplomacy, and peace from the eighteenth century to the present to explore their wider significance in the development of U.S. foreign relations. The series editors welcome new research in the form of original monographs, interpretive studies, biographies, and anthologies from historians, political scientists, journalists, and policymakers. A primary goal of the series is to examine the United States' engagement with the world, its evolving role in the international arena, and the ways in which the state, nonstate actors, individuals, and ideas have shaped and continue to influence history, both at home and abroad.

Advisory Board Members

David Anderson, California State University, Monterey Bay
Laura Belmonte, Oklahoma State University
Robert Brigham, Vassar College
Paul Chamberlin, University of Kentucky
Jessica Chapman, Williams College
Frank Costigliola, University of Connecticut
Michael C. Desch, University of Notre Dame
Kurk Dorsey, University of New Hampshire
John Ernst, Morehead State University
Joseph A. Fry, University of Nevada, Las Vegas
Ann Heiss, Kent State University
Sheyda Jahanbani, University of Kansas
Mark Lawrence, University of Texas
Mitchell Lerner, Ohio State University
Kyle Longley, Arizona State University
Robert McMahon, Ohio State University
Michaela Hoenicke Moore, University of Iowa
Lien-Hang T. Nguyen, University of Kentucky
Jason Parker, Texas A&M University
Andrew Preston, Cambridge University
Thomas Schwartz, Vanderbilt University
Salim Yaqub, University of California, Santa Barbara

Books in the Series

Truman, Congress, and Korea: The Politics of America's First Undeclared War
Larry Blomstedt

The Gulf: The Bush Presidencies and the Middle East
Michael F. Cairo

American Justice in Taiwan: The 1957 Riots and Cold War Foreign Policy
Stephen G. Craft

Diplomatic Games: Sport, Statecraft, and International Relations since 1945
Edited by Heather L. Dichter and Andrew L. Johns

Nothing Less Than War: A New History of America's Entry into World War I
Justus D. Doenecke

Enemies to Allies: Cold War Germany and American Memory
Brian C. Etheridge

Grounded: The Case for Abolishing the United States Air Force
Robert M. Farley

The American South and the Vietnam War: Belligerence, Protest, and Agony in Dixie
Joseph A. Fry

Obama at War: Congress and the Imperial Presidency
Ryan C. Hendrickson

The Conversion of Senator Arthur H. Vandenberg: From Isolation to International Engagement
Lawrence S. Kaplan

The Currents of War: A New History of American-Japanese Relations, 1899–1941
Sidney Pash

So Much to Lose: John F. Kennedy and American Policy in Laos
William J. Rust

Lincoln Gordon: Architect of Cold War Foreign Policy
Bruce L. R. Smith

www.ingramcontent.com/pod-product-compliance
Lightning Source LLC
Chambersburg PA
CBHW030256100426
42812CB00002B/456

* 9 7 8 0 8 1 3 1 6 6 1 1 7 *